AGONY OF
DESERTION

AGONY OF DESERTION

MELISSA BARRON

JANUS PUBLISHING COMPANY
London, England

First published in Australia by
Tony Souleiman 1994

This edition published in Great Britain in 1996
by Janus Publishing Company
Edinburgh House, 19 Nassau Street
London W1N 7RE

British Library Cataloguing-in-Publication Data.
A catalogue record for this book is available from the British Library.

ISBN 1 85756 279 8

Cover design Harold King

Printed and bound in England by
Antony Rowe Ltd
Chippenham
Wiltshire

Acknowledgements

To my partner and daughter Sue who transcribed my life story and edited all works, and had many sleepless nights doing so.

Prologue

I was born in 1941, I have one brother and three sisters. I also have two half sisters (same mother, but two seperate fathers).

My father was a typical Irishman, who had two brothers and two sisters, all of whom were very strict Catholics. The Lynch Family were well known in Hollymount, Ballinrobe, County Mayo, for their independence, and the hard work they did on their farm where they lived. Only two of the boys ever married, the two girls and the youngest brother remained on the farm unmarried for their entire life.

My mother was the youngest of 14 children. Twelve of these children migrated to America, some before my mother was even born. One of the siblings married and stayed in Ireland, which left our mother who remained on her parents farm in Ballinatrasa, Ballinrobe, Co. Mayo. Mother hated her life, and could not get away fast enough.

She met our father and found her chance. He was twelve years her senior, hard working, and her meal ticket out of this god forsaken existence. She chased him until she was pregnant and so the story goes, our nightmare began........

CHAPTER 1

David sat at the long kitchen table on one of the two benches either side, watching his mother preparing breakfast. The bacon smelled good and he could hardly wait until the rest of the family came down to eat. All these extra activities must be giving me a larger appetite David thought. He smirked to himself as he recalled the events that had taken place in the fields yesterday with Winnie Walsh. Heavens what a name, what must have her mother been thinking about when she named her, but that young child was hungry, and not for food! At that point, the rest of the family started seating themselves, breaking Davids line of thought, bringing him back to the present. He had to find some excuse to lose himself for a couple of hours this afternoon as he was meeting Winnie again at four o'clock for another lay in the hay, which was the common expression used these days. He would have to be careful, after all she was twelve years younger than he was. He didn't want any mishaps and he certainly couldn't afford to be marrying the wee lass. Besides he wasn't even in love with her and he knew his parents would never agree. All else aside though, Winnie was a sweet young lass, quite a pretty little thing, and she sure knew how to please a man.

David's father entered the kitchen. "Good morning Leonard, how are you this morning?" asked David's mother.
"Good thanks Mary, and ready to eat a horse."
"Well it be taking ya long enough ta get down ere then" David interjected in his brogue tongue.
"That'll be enough of that back chat lad" his father replied, "I'll have no son of mine talking ta me like that"

Mary started to dish up the morning meal, while Kathleen and

Phyllis prepared the table, and served the meal to the men. Feeding the clan of six, including herself was quite an accomplishment for Mary each day. Leonard, David and Shamous all had hearty appetites, but they worked hard on the farm each day and needed substantial meals to accomodate the work load they encountered. Besides, Kathleen and Phyllis were a great help with the household duties. She had believed that when Leonard, her eldest son, (who was traditionally called after her husband, as were all first borns in Ireland) had left the farm with his new wife Bridget, her life would be that much easier. However, it had made little difference to her really. It had made it more difficult on the male members of the family though. Still Leonard and Bridget had a good and happy marriage and Bridget was a lovely girl. Leonard had met Bridget while he was working for the Board of Works in Dublin. They had returned for the wedding and stayed on the farm for a short while afterwards. Later they had decided to leave the farm and buy the local pub. This had given them a good start to their marriage. They were doing quite well for themselves. Mary was happy for her oldest son, he had been a good boy all his life.

Leonard suddenly turned to David and said, "Tell me son, where did you disappear to yesterday, after mass?"
"Oh I went for a walk, ya know how I hate hanging round those chatterboxes and all their gossip after mass."
"Like foocking hell ye did me boy, ya were out with that Walsh girl, playing around. I've been telling ye son, them kind ain't no good, they're tinkers lad, that's what they are. Out of 14 children, Peter and Heather, be having two left here. One being hitched, and Winnie left at home. They're tinkers, the lot of them, roamers. The rest all left to cross the seas to America."
"They're not tinkers pa," David replied, "their farm is larger

than ours by far."

"Don't be interrupting me lad, I won't be a standing for it, ye hear me, I won't."

"I'm not pa, anyways there's nowt between Winnie and me, I'm just having a little fun."

"A little fun me foot, I'lls know what ya be doing. That's what they are all talking about after mass and I'll not have me family name talked about. I'm a proud man son, and I don't like being the gossip item of the week. Ya be knowing how those tongues wag after mass, Now ya put an end to it, ya hear me boy, end it,"

David suddenly thought about this afternoons meeting with Winnie, He contemplated ending the meetings this afternoon, then thought about the lovely times they had together, but his father may be right, he had best heed his advice, before he got in too deep. But first things first, he thought. First I have to get away this afternoon. He wasn't sure how he was going to do this, but something would turn up. Pa was usually relaxing with a few stouts, while mother prepared the evening meal at that time of day, chances were he wouldn't even be missed.

Mary sat down to eat the morning meal with her family, she thought about David and Winnie, she hoped it wouldn't go too far, not that she disliked the girl personally, but the Walsh family wasn't the most respected in Ballinrobe. Oh their wealth was well noted, but they were tinkers in the sense they all scatterd. She also hated these quarrels at the breakfast table. She never interfered when Leonard chastised the children, she daren't, but she didn't always agree with him either. He was such a proud man, and a hard worker. He was also a good husband, considerate of her feelings, and basically a good father, even though he was as stubborn as some of the mules they kept on the farm. She also knew that David had inherited his father's stubborn streak. She had to agree with Leonard this time though. Even though she was not voicing these opinions, this business with Winnie Walsh, must come to an end. Winnie really wasn't good enough for her David. She decided that she would talk to David privately later.

Kathleen and Phyllis commenced cleaning away the morning dishes, while the men washed their faces in the bowl of icy cold water. As Leonard dried himself and put on his jacket to commence the daily duties on the farm, he issued his orders to his two remaining sons David and Shamous.
"David, you can give the cattle their feed today, I need Shamous ta help me fix the fence on the East Boundary. Those rocks can get mighty heavy, as you know lad. When you finished that, you can busy yourself with painting the barn, we'll need it completed and dry before the making of the hay, so we can store the feed for our own cattle. I don't wanna be waiting till the last minute, and son remember what I said, stop all this baloney with that Walsh girl and stop it fast."
"Yea dad." replied David.

Leonard and Shamous left to repair the wall on the East Boundry. As they walked along Shamous thought to himself, why does he always choose me to help him with these jobs. David is the oldest and I get all the hard work. Suddenly he said, "Pa maybe ya should've got David ta help ye taday, I mean ya can at least keep an eye on him, make sure he's around, ya know what I'm saying."
"Now don't be talking like that bout ya brother Shamous, he's a good lad. I've told him to put a stop to this Walsh girl lark, and that he'll be doing. He's a good boy, I'm saying.'

Shamous thought, David's brain is in his groin at the moment, and he'll not be abiding dads word, that I be knowing for sure, but he said nothing except "Yeh dad, maybe ya right".

They walked for the next twenty minutes to the East Boundary in silence, both occupied by their own thoughts. Shamous thinking about the heavy rocks they would be lifting all day, and Leonard regarding his son David's fling with this Winnie girl. He hoped deep down that his son would abide by his rules and end it, before something serious happened. He was hoping that David would take over the farm one day, since Leonard his first born was now happily married. He sure as hell didn't want David marrying that tinker. No, his plans were to have David own and run the farm for him when he passed on to greener pastures.

His son Leonard had been lucky when he purchased the local pub, his future was set. However most young people couldn't afford to be getting married., Apart from farm work, there was little, if any employment for youngsters, and the farms in these parts weren't for sale, they were passed on down the line to the children. Besides from what he-had heard, that Winnie was a lazy little thing, although seventeen now and finished school two years ago, she done nothing but play truant from school when she had been attending. She averaged a three day week. Yea, I be remembering how they used to gossip about her, and how much trouble her folks be having with the guards calling on them all the time. Nothing but trouble they got from her. Then when she finally left school she wouldn't help her ma, would rather play around with the boys. No good, thats what she was. No, David had to end this now, what sort of a wife would she make. Then David had said there was nothing serious going on. He had to trust in his son's judgement and hope that he would stop seeing her, for his own sake.

Back in the kitchen, David was about to leave to give the critters their feed. Not one of his favorite chores, it was so boring, but it sure beat fixing the fence. As he turned to leave, his mother said, "David, I want to talk to you, could you wait a minute."
She turned to Kathleen and Phyllis, "That's fine girls, I'll finish up here, go into the parlour and polish the furniture, clean the floor and puff up the pillows please, the priest may be calling, and we want it clean. Then you can commence with the bedrooms."
"Now David sit down here with me and I'll fix you some tea." As she prepared the tea she gave some thought to how she was going to approach the subject and decided to be direct, it was the only way. She served the tea and sat down at the table with her son. "Now David, I want ta talk to ya bout this girl Winnie Walsh youv'e been going round with."
"Oh ma, don't ya be fretting yaself bout that, it ain't nothing to be alarmed about, really it ain't."
"Is that the truth me boy, it's not the way it be looking to me and ya father. Ya don't be hanging round much after the mass be ended, so ya don't be hearing those tongues wagging, but ya the gossip of the month. And it be hard for me and ya pa ta be listening to the gossip about our own."
"Then don't be a listening ma, ignore those wagging tongues."
"Now David, thats not possible, and ya knows that ta be the truth. Our family is dutied to the church, and their social events each week, we can't be ignoring the gossip, as well you know. Now take heed of ya pa's words this morning, and end this charade. It's killing ya pa. Ya know how proud he is, and ye aren't unlike him. If it's not serious, as ya be claiming it's not, just end it."

"Yea ma, I'll do as you say, but I just hate it, when those loose tongues control us so much."

"Well that's a fact of life in these parts as well ya be knowing. After mass comes all the gossip, and none of us can change that. So be a good lad, and give them something else to talk about."

"Okay Ma, I'll be doing me best." David finished his cup of tea, and left to do his chores. Before he left he kissed his mothers cheek and said, "Don't be worrying ma, I'll be a sorting things out this afternoon. I've arranged ta meet Winnie at four o'clock, so I'll be ending it then."

"Okay David, but ya had better not let ya pa know where it is ya are."

"Okay Ma, and ya will cover for me won't ya ma."

"Ya that I'll be doing for ya lad, but mark me words, it will be the last time I'll be doing it for ya lad, and don't ya forget it."

"I won't ma, and thanks."

Mary gave him a suspicious look as he left the kitchen, through the tall, back door. She went to the window and watched him walk down the long path, which led to the paddocks and wondered if he would end it today. Then she thought, yea he's a good lad, and his word is his honour, he wouldn't purposely mislead me.

CHAPTER 2

Winnie Walsh rode down the narrow lanes of Ballinrobe, on her push bike. She was going to the local store for groceries for her mother. She was also meeting her best girlfriend Francis O'Mally, which was far more important.

She first met Francis when she started school, and they had been friends ever since. Francis had been a good and loyal friend over the years, although a bit of a goody-two-shoes, who never played truant from school, but she was still good fun to be around. Winnie smiled as she reminisced about some of the good times they had had together.

Francis O'Mally's mother hadn't really approved of the friendship, believing Winnie to be a bad influence on her daughter. However, she had not stopped the friendship either. Winnie regarded this thought, and began to wonder why people saw her as no good. She had never done anything to hurt anyone around these parts. She knew that the town folk regarded the family as roamers, and she was often referred to as a tinker, but it was hardly her fault if all her brothers and sisters apart from Angela, had decided to migrate to America to make better lives for themselves.

"It's jealousy, thats what it is" she said out loud. She then wondered if her sister Angela had been called names when she had been growing up. To the best of her knowledge she hadn't, maybe she should ask her next time they were together.
"No, what the hell, it don't make no difference to me anyways", she answered herself. She turned her thoughts to meeting her friend Francis and instantly cheered up.

Francis was waiting outside the local store, holding up her push bike, waiting for Winnie to arrive. She liked Winnie, regardless of what others thought of her. Winnie had always been there when she needed her, and vise versa. The other town folk didn't know Winnie the way she did. They regarded her only by her family's background, and not as an individual, which Francis thought was extremely unfair.

Finally Francis saw Winnie approaching. With anticipation and excitement she waved to her girlfriend. She could hardly wait to hear the gossip that Winnie wanted to share with her. After mass yesterday, Winnie had said "Meet me outside the local store tomorrow at noon. I've got some important news to be telling ya." Then she had took off and left it at that. Francis had been thinking about the nature of the news all night. She did wish Winnie wouldn't keep her in suspense like that. Francis gathered it would have something to do with David Lynch, whom Winnie had been seeing over the past several months. He had also taken off after mass yesterday, coincidently within a short period of Winnie!

Francis regarded Winnie's morals for a brief moment. There is no waiting for marriage with our Winnie, she thought, and immediately regretted this line of thinking. "Thats none my business" she chastised herself aloud.

"Hi Francis," Winnie said, " and how are ya doing on this fine morning?"

"I be doing fine, thank ya Winnie. Now tell me ya news."

"Now hang on there a minute girly, I'll go get me ma's groceries as I be promising her. Then we can go for a ride, and I'll be telling ya all the news."

"Okay" Francis replid, "But will ya get ya skates on girl, the suspense is killing me."

"Oh have some patience Francis, it won't be taking me long to get these few things," Winnie said, as she referred to her short shopping list her mother had given her.

Winnie rushed inside the store, quickly got the things she was sent for and returned to her friend. After placing them carefully in the basket attached to her bike. she turned to Francis. "Come on then, lets get going if its in a hurry ya are."

Francis just looked at Winnie, and they both burst into an infectious laughter. They got on their bikes and began to ride down the lane.

"Now come on Winnie Walsh, I won't be waiting a minute more" Francis said.

Winnie laughed as she regarded her friend then she let her bombshell drop. "I'm going ta be a mum."

Francis stopped her bike and looked dumbfounded at her friends back.

Winnie also pulled up her bike, looked back at her friend and said "Now what is the matter with ya girl? What are ya looking at me like that for?"

"Oh Winnie, what are ya going ta do? Ya pa's going ta kill ya, and ya knows that to be the truth, and what about David, have ya told him yet?, It is David's isn't it?" she asked all in one breath.

"Well of course it's Davids," Winnie retorted. "What ya be taking me for girl, a whore."

"Oh no Winnie, I'm just trying to get all the facts, thats all."

"As for me ma and pa," Winnie continued "I'll not be telling them until I've spoken to David. I'm meeting him at four o'clock this afternoon. He's me main concern at the present time. I'm not real sure how he'll be taking the news. He's not told me he luvs me yet, but men are shy in them ways, and he sure does be treating me kindly. So I figure he'll be taking to the idea of marrying me quite kindly. It will have to be a quick wedding too, or else I'll be poking out all over the place."

Francis just stood watching and listening to Winnie. She was a bit shocked and also scared for her friends predicament and quite truthfully at a loss for words. She opened her mouth to make some sort of reply when Winnie broke in, as if detecting her discomfort.

"Now don't be fretting for me Francis, that ain't gonna change nowt. The facts are the facts, and there ain't no one can be changing them. So what will be will be. Now come on, we'll sit over yonder on the grass, and eat these here sandwiches I packed this morning, and have a chat while we have some tucker."

Both girls rode in silence to the park a few seconds away. They got off and parked their bikes against a tree. Then Winnie took the sandwiches and drinks from her basket.

"My I'm hungry," Winnie stated, "it must be the bun in me oven." she said with a giggle.

"Oh Winnie" Francis said, "I don't know how you can be a joking about it. What if David won't be a marrying ya, and don't ya care what ya ma and pa will be a saying. The whole village will be bad mouthing ya, and ya sit there and laugh."

"Well it's like this Francis, like I said before, the facts are the facts, and the whole village is bad mouthing me now anyways. I do feel a bit sorry for me ma though, and me pa's gonna give me hell about this."

Winnie paused for a minute reflecting on her fathers bad temper. "Boy is he gonna hit the roof, but I'll have David there with me, and he won't be a beating a pregnant women, especially if Davids there.

Winnie turned to her friend and continued "As for David, of course he'll be marrying me. He's a Catholic man and he'll not be leaving me in the ditch and his child a bastard, and that's the truth. That's why I'm not too worried about all this, and you shouldn't be either Francis. In fact I'm quite pleased ta be getting away from home at last."

"That's hardly fair Winnie," Francis said, "Besides he's twenty-nine years old and your only seventeen, that's twelve years difference Winnie, and it is sort of trapping him."

"It's not trapping him,' Winnie retorted, "it's just hurrying him up a little. He's well an truly had his hay days. It's about time he settled down and made a life for himself." Winnie hoped that he would see it the same way as she did. She was being very brave in front of Francis. She wasn't entirely as sure of herself as she was making out to be. She finally said "Besides, I'll be making him a good wife and I'll be a good mother too, regardless of what the townfolk be saying. I'll prove them all wrong."

As the girls finished their lunch, Francis said, "Look, Winnie, I'd better be running along. I told me ma, I wouldn't be taking too long. If ya need me for anything, call round ta my place, and if I can help ya, ya know I will. Let me know how things went with David next time I see ya, okay?"

Winnie stood up and hugged her friend and said "Thanks Francis, you really are the best, and will ya be me matron of honour when the time comes?"

"Of course I will, and proud of it' Francis replied."

Both girls packed up the mess they had made and jumped on their bikes. After waving their good-byes they rode off in separate directions.

Francis started to ponder on her friends predicament with pity. Poor Winnie she thought, things never seem to turn out quite right for her. She really has herself in a mess this time, and it's really all her own doing. Sex out of wedlock was against their religion, maybe this was God's way of punishing her. She hoped David was the man Winnie thought he was, for her friends sake.

CHAPTER 3

Winnie sat waiting in the field, where she and David always met. Since leaving her friend Francis earlier in the day, she had spent most of her day re-hersing how she was going to tell David that she was pregnant. She was still no wiser now, than she had been all day.

Winnie looked at her watch, and noticed it was four-fifteen, and David had still not arrived. Blow him she thought, no consideration at all. Arrives when he feels like it, and never a sorry coming from him. Still I had better not chastise him today, I must be loving, and understanding. The last thing I want to be doing is up-setting him before I tell him the news. He may storm off before I can tell him, like so many other times in the past when she had snapped at him. No she decided, today she would be carefree, and easy to be with, she had no choice, she had to make him love her, or at least like her.

David walked along, deep in thought about how he was going to end the relationship with Winnie. Although David was a man of twenty-nine, he still did his parents bidding, and respected their wishes. That was the way it was in Ireland, for most anyway. Winnie was an exception to the rule, David thought, our Winnie does what she pleases, but she means no harm to anyone, and she can be a sweet young lass if the mood takes her. David looked at his watch, and quickened his pace across the fields. He didn't want her being upset before he got there. His Winnie had quite a fiery temper when the mood took her. They say all red-heads are hot tempered, David mused. Her father was also a red head. He also had a hot temper, and he was built like an ox. It was now four-thirty, she would be screaming mad, but he was almost there now, another five minutes or so. He had tried to leave earlier, but his father had still been alert and watchful. Leonard had finally retired to the small, but comfortable lounge room. He had sat in front of the open fire, dosing with his stout, when David had made his escape, reminding his mother as he left to cover for him. She in turn, reminded him in no un-certain terms to finish his relationship with Winnie.

This wasn't going to be easy for David. Although he was not in love with Winnie, he did have a certain affection for her, and really didn't want to be hurting her feelings. He wished now that the relationship hadn't gone so far. He didn't particularly like his present situation, but he also knew he had to be strong. The longer this went on, the harder it was going to be to get out of.

Winnie heard David's footsteps approaching and stood up, telling herself to keep calm, and not to start yelling. She busied herself with straightening the blanket she had been sitting on. As he approached, she said "Hello David," with her sweetest smile intact, even though she was quite put out by his being late.

"Hi there Winnie me girl" David responded in a friendly tone, as he contemplated how he was going to tell her it was over. Winnie rushed over and gave him a big hug, and kissed him affectionately on the cheek. "Come over here and make yaself comfortable David, I've brought along some Stout for ya. I was beginning ta think ya weren't coming, but it don't matter none, ya here now, and thats what matters."
David thought, well at least she's in a fine mood today, that'll make it easier on me, I hope. He settled himself down on the

blanket, she had laid out. Winnie sat down beside him and snuggled in close, and started to undo his shirt buttons and caress his chest in a loving way, lowering her hands to his taunt stomach muscles. David stopped drinking, and put his hand on top of hers to stop her caressing hands. He knew it wouldn't take long for him to get excited and he had best give her the news before anything happened.

"Winnie" he said, "look there's some bad news I have ta be giving ya lass, and I don't know how ta be saying it in a nice way."

Winnie sat up right and stared David in the face, somehow she knew by his tone what was coming, and panic set in.

David continued, "I'm afraid we'll have ta be stopping our meetings like this, the whole town is talking about it, and...

Winnie cut in and in an almost hesterical voice said "No David, ya can't be doing this ta me, ya can't. I luv ya David. I thought ya felt the same way. I thought ya were going ta marry me one day, that's why I've let ya have me the way ya have."

"Now wait there a minute girly," David said, "I've never given ya any cause ta be thinking like that, and that ya know ta be the truth. I've never been declaring I've loved ya, or promising ta take ya to the alter."

"No David, you've just made love ta me twice or three times a week, thats all isn't it." Winnie screamed at him. "You bastard," she continued "you've been using me."

"Now don't ya be talking ta me in that manner girly, who the foocking hell do ya think ya talking to. An I ain't no bastard either, so ya watch ya tongue."

Winnie tried to calm herself down, she had paniced, but she didn't want him storming off before she had told him.

"Look David, I'm sorry I didn't mean ta be losing me temper, it's just that I luv ya so much and I don't wanna lose ya. It don't matter what the town folk are saying, it's none of their god damned business. Besides when we get hitched, it won't be making a difference anyhow, and then they'll be finding someone new ta talk about."

David shook his head, and said "But Winnie we're not getting hitched. I'm sorry lass, but like ya as much as I do, and I really do, I'm not in luv with ya. Look even if I was in luv with ya lass, ya know we can't afford ta be getting married. What would I do ta support ya, there's no work in Ballinrobe, as well ya be knowing. Look Winnie, its best if we don't be taking this relationship any further. I told me folks that I'd be ending it today, their not happy with me seeing ya, so ending it I'll be doing."

He stood up to go and Winnie jummped to her feet, grabbing hold of his arm.

"You're not leaving me David" she said with ferocity, "You've got to marry me whether ya like it or not. I'm going ta ave ya baby!"

David was momentarily stunned, and he searched her face for an explanation. He wasn't even sure if he had heard her right. The words flashed across his mind, like thunder, but all that keep ringing home was baby, baby, baby, what was she babbling about. "WHAT," hc finally managed, in a shrill, more than a shout.

"Ya heard me David, I'm pregnant, so it's not leaving me you're going ta be doing, it's making an honest women out of me." She calmed down for a minute, and in the softest voice she could muster she said, "Look David it's not that bad, really it's not. I luv ya so much, and I'll make ya a good wife, and I'll be a good mother to our child as well."

"You don't understand what ya saying girl," David said. "How can I be looking after a wife and baby, I've got no money, and what will I be doing for a job?"

"Things will sort themselves out David, ya know they will. Ya can continue ta work at ya pa's farm for a wage, and I'm sure we can live there for a time, until we get on our feet."

"Haven't you heard anything girly." David said, "They don't approve of ya, they wanted me to finish up with ya today. I've been telling ya that all along."

"Well they will just have ta get used to me, won't they" Winnie yelled. Oh how she hated them, they are all up themselves she thought. She would get them back when she was married to David, you just wait and see, but for now she had to hold her tongue. "Besides, they don't even know me," she continued, " they will come ta love me, as you will David. I will make ya a good wife, that I'll be promising. I can also get some work in for ya, I'm a very good knitter, and I can handle the sewing pretty good as well. I'm already doing some work for some of the town folk."

"No" David said firmly, but he regarded her with fondest, thinking how kind she was trying to be. "I'll not have any wife of mine working. On no account would I allow that, I'll put the bread and butter on my table, and don't be forgetting it.

Winnie smiled inwardly, although he was not happy about the situation, he had just accepted they were getting married, and she would be his wife. She continued with more confidence.

"Look David, things look pretty grim at the moment, but there's always a silver lining luv, maybe god wanted us ta be together and that's why he blessed us with this child."

"Or maybe he is punishing us" David interjected.

Winnie decided to change her tactics, and ignored his last statement.

"I'll be a good wife, you'll not want for anything", she started to caress him again, kissing his chest sensually. He pulled her away from him in disgust.

"Is that all ya can be thinking of at a time like this Winnie, have ya no shame." Winnie flinched under his condemning stare, and backed away feeling a little ashamed of herself, and hating David for making her feel that way. She turned from him, and looked down on the blanket they were standing on waiting for David to say something. David regarded her for a moment, and was suddenly overwhelmed with pity for her, and instantly regretted his harshness towards her. He came towards her slowly and wrapped his arms around her tummy, patting it softly.

"I am thinking maybe it's a boy Winnie," he said.

Winnie turned and threw her arms around his neck, kissing him in a feverish manner, thankful of his understanding, and pleased with herself, declaring her love for him over and over. Through her kisses and tears of joy she said, "If it's a boy we have, we shall call him David after you."

"Of course we will lassie, and what else would we be calling him."

Finally he pulled her away gently, not wanting this show of affection to go any further, not today, he had too much on his mind.

"Winnie", he said, "have ya told ya folks yet that you're pregnant?"

"No David, I wanted you ta be the first to know, since you're the father an all," she lied, then followed with the truth, "besides, I'm not sure how me pa's going ta be taking the news. I was kinda hoping ya would come with me, and tell him ya plan ta marry me and all. I sure could be using the support David."

"Okay" David said, "You be running off home now Winnie, and don't be saying anything to them tanight, I'll come over tamorrow morning, around ten, and break the news meself."

"But what about ya folks David, won't ya be missed at that time of the morning."

"Well that hardly matters now girly, does it, if we're going ta be hitched an all, there's nowt they can be saying. Still I'll try and get away un-noticed if I can help it. I'd prefer ta be talking this through with your folks before mine. Now you get along home, and don't be given them a reason to be yelling at ya. If ya home early, they won't be chastising ya, which will make it easier on us both in the morning."

He kissed her gently on the cheek, gave her a loving pat on the bottom and turned to leave bidding her farewell.

Winnie emptied the remaining of the stout beer which David hadn't drunk, threw the empty bottle into the field, and picked up the blanket. As she folded the blanket, she thought, Well that's that then, I'm getting married, no one telling me what to do anymore. Now maybe I'll be getting a bit of respect round here. I'm going to be a married women now, and a mother shortly, that should shut those townfolk up. Suddenly Winnie thought, I must go and see Francis straight away, I can't wait till later, I have ta tell her the good news. I'm going to be Mrs Lynch. I'v finished up early here taday anyway, so another hour or so won't make any difference. Besides, David will be none the wiser. She got on her bike and headed towards Francis's place, as usual doing what she wanted to, ignoring David's advice about going straight home.

CHAPTER 4

David rose early the next morning. He hadn't slept well the night before, and felt dazed and groggy. He had been distressed about the circumstances he found himself in. He wasn't sure how Mr Walsh was going to take the news about his daughter's pregnancy. It was all well and good to tell him that he planned to marry her, but the fact remained, that his daughter had been sleeping around. David also knew that his own parents were going to be terribly hurt and disappointed. David hurt for them also, even more than for himself. However the facts as they were, he had no alternative but to marry Winnie Walsh. He half laughed to himself as he reflected on Winnie's name, "At least that will be improving, Winnie Lynch sounds far better," he said aloud.

David prepared to go down stairs, as he left the room, he turned and studied his bedroom, and thought to himself how happy I've been here. For the first time he took note of the white-washed walls, and the clean vinyl floors, and his single timber bed. Such a simple room he acknowledged, but the room I've grown up in, and it's been home for me. David started to get emotional and walked out of the room, and downstairs to have breakfast. He had to keep a clear mind, and try to avoid any conversation about Winnie this morning. David walked into the kitchen with a false, but wide smile on his face, and gave a cheery hello to everyone present. He sat down without saying anything more. When his breakfast was placed in front of him, he ate in silence while the rest of the family talked about trivial matters. David made sure, not to be dragged into any conversation at all. After he had finished with his plate, he stood up and excused himself, explaining that he wanted to get an early start on the barn, which he had started the day before and left through the back door, before this could be questioned.

It was seven-fifteen, he quickened his stride, he wanted to get as much of the barn painted, before going to Winnie's place. He certainly didn't want to be getting there late. If Mr Walsh, was any comparison to his father, about ten in the morning was time to have a cuppa and some scones, after completing the morning chores. David decided he would go there a little earlier and wait around until he had morning tea.

David reached the barn, and got straight into the painting, all the preparation work had been completed yesterday. If he could finish one side at least, it would look like he hadn't moved from there, or so he hoped.

David finished the back of the barn, and got down from his ladder, and stood back to admire his mornings work with proudness. Then he glanced at his watch, it was nearly nine-thirty. My how the time had passed he thought. He pulled off his overalls, replaced the lids on the paint tins quickly, then he rinsed the paint brushes and left them sitting in turps. David got on his bike and left for Winnie's place. He wasn't exactly looking forward to this confrontation. However he had got himself into this mess, and now he had to see it through. He pondered this though, and self-pity engulfed him. How am I ever going to cope, I don't even love the girl, he thought, but there's no use crying over spilled milk. I'll have ta make the best of it now. I've made me bed, now I have ta lie in it. Perhaps Winnie is right, maybe things would turn out okay. Only time would tell. He was getting married and he had to make the most of it.

When David arrived, Winnie was standing at the front gate.

They said their hello's as David unseated his bike and parked it at the side of the house. Winnie grabbed his hand, and squeezed it gently.

"Pa's already inside" she stated as she walked him around to the back door.

"What sort of a mood is he in Winnie?" David asked.

"I'm not really sure David, I've stayed clear of him this morning, but we're about to find out."

"Come on then," David said, "lets get this done with girl."

Winnie led David through the back door, only the priest, or overseas visitors ever used the front door in Ireland, that's just the way it was. Winnie's folks looked up from the table when David and Winnie entered the kitchen, and David saw the surprise on their faces as they regarded him standing beside Winnie.

"Good morning, to ya" David said, as he approached Mr Walsh, with his hand outstreatched to shake his hand. Peter Walsh stood up and took David's hand in his, and smiled as he indicated for David to take a chair.

"Ta what do we owe this unexpected visit boy?" Peter said, looking David straight in the eyes, with a questioning look on his brow.

David flinched slightly under Mr Walsh's stare, then proceeded to answer him.

"Well there's a slight matter I've got ta be discussing with ya sir. It's regarding Winnie and meself."

Peter turned his gaze to his daughter who was standing behind David's chair with her hands rested on David's shoulder. Then he turned back to David and said

"Well boy, out with it, I'm a busy man as ya know, say what ya have ta and be gone with ya."

David resented his abruptness, but continued in a fairly firm tone.

"Well it's like this sir, Winnie is pregnant, and we..."
"WHAT" Peter interjected. He turned his gaze back to his daughter.
"You whore" he yelled. "I knew no good would be coming of ya, always galavanting round the way ya do. I told ya mother so, that I did."

Heather Walsh, just stood frozen to the spot near the sink, her hands over her mouth in shock horror. She could hear what was being said, but somehow it was like a dream, just not penetrating her brain. Almost there, but never quite reaching her main thought system. She turned and searched her daughter's face, looking for some sort of denial on her part, then started to shake from head to toe as she realised her daughter was really in the family way. What would the neighbours say, and what about the priest, he would be horrified. This couldn't be happening, it was a dream she keep telling herself. The screaming brought her back to her senses again, and she looked up and regarded the scene in front of her.

David cut through the obscenities Peter was verbally throwing at his daughter and said, "Mr Walsh, I've got every intention of marrying ya daughter, and making an honest women out of her."
"Lad ya can do what the foocking hell ya like with her, it's not my concern. Please ya self if ya marry her or not. As far as I'm concerned she's foocking dead. She's not my daughter from this day on. Now take this piece of shit outa me house, and don't let me set eyes on her again. She was born a piece of shit and that's how she'll end up me boy, you mark my words ere today."
Heather rushed over to her daughter, she was now reduced to babbling tears, she threw her arms around Winnie, hugging her

as if not wanting to ever let her go. Peter grabbed Heather's arm and violently pulled her away, screaming as he did so, "Let the tramp go, get her out of me sight, before I kill her with me bare hands. Go on" he yelled looking at David, "get her out of her. Now, NOW I say."

Winnie spoke for the first time, "What about me clothes and things pa?"

"What about me clothes and things Pa," her father mimicked, "me and my, that's all ya think about isn't girly, well ya came inta the world with nowt and thats the way ya can be leaving me house, now get out, go on get, I say."

Winnie now reduced to tears like her mother, ran from the house.

David looked at Peter and said, "We'll talk later about the wedding plans, when you've had a chance ta settle down, Winnie can stay at me ma's place for the time being."

"Are ye deaf, or just dumb boy?," Peter said, "I've just finished telling ya, I don't want ta be seeing none of ya faces ever again, and I mean it lad, stay away from me. Now get out, and follow that piece of trash that just left." Peter turned his attention to his wife and started to caress her, cooing to her like one would a baby, hugging her gently whilst rocking her to and fro.

David turned on his heel and left through the back door, the way he had entered feeling a mixture of feelings, hurt, ashamed, but mostly angry at Mr Walsh's attitude and stubbornness. He Looked around for Winnie wondering where on earth she had took off to now. He felt sorry for her in a way. Her father had been terribly hard on her. He finally found Winnie curled up in a ball in the field, crying like a baby. He ran to her and pulled her up into his arms.

"Now now, deary don't be carrying on in this manner. Ya

folks will come around. It's just the shock of it all."

"No they won't David, ya don't know me pa the way I do. He's a stubborn man, you'd better believe it. I hate him David, I really do. He's never had no time for me."

"Now don't be talking like that Winnie, he's been a good pa ta ya, you've always eaten well, and been well clothed. So don't be running the man down when he ain't here ta defend himself."

'Oh David, what am I going to do. I've got nowhere to go, no clothes, nothing."

"We have each other Winnie. First of all lets stop ya tears. Come on dry ya eyes or you'll not be piddling for days."

Winnie gave a small smile at this statement.

"Thats better, now pick yaself up and we'll make our way over to my place. We have ta face the music there too, so don't be wasting all ya tears and energy yet."

Winnie laughed this time, and David continued, "Like I said before, ya folks will change their tune in a few days. In the meantime ye can lodge at me ma's place. Under the circumstances I don't think their be making any objections."

But David had never been more wrong in his entire life. Winnie's parents didn't get over it. David and Winnie did get married a few weeks later. Heather Walsh had come to Davids folk's place a few days after the argument, and dropped of Winnie's clothing and wished them both all the very best in life. But neither of them attended the wedding, much to Davids disgust and Winnie's sadness.

I now believe, that this was the time when our mother's first brick was cemented in. The first brick in a wall so strong, no one or anything could pass it and hurt her again.

CHAPTER 5

The next few weeks leading up to the wedding were hectic for everyone. The pressure was building by the day. David's parents made it quite clear that they were unhappy about the approaching wedding. They were always snaping at Winnie for the slightest thing. David was the unfortunate one really. He had Winnies whinging to contend with, plus his fathers disapproval. David on many occasions had tried unsuccessfully to discuss matters with his father. However his father seemed distant and unwilling to enter into any discussions. This made Winnie very bitter towards them, and a few more bricks were added to her brick wall. She held her tongue though, and never gave them any further cause to make their lifes misery. She would take out her frustrations on David when they were alone, not realising that he was also under extreme emotional pressure.

David decided to let things ride for the present. He frantically looked for a cheap place to rent for himself and Winnie after the-wedding. He spent a lot of time with his brother Leonard, drinking at the pub. David had always enjoyed a few stouts, but of late he had been drinking on a daily basis. It was his way of relaxing he told himself, and getting away from all the tensions at home. He would get up in the morning, go about his chores without any instructions. Then in the afternoon he would say that he was going out to try and find somewhere for them to live. At first Winnie would want to go along with him, but she soon got the message that he was trying to get away. To be by himself for a few hours. He started coming home later and later as the weeks went by. Winnie started to resent Leonard and Bridget also. Feeling that they were the reason David didn't want to be at home with her. That in someway they were encouraging David to stay out late, leaving her at home with his hateful family.

One night David came home from the pub, and he was in a fine mood, singing and happy. He was also quite drunk. Winnie as usual was up waiting for him. The rest of the family had retired for the nite. David burst into the kitchen.

"Hello Winnie me luv."

"Be quiet David, ya'll have the whole bloody family down ere with all ya racket"

"Now don't be worrying ya self about that deary, I have wonderful news for ya luv," David slurred as he plunked himself down at the kitchen table.

Without asking about the news, Winnie went off on one of her tantrums.

"David, where the hell have ya been. It's not fair leaving me ere everynite by meself. Ya know how they treat me. I need ya support round ere."

"Oh stop ya foocking whinging lass, I'm sick ta death of it. There's nowt coming from ya anymore but moan moan moan. I'm sick of it, can ya hear what I'm saying."

"I'm sorry David, I don't mean to be nagging ya. I just get so lonely ere all day and all nite by meself. Ya out working all day, then ya take off looking for a place for us, and ya arrive back at eleven o'clock at night. Ya know that I'm not all that welcome round ere, and I need ya here with me. I only see ya at meal times if I'm lucky."

"Well like I was trying ta tell ya lass, I have good news for ya. Taday I found somewhere for us ta stay after the wedding. It's close ta here too, so I won't have ta come far ta work. Also when our little bundle arrives, ma will be close enough ta help ya out."

David had just spoiled his good news with his last statement. In Winnies eyes she saw Mary interfering, not helping with the baby and she just couldn't hold her tongue.

"Now hang on a minute David, I don't want ya ma helping me none, I don't care if I never see her again after we're married. After the way she's been treating me an all."

"Now don't be talking like that against me ma Winnie. She's doing the best she can under the circumstances, everyone is, and I'll not have ya bad mouthing them."

"Oh that's right isn't it David, they can bad mouth me, but I must keep me mouth shut. Why don't ya tell them ta have a little respect for ya future wife, instead of chastising me all the bloody time."

"Oh go ta hell Winnie, I'm sick of all this ere fighting. I'm going ta bed, I don't need these hassels."

Winnie sat in the kitchen and watched David storm off up the stairs. She regarded him with contempt thinking you really are a mummies boy aren't ya David, but she said nothing and let him go. She sat there for a while hating his folks and his brother Leonard. He should send him home early in the nite instead of giving him more free drinks. Things will change after the wedding and thats the truth she thought. After a few minutes she calmed down and decided to retire herself. She had been sleeping in the lounge room since she had been residing here. It didn't make sense to Winnie. She was already pregnant, and they were going to be married shortly, but still Davids folks insisted on separate rooms until after the wedding. You didn't add wrong to wrong as far as they were concerned.

"Bloody stupid," Winnie said to herself. Winnie went got up and went onto the couch and lay down. As she did so, she thought, gee I do wish I had found out more about the place David found for us, me and my blood temper. Never mind she would find out all about it tomorrow. The wedding was in a few days now, she and David would be more relaxed and happy after the wedding she told herself. Then turned over and went to sleep without any trouble at all.

David lay in his bed regarding the argument he just had with Winnie. My, she was a nasty peice when she wanted to be he thought. Then he realised he hadn't given her all the details of the house he had found for them. Let her wait and find out now he thought. He wondered what his life was going to be like after the wedding. He hoped that they would be happy for both their sakes. He did try to be patient with her, but whenever he seen her lately she was complaining, mainly about the way his folks were treating her. He had told her on the day he had found out about her pregency that they didn't approve of her. So why was she expecting to be treated any differently, then what she was. His mother was at least civil towards her, and his father didn't talk to her at all. His father wasn't talking to David either unless he really had to. David worried about this, he had always been so close to his father. Now his father was either avoiding him or ignoring his presence altogether. David thought to himself I'm the one stuck in the middle. I'm copping it from both sides. I wish Winnie would try and understand my point. Why I feel the need to get away from here. Hopefully things would improve when Winnie and himself were in their own place. Everyone would have a chance to adjust to the situation at their own pace. David looked at his watch, it was Twelve Fifteen., He turned off the nightlight to go to sleep. However he didn't find it as easy as Winnie had. He spent several hours that night tossing and turning, his brain on overload, thinking about what had past and what was coming. Wondering if the future would be even worse than the past.

The next few days flew by, and the wedding day arrived. It was a small quiet wedding, and as Winnie had promised,

Francis O'Malley was the Matron of Honour. It was David's father who walked Winnie down the isle, because her own father had refused to attend the wedding, even after several invitations. However on the whole the day went smoothly and everyone seemed to be relaxed and at peace with one another. After the wedding everyone went to Leonard and Bridget's place for a small celebration, where they all toasted the bride and groom.

David believed that finally everyone had come around, and he drank with happiness for the first time in weeks. Everyone became quite merry and drank and danced all night. Everyone except Leonard that is. The truth was he never drank, but Winnie took this the wrong way, thinking that he still held a grudge against her and she hated him for it.

Later in the evening David and Winnie left the pub and went home. It was quite exciting for Winnie and David to be going to their own place. David by this time had had a few beers and was quite drunk, as he had been nearly every day for the past few weeks. However Winnie was too happy to say anything to him. He carried her over the threshold and nearly dropped her twice. They giggled with each other over this, plus everything and anything else. They were actually happier tonight , than they had been since that day in the field, when Winnie had told David she was going to have his child.

"Well Winnie, how do ya like ya new home lass?"

"It's wonderful David, I'm so happy. I just know things are going ta turn out fine."

"I am thinking ya right deary, now lets be getting ta bed. We're honeymooners ya know. I stocked up on some beer for me and some wine for you. Leonard gave 'em to me."

"Oh David, lets not have anymore to drink lets just go ta bed and have us some fun," Winnie said with a giggle.

The next morning Winnie rose early and went straight out to the kitchen to prepare David some breakfast, she wanted to surprise him and give it to him in bed. David's mother had stocked the kitchen with food from the farm so they had plenty to eat.

Winnie looked about the kitchen and thought to herself, this place ain't much at the moment, but I'll fix it up slowly.

It was already furnished although the furniture was quite old and grotty, and the bed they had slept in was not the most confortable, but it sure beat the couch Winnie had been sleeping on at the Lynches. Winnie got on with what she was doing and she had almost completed breakfast when David came out.

"Good morning David" Winnie said, "Now get back ta bed, I'm going ta spoil ya this morning with breckie in bed."

David laughed and said "Alright deary, that I'll be doing, but first I gotta go to the toilet."

David went outside into the fields and crouched down. He had woken with terrible pains in his stomach. It must have been all the food yesterday. He finished emptying his stomach then looked around for a nice wide leaf referred to as a docket leaf in Ireland. After cleaning his rear to his satisifaction he return inside. My, he thought, I do wish I had a toilet like the one in Leonards pub. I wonder why ma and pa never got one, it gets so cold out ere first thing in the morning. When he got inside he washed his hands and returned to the bedroom where Winnie was waiting for him holding the tray of food.

"Come on then" Winnie said "get undressed again and hop inta bed."

"Well Winnie, thank ya an all, but I may as well stay up now and eat it in the Kitchen. I have ta get dressed anyway and make me way up ta the farm."

"What," Winnie yelled, "ya going up there taday, on our first day of marriage"

"Now don't start ya yelling Winnie, how do ya think I'm going ta be paying the rent on this place if I'm not working."

"They could ave given ya a couple of days off David, just being married an all."

"An why would they be doing that lass, the chores still have ta be done up there, and their paying me ta do them now, plus the're giving us the food we'll be eating."

"Well I don't want it, or need it, they can keep their charities. Besides it's just so they can have a hold on ya, and still keep telling ya what to do."

"Now that's nonesense Winnie, and ya know it. Their trying ta help us out as much they can, and ya should be thanking them, not critising them girl."

"Oh get out, go ta them, see if I care." Winnie snapped back.

"Shut-up Winnie" David said. He got up, leaving the tray of food, and Winnie sitting on the bed. He washed his face in the kitchen and left for the farm. After work he went to the pub and returned home late at night. Winnie ate alone on her first night of marriage, and a few more bricks were cemented in.

CHAPTER 6

As the months passed Winnie and David settled down together. They continued to fight, and always about the same things, David's family and David's Drinking. They went hand in hand. First Winnie would complain about David's family, then David would stay out all night drinking. Slowly Winnie started to keep her mouth shut in hope that David would come home at a reasonable hour. But by this time it was too late. David would avoid coming home to save having an argument.

Winnie avoided David's family as much as she avoided discussing them with David now. She hated them with a passion. She felt it was them that had caused all the friction between her and David. She would imagine that Leonard and Mary Lynch were bad mouthing her all the time to David while he was over there with them. The truth was she was totally wrong. They, like the rest of the Lynches, had now gracefully excepted the marriage and were genuinely trying to help them out.

On some occasions Mary would visit Winnie to see how she was keeping, and if there was anything she needed. She would be met with coldness and reproach. In Winnie's eyes Mary was only there to check up and see if the house was clean, which it never was. Oh at first Winnie had been very good and cleaned the house everyday, but the more David had retreated to the pub, the less Winnie had done. It was all a waste of time to her. Winnie got lazier and lazier. She always cooked David's meal for him and nine out of ten times it stayed in the oven until it was burnt to a sinder. But if he did make it home at a reasonable hour the food was always ready for him. He expected that. Apart from that she did nothing but knit all day.

Even though David forbid her to do knitting for the townfolk before they were married, Winnie continued to do it. If David happened to come home early and found her knitting she would say it was for the baby she was carrying.

However as time passed, some things did start to improve. David still spent most of his spare time at the pub. Winnie still avoided his family, (except on Sundays when she would see them after mass). But the fighting when Winnie and David were together seemed to be easing at least. This was due to the fact that they, rarely were alone for any long period of time. One day David arrived home at four o'clock, and found Winnie knitting as usual. The house was a shambles, and as David entered, and saw the scene in front of him he was disgusted. However, he said nothing of his feelings except, "That there child ya carrying will have more clothes than the queen herself"

Winnie looked up, and was surprised to see David home so early.

"Hello David, what a pleasant surprise. I'll get ya dinner out of the oven for ya luv. How come ya home so early?"

"Well I've got some wonderful news for ya actually. I think ya were right when ya said things would be turning out fine. Me pa's come round now, and things are just like they used to be."

"Well that's good" Winnie said in the sweetest of ways, but she was thinking that's all ya worried about isn't it David. Bugger how I feel, just worry about ya folks. Jesus it made her mad.

"Anyway Winnie, getting to the point, while we were having morning tea this morning at the farm Leonard and Bridget arrived. As ya can imagine I was quite taken aback, as was the others. Dad told em ta sit down, that he had a family matter ta discuss, and guess what it was all about?"

"Well how would I know David, I wasn't there" Winnie said.

"Well it was about the farm. He addressed Leonard first and explained he was the oldest and by rights the farm should go ta him one day, but since he was already well off in his own right with the pub an all, that he and ma had decided ta leave the farm ta us and our kids, since we needed the help more."

"Oh that is good news luv, I bet ya feel good after that news." Winnie said.

"Yea I sure do luv. There was one condition though, which was, I'm never ta put Shamous, Kathleen or Phyllis off the farm while their still on this earth. Nevertheless the farm goes onta me and me kids later."

"Well of course there's a condition, there always is. In other words it's ours but we can't live there until everyone dies. Big deal."

"Winnie, ya nowt but an ungrateful bitch. Can't ya see their trying ta make up for what they said about ya. They're trying ta except ya inta the family."

"Well ya can tell em I don't need their bloody acceptance, and I don't need their stupid farm either, they can keep it. I need nowt from any of em."

For the first time, David really felt like slapping Winnie across the face. He rose from the kitchen table and stared at her, trying very hard to control the temper that was flaring up inside of him.

"There's no reasoning with ya Winnie, sometimes ya really make me sick. This place is a mess, you're a bloody mess, and all ya can do is turn ya nose up at everything me folks try and do for us." David paused for a brief moment, in an effort to control his temper, then he continued, "I'm going out now Winnie, and when I come back make sure this place is looking like a home, and not a bloody pig sty."

Winnie watched him leave and regretted instantly her words,

but it was too late to take them back now. She would try and make it up to him later. Since their marriage they rarely made love. Even when they had, he was usually drunk, as she was sure he would be when he returned home again. Tonight she would endeavour to make things right between them and apologise to him for her attitude.

David returned in a terrible state that night, and although Winnie attempted to make love to him, it was impossible, he wasn't even capable of getting an erection. Winnie gave up in the end and let her husband sleep. She decided that she would try and make this marriage work and stop all her complaining. She would still avoid his family as much as possible, but if they did come for a visit she would at least be civil towards them, and try and make them feel welcome.

Winnie done as she vowed that night in bed, and slowly things did start to improve. The gossip started to die down and slowly Winnie felt more comfortable around everyone, even the neighbours. The neighbours had obviously found some new sourse of gossip to talk about. They even stopped staring at them the way they used to. The Lynch family were slowly uniting. David was less conscious of the gossip, and he no longer felt that his name was being dragged through the mud. Winnie started to keep clean house again, and David started slowly to return home earlier, unless of course they had been fighting, which was much less frequent now.

Winnie actually started to enjoy her life now. Since she had made a conscious effort to stop all the bickering, things had really improved. Winnie as if growing up suddenly, realised that all she needed to do, to keep David happy was, not be in bed when he arrived home, no matter how late. Have a meal ready for him, and keep the house clean. They were really starting to get along.

As Winnie reached her ninth month of pregnancy, life became pretty hectic, preparing for the new baby. Winnie even started visiting Mary and Leonard Lynch. She still held the bitterness in her heart, but she really wanted her marriage to work, and most of all she wanted David's love and respect. Slowly she began to get this too. He ignored the gossip completly, and if his family happened to talk or say something against Winnie, he began to jump to her defence, which naturally made Winnie feel over the moon with pride and joy. David and Winnie really were starting to be a family. Even David was looking forward to the birth of the child, forgetting about the financial side of things altogether. Winnie continued to keep house, which was reasonably hard work since there were no electrical appliances. The washing was done by hand. The ironing was done with a heavy iron which was heated on the range. To test if the iron was at the desired heat, Winnie would spit onto the base of the iron, if the spit rolled off, the iron was hot enough.

David still had his drinking binges, but Winnie had well and truly learnt to keep her mouth shut. Which in turn made David happier and spend more time at home.

CHAPTER 7

As the birth of the child approached Winnie grew more and more excited. She knew that David would prefer a boy. However Winnie wanted a little girl more than anything in the world. She had decided to call the baby Francis after her close friend Francis O'Mally. If it were a boy she could still call him Francis, but she knew from now, that this would cause friction between herself and David all over again. In Ireland the first born was always called after the father or mother. It would be easy to break the rule for herself, she had never liked her own name anyway. It had often got her into quarrels at school when the children teased her. Winnie hoped with all her heart that it was a girl for other reasons too. She could dress a little girl in pretty little things, and play with her hair all day. She didn't really know how to dress a little boy.

It was four o'clock in the morning when Winnie went into labour. Not knowing what to expect she became frightened, and woke David up on her first twinge.
"David, David, wake up, it's coming."
"What, what's coming" David replied, still half asleep.
"The baby, the baby is on it's way. Be a pet and go get the midwife."
David rose, startled. He too was new to all this. He jumped out of bed, and grabbed for his pants and shirt. "I'll be back in a jiffy with her, ya hold on there now. Take it easy. Don't be doing anything till I get back".
"Well I can hardly be controlling that now, can I David?"
"Ain't that the truth" David replied as he finished getting dressed. He kissed Winnie and ran to the midwife's house.

Both David and the midwife returned to find Winnie in the

kitchen having a cup of tea and some home made scones, with piles of fresh cream and jam.

The midwife turned to David and said, "Why are ya getting me outa bed at this ungodly hour lad?, ya wife ain't in no pain, and from the looks of her appetite it'll be a few hours yet before the babe is born. I'm going back home. Come back and get me when the pains are regular like, about five minutes apart".

Just than Winnie let out a scream, and both the midwife and David turned to see her bent over with pain. Then came another yell from Winnie's mouth.

"Quick" said the midwife to David. "Looks like the little mite is on the way after all. Help me get Winnie back inta the bedroom. Then ya can commence boiling me some water on the range. I also need plenty of clean cloths."

Winnie interjected and said. "David, I've been boiling some water already, and the cloths ye'll find in the bottom draw over yonda."

The midwife continued, "I'll also need something ta wrap the baby in, when it arrives."

They carried Winnie through to the bedroom and laid her on the bed. While David prepared the things he had been asked to, the midwife settled Winnie down, giving her some breathing exercises to do, designed to control the pain. David returned to the bedroom, but he was sent packing by the midwife.

"Go about ya business now David, and I'll be bringing out ya babe ta ya when it arrives."

David left the bedroom and the midwife closed the door behind him.

David sat in the kitchen by himself in anticipation of the baby's birth. Well the time has finally arrived he thought, the baby will be here soon. He was suddenly very excited, and stood to get himself a stout from the fridge. As the hours passed, he began to wonder what the hell was going on in the bedroom. He could hear the screams coming from Winnie. Occasionally he knocked on the bedroom door, and asked what was going on in there. The response was always the same. "It won't be long now."

After approximately eight hours or so, and several stout beers, David heard the cry of a new born baby. He jumped up from the chair and ran to the bedroom. As he went to open the door, the midwife came out with the bundle in her hands.
"It's a boy" she stated flatly.
David looked at his son. What a beautiful boy he is, he thought, and took the child from the midwife. She watched over him carefully for a few minutes than said, "I'd best be taking him back ta his ma. I'll clean Winnie up a bit and get her comfortable, than ya can make ya way in ere. Perhaps ya can make us all some tea in the meantime" she said.

The midwife returned to Winnie. "How ya feeling lovie" she said, as she handed the baby back to Winnie.
"Oh fine now, thank god thats all over." She turned to the baby in her arms and thought, why did ya have ta be a boy. Then as she studied him more closely, she thought, my ya are a pretty wee thing though, with ya vivid blue eyes, and what a mop of jet black curley hair ya have. Suddenly she felt very happy, and held her baby close to her kissing him gently.

The midwife gave Winnie a wash down and cleaned the room up to it's orginal state. Then she changed the sheets on the bed, asking Winnie to sit in the armchair as she did so. Shortly after David knocked on the door. After being told by the midwife it was alright to come in, he entered with the tea tray, put it on the bed and went to Winnie's side and kissed her gently.

"He's beautiful isn't he lass" he said to Winnie.

"Yea, he is David."

"I'm glad it's a boy Winnie". He looked down at the baby as he said this, then added, "Me little son, David Jnr." Winnie froze suddenly, and sensing the tension David looked up at her.

"What's the matter with ya girl?" he asked

"Oh nowt David luv, it's just I was kinda thinking I'd like ta call him Francis after me girlfriend."

"No bloody way Winnie, he'll be called after his pa, the same way Leonard was called after his, and his father before him."

"Well why da we hav ta be following that old tradition anyways" Winnie responded. "Why can't we do our own thing an all. It's confusing having two people in the same house with the same name. We'll start a new trend".

David stood up abruptly "Do what the hell ya like Winnie, ya always do anyway, all ya think about is yaself. I really thought ya were beginning ta change lately, but I guess I was wrong" He turned and left the room. Winnie regarded his words for a moment, and considered changing her mind and calling the baby David after all. Then she had second thoughts, na he'll get over it, she selfishly thought. It's only a name.

The midwife who had been present during the whole conversation finished up what she was doing and turned to Winnie, "That's not the way ta be starting a family life girly. Ya son should be called after his pa, as well ya be knowing. Besides what kinda name is Francis for a boy."

"It's a lovely name, it can be shortened ta Frank. Besides it really ain't ya business. It's between me and me husband."

"That I be knowing, without your cheeky tongue telling me, but I'm telling ya it's not right, and I'm telling ya for ya own good too, not mine. Now I'm finished up ere so I'll be getting meself home ta me own family, but remember what I'm saying, ya'll have the whole town gossiping again girly, ya mark me words."

"Who gives a damn" Winnie replied with vengence.

"Ya husband does, that's who. Ya know how proud he is. When ya first got married, and everyone was talking about ya, it affected him pretty bad as ya know. Why do ya think he spent most of the time in the pub luvie. He was drowning his sorrows, and his shame."

"How da ya know about that?" Winnie asked.

"I go ta mass every Sunday dearie, that's how I know. Everybody knows everything about everyone round these parts." She paused for a moment and then went on. Look all I'm asking is ya think about ya husband, then do the right thing." Then she turned and left saying her goodbyes and congratulations to David in the kitchen on the way out. Winnie heard them both in the kitchen and then heard her leaving. Nosey old cow she thought, I wish everybody would mind their own bloody business.

David seen the midwife out. Then he sat down again, and thought about what Winnie had just told him. "Oh what does t matter anyway." He said to himself . "It's only a name." He rose and went back into the bedroom. Winnie was now settled back in bed feeding young Francis. He went over to the bed and kissed them both gently.

"How ya both doing?" he asked.

Winnie looked up and smiled realising that David was happy again. Then she said,"We're just fine David and very happy."

"David" she added "Ya don't really mind about the baby being called Francis do ya?"

"Na, I'll get used ta it" he responded.

They sat there in silence for a while just watching young Francis sucking away at Winnies breast. Suddenly David said, "I'd best be going ta give the news ta me folks then, this is their first grandchild ya know."

"Yea David, that's a good idea. I'm feeling pretty tired anyways. I think I'll have a nap while ya gone."

"What about your folks Winnie, should I drop over and tell them too?"

"Na don't bother. They don't give two shits about us. Not even me sister comes near me any more, so why should I worry about them. I still can't believe none of em came to our wedding. They can all go to hell as far as I'm concerned. Besides they'll find out at mass on Sunday, so don't be wasting ya time on em.

"Ah Winnie, don't be like that lass. Maybe the baby will change things."

"I told ya before David, ya don't know me pa the way I do. The baby ain't gonna change nowt, believe you me. Besides I kinda like things the way they are. You, me and the baby, everyone else can go and jump."

"Okay Winnie, we'll talk about it later, when ya well rested an all. Well, I'd best be on me way then, and tell me folks the news. You get some rest, and I'll be back soon."

David kissed them both again before leaving.

CHAPTER 8

David took the bike out of the shed and rode up to the farm. He was excited about the news, and he felt a certain peace within himself. He considered how his folks would take to the name of his first born. Then realized, well I'm a married man now, and it's really between me and me wife. However, he still knew that they would have something to say about it.

It was one o'clock in the afternoon when David arrived at the farm. Good he thought everyone should be inside. He burst open the door and screamed
"It's a boy"
Everyone turned, and there was talking and noise coming from every direction. Clapping, laughing, congrutulations, questions, kissing and hugging. The atmosphere was ecstatic. Finally everyone calmed down, and David relayed the details of that morning's events. How long the labour was etc, etc, etc. Then he described his new son, telling of his thick curly black hair, his tiny toes, and his beautiful deep blue eyes. Everyone was spellbound with David's description of his new baby. Then suddenly David said,
"We ave decided ta call him Francis."
Just as suddenly, the atmosphere seemed to change. Everyone started to look from one, to the other, and then back to David.
"What's wrong with ya all?," David enquired.
"Well, shouldn't ya be calling him David, after yaself?" Phyllis asked.
"What on earth for, one David in our family is enough, don't ya think." David said in a light tone, and a slight laugh. Leaving out, that it was Winnie's idea, and not his, to call their son Francis.
Leonard Snr broke in and said, "Well that's your business son,

it does seem a trifle strange ta me though. I mean the way I see's it, ya should be proud ta have ya first born named after ya."

"Ah that's old fashioned pa, that's what Winnie said" he lied, "but I told her the same as I'm telling you lot now."

Leonard stood up, and went over to David and extended his hand, "Congratualations son," he said, as he shook David's hand, and slapped his back at the same time. "Let's ave a drink in the parlour taday, and wet the baby's head."

"Well okay pa, I'll have a quick one, but then I'd best be getting back ta Winnie, she may be needing me help."

Everyone followed Leonard into the parlour. David had only been in there once before, when his brother had been married. It made him feel somewhat important, and he liked the feeling. Everyone had something to drink. The women were drinking sherry, and the men drank the scotch that was saved for special occasions such as these. After a short period of time, David announced that he should be making a move. There was once again kisses and hugs all around.

David's mother went upstairs, and came back down with a big box full with baby's clothes, and knick-nacks for the baby.

"Here ya are David," she said, "this is for ya baby, and I'll come over later, and bring ya some cooked food for ya supper."

"Ah thanks ma, ya a doll"

"Oh be off with ya lad," Mary replied, slightly embarrassed at this show of affection. "Now get going back ta ya wife, I'm sure she'll be needing some help back there."

"Yea, ya right ma, I should be going. I'll have ta walk back home though, I'll never be fitting all this stuff on me bike."

"That don't matter none, the exercise will be doing ya good. Now off with ya lad."

Again David said his goodbyes, but this time he left.

When he got back home, he crept in quietly in case Winnie was asleep. However he found her in the kitchen by herself.

"Wheres the baby luv?" he asked.

"Sleeping, what's that ya holding?" she said, as she looked at the big box in David's hands.

David put the box down on the table, and said "Ma sent it over, it's some stuff for the baby." He opened the box and looked inside for the first time. There was knitted clothes, blankets and bedsheets for the cot, rattles, and all sorts of goodies. He was overwhelmed at his mother's kindness.

"I've got all that stuff meself" Winnie said, without the slighest bit of gratitude. "It would have been more sensible ta give us some money instead of all this stuff David".

David looked up, and the disappointment reflected in his eyes.

"It would pay ya ta show a bit of gratitude Winnie, It's the thought that counts ya know."

"I, I know that David, and I didn't mean ta be ungrateful, I'm just trying ta be sensible about matters, there's lots of things we need, as well ya know. I can make all this stuff meself, and ya ma knows that only too well. What we need is a pram, or a cot, and things like that. So the money would have been of better use ta us, that's all I meant, so don't be getting all upset with me."

"I lass, ya right, but it was still ever so nice of her, don't ya think?"

"Yea, I think" Winnie repeated, then started looking through all the stuff. It was all red, white and lemon. All the neutral colours. No pinks or blues. Some of the things were really lovely, and Winnie became happy again as she rummaged through the goodies. David also had a better look at everything, and they laughed as they showed each other the different items from the box.

Yes, David and Winnie seemed very happy. Things were going wonderfully well for them both. Winnie became more confident in herself. She paraded up and down the street with her new baby in her arms. She dressed Francis in Red and White mainly, and refused to cut his hair. Whenever someone commented on how beautiful Francis was, and that he should have been a little girl, Winnie glowed with pride, and stroked his long black curls lovingly. If they commented on his name, or refered to the fact that he was not called David she would reply.

"I'm sick of the Lynch's names, I ear em everyday, so David and I decided ta be individuals, and change that silly old tradition."

She would state this as cool as a lord. The real fact of the matter was, she wanted a girl so desperately, she decided to give him her girlfriend's name regardless of his sex. Winnie was even dressing him like a little girl. David would often comment about this saying, "Ya turning that boy inta a foocking cissy."

But Winnie had learnt how to ignore David, and go about her own business. She continued to do her knitting and some sewing for the townfolk. With the money she slowly started buying things for Francis. Oh she loved him dearly. She felt that for the first time in her life she had something that was truly hers. Something that nobody could take away from her. Her whole life revolved around him, and David noticed this. In one sense he was proud of her, but in another sense he felt left out, and he started going to the pub more and more frequently. However Winnie didn't seem to mind. She had her Francis now, and that was all that mattered. She was really quite content.

One day, one of the neighbours gave Winnie an old, battered

up pram. When David came home from the Leonard's pub, Winnie was merrily cleaning it up.

"What the hell is that old thing?" David remarked.

"The Hickey's gave it ta me for Francis, David. It will look a hundred percent when I've finished cleaning it up luv."

"Well ya can bring it right back. How many times do I have ta tell ya woman. The Lynch's never take from no one except family. We're not beggers. The Lynche's buy their own stuff when they can afford ta, and not before. Do ya hear me, do ya understand what I'm saying."

"Yea, I understand ya David, but ya talking noesense, the way I see it,....."

Without letting Winnie finish what she was about to say, David said, "Don't go arguing with me Winnie, not this time. Furthermore, I don't like ya mixing with the townfolk. It only gives em things ta talk about. Now take that foocking pram back tamorrow, and tell the Hickey's ya will buy a pram when ya can afford ta."

"And when will that be David, when Francis is too old for one."

"Winnie, I've had about enough of ya tanite. Stop back chatting me women."

Winnie glared at him, then shouted, "If ya foocking folks had given us money instead of all that knitted shit, we could ave brought a pram, then we wouldn't be having this bloody fight."

David jumped to his feet, and for the first time slapped Winnie across the face.

"Don't ya know what's enough," he growled "ya can't keep ya mouth shut, can ya. Now get outa me site before ya get more of that, and if I find that pram ere tamorrow nite, I'll break every bone in ya foocking body.

Winnie ran off to the bedroom, she did not shead a tear. She rarely cried, it wasn't in her nature. She was becoming as hard as nails. Just building up her barrier of hatred for everyone except her Francis. Even David held no special place in her heart anymore.

The next day David came home late. He was quite plastered, and seemed to be in a shocking mood again. Winnie decided to try and soften him up. She was becoming quite shrewd lately. She knew just how to turn him around to her way of thinking.

"How are ya David, and how are Bridget and Leonard?."

"We're all bloody fine girl, as if ya care". David was still in a bad mood from the pram episode yesterday.

"Of course I care David, why are ya being so ugly tawards me pet?"

David mimicked her last statement, then added "and when are ya gonna get that foocking cissy son of yours baptised women?"

Winnie gathered that there had been talk at the pub about her and Francis, so she answered with caution, disregarding the cissy statement altogether.

"We can do it on Sunday if ya like. I've been thinking we should ask Francis O'Mally ta be godmother."

"Don't be stupid Winnie, we'll ask me brother Shamous, and me sister Kathleen ta stand in as godparents."

"I think Francis will be happier ta do it, David," she replied, resenting the fact that David wanted his family to be involved.

"I don't care what ya think Winnie, this time ya be doing as I say, and I'll hear no more about it."

"Okay David, if ya feel that strongly about it, we'll do as ya say." Winnie hated losing, but she had learned by now, that when David was in this mood, there was no use arguing with him. David was often in one of these moods lately. His drinking had become a problem again. He would often have a dig at Winnie about her folks. Whenever he went to the fair he would come home saying,

"I seen ya foocking red headed, red faced pa taday. He didn't even acknowledge me. The foocking old bastard."

Winnie would never defend her father. She hated him too, but somehow it still hurt when David said such things. Maybe it hurt because she realised that he was trying to offend her and not her father. However, she always stayed quiet and let David mutter away to himself in his drunken state.

CHAPTER 9

Winnie's folks never came near them, even after the birth of Francis. Winnie felt angry and hurt by this, but she was also stubborn, and never tried to talk to them either, or sort things out.

David would see Peter Walsh every Thursday at the fair, where all the farmers meet to sell their goods, have a few drinks, and a chat. It was quite a big, and regular event in Ireland, like mass on a Sunday. However David and Peter never conversed.

On Sundays they went to different mass services, that way they never ran into each other. Winnie's parents went to the earliest mass, with Angela, (Winnie's sister). Angela's husband and children went to the middle mass of the day, which gave the children extra sleep in the morning, and made them less cranky at mass. As for David, Winnie and Francis, they went to the last mass of the day with the rest of the Lynch family.

One Sunday morning Winnie was busy getting breakfast for David. While he ate, she polished his shoes, and got Francis dressed and ready for mass. Suddenly there was a knock at the door. Winnie looked up startled wondering who would be knocking at the door on a Sunday morning. She went to the door and opened it to find Mary Lynch standing there looking somewhat shocked.

"Come in Mary," Winnie said, "we were just about ta leave for church."

"Oh Winnie, I carry terrible news ta ya luv."

"What is it, what's the matter?"

"It's ya sister Angela, on her way home from mass this morning, she was knocked off her bike by a truck driver. It was a very bad accident. Apparently the truck driver must have swerved after hitting her, and he smashed into a cliff, in the bend. He died instantly. The police believe that he was drunk, because he smelled of whisky."

"What about Angela?" Winnie asked, "Is she okay?"

"Well she's alive, but in a critical condition. She has been rushed to the hospital, her head has been badly smashed in."

"Oh" was all that Winnie managed to say. There were no tears, and little emotion after receiving all the details.

Suddenly David spoke and said, "Do ya wanna go and see her Winnie?"

"Ah,...yea, I guess we had better go, hadn't we," she replied.

"Come on then, get ya jacket and let's be on our way."

Winnie turned and continued getting Francis ready when Mary said.

"Don't worry about Francis luv, I'll tend ta him while ya gone."

Winnie looked up sharply and said, "Like bloody hell ya will, he's my son and I'll be tending to him."

Mary looked taken aback, but then thought, the poor child is in shock about her sister. So she ignored the dagger eyes that Winnie had given her, and the look of hatred that shone from them. Mary put Winnie's reaction down to the shock she had just received, with the news of her sister's accident. As for David, he said nothing about Winnie's outburst at his mother, he too believed Winnie was in a state of shock.

David, Winnie and Francis went to the hospital where Angela was. When they arrived Peter and Heather Walsh were there with Angela's husband Patrick. They were all sitting slumped over, on the bench which ran the full lenght of the hospital corridor. Patrick was the first to look up, as he heard David and Winnie approaching. He stood and extended his hand to David.

"Hi," he said sadly, "we ain't got any news at the moment. She's in surgery now, but I'm afraid the doctors don't hold any hope for her survival."

"Don't be giving up yet Patrick, only time will tell us what the outcome will be," David replied, "at the moment all we can do is pray."

Suddenly as if just realising someone else was present, Peter stood up. When he saw Winnie standing there he looked startled.

"What the foock are you doing ere?"

"I'm here ta see me sister," Winnie stated bluntly.

"Ya don't have a foocking sister, now get out of ere ya tramp."

"Hush, Hush, luv," Heather said, "this ain't the time, nor the place for talk like that."

Peter ignored his wife and continued, "Get her out of ere."

Then David spoke up. He was sick and tired of Peter's attitude, who the hell did he think he was anyway.

"Why don't ya shut ya mouth for once" he said. "I'm sick ta death of ya bad mouthing Winnie. She has as much right ta be ere as you do. Furthermore she ain't no tramp, and I'd like ya ta be remembering that. She's my wife, and the mother of me child, and I'll not have anyone talking to her in that tone, including you, red face."

Peter was dumbfounded, he couldn't believe that David was talking to him this way. Finally he found his tongue, and said, "You get ya so called wife outa me face then, cause I don't wanna see her face again, and that goes for you too. Ya both make me sick."

With all the shouting that was going on Francis started to cry. Heather went to go over to Winnie and the baby, but Peter grabbed her arm.

"Stay where ya are women" he ordered.

Winnie looked at her father, then looked back at Francis, whom she held in her arms, and said, "That mean, self-centered man over there is ya grandpa, what a pity he'll never hold ya in his arms, or even know ya, for that matter."

With that she turned on her heals and said,

"Come on David, we should never ave come, let's get outa this god forsaken place."

David grabbed Winnie's hand and they walked out proudly together. For the first time in a while, Winnie cried tears for the loss of her family. She asked David

"What have I ever really done wrong, except fall pregnant. Why does he hate me so much?"

"Oh don't be worrying about em Winnie, we ave each other luv, and I was proud of ya back there. Ya stood so tall and proud. Ya were like a real Lynch."

"I did, didn't I" she said cheering up a little, "and thanks for standing up for me David."

She knew she would never have anything to do with her folks again,. but she didn't mind anymore. She didn't even hate them any more, the truth was she no longer cared. She had finally let go of them forever, they meant nothing to her. She still felt sorry for Angela, and hoped that she would be okay. She knew she wouldn't be able to go and see her in the hospital again, but she didn't really care. Mary Lynch would keep her informed about all the news. She also had David, and he was starting to be a really caring husband and father, even if he did have the occasional bad mood. That was common of everyone. Anyway she had learned to handle his bad moods now, quite effectively, all she had to do was humour him, and don't answer him back. This procedure had also become easier. Yes, Winnie knew she could depend on David, she had just witnessed that in the hospital, and it made her feel good about herself.

Angela O'Reilly did come out of surgery okay in the sense she was alive. However she suffered severe brain damage, and was shortly transfered to the Castlebar Mental Hospital, which was a section of the Castlebar General Hospital. She didn't recognise any of her family, including her two daughers Heather and Mary. Patrick hoped that with the correct medical treatment that some day she would return to her former self. However, the doctors thought that due to the extent of the damage, this was doubtful.

Winnie's family in America, were all notified of the tragety. None of them came over to see their sister Angela, but the money started rolling in on a weekly basis for both, Angela's medical expenses and the support of her two children. Heather and Mary O'Reilly went to the finest schools and were very well kept, so even though, in a sense, they had lost their mother, they were extremely luckly children. (A lot luckier than we were going to be). Both girls grew up, and married local farmers. Their uncles and aunts in America purchased tractors and other major equipment for both their farms. Old man Walsh, also devoted time, and money to Angela's children, but never anything to Winnie and her family. When Mary, the youngest child had been married for six months or so. Patrick died. Some say he only hung around to see his daughters settled in life. Once he achieved this, he died of a broken heart. He and Angela had been extremely happy together, and he loved her dearly, but since the accident she didn't even know who he was, and he was crushed.

After Patrick's funeral, Heather and Mary, along with their husbands, were taken to America, at their own request. As for

Angela, she lived out her entire life in the Castlebar Mental Hospital, alone, except for her parents, and of course Winnie, who because of the situation never visited her anyway.

When Winnie received the news that Angela's daughters had migrated to America, she cursed them for leaving her sister, their mother, behind. On the same token she was happy. Her father had no one left now. He had disowned her, and Angela didn't know him from a bar of sope. My parents are finally getting just what they deserve she thought, and they have no one else to blame but themselves. God really did work in mysterious ways. Now they would die lonely old people without any loved ones around.

"Just let em come near me now," she said to herself, "and I'll kick em, from ere ta kingdom come."

David felt quite sorry for Winnie's folks when he heard the news. But like Winnie, he agreed that they had brought it all upon themselves. His heart melted for poor Angela too, who had been left to die in the mental hospital. Then there really wasn't any hope of her ever recovering. There was nothing anyone could do for her now. It was depressing having to think of her this way though, according to Mary Lynch, she was reduced to a skeleton now. Not that he had ever really known Angela, she had been married when he and Winnie had become involved, and then she had stayed away. However, he remembered she had been a happy, energetic type of person and a pretty wee thing. She had been much smaller in frame than his Winnie, but with the same striking facial features. Now she was reduced to nothing, just skin and bone, with no mentality at all. What a waste of a perfect human being, David thought.

CHAPTER 10

Life for Winnie and David went along as normal. The day to day routines were without change. Francis was now six months old and Winnie had a sneaky suspicion that she was pregnant again. However, she kept it to herself. She never went to visit Angela in the hospital, for two reasons. One, that she may run into her parents while she was there, and two, that David had forbidden her to go because he didn't want her to be lowered again, by her folks.

Winnie withdrew into herself more and more, until in the end, you never knew what she was thinking. She spent most of her time doting on Francis, admiring his beautiful blue eyes and long dark lashes. His hair was thick with curls, and growing quite long. She would sit for hours, just playing with those curls, and brushing his hair. Everywhere Winnie went, Francis was right by her side. Francis wanted no part of David, only his mother. Which was just the way Winnie wanted it. She wanted her Francis, all to herself.

When Winnie was four months pregnant she decided that David had best be told. One night when he came home she served dinner as usual, then took her place at the kitchen table. After both of them started eating, she blurted out her news, thinking the quicker I do it, the quicker it's over.
"David I'm with child again," she stated flatly.

David looked up at her, and suddenly lost all control, he threw his dinner up in the air, and everything else nearby went flying. Winnie in fear of being hit herself, rose, and flew from the room.

The next morning Winnie was relieved that she had got it off her chest. However she was dubious about what mood she would find David in. She went out to the Kitchen, thinking David would be out there, waiting for breakfast. However David was already gone. Oh dear, Winnie thought, he must be in a mood, an a half. Never mind, I'll make him a lovely dinner tanite, and try and cool him down.

All day, Winnie was jittery, wondering what David's manner would be when he came home. Normally after an arguement, everything was fine the next morning, and the arguement was forgotten about. He had never done this before. That day, Winnie couldn't even be bothered combing her son's hair which was really abnormal. All she could think about was David, and what would happen when he returned home that evening. She gathered he would be drunk, but that was the least of her worries.

To Winnie's surprise David returned home early that night. He had been drinking, but he wasn't drunk. She had made an Irish stew for him. She turned to the range after he came in, to re-heat the stew, when he yelled out to her,
"Woman, come over ere, we need ta talk."
"Yea, that we do" Winnie replied, in a mild tone of voice, "We have ta get this sorted out, and get on with our lives."
"Get on with our lives. Fat foocking chance of that happening now, is there. Just when we were getting our foocking feet on the ground, ya spring this on me. What the foock are we gonna do for money Winnie?" he asked.
"We'll manage somehow David, sure we will, I'm sure things are gonna be fine."
"Yea, that's what ya always say girl."
"And I've been right, haven't I luv."

"Yea, ya have been, but it'll be harder now, with two little un's ta look out for."

"Look David, I could write ta one of me sisters in America, and ask em ta help us out, if ya want me too. I mean they helped Angela's kids out. It's about time they did something for me, don't ya think?"

That was the final straw, as far as David was concerned.

"No I don't foocking think," he screamed. He started throwing things around again, breaking everything in sight. Winnie was terrified, too terrified to even move, or run, as she usually did. She just looked at him wondering what the hell had set him off.

"David" she said, "What is it, what ave I done?"

"It's you woman, what the foock are ya trying ta do to me. Send me round the bend or what?"

Winnie was dumbfounded, but made no reply, she just sat there, horrified, watching David.

"Ya really want ta blacken me name, don't ya? Blacken my name, the way your name is blackened with ya family. Well ya won't do it, do ya hear me, not to a Lynch. We're a proud family, as well know. Furthermore, we want nowt from no one, especially your rotten, stinking, so called family. Now hear me Winnie, and ear me good, if ya ever, even suggest a thing like that again, I'll break every foocking bone in ya body." David went on, and on, and on, while Winnie just sat and listened.

"Remember" he continued "I don't want nowt from ya family, not now, or ever, even if we have ta starve. I want ya ta stay clear of the lot of em. And let this be a lesson to ya, don't ever mention any of ya family in America ta me again."

All of a sudden, David saw Winnie for the first time during his tantrum. He suddenly realised that she hadn't meant any harm, she had been raised different, that was all. He didn't want to go soft though, he wanted her to remember what he had said, and abide by his wishes. However he did feel sorry for her, and wanted to end the quarrel. He continued in a more gentle tone of voice,

"Now be a good women, and serve me up some more dinner."

"I can't David, ya just threw it off the range." Winnie said, half scared to mention it at all. "But I can make ya something else if ya want."

"Na, don't worry yaself, I'll grab a sandwich or something, ya have enough ta do, cleaning up this mess, then perhaps ya might like ta go warm up the bed for us lass". He laughed, then continued,

"We may as well take advantage of the situation, while the buns in the oven an all, ya can't get pregnant twice, can ya."

Winnie laughed also, but it was a false laugh.

"Yea David, ain't that the truth" she said, then she went about her chores, as though nothing had happened, thinking to herself, well at least that's over with.

About a week later, David came home and said, "Look, tamorrow nite don't worry about cooking tea Winnie, Ma's invited us round for tea. She reckons we never go there no more, and she's right ya know."

"Oh David, I've been feeling right poorly lately."

"Yea, ya always are when we have ta go visiting me folks Winnie. With ya mouth, ya say ya don't hold any grudges tawards em, but ya actions tell me different. Well we're going, and that's final."

Winnie didn't say another word. David was right of course, she hated going to see them. She still really hated them, even though she made out not too. She had to pretend to David that all was well in that area, but only she knew the hate she felt for them.

The next day David came home from the farm, and collected Winnie and Francis. As they arrived back at the farm, the smell of freshly made bread reached Winnie's nostrils, she suddenly forgot her animosity for the people inside, and started to think about her stomach. She suddenly felt quite hungry. They went inside, and Winnie enjoyed a good hearty meal, thinking to herself, it always tastes better when someone else does the cooking.

Phillis was holding the baby, and cooing away with him. Suddenly she turned to Winnie and said,
"When are ya going ta cut this lad's hair Winnie, he's getting more and more like a girl by the day. Even the way ya dress him in red and white makes it difficult ta tell if it's a boy or a girl. Cut his hair, and dress the poor lad in blue will ya."
Winnie lept up from the table, grabbed her son, and said, "Phyllis I wish ya would mind ya own bloody business. If ya know so much about it, why the hell don't ya get married, and have ya own kids. Then ya can dress em the way ya bloody want." With that she stormed out of the house, with Francis, and slammed the door behind her, leaving David where he was.

David also rose, and followed Winnie outside, without saying a word to his family. When Winnie heard him coming, she thought. Oh no, here comes trouble, however all he said was, "Get the foock home women" and he followed closely behind her. Winnie was thankful of this, but she knew this wasn't the end of it. She knew there was going to be trouble when they did get home.
When they arrived, and went inside, David slammed the door behind them.
"Get rid of that foocking cissy child of yours, get him inta bed now" he screamed.

Winnie done as she was told, and when she returned to the kitchen a short time later, David grabbed her by the arm violently, and began to shake her, and scream at her at the same time.

"How dare ya talk ta me sister like that, who the foock do ya think ya are, and while me ma and pa were present too. You'd best be remembering that their the ones feeding us each day, ya dirty little tinker. When no one else wanted ya Winnie, it was me folks that excepted ya, and this is the thanks ya give em."

David was in a violent rage at this point, and there were no holds bared, it was as if he was releasing all his anger and frustrations of the past year and a half.

"Ya were the one doing all the chasing in the beginning Winnie, ya were like a wild cat, till ya got what ya wanted in those fields. God only knows how many other men ya had in the fields, before me. But I was the sucker ta marry ya."

He paused momentarily, then continued "As for ya foocking red headed pa, he should ave been thanking me for marrying ya, but no, not that old bastard, he still turns his nose in the air everytime we see each other. Ya whole foocking family are tinkers, and rotton ta the core. Yet ya have the cheek ta treat me family with rudness. Well things are about ta change Winnie, you mark me words. If ya ever speak ta any one of them again like that, I'll foocking knock ya out. Now get out of me sight." he said, as he gave her one final push, releasing the hold on her arm at the same time.

"Ya make me sick just looking at ya, go on, piss off." he screamed.

Winnie ran of to the bedroom without saying a word, just thankful that he hadn't hit her, although her arm where he had held her was badly bruised, and she felt like her head was going to fall off, after all the shaking it had received. Winnie fell on the bed exhausted from all that had just happened. She knew he would be okay again in the morning though. She rolled over and went to sleep, and as she done so, her hatred for the Lynch's increased a little more.

David got a beer out, and sat at the table. He knew tomorrow he would have to face the music with his family. He still didn't answer his family back, and for Winnie to do it, was even worse in their eyes. No he wasn't looking forward to tomorrow one bit. What made it worse was he knew he had to stand by Winnie, even though he thought she was wrong. David sat there till the early hours of the morning, having one stout after an other, until he finally collapsed across the kitchen table.

A few hours later, he awoke with a dreadful hangover, and decided he'd walk over to the farm early, he could have breakfast there. He needed the walk, and the fresh air, to sober him up a little. He wasn't in any hurry to face his parents, but he was in less of a hurry to see Winnie. When he arrived, he walked in and approached Phyllis first, by saying "Phyllis, please don't be passing any remarks ta me wife about the way she chooses ta dress our son," and he emphasized the "our son." Leonard and Mary regarded their son in bewilderment, wondering how he had the nerve to defend Winnie, after what she had done yesterday. David acknowledged their amazement, and turned to them saying.

"I'm sorry, but she is me wife, and it's me duty ta stand by her. Please try and understand that."

He turned back to Phyllis, and put his arms around her shoulder's, and said,

"I luv ya, and I hope ya not hurt by what I'm saying, but it's me wife, and the mother of Francis, and she'll dress him the way she see's fit."

"No, I'm fine." Phyllis replied, and attempted to smile at her older brother.

The breakfast was ready, and the family sat down to eat inviting David to join them. Then they all went about their business, and the bad feelings were once again pushed aside.

CHAPTER 11

Leonard, David, and Shamous worked on the farm. It was a hot sticky day and the boys were busy bundling the hay for the fair. At about two o'clock Leonard said, "Let's call it a day boys, I'm not feeling too well, I think the heat getting ta me." David looked at his father a little alarmed by his statement. Leonard never called it a day, until the job at hand was finished. Not for as far back as David could remember.

"All right pa" David said, "you go on back ta the house, me and Shamous can finish up ere, I'll see ya down the pub later for a few beers"

"Na son, I'll give it a miss taday, I may go home and get meself inta bed, I must be coming down with something."

"Okay pa," David replied, "I'll be seeing ya tamorrow then."

As his father walked away David watched after him. Maybe he's just tired with the heat an all, David thought, and carried on with the work at hand. After the work had been completed for the day, David and Shamous made their way to their brother's pub. They never drank anywhere else, for two main reasons. One they liked their own company and didn't like mixing and two, the beer came cheap! That night David drank the pub dry, so to speak. He staggered home after closing. He fell in a heap on his bed, and fell instantaneously asleep. Winnie heard him snoring, and laughed to herself. He'll have some hangover tamorrow morning, she thought.

In the early hours of the morning, there was a very loud banging at the front door of David's place. David staggered out to answer the door still half asleep, and with a pounding headache.

"Hold on, hold on," he yelled as the banging continued, making his head, ache even more. When he opened the door, he saw Shamous standing there.

"What the foock are you doing ere at this time of the morning lad, have ya no brains?" David asked.

"Come quick David, Pa just passed away in his sleep," Shamous said, trying hard to hold back his tears.

David staggered backwards, and sat down on the nearest chair, letting the news digest. He put his face in his two hands, and suddenly began to weep like a young lad, for the loss of his father.

Winnie came into the kitchen wondering what all the commotion was about and saw both David and Shamous crying.

"What's wrong?", she asked "What's happened?"

David looked up, and said, "It's me pa, he died, passed away in his sleep, he did."

"Well ya best get over there then, hadn't ya, I'll stay ere with Francis, and follow ya up in the morning when he wakes up, and I get him organised."

David rose, went to the bedroom, threw on his clothes, and left with Shamous. When they arrived, they were naturally meet by great sadness, at the Lynch home.

David took the news of his father very badly, and as usual began drowning his sorrow with alcohol. The next few days were very trying for the whole family, but the day of the wake was the worse. Leonard Lynch was laid out in his coffin in the parlour. The neighbours made cakes and biscuits for the guests, and they prepared the tea and coffee for everyone who came to pay their last respects. The townsfolk would look in the coffin, and say to the remaining family members, "Sorry for ya troubles".

On the third day after Leonard's death, he was buried. Everybody for miles around came to the funeral, which was the custom in Ireland. Winnie and Francis accompanied David to the Funeral. David was astounded at Winnie's demeanour, she showed no remorse at all. It was as if she was made of steel. However David made no comment. She also dressed Francis in brand new, all red clothes. This didn't go un-noticed by David, or the other members of his family. But nothing was mentioned, not that day anyway. However it was thrown back at David in years to come, by his brothers and sisters.

After the funeral, everyone meet at Leonard and Briget's pub. (Which was the usual event after a burial in Ireland.) They drank, ate and discussed old times and their growing up days, etc. They also discussed how wonderful Leonard Lynch had been, as a father, husband, and person. The pub stayed open all night that night, Briget and Leonard let everybody help themselves to drinks, while they relaxed for the night, along with everybody else.

Over the next few days David spent all his time at the pub, not wanting to see Winnie at all. He still couldn't believe how hard she was. Then on about the fourth day after the funeral he staggered home at a reasonable hour.
"Where's me dinner?" he demanded, as soon as he walked in the door.
"It's in the oven dear."
"Never mind the dear business," he retorted, "Ya nothing but a bitch Winnie. What the hell are ya made of anyway, don't ya have any foocking feelings at all. And another thing, don't think I didn't notice ya dressed that son of your's all in red the day of the funeral, as if ya were trying ta spite me family again. I'm not completely foocking mad ya know. Well ya can do

what ya foocking like from now on, with ya cissy boy. Ya can put a foocking pink dress on him for all I care, but stay out of me foocking sight, da ya ere me."

Winnie didn't respond, as usual, she knew when to keep her mouth shut. David kept away from Winnie, and vise versa for a good week or so. David wasn't eating much at all these days, just drinking. He still went to work every morning, but spent his nights drinking, and then sleeping. He was still mourning his father's death.

The months passed quickly, and the time for Winnie's second child to be born was approaching. Francis was eleven months old, and his long curls were still fully intact, and at shoulder length. He was walking now, and a happy little soul. He was also very devoted to Winnie, but still had little to do with David.

One night after David returned home, he seated himself at the table, and began eating his dinner. Then suddenly he spoke to Winnie, which was quite rare, since the funeral.
"Winnie," he said, "the babys due any time now, I've been talking ta ma, and we think it's best if ya pack yaself and young Francis up, and go stay with her for a bit."
Without thinking about the consequences Winnie objected to the idea. "Oh no, that's not such a good idea David, I'll feel much more relaxed in me own home." she stated.

David's eyes blazed at her. "Why, ain't me ma good enough for the likes of you then?"
"Oh, it's not that David, ya know it's not. It's just I'd feel more comfortable ere that's all."
"Well Winnie, ya going, and that's all there is to it. I've

already made all the arrangements, and I'll not be offending me ma no more on your account. She's coming ere tamorrow, ta help ya pack ya things."

Winnie knew it was pointless to argue with him anymore. She hated the fact, of being forced to stay with that old women, which was how Winnie regarded her, but she said no more on the subject. Regardless of what Winnie thought, Mrs Lynch was a very nice old lady. She would give anybody her last bit of food. She would help everybody who needed it. Her only fault was she didn't think anybody was good enough for her children. Her other siblings, apart from Leonard, never married, in fact they remained on the farm for their entire lives.

She had been dead against David and Winnie's marriage though, and had told Winnie this, straight to her face. Winnie still remembered her exact words which were, "Ya not good enough for me son Winnie Walsh, you're from bad stock. Furthermore if ya weren't pregnant I'd run ya back ta where ya came from, as quick as lightning."
Winnie couldn't forget those dreadful words, no matter how hard she tried, and this was the real reason Winnie hated her so much. And that hatred had only grown over the last couple of years.

However, Winnie's biggest fear now, of staying with her mother-in-law, was that she might force her, or even take it upon herself to cut her son's hair, which would kill Winnie.

The next morning Mary came as arranged, and after a little while Winnie suddnely burst into tears.
"What's the matter with ya child?" The alarmed Mary asked.
"Oh it's just I'll be missing David while I'm gone."

"What are ya talking about, didn't David tell ya nowt. He'll be staying with ya, up at my place. What would he be doing coming home to an empty house. Now dry ya tears, and let's get back before lunch."

"There is something else that's been on me mind Mary."

"And what's that child?" Mary asked

"Ya won't be cutting me boy's hair will ya?".

"Look, Francis is your son Winnie, and if ya want him looking like that, I'll have nowt ta say about it."

Winnie felt at ease now, and hurried getting her things together.

Mary did look after Winnie, as she would have one of her own girls, maybe even better. She washed, cooked and cleaned after her. She nursed her grandchild, whom she loved dearly, and let Winnie rest as much as possible. However, instead of taking advantage of the situation, and being grateful for the help she was receiving, Winnie resented the fact, that Francis was with Mary so much. She felt that Mary was trying to take over him. Winnie couldn't wait to have her baby, and get back home, away from Mary's influence.

CHAPTER 12

Winnie gave birth to her second child. It was a baby girl, but no where near as beautiful as Francis had been. She had red hair like her mother, and pale blue eyes. However to David she was the most gorgeous thing he had ever seen. Who would have imagined that the drunken David Lynch, (which was what he had become.) would pick up, and nurse a new born baby with such tender loving care. He continuously talked to her, telling her how lovely she was all the time.

Winnie watched him carefully one day, a couple of days after she was born, and wondered why David was making such a fuss over this ugly baby. It was her understanding that all Irish men wanted boys, this hadn't been the case with David. He had paid little, if any, attention to Francis when he was born. What she didn't realise was that her possesiveness with Francis, had turned David away from him, not to mention the fact that he had been thrown into fatherhood, and marriage for that matter, all too quickly. He was old hat at it all, now.

Nevertheless Winnie felt proud and content as she watched David with the new baby. She knew that this little girl was the apple of David's eye, even though she was only a few days old. Furthermore, he didn't mind playing with her. regardless of who was watching.

Suddenly David broke into Winnie's thoughts, "Come on" he said, "lets go down ta the pub, and wet the baby's head. I'm paying," he joked.
"Who, me" Winnie said.
"Yea, you women, who the hell else is ere."

"Na David, I can't be doing that, what about the baby and Francis."

"Ah don't worry about that. Ma can take care of em for a couple of hours."

Winnie didn't like that idea, at all.

"No," she said, "but you go luv, and thanks for the offer."

"Okay Winnie, I'll see ya later then." he said, and then he left.

Winnie watched him go, thinking that's the last I'll see of him tanite, but she didn't mind. David and herself had been getting along so well the last few days, since the birth of the baby.

Winnie was wrong, David didn't stay out all night, in fact he was not out long at all. The truth was, he was over the moon with his baby daughter and was quite eager to return home to see her. When he did return home, Kathleen and Phillis were in the kitchen. They all had a general chat, and then Kathleen asked, "What are ya going ta call the baby David?"

"I've got no idea really, we ain't discussed it."

"Well the lass is three days old, don't ya think she needs a name?"

"Yea, I guess so", David laughed, "I'll go talk ta Winnie about it right now in fact."

As he went up to Winnie's room he thought Kathleens right, I'd best be getting it sorted out quickly, knowing Winnie she'll give the poor wee pet a boy's name. He laughed to himself, as he entered Winnie's bedroom. Winnie was sleeping, so he went straight to the baby, and looked in on her. What a sweet wee thing ya are. I think Caroline is a beaut name, for a beaut girl, he thought.

David went over to Winnie's side, and sat on the edge of the bed. Winnie opened her eyes, and smiled at him.

"Hi luv." she said.

"Hi yaself, did ya have a good rest."

"Yea, what's the time?"

"It's only four-thirty."

"How come ya back from the pub so soon?"

"I couldn't wait ta get back ta the baby."

"Oh really" Winnie said with a laugh, "and what about ya wife and son".

"Yea, them too" David said as he tussled Winnie's hair.

Then he continued, "Listen Winnie, what do ya think we should call the baby?"

"I dunno David, I've not thought about it."

"Well, what about Caroline then, I thing that suits her well enough. I'm sure she'll grow inta a beaut young lady one day ya know."

"Yea, that does ave a nice ring ta it, and it sure beats Winnie."

"Ya can say that again." David mused.

"Don't be cheeky now, David Lynch," Winnie teased, and then continued, on a more serious note.

"Oh, by the way David, how is young Francis?. I ain't seen him much since I've been ere ya know."

"Oh he's fine Winnie, and being well taken care of, don't ya worry yaself about that. Ya ave the baby ta care for just now.

"Yea, I know that, but I'd still like ta see him, once in a while.

"Well, I'll tell ya what then, I'll bring him up ta ya later, when he wakes up."

"Okay David, thanks luv. I may go for another nap now then. Wake me up later, when ya bring Francis in ta me.

"Yea, that I'll do."

David got up, and went over to the baby for another look, "Caroline", he said, "yea that suits ya just fine." Then he left the room.

Later that evening, after Francis had been fed and changed, David brought him up to see Winnie, as he had promised. Winnie was already awake when David entered the room. She smiled, and held out her arms to Francis. He ran forward, and hugged his mother, as he always did. Oh she loved him so much. She covered him with kisses, and as usual started playing with his long curls. He was nearly one year old now, and had never had a hair cut. Winnie asked David to bring over the baby, so Francis could see her. However Francis showed little interest in his new sister, so baby Caroline was put back in her crib, while Winnie continued to play with her darling Francis.

A few days later Winnie returned home, despite questions about her health from Mary. Winnie insisted that she was strong enough and should be getting settled back home in her own place. The truth of the matter was, despite all the help she had received from Mary, she still didn't enjoy being around her.

When they got home, Winnie made some tea, it felt great being in her own surroundings again. David was also in a very happy mood. Somehow the birth of Caroline had made him happy, and in turn Winnie also seemed happy. After they had drank their tea, and Winnie was settled in, David said he had to return to the farm to get his work done. He kissed Winnie and the children goodbye. Then he told Caroline how beautiful she was, yet again. Winnie didn't understand how he could say that. The child was ugly!

Caroline changed David's life, well everyones for that matter. He was coming home straight from work most nights and would spend hours playing with Caroline each night. He became closer to Francis, and Winnie also, but it was obvious that David loved his daughter more than anyone else in the world. He was a fair man though, and never brought anything for Caroline without getting something for Francis as well. On Thursdays when he went to the fair he always came home with something for the pair of them. This was something he had not done before Caroline had come along.

Thursdays had become a special day for the children and even Winnie received a small gift from time to time. Winnie and David joked all the time, and seldom argued. Caroline had really changed things for the better, or so it seemed.

One Thursday evening David returned home empty handed, much to the children's disappointment, and Winnie's surprise.

"Did ya forget us taday luv" she asked in a lighthearted manner.

"No luv, but I've had other things on me mind. We've been so happy together since Caroline came inta the world, and I don't want ta change nowt, but I've got some bad news for ya luv."

"Oh nowt can be that bad David. We can sort it out tagether."

"Yea" David answered only half believing his own answer.

"Okay out with it David, what's the bad news?"

"Well it's about ya pa Winnie. Ya see he wasn't at the fair taday, so I asked around, ta see how come an all."

"Ya, and what did ya find out?"

"It seems he's very ill. The word is he's got cancer and only has a couple of weeks ta live"

"Did ya find out if any of me sisters, or brothers are coming over from America ta see him."

"Na, that was the last thing on me mind, I was too shocked when I found out. In fact I said very little at all. But ya know something Winnie, I pity the poor devil. I also feel terribly guilty about all the names I've called him in the past."

"Don't feel guilty David. He wouldn't feel guilty if the shoe was on the other foot, he wouldn't be feeling any pity neither. Na he's got what he deserves, the old bastard."

"Winnie that's a terrible thing ta say. Ya really are made of stone aren't ya. Ya really have ta let go of the past Winnie. It's no good for ya ta feel this way, he's still ya pa ya know."

"Yea me pa, and what's he ever done for us. He beat me nearly every day for nowt, ma couldn't defend me, she was too scared of coping a blow herself. That's why I was asking ya, if the rest of the family will be coming over, cause they were in the same boat as I was, that's why they all pissed off, and ya know what, I doubt if any of 'em will come , and if they do, they're all bloody mad."

"Oh Winnie, have some compassion for the old boy. Cancer is a terrible thing ta have, and he is ya pa after all."

"Yea, well I never asked ta be born, especially ta the likes of that man."

David realised he was getting nowhere with Winnie, so he dropped the subject, for the time being anyway.

Later on in the evening he brought it up again.

"Look Winnie, even if ya don't go and see him now, while he's alive, we'll still have ta make an appearence at the funeral."

"Like hell we will."

"Look Winnie, I'll not let ya show me up, or embarrass me."

"I'm not trying ta do that David, but why should I pretend ta mourn for someone I hate."

"Because he's ya father, that's why. Look, he's not my favourite person neither, but I'll give him he's due, when me pa died, regardless of the situation, he showed face at the funeral, and we'll be doing the same, along with the rest of me family."

"Okay David, I'll do as ya ask, I don't like ta argue with ya luv, but remember I'll be doing it for you, and not out of luv for that old bastard."

"That's enough of that language too madam" David said laughing, then he rolled over, and started tickling Winnie, until tears of laughter rolled down her face.

On the face of it all, life seemed pretty good, but David didn't realise how much hate Winnie really harboured inside. To David, Winnie was happy and content. The truth was, Winnie was filled with anger, instilled in her from childhood, and it grew stronger and more distructive as the years passed. She had learned to hide her feelings well and she did appear happy and content around David, and in a way she was at her best when he was around. However he was correct when he referred to her as being as cold as stone, but this was Winnie's defence barrier. It was something that she had build up over the years, stone by stone, and it was now, as solid as rock, and getting stronger by the day.

Old man Walsh passed away four weeks later. Winnie and David did attend the funeral. However she refused to go to her mother's house and pay her final respects and David did not force the issue. He ignored the fact that the rest of the village would be attending, regardless of their feelings towards the old boy.

The funeral was a sad and lonely one. It was ironic really, out of the fourteen children that Peter had brought into the world, only Winnie, the one he had disowned attended his funeral, and if it hadn't been for David she wouldn't have been there either. Most of the village people did make an effort, like David's family, all except his mother who had stayed home to mind her grandchildren for the day. No one shed any tears either, except for Winnie's mother.

In a way, it may have been better all round if Winnie hadn't attended the funeral after all, because her name was to be dragged through the mud once again and David was going to be embarressed anyway. As they lowered Peter into the grave, Heather let out a cry of anguish, turned and faced Winnie holding one hand over her mouth, as if trying to hold back her screams, and said, "Winnie, ya all I have now luv."

Winnie regarded her mother's words with disbelief, and then answered her mother with vegence, "Go ta hell mother, you lost me, the day ya gave birth ta me" she screamed on the top of her voice.

Everyone's eyes turned towards Winnie and her mother. The look of disgust for Winnie, was more than apparent in their eyes and expressions, they didn't have to say a word. However, this didn't worry Winnie, in the least. Her mother began to cry and plead with her daughter hysterically.

"Please Winnie, what am I supposed ta do luv, I've got no one, what am I going ta do on me own."

"Well ya should have thought about that the day I came home, and told ya I was getting married ta David. Do ya remember that day ma, the day ya disowned me. Well I've got me own life now, and their ain't no room in it for you. Why don't ya try writing ta ya other kids in America and see if they bloodly want ya, cause I sure as hell don't."

Heather, started to grab at Winnie's sleeve, pleading and begging her daughter to forgive her, but Winnie was too hard and to cold to warm to her mother's plea's of forgiveness. The village people looked with horror and mumbled amongst themselves about how terrible Winnie was.

David couldn't take any more, he was so embarressed and

ashamed, but still he stood by Winnie. He yanked Heather's hands away from Winnie, and said, "Come Winnie, I'd best be taking ya home now."

They both turned and left. David's head sunken and looking to the ground, Winnie's head held as high and as proud as a peacock.

As they made their way back to Mary's house to collect the children, David turned to Winnie and said, "Winnie, ya ma can come stay with us, if that's what ya want. (Half believing that Winnie had been so hard on her mother because she thought he had not approved of having her stay with them.) She would be a help with the children too."

"No David, like I said back there, I've got no room in me life for her now. When we needed her, she wasn't there for us. Now she can go ta hell. I don't even want ta see her."

"Alright Winnie, what ever ya say, but she is ya ma and ya should have held ya tongue at the funeral, that's not the place ta be hanging out ya dirty laundry. Not that I'm angry with ya girly, I know ya have been through hell as a child, but there's a place for everything, and that wasn't the place."

"Yea I know that's the truth David, but it's hard for me ta control me anger sometimes, that's all."

"Yea, I know luv, me too."

As they approached Mary's place, Winnie said, "David ya best be telling ya ma what happened at the graveyard, before she's told by the townfolk. Ya know what they're like, they'll make it sound ten times worse then it really was."

"I was thinking the same thing Winnie. I'll let her know your side of the story too, and ya reason for acting like that. I'll do me best ta make her understand how you feel."

Mary listened intently to the events of the morning, then had her say.

"Well Winnie, it's still ya ma and nowt's gonna change that, but ya right child, ya do have ya own life now, and it's not for me ta be making any judgements upon ya, that's for god ta do. What do ya think she'll be doing now though?"

"I'm not sure," Winnie answered, "maybe she'll pack her bags and go off ta America like I told her to. Who knows, anyway that's not my concern."

Neither Mary nor Winnie said any more on the subject, but Mary was secretly thankful that Winnie wasn't her daughter. She wondered how Winnie could be so heartless, especially at a time like this. Most people would forget their differences when there was a death in the family. But Winnie wasn't most people, as everyone was soon to find out.

About one week later, Winnie and David were playing with the children in the back garden when suddenly Winnie's mother arrived on the door step.

"What the hell are you doing ere?" was the only hello Heather received.

"Look Winnie, please forgive me and forget the past. Ya know I did the best I could luv." she said, on the verge of tears. "I need ya luv, I'm so lonely in that big old house by meself, and I can't manage it by meself either. Please Winnie, have some pity on ya poor old ma."

"Have some pity, that's a joke, what pity did you have on me when that old bastard used ta beat us? None, that's what, so now we're even ma, cause I ain't got none for you either. Now get away from me door, and don't be coming round ere again."

"Please Winnie luv, I'm begging ya honey. Look I'll sell the farm and house, and ya can ave the lot. It's yours, just let me stay with ya,... please, I'll die if I'm left alone any longer."

David finally spoke up, he felt so sorry for Heather Walsh, she was actually begging, and no one should have to do that. Yet he knew Winnie well enough to know she wouldn't back down.

"Look Heather, it's no use ya keep asking, it's not possible ta have ya here, and we don't want ya money either. All we really want is a little peace and quiet in our home. If ya were ta come stay with us, you and Winnie would be fighting with each other day and night. Look luv, do yaself a favour, sell ya farm, and everthing else ya don't want, and go over ta ya daughter Nancy's place in America. She's well off enough ta be taking care of ya, and you've had no quarrel with her.

Heather was devestated, but realised that David was speaking sense. She looked up into his face with admiration for his honesty, and said,

"Yea David, ya right lad, thanks." then she turned and left, ignoring Winnie completly. Winnie never heard from any of her family in America, including her mother, for the next twenty five years, but she never gave it a second thought.

Heather Walsh sold her farm and belongings and went to say a final farewell to her daughter Angela, before leaving for America.

The townfolk were cold, and nasty towards Winnie, because of what had happened. However this didn't bother Winnie either, she walked around with her head held high. The only one she had time for, apart from David and the children, was her childhood friend Francis who she had coffee with on a regular basis. The rest of the world could go to hell, for all she cared.

Time passed quickly, the days into weeks, the weeks into months and the months into years. David and Winnie were very happy and the children were growing. Winnie and David now were free to visit Angela anytime they wanted to, which they did every fortnight. Angela was like a dead lump of meat now. She had to be spoon fed and was totally dependent upon others. She was thin and very weak. She still didn't know any one including Winnie. She was just waiting to die.

David still enjoyed the occasional drink after work, and would go every couple of days for a quick one, as he liked to refer to it. This quick one, usually meant two or three, but he always came home for dinner. One night he returned home and said, "Winnie, it's been some time since ya pa died, and we ain't been there ta visit his grave yet. What if we go this Sunday, after mass?.

Winnie looked at him in shock, and then said, "Are ya feeling alright David or ave ya gone mad. I've got no desire ta go anywhere near him. I'm only glad that he's dead, and outa me life."

It was David's turn to look shocked, "Winnie don't be talking like that about the dead. Ya dreadful sometimes, really ya are."

Winnie just laughed and said, "I can't help me feelings David."

"Ya should be able ta find some forgiveness in ya heart by now Winnie. Besides it's a terrible sin ta hold a grudge for so long."

"Yea, well if that's the case, the old boy died with his sin, he certainly held his grudge for long enough didn't he, till the bloody day he died."

"That may be so, but you shouldn't. Two wrongs don't make a right, ya know."

"Well maybe I'm more like him than I thought, cause I know I'll hate him till the day I die."

"Oh, why the hell do I waste me breath on ya anyways. Ya know what they say Winnie, no sense, no feeling, and that's you to a tee."

Winnie only laughed at his last statement, then continued

dishing out the evening meal.
David gave up and said no more.

CHAPTER 13

Five years passed quickly and Winnie realised that she was once again pregnant. She delayed telling David until her fourth month of pregnancy, not wanting his disapproval yet again. However when David did find out, his response was, "Oh well, not much we can do about it now."

Winnie had sensed a slight disapproval in his tone, but he had still been quite calm about it. Winnie was relieved, and glad the news was out in the open.

Francis and Caroline were now both at school. Francis was six years old, and Caroline was five. It was getting difficult to tell if Francis was a boy or a girl, because his long curly locks were still fully intact. The other children at school made fun of him all the time, but it didn't seem to worry him, or Winnie. Having the curls was far more important to both of them. However, David did not have the same regard for his son's hair. He hated his hair, and the remarks that came about because of it. It was so damn embarrassing.

One night while Winnie and David sat relaxed in front of the fire, David approached the subject. He was hesitant, because he hated fighting with her and he knew how precious Francis, and his hair, was to her. However the situation was really starting to get on his nerves and something needed to be said.

"Winnie", he said, "I know I don't usually say much, bout the way ya look after the kids, but Francis is six years old now and far from a babe. Don't ya think it's about time ya gave the lad a haircut?"

"What on earth for David, he looks so fine with his lovely curls."

"Yea, he would if he was a girl, but he ain't. Look the other kids are making fun of him all the time, Caroline has told me a few times how the lad is always fighting because of it. Besides the folks round town are getting on me bloody nerves, with all their smart remarks."

"Well the townfolk can go ta hell David. They should mind their own bloody business. As for Francis, the fighting don't worry him none, he's not even complained about it ta me. Besides all boys fight, it's part of growing up. As for Caroline she has a big mouth, and should learn to keep it shut."

"Now don't be blaming the lass Winnie, Francis is a boy, not a girl, and it's about time he got his bloody hair cut, and another thing stop getting him ta help ya with the housework, Caroline can help ya. On Saturday I seen him helping ya hang out the bloody washing for Christ sake. That's not a boy's job.

Winnie realised that David was getting angry, and said, "Alright David, I'll cut his hair tamorrow night after school. Don't start losing ya temper now."

"That's fine Winnie." David responded, in a final manner, leaving no room for Winnie to worm her way around him again.

The next morning Winnie brought the children to school, she didn't mention anything to Francis about cutting his hair that evening. She hated the idea of having to do it, but she knew David well enough to know that he wouldn't soften once his mind was made up, and this was one of those times.

That evening when Francis and Caroline got home from school she sat Francis down on a stool, and put a cloth around his neck. As soon as Francis realised that his lovely hair was going to be cut he began screaming, "No ma, please ma, don't cut off me hair. Mummy please, I luv ya ma, don't cut off me lovely hair."

Winnie's heart was breaking for her boy, and she hugged him tightly. Tears pricked the corner of her eyes as she said, "Now don't cry lad, listen ta me. I'll only cut of the tiniest piece of hair, and I promise ya, you'll still have plenty of curls left. Last night ya pa told me that ya have ta have it cut. Ya six years old now lad, not a babe any more. So you be a big brave lad now, and sit back on the stool for me, okay."

"Okay ma," he answered, but the tears rolled down his face the whole time and it tore at Winnie's heart. No one else ever got this reaction from Winnie. Yes she had cried before, but not out of sorrow, or love for someone else. At this stage of her life, Francis was the most important thing to her. Winnie kept to her word, she only cut a little of his hair, just enough for David to realise, that it had been cut.

David returned home shortly after. When he saw Francis he said,

"Lad I do believe ya ma's actually cut some of ya hair."

"Yea she did, and I hate it pa, why did I have ta have it cut anyway?"

"Because ya a boy, not a lass. Besides she cut so little, ya still look like a bonny wee lass. I think ya should cut it a bit shorter, then ya would look like ya old man."

"No pa, please."

Winnie intervened, "Leave the lad alone David, he went through hell tanite getting that much off. He really was distressed about it coming off."

"Okay Francis, be a little sissy, see if I care." David snapped.

Francis ran off to his bedroom, totally ignoring David's comment, he was too relieved about keeping the rest of his hair. Being called a sissy didn't have any effect on him at all. The trouble was, Winnie had made him feel that his hair was the best asset he had, from the day he was born. To him his hair was far more important than any name he may be called by his father, or anyone else for that matter.

Caroline was at the other end of the scale. She had no curls, but it was slightly wavy and as red as apples. The only person who ever told her she was pretty was David. The truth was she wasn't a very attractive child at all. Especially if she stood next to Francis.

The next morning when Winnie had packed the children off to school, she began to think about the previous nights events and cringed as she thought of how upset Francis had been. If people would mind their own bloody business and kept their mouths shut it mightn't have happend she thought. My how I hate the lot of em. Then her line of thought shifted to her so called neighbours and her hatred grew. Since her mother had left for America things had been even worse. The townfolk blamed her for that too, they thought she was heartless and cruel, but they didn't know everything, "That's their trouble, what they don't know they make up." she said out loud, "Anything for a bit of gossip."

Winnie was not an intelligent person when it came to reading and writing. She had very rarely attended school, and when she had made the effort she paid little attention to what she was being taught. However she was a cunning person, with a good tongue. She could talk her way out of anything or lie straight to a person's face, without feeling a bit guilty. Sometimes she would argue with someone, and abuse them terribly. While at other times, she would be like a mouse. It depended on what suited her best, and what would be more beneficial to her needs at the time. In fact Winnie was really quite complex, and no one really knew how to deal with her. The best way to describe Winnie was dangerous. If by chance, Winnie did have an argument with anyone, god help that person, because no matter how long it took, she would have revenge. She could be quite spiteful when she wanted to be. Perhaps this was why everyone avoided her, and talked about her. They were frightened of her. They weren't sure how she would react to them. She was just so unpredictable, except with David. With him she was as sweet as pie. He was all she had, she had to be nice to him.

Time passed, and the haircut issue was forgotten. The time approached for the birth of her third child and panic began to set in. She didn't want to be going up to stay at Mary's again. She had no control there, none at all, and that worried her. Winnie had to be in control of the situation at all times, otherwise she began to weaken and feel insecure. She thought about the problem for a week or so, then cunningly came up with a solution that would not only solve the problem, but not alarm David about her reluctance to spend time with his precious mother, whom David thought was so perfect. Winnie really resented her sometimes, but she kept her feelings well hidden from David.

One day after the evening meal, Winnie decided to approach the subject. (Winnie always got her timing right by buttering David up with his favourite meal, and poor David never seemed to fall in. If he did, he ignored it). "Look David, I've been thinking about ya ma luv. It don't seem fair that I go stay with her this time ta have the baby. She's getting on now ya know and Francis and Caroline can be a bit of a hand full as ya know. So I've been thinking, don't ya think it would be far better if one of ya sisters came ta stay ere with us. They're far younger than ya ma, and it would make things better all round." "I think that's a wonderful idea Winnie. I'll talk ta ma tamorrow about it and see what she thinks. I'm sure she won't mind giving up one of the girls for a week or so. Like ya said, it would be easier on everyone."

Winnie was quite pleased with herself, it had all gone according to plan. A week later, Kathleen came to stay, and shortly after Winnie gave birth to another red headed daughter. She was named Maureen. Maureen was only very small when she was born, and the midwife didn't hold much hope for her survival. They had her baptised when she was only a few days old in fear of losing her. But survive she did, and although she was always small and skinny, there was nothing else wrong with her. Kathleen stayed with Winnie until after the baptism. Then returned home, leaving Winnie in complete charge, but Winnie had her hands full this time. Maureen really made the difference to the household. She did nothing but cry from morning to night. Winnie spent most of her time nursing her. As for Caroline she was a terrible tomboy and into everything. Winnie had no control over her at all. Francis on the other hand was her backbone. He helped Winnie with everything, including the washing and the cooking. David also helped occasionally on the weekend. His help was taking Caroline off Winnie's hands. For some reason though, Caroline always behaved herself for David. David had installed an extra seat on his push bike, and the pair of them would go bike riding for a few hours. One day, David was sick of all the screaming going on, and he said to Winnie, "I'll take Caroline out for a while luv."

"That sounds like a good idea David," Winnie said over Maureen's screams.

David saddled up Caroline, and they left. He was thankful to be out of there. Since Maureen had come into the world, the house had been upside down. Everytime he came home from work the place was a pig-sty, the evening meal was rarely ready, and the baby was always screaming. Winnie seemed to have little, if any, control over Caroline yet she was such a sweet child for him. David was lost in his thoughts, assessing the current situation at home and wasn't concentrating on the road. It had been raining and the roads were slippery, he turned a corner too sharp, hit the curb and Caroline came flying off the bike. She fell into the ditch at the side of the road right into a mud puddle. David got off the bike and ran to her. He was frantic with worry. Caroline looked up into David's face and burst out laughing as she looked at his worried expression "That was fun Pa." she said.

"Fun was it luv", David said, relieved that she was not hurt, "just look at the state of ya, what ever will ya ma say."

Caroline looked down at herself. She was covered with mud from head to toe. She laughed again, and replied,

"She'll do her nana pa, but it was still fun. She's always telling me off for getting dirty. On the way home from school Francis and I jump the ditches, and Francis always falls in. He can't jump very high ya know, ma always blames me though." Caroline said, with a small giggle.

"Come on pet, we'd best get ya home and cleaned up." David said, as he wondered why Winnie was so hard on Caroline, and so easy on Francis.

When David walked through the door with Caroline, Winnie just stared at them, and burst into laughter,

"What on earth happened?" she asked.

David started laughing too, "We had a small accident" he answered.

"Here take Maureen, Winnie said, (only too glad to be rid of her for a while) "I'll get Caroline cleaned up. Then I'll start us some dinner. This baby takes up me whole day David, she's really getting me down ya know."

"Oh don't fret luv, she'll grow out of it soon enough."

"Yea, I guess ya right, I just wish she'd hurry up." "Come lass," she said to Caroline, "Let's get ya cleaned up."

CHAPTER 14

A few weeks later, David came home from work, to find Winnie sitting in the lounge nursing Maureen and Caroline up on the kitchen bench playing a dangerous game with her brother. She was jumping around while Francis grabbed at her feet. He was trying to catch them, while she tried to dodge his hands.

"Get the bloody hell down from there, this instance Caroline," David yelled.

"It's okay Pa, we play this all the time, mum never tells us off." But Caroline lost her concentration while she had been talking to David, and Francis suddenly caught her feet and pulled at them. Caroline went flying backwards, straight through the kitchen window. David ran out the door, to her side. Her tongue was half off, and half on. He picked her up into his arms, and carried her all the way to the hospital screaming at Winnie as he left.

"It's her tongue, I'm taking her ta the hospital, stay ere with the kids."

Caroline received seven stiches in her tongue. On the way home David was fuming. If that bloody Winnie spent more time on the older two kids, and not just Maureen, this wouldn't have happened, he thought.

When he walked in the house Winnie came running to them,
"Is she alright, what happened?"

"If ya were out ere supervising the kids, like ya supposed ta, nowt would have happened, but no, ya park ya arse on that bloody couch all day with the baby and the rest of the house falls ta pieces. If ya must foocking sit down all day, keep the foocking kids in the same room with ya women. Not galavanting round where ever they please."

"David that's not fair, ya know how the baby plays up on me."

"Look Winnie, I don't want any foocking excuses. Ya home ta look after the foocking children and keep the house clean. This place is like a foocking pig-sty all the time. Dinner's never cooked anymore and the older two kids are out of control. Now start foocking looking after em properly. If ya had stopped Caroline from getting up there the first time she done it, this wouldn't have happened. She could ave split her foocking head open."

"Well what about you David, when she fell off the bike. That was an accident, the same as this was. Caroline is always getting hurt, she's a tomboy."

"Well it's your foocking place ta teach her some lady like manners then, ain't it."

Winnie didn't respond, she just nodded and started the evening meal, with Maureen in her arms. David turned and walked into the other room, as he did he said, "And get this foocking house cleaned up women, it's starting ta stink. The kids also need cleaning up, they're always filthy, it was bloody embarressing at the hospital. It looked like she hadn't been washed in weeks."

Winnie ignored him and carried on with what she was doing. What the hell did he know anyway, she thought. I've got this dammed baby in me arms all day, and when she does finally go ta sleep I'm just too tired ta do anything. He's only ere on the bloody weekends, and then he usually disappears with Caroline. A few weeks passed, and Winnie tried a little harder to keep the place clean, but Maureen took up so much of her time it was impossible to do everything.

One day Winnie settled Maureen down in the early afternoon and with relief sat down for a rest. She decided to do some knitting, while she sat there. She enjoyed her knitting, and done it most nights after the children were settled. She still insisted to David that it was for her own children. While she sat there knitting, Francis and Caroline went outside. Winnie, in a world of her own, didn't even notice them gone. Winnie was so relaxed and comfortable that she forgot all about the time, until Maureen began to wail. Winnie frowned and looked down at her watch.

"My it's five o'clock already," she said to herself "David will be home soon and I've not even started the dinner yet." She got up quickly. She ignored the crys of the baby and went to call the older kids to give her a hand. She had it all planned out, Caroline could nurse Maureen and Francis could help with the evening meal. She called their names several times, but there was no reply. Where the hell are they she though. She went out to the back yard, no kids. Oh shit she thought, where the hell have those brats gone. Davids gonna hit the roof when he comes home. That's all I need another bloody fight. She went back inside and picked up the now screaming Maureen. Then she began searching each room, one by one. Nothing! She went out to the front of the house, and began screaming their names again, "Francis, Caroline, where are ya?" but no one answered. Then Winnie saw David arriving home. Oh shit she thought, now there's gonna be trouble.
"What's going on" David asked, as he saw Winnie's worried face.
"It's the kids, they're missing David."
"What the hell are ya talking about, missing?"
"They were ere half hour ago David," she lied, (She hadn't seen them in hours.) Playing in the back yard, and now they're gone."
"I'll go look for em, you stay ere in case they come home."
David returned home four hours later, with the children to

Winnie's relief.

"Where were they," Winnie asked.

"They were bloody miles away Winnie. I found Francis stuck in a drain pipe, with Caroline bent over him laughing her head off. When I asked him how long he had been stuck down there, he told me since just after lunch. Ya foocking told me they were ere half hour before I got home, ya a foocking liar Winnie. The boy could ave got killed," he continued, "why weren't they at school anyway?"

"Because they said they were feeling poorly this morning, so I kept em home."

"If they were feeling poorly, why the hell weren't ya looking after em. Ya too foocking careless with these ere kids Winnie. I don't know what's come over ya lately. Listen ta me Winnie, and listen good. Ya pull ya foocking socks up quick smart women, cause I'm not standing for this any longer. Start looking after ya foocking kids the way ya used ta, or there'll be trouble round ere, ya hear me, big trouble."

"I can't cope with it all David. Caroline's inta everything, I can't turn me back for a minute or she's up ta something else. As for the baby, she never shuts up with her crying."

David cut her off, "Look I don't want no more excuses Winnie, ya the mother of these children, bloody look after em. They're like walking tramps all the time lately, and it's just not good enough. Me Ma had five of us and coped, what the hell's the matter with you?"

This last statement made Winnie's blood boil, but she said nothing. Why the hell does he always have ta bring her up, she thought. Silly old bitch that she is. Winnie took heed of David's words though and tried harder to get things back into order. She hated these quarrels happening again, things had been so good for so long, before Maureen had come along. She wanted things the way they were. Her efforts were rewarded too. Slowly the house became more organized and relaxed. Maureen was becoming stronger and cried a lot less. David seemed happier and the quarrels were non existent, for the time being anyway.

CHAPTER 15

When Maureen was five months old, Winnie began to feel that old familiar feeling of being worn out. She tried hard to ignore it though, not wanting to start David off again. However she finally faced the un-bearable truth that she was pregnant again. Winnie really didn't want this child. Maureen had taken too much out of her, and she knew that David would feel the same way. She dreaded telling him the news, however she knew it had to be done, and she may as well get it over with. That night when David came home all the children were already in bed, settled for the night. His meal was also ready for him.

"Where's the kids?" David asked.

"Oh I got em down early tanite luv. They've already eaten and I'm so bloody tired, I thought we could ave a peaceful evening for a change."

"That's all I ever ear from ya lately Winnie, that you're tired. The bloody kids are at school all day, and the baby has settled down now. Ya should try working out in them fields all day, then you'd ave cause ta be tired" David said.

"I think I'm tired, cause I'm pregnant again," Winnie blurted out.

David's two fists clenched, and he pounded them down on the kitchen table. The meal he had been enjoying went everywhere.

"Oh Winnie, what the hell am I supposed ta do now. We're not bloody millionaires ya know. We can't afford another kid, and you can't bloody cope with three, let alone four."

Winnie didn't answer, she knew he was right, but she also knew there was nothing they could do about it. As if reading her mind, David said,

"Oh Winnie, I'm sorry luv, I know it's not just your fault. It takes two ta tango as they say, but Christ, Maureens only five months old, and we really can't afford another one. The little amount I earn on the farm is hardly enough ta keep us all, and ma can't afford ta be paying me any more."

"I know David, and I hate fighting with ya, but there's nowt we can do about it now."

David put his head in his hands, and gently massaged his scalp, then he looked up at Winnie again, and said,

"Look we've been struggling for a while now Winnie, but I didn't want ta alarm ya, cause it's my job ta pay the bills, and do the worrying. However, there's an idea I've been fiddling with since Maureen was born, now it's time we looked at it more seriously. What do ya think of me going up ta Scotland ta find some work after this next child is born. I'll get more money up there than I can on the farm, and things won't be so strained between us."

"Oh I don't know David. It's such a long way an all."

"Yea, well we really don't have much choice now, do we. We just won't be able ta survive once the baby comes. On the wage I'm getting, it's just not possible."

"Yea, maybe ya right David, I just don't know."

"Look let's not discuss it any more tanite, I'll talk ta me family about it tamorrow and tell em what our plans are. Let's see what they have ta say about it."

Winnie was annoyed with David's last statement. What difference should they make anyway. Christ if he had ta go, like he reckons he does, then he had ta, what they thought didn't make a difference, Winnie thought. But she said nothing except, "Okay David, what ever ya say."

David's family wasn't really impressed with his idea, but they excepted it. So over the next several months, David began to save hard for his journey to Scotland. He needed enough money to see him through, until he found work and he wasn't sure how long that would take.

David and Winnie's fourth child came into the world. (That was me.) I was not welcomed with open arms, in fact I was really a burden on the family. I was named Josephine. Like Maureen, I was baptised within the first week of my life. This time the reason was because David, my father, wanted to get away to Scotland to start earning his fortune. Well at least a living for the family.

The night before David left for Scotland the whole Lynch family got together for dinner, at Mary Lynch's. Winnie objected to this at first saying, "I want ya all ta meself on our last night David."

David felt flattered, but said, "Ah what's the difference luv, if we all eat tagether, no one misses out."

Winnie reluctantly agreed. After dinner was finished, Mary stood, and got the attention of the family.

"Tanite is the last time we shall see David for quite a while" she stated, and paused before going on, "I think I speak for everyone here, when I say that he shall be greatly missed. There is something else I want to stress again, before he goes. I know we have discussed it before, and I'm sure you are all well aware of what my will states. However since we are all together, I am going to say it again." Mary took a drink, and then continued.

"When I pass on, ta be with ya pa, just in case it happens while David's still away. The farm and house must go ta David, Winnie, and their children, my much loved grandchildren. Furthermore it must never be sold ta an outsider. Does everyone understand that."

The Lynch family nodded their understanding and agreement, but none present were happy about it, except Winnie. David himself was indifferent, as far as he was concerned he would never live there anyway, so it made little difference to him.

The rest of the evening continued merrily and everyone seemed relaxed and happy. Except Winnie!. Finally the time came for David to leave. David's brothers and sisters hugged him and wished him good luck. Then it was Mary's turn to say goodbye.

"Well David, this is it I guess. Take good care of yaself son." Suddenly she was overwhelmed with grief and she hugged him with all the emotion she was feeling. Soft tears fell gently down her face, and she said,

"I do wish ya weren't going lad, I'll miss ya so much."

Then, to change the atmosphere, she turned to Winnie, and said,

"If ya need anything while David's away lass, just let me know."

"Yea, I'll do that." Winnie replied, but thought to herself, you crafty old bitch, you made sure ta say that while David was around, didn't ya.

"Come on David," Winnie said, "we had best be getting along. There's still a lot ta be done back home."

Mary grabbed her son again and the tears flowed fast and steady. "Oh David, I do wish ya would change ya mind luv."

"Oh ma, ya know that's not possible, I've got four kids now, and I really can't manage on the wage I'm getting. I also know ya can't pay me any more. Not that I expect it mind. This is the only solution ma."

"Yea lad, I know it's the truth ya speaking, but I luv ya so much, and I'm going ta miss ya terribly."

"Don't be fretting ma, I'll be fine, sure I will. Come on Winnie get the children ready, we had best be on our way luv."

....As they walked home, Winnie felt sick to her stomach, what a painful women that Mary is, she thought to herself. All those tears, over nowt. She really makes me sick the way she carries on sometimes.

The next morning was pretty hectic for David and the family. He had to leave home at 7am to catch the 8.15 train to Scotland, so it was an early start for everyone. The baggage had all been packed the previous night, so only the basics were left, and of course the farewells. This was the hardest of all for David. He looked down at me, his new born child, and said, "I've not even held ya for more than a minute and I'm leaving ya already. But I'll be back soon me little darling and ya ma will take good care of ya till I return."

Then he kissed us all one by one, and bid us farewell. First Maureen, and then Caroline. He hugged her the longest, and said, "Now ya help ya ma round the house lass, and don't be getting yaself inta any trouble. It's your place, being the oldest girl ta help ya ma, and don't ya be forgetting it." Then he turned to Francis. "As for you lad, ya the man around the house, for the time being anyway till I get back. I want ya ta be doing ya ma's bidding like a good lad, and look after the family for me."

"Yea pa", Francis said, and began to cry as he hugged his father goodbye. That started everybody else off, even mum shed tears that day.

"Now that's enough of that," David said, "I'll be back before ya know it." Then he turned to mum and said,

"Well this is it luv, I'd best be on me way. Take good care of the kids for me, and I'll send ya money every week, as soon as I get meself a job like."

"I will David", mum replied, "and take care of yaself luv. I'll miss ya terribly, but I know it's for the best."

"Well I'd best be on me way then or I'll be missing me train. Look ere's some money ta keep ya going, till I get meself a job. Now don't be fretting for me cause I'll be back in a few months, and the time will fly by. In the meantime, if ya need any thing just call on me ma, ya know she won't mind."

David kissed her, picked up his luggage and left. Everyone stood at the door waving to him. Everyone was crying, except for me, I knew no better. Even dad had tears in his eyes. It was one of the saddest days of his entire life, watching his whole family in front of him, crying for him. Francis and Caroline were sobbing their little hearts out and it was tearing dad apart to see it.

After arriving in Scotland, it only took dad a couple of days to find work. He found accomodation in a nearby hostel and was quite happy and doing well. He had also made a friend which was unusual, because dad, like the rest of the Lynch's preferred to keep to himself. His new friend's name was Patrick Rooney. He was also from Ballinrobe originally, but hadn't lived there since he was a very small boy. Dad wrote to mum often telling her all the news, and asking her how we were. He missed us all deeply, especially Caroline.

As he had promised, he sent home money to mum every week. Mum was beginning to enjoy this being by herself business. She had plenty of money, and was in control of it. Yes this was a great life, there were no responsibilites about meals. She fed us when ever she felt like it, or when we were starving, which ever came first. She was very happy indeed. Grandma was helping in every way she could too. She would quite often take Caroline and Maureen off mums hands for the weekend, leaving only Francis and myself for mum to look after. Grandma would also bring us most of the food for the week, which left little for mum to pay for at all. Dad also wrote to grandma on occasions, and she would write back telling him all the village gossip and how mum was coming along.

As for mum, she didn't write back often. She was too lazy.

Her excuse was the children kept her too busy. The truth was, she gave little time to us at all. She spent all her time knitting for the townsfolk. She could do it freely now, without any questions from dad. We went un-washed for weeks on end sometimes, and our hair was never even combed. For some reason I was the worst neglected out of all of us. Maybe because I was the ugliest child she had. I had black hair, and green eyes, which were always filled with green crispy gunk, and were very sensitive. I was also very fat. Or maybe it was because, I just wasn't wanted, from the day I had been conceived. Perhaps it was a little of both, I really don't know. What I do know was mum got lazier, with each and every day.

Grandma began to notice this, and felt it her duty to let David know the state we were always in lately. So in one of her letters to dad she mentioned it. Shortly after, mum received a letter from dad stating that if all went well, he would to be home in a couple of weeks. He had been quite distressed after reading his mother's letter. According to the letter, Winnie had been going out at night, leaving Francis home to mind the rest of the family. He had decided then to go and check it out for himself. (Dad's only mistake was letting mum know he was coming.) Besides he was earning good money now and a few weeks with the family would do him good. He had been away several months now and he convinced himself that it was time to go home for a spell. Dad didn't like to listen to gossip though, and he wrote back to his mother, saying, he found it hard to believe what she had written about Winnie, and that she should stop telling tales. However in his heart, he felt that there may be some truth in her words.

So dad, after six months of being away, returned home. Caroline was so happy to see him, and she leapt up into his arms. He had brought presents for everyone. Mum had cleaned up the house, and we were all clean and presentable, which made his mother appear to be a liar. He didn't even question mum about going out at night, he had no cause to. Everything looked perfect. He told mum how much he had missed her and the children and how glad he was to be at home, even if it was only a week. That week went by as quick as lighting and it was time for our dad to leave again, but he left his trade mark with mum. She was pregnant again!

Back in Scotland, dad threw himself into his work. He was getting used to being alone now, however he still missed the family. He spent most of his spare time with Patrick who, like himself, liked a few stouts and they had a lot of fun together. Patrick was a single man, but had a girlfriend named Elizabeth. They were saving to get married.

Meanwhile back home, mum discovered she was pregnant again. She wrote and told dad the news straight away. She also told him how unhappy she was about the pregnancy. However dad wrote back and congratulated her, saying that it wouldn't make much difference now. He was making good money, and one more child sounded just fine to him. After reading dad's reply, mum screwed up the letter, and threw it across the room in temper. Congratulations she thought, just what I need, another little shit ta tend to. Mum was getting quite used to being by herself. She had started going out with her girlfriend, Francis, who was still unmarried. They went to the local dances together and had a lot of fun. Another baby would put an end to all that. She had been saving most of the money that dad had sent. There was no need to spend much. Grandma was feeding us. As for our clothes we made do with what we had. So all she really had to pay for was the rent each month. Mum had started sleeping in each morning and Francis and Caroline began missing a lot of school. When the police guards would come to find out why the children hadn't attended school, she would lie to them and say "Oh they weren't feeling well." or, "They have a cold." and she would always get away with it. She just lied so well, everyone believed her.

By day mum knitted for the townsfolk, and most nights she went out with her girlfriend. Then one day she got a knitting job for the wife of the local doctor. His name was Doctor John Flannery and his wife's name was Rose. They had no children but were happily married. Winnie started delivering the finished garments to the doctors office, at Rose's request, (so that her husband John would pay for them.) But that was a mistake on Rose's behalf. Mum started flirting with John Flannery and soon they were having an affair. They would meet in the middle of the night and make love. Sometimes it would be at the surgery, sometimes in the car, or even at the bus stop, but he never came to our place because Caroline had a big mouth. Mum knew she would repeat everything to grandma, who in turn would tell dad.

Mum was so brazen about the affair though, sometimes she would go to Rose's house to give her a knitted garment, just as a present, and allow herself to be entertained by Rose. Poor Rose, she was completely blinded by mum, as was her husband John. She believed that Mum was a lovely person and would enjoy her company immensely. These meetings went on the whole time the affair did.

Mum was well and truly expecting with her fifth child now, but it made no difference to her, or her doctor friend. In fact, mum regarded her pregnancy as a blessing in disguise, because no one would expect her to be having an affair firstly, and secondly, she couldn't get pregnant twice, so dad would never find out either.

However mum was wrong. The situation became more involved than they thought it would. John Flannery actually fell in love with mum, even in her pregnant state. What's worse is, mum fell for him too. All she could think about was him. She didn't stop to think for a minute, about us and her husband. No, she was far too selfish for that. If only dad had taken a little more heed of his mother's letters, just maybe things would have turned out different. He should have just come home unexpected. Then mum would have been caught out. But she didn't get caught out, not until it was too late for us anyway!

A few months later, mum received another letter from dad. It stated that he would be returning home at the end of the month (again giving her ample warning) for a short time to see us all. Mum was very disappointed and again screwed up his letter and threw it. David coming home meant that she couldn't see John for a while and that was agony for her. Mum had plenty of time to clean up the house again, and get us looking respectable. As far as dad could tell his family were all well, and so was his marriage.

Mum smothered him with hugs and kisses when he arrived, making believe that he was her whole life. We were so happy to have our father back and dad seemed the happiest of all to be back. Caroline jumped into dad's arms as soon as mum had released her hold on him. She was so excited, she had missed him more than anyone. Dad laughed at her excitement and tickled her until she was screaming with laughter, before putting her down again. Then he turned to Francis, who extended his hand in a gentlemans manner. Dad laughed again as he shook his son's hand. He still looks like a girl, he thought, his hair is as long as ever. As if on impulse he rubbed the top of his son's hair, and said.

"When on earth is ya ma gonna cut this head of hair lad?"

"Never" Francis answered, and ran inside the house before David said anymore on the subject.

"Come on," David said "let's all be going in, we can't stay out ere all day."

Everyone went inside and Caroline jumped back into dad's arms again. Mum was beginning to panick, she had to get Caroline away from David. Caroline had such a big mouth and she couldn't risk her telling David that she had be going out a lot at night.

"Come on Caroline", she said, "get down of ya Pa, and let him say hello ta the rest of the family".

Caroline jumped down from her father's arms and dad picked me up.

"Hi there Josephine," he said, "how are ya, me little darling. I'm ya pa."

I began to cry. (I was only 14 months old and had only seen him once before on his last trip home). I was handed back to mum quick smart.

Dad turned to mum, "What's the matter with her eyes Winnie?" he asked, "They're all puffy and sore looking."

"Oh they're fine David", mum said, "It's just cause she's been crying, that's all." How well that women lied. My eyes were always like that and she had never bothered getting them checked.

Then dad picked up Maureen, and with a gasp, he said, "This child weighs nowt, sure the baby is heavier then her. She looks like the wind could break her bones Winnie. What's the matter, aren't ya feeding the child or what?"

"Ya can't be comparing weights between Maureen and Josephine, David," mum answered with a forced laugh. "Josephine, is ten tonne tessy, can't ya see how fat the child is, she's like a baby elephant. As for Maureen, she never puts on any weight. Don't matter what she eats, she stays the same. That's just the way she is. So don't be fretting yaself with the kids luv, they're just fine. Now sit yaself down ere at the table, and I'll make ya a nice cuppa, before I get the dinner ready."

"I'd prefer a guiness, if ya ave one luv."

Mum frowned. She had forgotten to get some, she had been too busy trying to put the house into a bit of order. She turned and said,

"Oh David, I've been run of me feet, with the kids an all. With all the excitement of ya coming home, I plain forgot ta get some, I'll nick down later for ya luv."

"Okay, tea will do, but ya know I luv me guiness, I thought ya would have got a couple for me at least."

"Ah, I'm sorry luv, I'll go get some now." Winnie said in her sweetest tone. Inside she was cursing him for her trouble. But she put on her coat, to go out and get him his stout. She had half hoped he would tell her not to worry, that he'd go down later, but he didn't. As she was about to leave she said to Caroline, "Come on Caroline, ya had best come with me, and help me carry em home."

"Ah mum, I wanna stay ere with pa" Caroline answered.

I bet ya do, ya big blabber mouth, Winnie thought, but said, "Leave ya pa be, we'll be back in a jiffy anyhow. Now get ya coat, and let's go."

Caroline done what she was told, and they both left. As they were walking Winnie was deep in thought, I have ta keep this child away from David as much as possible, otherwise all hell could break loose.

When they got back home, dad was on the floor playing with

us. Francis was jumping all over him and Maureen and I were in fits of laughter. Mum would have been happy to see this a couple of years ago. Now it irritated her. Dad was a burden now, just like us. What was worse, she was stuck with it for the time being, at least until dad went back.

"Here's ya beer David," mum said, "now come out ere and talk ta me for a while."

Dad got up and sat at the table. Mum prepared herself a cup of tea and sat down with him.

"So how ave ya been Winnie, ya look like ya bundles about ta drop any day." David said.

"Na, I've got another four weeks ta go till the baby comes. I do wish ya could stay for the birth David." She lied, knowing he could only stay a week without losing his job.

"Yea, I wish I could too, but I can't luv, I'm doing so well in Scotland now, and we can't afford for me ta be losing me job now, can we. The worst of it is when I go back this time I won't be able ta come back for a while, maybe a couple of years."

"Oh David that's terrible, the new baby won't even know ya luv, and I miss ya so much when ya gone. I get so lonely with just the kids."

Mum spoke her words with such emotion, yet inside her heart was dancing with joy at the news he had just given her. Only one week she would have to put up with him, then peace for two years. She looked at him, and wondered how she had ever got stuck with an old man like him. Then she smiled her loving smile, and said, "Don't look so guilty David, I'm sorry for asking ya ta stay. I know ya do the best ya can for us. Just forget I mentioned it. I'll manage just fine on me own luv. I won't like it much, but I'll be okay."

"Oh Winnie, I wish there was some other way, but there ain't luv. The way I figure it, if I go back, work for a couple of years, and save hard, we can be settled for life with no worries. We can buy a house, maybe even around these parts if we're luckly, and I can work locally, without worrying about the rent, and so on."

"Oh it does sound good David, and I'll manage by meself, so don't ya worry about it luv."

That week, (The last week we would ever spend together, as a whole family,) passed all too quickly for dad, and us, but I guess it dragged for mum. All the cleaning and cooking was driving her mad. As for us, we were really grinding on her nerves. She just wasn't used to us anymore. Always asking for things, and having to look after us. Mum watched Caroline like a hawk. Everytime she saw her on dad's knee she would call her away to do something, or go somewhere. My sister didn't realise what she was up to at the time, but now, looking back at it, it's all very clear. Sometimes dad would try and keep Caroline with him if they were playing, but mum would insist that she needed Caroline's help.

Dad made a few comments regarding my eyes too, (which he felt needed immediate attention). But mum would pass it off lightly, assuring him that she had them checked on several occasions and I would grow out of it. Dad believed her lies, and dropped the subject, feeling that mum knew best. He didn't know just how neglected I was, or should I say, we all were. How could he, she hid it all so well. When dad was around she was the perfect wife, and mother.

The day came for dad to return to Scotland, and he hated leaving. Caroline was sobbing and Francis was close to tears also. Maureen and myself were also screaming, but we didn't know why, we were just copying Caroline. Dad kissed us all, leaving mum till the last. He told her to let him know when the baby arrived and added that he hoped it was another boy to help balance the scales a little. Then he kissed us all again and left. Mum was glad to see the back of him. She was looking forward to seeing her lover again. Dad on the other hand, left broken-hearted and with a great sense of loss in his heart. He didn't realise though, just how much he was going to lose.

CHAPTER 16

Dad returned to Scotland to continue providing for his family and to someday have a happy life with us. That was dad's only dream in life, but some people's dreams never come true. Dad was one of those people.

Mum returned to her lover. The fact that she was giving birth to a baby, in three weeks or so, made little difference to their love making, neither of them seemed to care. Mum was fat, unattractive, and very dirty. The only piece of mother's body that ever saw a bar of soap was her face. But John still found her exciting. Yet his wife Rose was a beautiful, well bred and respected lady. It doesn't make sense when you think about it, but that's the way it was, John preferred Winnie.

Two weeks passed and mum went into labour unexpectedly. She had always been on time or a couple of days late, but this baby was eager to come into the world. If only it had known what it's life was going to be like, it wouldn't have been so eager.

Mum gave birth to a beautiful baby girl. This was by far her prettiest baby. Like Francis she had thick curly hair, but it was pure white. She had big blue eyes, with very dark lashes. She was like a doll in every sense of the word. She was named Pauline. Everyone who saw her, took to her straight away. Everyone except mother that is. If Pauline had died at birth, it may have been better, for all the love she was going to receive. She may as well have been dead for all mum cared. Even Francis got on mum's nerves now. All she cared about was her Dr John Flannery.

Mum wrote to dad when Pauline was born and told him that

they had another baby girl. She described her with love and affection, but they were only words. They had no meaning. Mum's only concern was getting her figure back into shape for her lover.

By day, mum slept. We had to take care of ourselves. Francis was eight, and Caroline was seven, nearly eight. They were quite capable of looking after themselves. Caroline had the added burden of looking after us three as well, with some help from Maureen. Francis was keeping to himself all together. During the day, while Caroline was at school, Maureen fed the baby. Maureen was only two and a half years old herself, and a very small two and a half at that. When Pauline cried Mum would ignore her. It didn't matter if she was hungry, or wet, she was still ignored by mum.

Because Maureen was so small, and incapable of lifting Pauline out of the cot, she would feed her through the bars of the cot, giving her bread, or what ever she could find, until Caroline returned home from school. The cot which Pauline slept, ate and drank in, was filthy, just like the rest of the house, and us too for that matter. Caroline did what she could to take care of us, but that was little. She was only a child herself.

When mum finally got up each day (usually mid to late afternoon) she would either start her knitting, or start getting herself ready for her evening out. That depended on what time she got up. If we were really luckly she would prepare us some food or change Pauline's nappy for the day. (Mostly these two chores were left for Caroline, after school). However mostly we ate bread and dripping, which was prepared by Caroline.

One Friday after school, grandma called to take Caroline and Maureen home for the weekend. When she arrived mum was still in bed. The baby was screaming and the rest of us were running wild. Mary went straight to the baby and picked her up from the cot. Pauline was soaking wet and stunk to high heaven of shit and urine. Mary was flabbergasted. She asked Caroline, "Where on earth is ya ma child?"

Caroline looked up at her baffled, as if to say, where she always is, and said, "In bed grandma."

Mary marched straight into Winnie's bedroom with the baby still in her arms, and burst open the door.

"Winnie," she said in a stern voice, "It's 4.30 in the afternoon. What's the matter with ya, are ya sick or something?"

"No I'm not bloody sick" mum snapped back at her, annoyed at being woken up. "What the bloody hell are ya doing ere anyways?"

"I came ta see if I could take the two older girls home for the weekend, and I think ya need ta change this child in me arms," Mary said, changing the subject completely, "she stinks and is absolutely saturated."

"That's none of ya bloody business, besides it's Carolines job ta change the child."

"Oh Winnie, Carolines but a child herself, you're the babes mother, not her."

"Oh why don't ya mind ya own bloody busines Mary. You raised your family, now let me raise mine. Ya nowt but a bloody busybody. Now foock off outa me house, and mind ya own bloody business for once."

"Now Winnie, there's no need ta be talking ta me like that. I'll take the girls, and let ya calm down."

"You leave the girls where they bloody are, I don't want ya touching none of me kids again." She jumped up out of bed,

- 114 -

and snatched Pauline out of Mary's arms, pushed by her, and practically threw Pauline back into her filthy cot.

"Now get outa me house, I've always hated ya, ya bloody old cow. I never want ta see ya again, ya hear."

Caroline and Maureen started crying, and the baby was once again screaming. Caroline started to speak through her tears, "Oh ma, can't we please go ta grandma's?"

"No ya bloody can't, not taday, and not ever."

"Oh please ma, I'll be good, I promise."

With that, mum gave Caroline such a slap in the face, it sent her flying, and she screamed out at her, "Shut-up child."

Caroline held her tongue, and the side of the face where she had just been slapped. She knew that when she went to grandma's, Maureen and herself ate well, and could relax, and play. It was fun there, but she still didn't say another word. Maureen was also trying to say something,

"I've been good, I feed the baby for ya," but her speech was slow, and she couldn't make herself understood. She was also told by mum, to shut up with her babbling.

Mary went to Caroline's side and tried to comfort her after her slap in the face. This started mum screaming again.

"Take ya filthy hands off her, bitch."

"Look Winnie I'm only trying ta help ya luv." Mary said in a nice calm tone, realising that mum was losing all control.

"Ya can't manage all of em by yaself luv. Let me help ya, that's all I'm trying ta do, ya know."

"Oh just get out of ere, ya silly old bitch." mum screamed, "Don't ya understand, I don't want ya foocking help. We can manage fine without ya, and ya can write and tell ya son what I'm saying too, I don't bloody care." Winnie bluffed.

"I won't be telling David nowt. I'm sure we can work this out between ourselves. Besides, I'm not sure he'd believe me anyway Winnie. It's best if he finds out for himself, how nasty ya can really be. One day, David will open his eyes Winnie, I just pray ta god it won't be too late. Look Winnie I'll do as ya ask, I'll never enter ya lives again from this day on. If that's the way ya want it, who am I ta argue, but remember, I tried, I really tried me best."

"Oh just piss off, will ya." Winnie answered her.

Mary released her hold on Caroline, and sorrow overwhelmed her as she looked, first at Caroline, and then around at the rest of us. She turned to hide her tears, and left the house. That was the last time any of us ever saw our grandmother. Caroline can still remember that day clearly, even now, fifty years later. I believe she was the most affected by the loss of our grandmother. She remembers her as a sweet, loving old lady, who loved us all dearly.

Mary never told her son about the argument, or the way his children were being neglected. She was getting old now, and just wanted a bit of peace in her life. Maybe if she had told him again, things would have been different. Then again maybe she was correct, dad probably wouldn't have believed her, or at least have thought that she was exaggerating the whole thing.

The situation just got worse for us. Mum even received letters from the school, informing her that Francis and Caroline were badly infested with head lice. She had the cheek to go to the school and blame them for the situation. Knowing that she never bothered to even bath us, not alone clean our hair. The truth was, we all had lice, even Pauline, who had never even left the cot. Mum could change any situation around to suit herself though. The school actually apologized to her, and saw to it that their heads were cleaned. If it had been left to mum, it wouldn't have been done. It was a useless effort anyway, because Francis and Caroline caught them again from us. At this stage we were getting little food at all. Our whole diet was bread and dripping, or bread and jam. Sometimes we got milk to drink, but mostly it was water. Sometimes we got nothing at all, because mum hadn't even brought bread. There were times when Pauline would be screaming, and mum would scream out to Caroline,

"Caroline, shut that baby up."

Caroline would answer "She's hungry ma."

"Well why ain't ya feeding her then?"

"There's nowt ta feed her ma" Caroline would answer. Then we would get some more food. In a way, Pauline was even helping to feed us.

Pauline was ten months old now, and had been terribly neglected. If it wasn't for Caroline, and Maureen, I'm sure my sister would have been dead today. As for Francis he was never around. As soon as he came in from school, he went out to play. When he came back, he went straight to bed. He seemed to go into a world of his own since mum had turned her back on us. Maybe it was his way of protecting himself against our mothers denial of love. Or maybe he just couldn't bear to believe what she was doing to us. He loved her so much. He always had. Who knows for sure what he was thinking, he never discussed it with us.

As for me, I was just there, just another burden for Caroline. I was too small to help with anything, and I was too young to play with. I was the ugly ducking of the family. My eyes were still badly infected and I was still very fat, even though we ate very little. I never cried, or laughed much. I really only existed, I was there, and that was all. Out of all of us, I guess Pauline had the worst treatment. The only good thing was, she knew no better, that was life to her. She was born so healthy, like all of us, but she was also beautiful. It hurts me when I think of the damage that was done to Pauline, by being left in her cot for ten months without exercise. Due to lack of exercise, from crawling and movement she had become a cripple, and no one realised it yet. We were all too young to realise, and mother just didn't care enough to notice. Some people try all their lives for children, and have no success, while others have badly deformed children, and love them with all their hearts. Our mother had five healthy children and rejected them completely. I often ask myself why god lets this happen, but there is no answer.

By the time Pauline was 16 months, her condition had worsened. Most of the time she just lay there. She didn't even cry much any more. She had gotten used to being hungry, and dirty. Maureen was a little over four years old now. She had taken over Pauline's feeding completely at this stage. Everytime she ate herself, she automatically fed Pauline. But Pauline had lost weight and looked pale all the time. She hadn't grown much at all, because she was suffering from malnutrition. Maureen can still remember the smell that used to come from Pauline's cot as she feed her. Pauline had never been toilet trained, so everything was done right there in the cot. Caroline cleaned it up occasionaly, (usually when she saw Maureen heaving as she fed Pauline through the bars of the cot, Pauline's little prison.) But Caroline did little else for her, she was too busy with the rest of the chores she had to do, and going to school.

School was Caroline's only escape from home. At school, she was like everyone else, just a child. At home she was totally relied upon by us, and that was a strain for a child who was only nine years old herself.

As each day passed, mum had less and less to do with us. She was always too tired. She would snap our heads off whenever we even spoke to her and went really wild if we asked for something.

Finally it happened. It was bound to eventually. Mum became pregnant to Dr John Flannery. Our futures were about to change drastically, and there was nothing we could do about it.

CHAPTER 17

A month later, when mum first realised she was pregant, she was quite upset about it. She didn't want a baby upsetting her relationship with John. She also knew that all hell would break loose when David found out. She couldn't even palm the child off as being his, she hadn't seen him in sixteen months. She had no alternative but to face the music, or convince John to run away with her. Winnie wondered how John would take the news. She knew him well enough to know he would stand by her. But would he leave his wife for her. One thing for sure was, she needed to tell him straight away, before she started to show.

She didn't even consider us, just herself. She was quite prepared to leave us, all five of us, for the one she had in her womb. I can't understand that, even today. Her love for the doctor must have been very strong, that's all I can say.

On the Friday night of that week, mum went out and met John at the surgery. She had put plenty of effort into her appearance that evening, and knew she looked attractive. Her figure had returned, and her face was, as always, appealing. Tonight she was going to seduce her lover into running away with her.

Mum succeeded too, worse luck. After she outlined her predicament, and the fact that facing David would be hell itself. Dr John Flannery agreed to leave his wife. He went along with it, like a lamb to the slaughter. His main concern was, what would happen to us, HER CHILDREN. She assured him that we would be fine. That she planned to bring us to our grandmother's place, where we would be well taken care of. John, convinced that everything would be fine, looked forward to having a child of his own. Which his wife Rose had never been able to give him. Mum was very cleaver, she had made sure to mention the fact that he would now be a father, knowing full well that he had always wanted a child of his own.

One thing I still can't understand though, is why she didn't bring us to grandma's place. That would have been far better than just leaving us to starve by ourselves. Maybe she thought that Mary might have tried to stop her, or contact dad. Who knows what her reasoning was. One thing I do know is, I hate her for doing what she did to us. We never asked to be born, and no one deserves that kind of treatment, especially five helpless children.

The next day mum went out and got some shopping. Well she got milk, bread, and jam. She also brought some roasting meat, something we hadn't had since dad went away. She came home and cooked a roast meal for dinner. Was that her way of making up for what she was about to do. When Caroline and Francis came home from school, she told them that dinner was in the oven. Caroline looked at Mum and said,
"Meat, how come ma, ya always say ya can't afford it."
"Well I saved for it Caroline. How come ya always have ta ask questions anyway child."
"Sorry ma, I was just wondering, that's all."
Francis sat down at the table, he usually came home, dropped off his books, and took off. Maybe he thought that mum was going back to her old self and wanted to be around to see it. Or maybe, like Caroline he sensed that trouble was about to break. We never did find out what he was feeling that day. He never would discuss it. However Caroline has discussed it with me, on many occasions. She knew that something was going on,

and she knew it wasn't going to be good for us, but good sense told her not to question our mother. Mum's hands were very free lately, and the slightest wrong word, or action, was likely to bring a hard slap on the face.

It was a Friday evening. Winnie had planned it well. The school guard wouldn't call over the weekend, and probably not until Tuesday or Wednesday, to find out why the kids hadn't been to school. She hoped they wouldn't go on Monday, but she couldn't be sure of that either. Either way, she had the weekend at least to make good her escape.

Mum sat down and had the evening meal with us, in a sense it was the last supper. It was the last one we would have with her anyway. After dinner she rose, and said to Caroline,

"You can clean up later, Caroline. I have ta go out now."

Then she got up, and did something strange. She kissed us all. Then she said to Caroline,

"Caroline, listen closely girl, no matter what happens, don't be going near ya grandma, da ya hear me child. Stay away from her, or so help me god, I'll kill ya."

"How come ma" Caroline asked.

"Don't be asking me all these quesions child, just do what I'm telling ya for once in ya life."

"Okay ma " Caroline answered, but Caroline knew at that instance what was happening, she knew her mother wasn't coming back, but she didn't have the guts to ask her why.

Mum, with only a small bag in her hand, left the house, and us. Caroline jumped up on the kitchen bench, and looked out the window. She watched our mother walk down the path to the gate. Mum actually turned, smiled at her and waved goodbye. Caroline has her smiling face etched into her memory. She can still see her waving goodbye to us. She can still remember the silent, hot tears rolling down her face, as she waved back at our mother. Caroline turned to Francis, and was about to speak her fears with her big brother, but he got up from the table, and ran to his bedroom, before anyone could say a word.

Winnie met John outside the surgery, all packed and ready to go. They were going to Dublin. Winnie was in fine spirits when John drove up to collect her. She was starting a new life, with her new boyfriend, and was very happy about it. She had no bad feelings at all about the five children she had just abandoned. She was much too excited for that.

As soon as she entered the car, John asked her how it had gone with Mary Lynch, and if she had taken the children. Winnie looked him straight in the face, and said,
"Yea, it went like a breeze. I knocked at the door, and when she opened it I said,
"Here are ya son's kids. Now you can ave em. I'm off ta make a better life for meself."
"Ya didn't tell her it was with me, did ya Winnie?"
"Na, I didn't say a word, neither did she. The old cow was too shocked ta say a word, she just stood there with her mouth open. Then I turned on me heel and walked off. As I walked off though, I heard her calling me back, but I just kept right on walking."
"Will ya miss the kids Winnie?" John asked.
"Yea I will," she answered, and started to cry. She was such a god damned liar, even the supposed meeting with grandma Lynch all sounded so real and convincing.
"Are ya sure ya want ta go through with this Winnie luv?" John asked, feeling guilty for making her leave her kids, when it was her idea to leave in the first place.
Winnie dried her tears immediately when he said that, in fear

he would change his mind.

"Oh of course I do, luv, I know it's for the best, besides I'll soon have another child. Our child John," she added, "and we will all be so happy together."

John hugged her, and said, "Okay then, let's be on our way."

He started the car, and they were off on their journey, to start new lives together. Poor John, he must have been horrified when he found out later what mum really did to us.

....The weekend passed slowly. The little food mother had brought us was gone. It had been, since Sunday. The snow was thick on the ground outside, and we were freezing. It was just as cold in the house, as it was outside. Caroline did what she could to keep us warm, but there wasn't much she could do really. At least when mother was here the house was warm, she liked her comfort. Now we were not only hungry, but very cold as well. We were like this until the Tuesday evening. Alone, cold, scared, and hungry. On the Tuesday evening, the school guard came around to enquire why Francis and Caroline hadn't attended school for the past two days. (They had not gone to school, just as mother had hoped, they had stayed home to mind us.) When the knock came to the door, Caroline leapt to her feet, hoping to see mum on the other side of the door, but she was still relieved and happy to see the guards face. Any adult face, was better than none.

"Hello lass, where's ya ma then?" the guard asked.

"She's not ere sir, she went out last Friday, and she ain't been back. I don't think she's coming back anymore sir." Caroline said.

The guard frowned, and pushed by Caroline to take a look around inside the house. As he went into the sitting room he saw Francis, Maureen, and myself all huddled in a ball, on the middle of the floor. We were trying to keep warm. The smell was overwhelming in there, and he began to look around in search of the vile smell. He soon realised it was coming from the cot, which Pauline lay in. He went over to her, she looks so pale, he thought, and wondered for a moment if she was dead, or just sleeping. He touched her face gently, she was very cold, but still alive. Maureen and myself started crying, we were not accustomed to strange faces. Francis tried to calm us down as best he could, but was getting nowhere. After covering Pauline up, the gaurd walked back to us.

"Now now, stop ya crying." he said, "Everthing is gonna be just fine. Ya can all come with me, and we'll get ya some nice hot soup, and some warm clothes, how does all that sound?"

I started screaming, "Don't wanna go, don't wanna go Cal's," I kept repeating to Caroline.

"It'll be fine" Caroline assured me. It all sounded great to her. "I'll be coming with ya Josephine, so stop ya tears right now, ya hear."

We were all bundled up, he even changed the baby's nappy, and put warm clothes on her before leaving. We were taken down to the local police station, where we were fed, and looked after, while the authorities tried to find somewhere for us to stay.

We never did find out whether our grandma was notified, but if she was, she didn't come for us. In fact no one did. We ended up in the Castlebar Mental Hospital. (Where our aunty Angela was). We were there a full week, before they could find a suitable place for us. We were to be placed in a Convent, for unwanted and orphaned children. Us with two healthy parents, still alive. But at least it was better than the Mental Hospital. Francis was sent to an all boy's convent called the "Christian Brothers Ophanage", and initally, the rest of us were sent to a place called "Our Lady of Mercy". It must have been worse for Francis than ourselves. At least we had each other, for the time being anyway. He had no one. The Irish papers printed the story, it was a very big disgrace for the Lynch family and poor dad knew nothing about it. Not until after the story was printed, that is.

CHAPTER 18

One morning, David lay in bed at the hostel. Lately he had spent most of his time there, or working. He really missed his family. He hadn't seen them in sixteen months. He tried hard to save his pennies, and get back to his family as quickly as possible. The women who served the food at the hostel, (and who was also very attracted to David) knocked and entered his room with David's breakfast tray. Her name was Edna Mitchell and she was an English women. She had been previously married with two children. However, her husband had constantly beat her during the marriage, so when her children had grown and left home, she left also.

Edna was six years older than David, but still an attractive women. She hadn't counted on falling for anyone else quite so soon though, and especially to a married man. She knew that David was totally devoted to his wife and children too, and that she didn't stand a chance with him, but she couldn't help her feelings. However, because of the situation, she keep her feelings to herself knowing it would only make them both uncomfortable, but she always looked after him, making sure he was well fed and had clean clothes to wear.

"Good morning David," she said as she entered the bedroom. "Here's your breakfast, eggs done just the way you like them."
"Thank ya Edna, just leave the tray over there," David answered, as he pointed to the dressing table at the far side of the room.
"Fine." she replied and then added, "I'm running a bit late this morning, so you had better make it snappy, it's already close to six thirty."
"Right ya are, I'll get up as soon as ya leave."

"Okay, David, I'll see you later then, at dinner."
"Yea, yea," David replied, still half asleep.

Patrick Rooney was already up and dressed. While he sat and ate breakfast, he broused through the Irish paper. Suddenly he saw it, his eyes opened wide with horror, as he realised the story was about David's children. Oh my god, he thought, these are David's kids. I wonder if he's seen it yet. With the paper in his hand, he jumped to his feet and went to David's room, two doors down. He didn't bother knocking, he just barged right in.

David was pulling up his pants, and turned sharply when the door opened, wondering if it was Edna again. When he saw Patrick he smiled with relief and said, "What ya doing ere so early Patrick, I ain't had me breakfast yet."
Patrick didn't answer, he went straight into the reason he was there, and said, "David ave ya seen the Irish paper this morning?"
"Na, can't ya see I just got up?"
"Well take a look at this, there's some real bad news about ya kids in it."
"My kids, what the foock are ya talking about, my kids," David said, as he snatched the paper from Patrick and began to read the article.

The article told how his five children had been abandoned by their mother, who was later arrested in Slygio, on the way to Dublin, and she was now in Slygio Prison. It told how the authorities had been unable to contact the father of the children, and that they had been sent to convents.
David looked up from the paper and tears filled his eyes. He looked at Patrick, and asked,
"Why Patrick? What the hell was the women thinking about?"

(David had no idea about John at that stage. They hadn't mentioned anybody else in the article.) "Why didn't me ma take em? I don't understand any of this Patrick. What the hell is going on?" David asked, trying to make some sense of it all.

"I know less than you do David," Patrick answered, "but we'll be sorting it out soon enough. Come on, get dressed. We can take the day off work, and find out what the hell's going on."

Patrick and David didn't find out much more than they already knew. They contacted the authorities in Ireland, but all they found out, was that he couldn't get us back. Not until we turned sixteen years of age.

Our mother spent eighteen months in prison. I wish to Christ she had been hung there and then, because she hadn't finished tormenting us. Even when we were much older, she remained a thorn in our sides. Always doing something to hurt us. As for the baby she was carrying at the time she was arrested, it was born in Slygio Prison. Mum named her Doreen Lynch. Using Dad's surname and not John Flannery's. Doreen was sent straight to the convent to be with her half sisters.

As for Dr John Flannery, I'm not sure whether he spent any time in prison, but I do know that his wife never took him back, and he disappeared somewhere, never to be heard of again.

Father did what he could to get us back, but to no avail. We were to be kept in the convent until we reached the age of sixteen, at which time dad would regain custody of us. Notifying the authorities in an attempt to get us back had been a total waste of time, and cost him money as well. Not only couldn't he get us back, but he had to agree to pay for our keep as well. Dad was a proud man though, and probably preferred it that way. He agreed to pay a fee of £5.00 per child, per fortnight, making a total of £25.00 per fortnight. However, he flatly refused to pay for Doreen, who wasn't his child anyway. He also promised to follow all the rules set out for him, but he had one condition of his own, under no circumstances were the nuns allowed to let our mother near us, either for a visit, or to take us out. Otherwise his payments would stop immediately.

Although they agreed, they did not honor their agreement. Mum did come to visit us later on in life. She also took us out for the day, but dad never found out about it until years later, when we were all out of there.

David became very depressed after all that had gone on. He began drinking heavily again, just like when his father passed away. Patrick Rooney was forever dragging him home from the pub, and trying to sober him up. Edna used to cover up for him at the hostel, explaining that he was depressed or unwell. She was frightened that he would be thrown out of there if they knew he was drunk all the time. She constantly tried to make him eat, but he refused most of the time. He really began to go down hill fast. Edna reminded him that he was no good to the children in this state, but all she got for her effort were insults. Most of the time he would scream at her, telling her to go away, and mind her own foocking business.

Edna also made sure that the £25.00 was always sent to the appropriate authorities, sometimes paying the money from her own pocket. She knew that if David fell behind in his payments, that he would be fined, and then he would never be able to catch up with the payments. So she always made sure the payments went off each fortnight. One good thing about David though, no matter how drunk he got, he never missed work. However, at the moment he was really in a slump and terribly depressed. (He referred to it as the worst time of his life, when he got us back.)

With time, and plenty of effort, Edna and Patrick got David back on his feet. It took several months, but they finally succeeded.

The day came for Patrick and his girlfriend Elizabeth to get married. David was asked to be best man and Edna to be matron of honor. It was a happy event for everyone, including David. Patrick moved out of the hostel to a place nearby, with his new bride. They were hoping to buy a place in London eventually, but in the mean time, until something came along that they really wanted and could afford, they were renting.

The Rooney's, David and Edna would often go out together, and generally life was good for David again. He had grown quite fond of Edna and realised that without her and Patrick, he wouldn't have made it through the bad times. However, he still wasn't ready for any commitments, and hadn't slept with Edna.

Finally, after several months, Patrick told David that he had found a house to buy in London. He was really excited with his news. David was also very happy for him, but he knew he was going to miss his friend very much. It was the only true friend he ever had, and they had been through so much together over the past few years.

That night at tea, David told Edna the news, and explained how much he would miss Patrick. Suddenly Edna came up with an idea,

"David, we could go to London too," she said, "maybe even get a place together."

At first David was shocked at her suggestion, but after a few minutes, it didn't seem like such a bad idea. She was a very good person after all, and they had a lot of fun together. So he said,

"Ah, I dunno about that Edna, what if it didn't work out an all."

"If it doesn't work out David, we can just as easily break it off."

David thought about it some more, and agreed, but he gave her an ultimatum.

"Okay Edna, it's not such a bad idea, but know this now, if ya ever become pregnant, you'll be out on ya arse so quick, you'll be wondering what hit ya, and with no help from me. Do ya understand that?"

"Yes David, that's quite acceptable to me luv. I'm too old for kids now anyway, and between yours and mine, we have plenty, don't you think?"

David laughed and agreed with her.

Shortly after Patrick and Elizabeth moved, David and Edna found a place in the West End of London. It was also close to Patrick and Elizabeth, which was an added bonus. David found a job on the railways, where he actually worked for the rest of his life. He was a hard worker, who never missed any time, unless it was absolutely necessary. Edna found work in a factory which made number plates for cars, and they were both very happy. Edna suggested that they buy a car, but David refused. He knew how to drive, he had driven trucks, and tractors back home in Ireland, on the farm. However, in his opinion he drank too much to drive safely. So he walked everwhere, not even using the buses or trains, which he had a free pass for. The truth was, he just enjoyed walking.

Winnie got out of prison and also went to London. (She had no idea then that David was there. As far as she knew he was in still in Scotland.) She found work in a hospital, as a nurse's assistant. She never told anyone about her past, or any of her black, dark secrets. Actually she didn't discuss herself much at all. She was well liked, and made plenty of friends, most of them nurse's at the hospital.

Eventually she met another man. His name was Richard, he was English and a Policeman. It didn't take her long to move in with him either. She conveniently forgot to mention that she had six children though, five of whom she dumped to run off with a doctor. Or that she gave birth to her last child in prison. No, Richard only knew her as a sweet, innocent girl from Ireland.

Winnie was still very cunning. She made sure never to associate with any Irish people, just in case her secret came out. She had changed though, she now kept herself clean, and well groomed. She always looked smart, and always wore make-up. She went to work every day, and worked hard while she was there. She was totally different now, not lazy at all. She loved her work, and her new life. Maybe prison had given her time to think about her future. However, her future didn't include us, she was making a new life for herself again. It was too late for us and our future's anyway. We were to be in our so-called prison, for years to come. She was out of prison, and she never bothered with us at all, not even a card for several years. I often wonder how she slept at night, or if she ever thought about us. Who knows for sure.

David and Edna were happy together, and were leading a good life. Then one day David got a letter from his brother Leonard, informing him that their mother had died. David didn't have much to do with his family, since the children had been taken away. In his heart he believed that his family could have done more to help his children, even though they said it was too late by the time they found out. He was especially disappointed with his mother. She should have told him what was going on. Especially after her arguement with Winnie. But now she was dead. David put the letter down and thought about all that had happened. He had always promised himself, that one day he would go home, and ask his mother all the questions he needed to have answer's to, but now it was too late. David sat and looked down at his feet. Suddenly he started to cry. He cried for the loss of his mother, for his children, and for the break-up of a once happy family.

CHAPTER 19

David returned home for the funeral of his mother. It was the first time he had been home since the break-up of his family. He wouldn't have returned at all if his mother hadn't passed away. He had debated going back even now and to be quite honest, if it hadn't been for Edna, he probably wouldn't have. So much had happened and he was so ashamed to face the people of Ballinrobe again. He knew that they would have had a field day, gossiping about Winnie, and how she left the children. He also knew that his presence in Ballinrobe would start those tongues wagging again, even though it was a couple of years ago. It had been such a hard decision for David, deciding whether to come back for the funeral or not.

Apart from the past being dragged up, he still held resentment towards his mother and family for not protecting his kids. If they had only taken the children from the authorities, he would still have them now, and they wouldn't be in that hell hole they were in.

So here he was, on his way back home, full of resentment and sorrow, but most of all embarrassment about facing everyone for the first time. Suddenly tears filled his eyes, he wasn't sure if they were for the loss of his children, or the loss of his mother. He was just so damn confused. Maybe it was just self pity, he thought. He dried his eyes, blew his nose, and held his head high again. I'll get through this he thought, it'll soon be over.

When David arrived in Ballinrobe, he went straight to the farm house where he had spent most of his life. He was glad to see it, but he wished it was under happier circumstances. He also dreaded seeing his family again. With that thought in mind, he suddenly stood straight, held his head high, and marched on through the door. Kathleen and Phyllis ran straight to him and hugged him affectionately, planting kisses all over his face. It made him feel good in a way, and some of his animosity was lifted. Leonard and Shamous then came forward, both extending their hands.

"Welcome home" they said.

"Not the best circumstances though, is it?" David answered.

They bowed their heads and turned away. They didn't want to be reminded about their mothers death, even though they knew that's why David was there.

Maybe it was their reaction to David's statement, or maybe David just had to clear his chest, but something snapped inside him, and he released all his anger.

"Why the foocking hell didn't ma do more ta help me kids", he stated bluntly, "and you Kathleen, have ya no compassion at all. Ya knew the way things were, why didn't ya let me know, for Christ sake."

Kathleen turned back and faced her brother, her anger to her brothers accusations flaring from her eyes and she screamed at him, "And would ya have believed us David? I doubt it. Not where ya precious Winnie was concerned. So don't come round ere blaming us for what happened."

"I'm not blaming anyone, except that bitch Winnie. But ya could ave saved me kids, I'm sure ya could. Didn't the authorities contact ya at all."

"Not me, I'm not sure about anyone else in the family. Maybe they contacted ma, I really don't know, but after that dreadful fight ma had with ya wife, she swore she wouldn't interfere no more. Besides maybe she thought that the authorities would find Winnie, and everything would be sorted out. I don't know

David, I just don't know."

"I don't know, I don't know," David mimicked. "Why don't ya foocking be honest and say ya don't care."

Leonard entered the conversation then and said, "That's not fair David, and ya know it's not. If any of us knew it would go this far, we would ave done something. As for me, I knew little about it, till it was too late, I'm always stuck in the pub as ya know."

"That's not good enough, they were your family, for Gods sake, your blood, how could ya let it happen," David suddenly slumped down at the kitchen table, and cried into his hands, "I just don't understand." he said trough his tears.

Phyllis went over to him, and put her hands on his shoulders,

"Look David, we're sorry, we didn't mean for it ta turn out like this. If we'd realised the consequences, we would ave done more. But it's past now, and we all feel as bad as you do, but none of us can do nowt ta change things."

"Yea, I know ya right, but you could ave done something from here. I didn't even know until it was too late. Even if ya had got hold of me, then I could have done something. But none of ya done a bloody thing, ya all stood by and just let it happen. That's so hard for me to understand."

He stood up, "I'll go freshen up," he said, "I need a rest, I'm worn out."

David turned and left the room, everyone just looked at him as he left. They knew he was right, but they couldn't do anything about it now and they just wanted the subject closed.

While David freshened up, he began to think about his family downstairs. Some family they turned out to be, he thought. He knew that the authorities wouldn't have allowed Leonard and Bridget to have the kids, because of them living in a pub. But he also knew that Shamous, the girls, and his mother could have brought them to the farm. He was convinced that they had been given the option. But he also knew that Phyllis was right, it was too late now. Even if he owned a castle, he couldn't get the kids back. Not until they came of age at least, so it was no use dwelling on it anymore . Being back here, and seeing them all again, just brought the memories all flooding back though. David decided to go back downstairs, and forget about the past. He was here for the funeral, not to fight. He had to try and forget the past, and think about the future.

He went back downstairs into the kitchen. Everyone was quiet when he walked in. Kathleen had made a pot of tea, and everyone was sitting drinking it, lost in their own thoughts. David poured himself a cup too, then sat down. As if he had no control over his mouth, he started up again. He just couldn't hold it back, he had to know everything. Oh he knew that they could have given the kids a roof over their heads and didn't, but he just wanted to get everything else clear in his head.

"Kathleen, ya know everything for miles around, ya as good as the local newspaper. Maybe ya can set a few things straight for me."

"Like what David?"

"Like what happened to the famous Dr Flannery."

"Well, I heard he went back to Rose. He admitted that he had an affair, but as far as he knew, from what Winnie had told him, the kids had been given to their grandma. He had no idea that Winnie had left them to fend for themselves. Apparently he felt quite horrified when he found out."

"So he's ere then, in Ballinrobe?" David asked.

"Oh no, Rose threw him out on his ear. After that, no one knows where he went." Kathleen paused for a moment and then added, "David, Winnie was really very bad, ya know. If ya had listened ta pa all those years ago, none of this would ave happened."

"Oh why don't ya shut-up Kathleen. Ya so bloody righteous, arn't ya. If you had taken me kids in, they wouldn't be locked away right now either, would they?"

Shamous rose from his chair, "Look David, if ya came ere looking for trouble, ya can take ya arse right out again. We're all ere to bury our ma, not ta bloody bicker amongst ourselves."

David was astounded at his younger brother's outburst. He stood up also and looked Shamous straight in the face.

"Now wait there a foocking minute. This is my house now, so don't be telling me ta get me arse outa ere, cause I won't. Furthermore, after the funeral, you can all get your arses outa ere. Then you'll see what it feels like not ta ave a roof over ya foocking head, just like me foocking kids."

David hadn't meant one word of this, but after Shamous's reaction he wanted to put him back in his place. That would put the fear of god in em, he thought. Shamous went quiet for a few moments, he was stunned by David's words. However, it didn't taken him long to find his tongue again. "Ya mistaken David, after ya stopped writing, and never bothered coming home for visits, ma changed her mind and said we were to ave the farm."

It wasn't David who answered Shamous, it was Leonard. He looked Shamous straight in the face, and said, "Shamous, when did ma tell ya this, she didn't mention nowt ta me."

Shamous blushed, but continued calmly, "About two months ago now, it was."

"Shamous ya a bloody liar," Kathleen said, "Only last Sunday after mass, ma told me, that if anything should happen ta her, ta make sure that David and the children got the house. She also told me, that her instructions were left with Fitzgerald, the

Solicitor. In fact, he will be coming ere after the funeral, to read the will to us."

David couldn't believe his ears,

"I don't believe you Shamous," David said, "trying ta cheat me as well. Ya foocking unbelievable you are. Typical Irish bastard, fighting over foocking land, and poor ma ain't even been put in the ground yet."

All that Shamous could answer was, "Well, you're the one who foocking started, not me."

Leonard spoke up, "Your disgusting Shamous, trying ta steal from David, and his kids. Don't ya think he's been through enough already, without this."

"What about him then," Shamous screamed, "It's alright for him to throw us out, ain't it." "That's up ta him ta decide, but mark me words, I'm behind him all the way. This farm is his, and while I'm alive, I'll not see em cheated out of it."

David broke into the conversation and said, "Look Shamous, don't worry yaself too much, I'll not be putting any one out, I don't want the bloody farm. It won't be doing me kids any good now anyway. Besides I'm quite happy where I am now, so ya can all stay right where ya are. But this I will say, and remember it well," David paused for a moment, and looked around at each and everyone one of them, making sure that they were listening, then he continued, "don't sell the bloody place. Ma never wanted it sold, and I want me kids ta own it one day. By God they deserve it, after all they've been through."

(They all agreed that day, but they never kept to their word. Years later the farm was sold by Shamous, to an outsider. My grandmother probably turned in her grave that day because she never wanted the farm sold. Furthermore, we never received a penny from the sale of the property).

The funeral all went according to schudule. David felt very self-concious being amongst the townfolk again, but apart from that, everything went well. Later in the evening Mr Fitzgerald came to the house for the reading of the will. True enough the farm and house went to David. Any other possesions or money was to split evenly between the remaining brothers and sisters.

Later on in the week, David prepared to pack for his return to London. He was asked to stay on a while but declined the offer, he was actually anxious to get back. He told them about his new lady, Edna, and how it was time he returned to her. They had been happy for him, until they had found out she was English. Then they had become righteous again, telling David that she could never be brought back to Ballinrobe. God they made him sick. David told them where to go and advised them that she wouldn't want to come to Ballinrobe and neither would anyone else in their right mind. It's a pity they weren't so righteous when it came to taking in their nieces and nephew, David thought. No, that lot changed their minds all the time, to suit them bloody selves. David said his farewells and returned to Edna in London, with great relief. However, he never advised Edna when he would be returning. In his mind he thought he might catch her with someone else. He had little trust in women after what mum did.

When he arrived home, Edna was still at work. When she returned she was so relieved to see David. In her heart she half expected a letter from him, saying that he had decided to stay in Ireland with his family. She wasn't very secure in her relationship with David. She believed, that she was just filling a place for his children, for the time being. However this wasn't totally true, David had grown quite fond of Edna, he just didn't show his feelings anymore. He was afraid of being hurt again.

He was too proud a man to let another woman, or anyone for that matter hurt him again. He had a favourite saying which was "I only like to see my own shadow coming and going, because that causes me no strife, people do." So Edna was always kept at a safe distance, along with everyone else in the world.

CHAPTER 20

When Francis first arrived in his new home, "The Christian Brothers School" as it was named, he was ten years old. I was three and a half. I never saw my brother again until I was eleven. Father wrote to him often, and sent money for Christmas and his birthday, but like us, he never received the money, only the letter. The letters were all read before we received them and any money removed. We had no privacy at all.

The first thing they did to Francis when he arrived, was to cut of his long, lovely curls, and clear his head of lice. Then he got a good scrubbing. (Which was well over due anyway.)

If our mother hadn't suceeded making a girl out of him, "The Christian Brothers" school did. He later told us that every night the other brothers, (as they were taught to call each other) attacked him and had sex with him. He told us that some nights they would queue in line, waiting to get up him. If he refused he would get beaten. Sometimes he would get beaten after the sex so he would keep his mouth shut. He had tried writing when he first arrived there, but had been beaten with a strap by his superiors for telling vicious lies. He was trapped, with another six years to go before getting out. After his whipping he had decided to get along with his superiors as much as possible. He didn't like the strap, or any beating for that matter. At least if he had his superiors on his side, things wouldn't be too bad. He often asked himself why his mother had done this to him. But the more he wondered about it, the more confused he became.

With time, Francis got used to the sexual harrassment. It really wasn't that bad, but he never learned to cope with the beatings. However he was trusted and well liked by his superiors (the priests) and would help them everyday. He learned a lot from them about the organization of the school. He also studied hard while he was in class. With time they even sent him out into the village on small errands. More importantly, Francis got to learn where the money was kept, and he used it to his advantage.

One day, when Francis was fourteen he was sent out on an errand. Before leaving, he stole all the money he could get his hands on, and ran away. He caught a boat across the channel to England, and landed on his father's doorstep.

At first David didn't realise who it was. Francis had changed, his hair was shorter, and he had grown so much. It had been six years since David had seen him.

"Dad," Francis said, and burst into tears, "I couldn't take it any more dad, it was terrible there."

David hugged his son tightly, it was good to have him back. He wondered if the authorities would be hot on his trail, but he didn't care, it would be worth it, to hold him like this was wonderful.

"Come in son, how did ya get ere lad?. My ya've grown. Let me take a look at ya?" David said, all in one breath, not giving Francis a chance to answer, or say a word. David held out his son at arms length, and took a good, long look at him, his eyes looked so large, and blue. They were the biggest part of his face, my he looked handsome David thought, then he pulled him close again.

"Come in ere, outa the cold boy." David said with tears in his eyes.

They both went inside, to the warmth of a cosy fire. Edna in the kitchen, was un-aware of who it was, and came in to find out.

"Who was it David?" she asked as she entered the sitting room.

"Come in Edna," David said, "this is my son Francis, it seems he took off from the home yesterday." "Francis, this is Edna, my good women now." David turned back to Edna. "Edna would ya mind leaving us alone for a while luv, till I get re-acquainted with me boy, and find out what the hell is going on," he said in a light tone.

"I wouldn't mind at all" Edna said, then turned to Francis, "We'll talk later lad". she added.

As Edna walked back to the kitchen she was nervous, she wondered whether Francis would make a difference to her relationship with David. She shrugged, "Don't be imaginative" she told herself, "Of course it won't, I won't let it. I'll be totally supportive of all the kids." Then she went about her business of getting dinner ready.

"Who is that?" Francis asked his father.

"That's me lady friend, and a fine women she is too. Helped me through the bad times, she did lad. I don't think I would ave made it without her."

"But what about ma, dad?" Francis asked.

"What about her lad, the bloody bitch dumped the lot of ya. She's rotten ta the core, and I want no more ta do with her. Let's not talk about her anyway, let's talk about you. How have ya been lad, were ya happy at the school?"

"Happy, you must be joking, why do you think I ran away."

"I'm not sure, why don't ya tell me all about it, and how ya got the money ta get over ere? "

"I stole the money dad."

"Ya did what, is that what they taught ya there, I'll have no son of mine, a bloody thief."

"I'm not a thief dad, I'll send all the money back, but I was desperate to get away." Francis began to cry as he told his father what he had been through, all the beatings, and the sexual harrasment. It wasn't long before David had tears in his eyes too. Francis also explained that he wrote to tell him once, and that he got in big trouble over it. He explained how they always checked the mail before it was posted, and before the children received theirs. David wondered, just what the girls were going through, and if they too, were not able to get word to him. He hoped it was different where they were. At the end of his story Francis began begging, "Please dad, don't let them take me back, I'm begging you, I'll be good, I promise I will."

"Now stop ya begging son, after what you just told me, I doubt if they'll even try and get ya back. But if they do lad, they'll ave a fight on their hands, that's for sure. I'll make it all public too. However, ya will have ta pay back all the money ya took, and if I ever ear of ya stealing again, I'll break ya bloody fingers. Do ya ear me lad?"

"Yes dad, I promise I'll never do it again."

"Right then, that's settled. I'll say one thing about the place though, ya English has sure improved. Ya sound more like Edna, than ya do me, right proper like."

They both laughed, and David asked, "Did ya eat on the boat lad?"

"No, I was too scared, I lay low the whole trip. The truth is, I'm starving."

"Come on then, let's go see what Edna's up ta."

Edna had just about finished the evening meal and they all sat and ate together, talking merrily between themselves.

The next day, David rang the Christian Brothers School, and advised them that Francis was with him, and that he intended returning the money, that Francis had stolen. He also told them, in no uncertain terms, that if they attempted to get Francis back, he would go public with the story Francis had told him. Neither

Francis or David heard from them again.

After the phone call, David went to work, leaving Francis at home to rest. He felt happier than he had in a long time. During the day David gave a lot of thought to his son's future. He was too young to work, that was for sure. Maybe he should send him back to school for a couple of years, David thought. He decided to discuss it with the lad tonight. He had been through enough in his young life. He should start doing what he wanted for a change, Christ, the boy deserved it.

That night at dinner, David asked Francis, "What would ya like ta do with yaself now Francis?"
"Well I'd really like to join the Navy dad, if that's okay with you, sir,"
"That's fine with me lad, if that's what takes ya fancy. But ya only fourteen, a mite young don't ya think." David answered with a short laugh.
"Yes I know that dad, I thought you meant when I grew up."
"Na, I was kinda thinking about now. Ya too young ta work. What about finding ya a school ta go to."
"Oh dad, I've had enough of school, I'd rather not."
"Well ya can't laze round ere for the next two years, can ya."
"I haven't really thought about it dad. All I wanted to do, was get back to you."
"Yea I know lad, well what about this then. It's only an idea mind, but see what ya think. What if ya stay ere with me, for two or three months, till we get ta know each other again, and you've had a good rest. Then ya can go back ta Ireland for a spell. Ya can work at the pub, with ya Uncle Leonard. I'm sure he won't mind, and he'll pay ya some pocket money an all. How does that sound ta ya?"
"It sounds wonderful dad, but will Uncle Leonard mind?"

"Na, I think he'll be only too willing ta help out, and glad ta have ya. I'll give him a call later."

David wondered, as he dialed Leonard's number later in the evening, whether he would agree to having Francis stay with him. Or would he let him down again, like last time his kids had needed his help. However, Leonard was all for it. He thought it was a great idea. Maybe he was trying to compensate for past events. Or maybe he could do with the help. Either way, he accepted without hesitation.

The weeks flew by quickly. David brought Francis nearly everywhere with him and Edna. Even down to the local pub, where Francis was allowed to drink soft drinks only. David's drinking place was right across the road from where he lived. It was called "The Nelson." Everybody knew David and Edna at the Nelson, believing them to be married. Not that David had ever lied about it, in fact he hated to lie. He always introduced her as "My good lady," they assumed the rest. David still kept his distance, as he always had. He never invited anyone back home, not from the Nelson or from his work. The only people that came to visit them were Patrick and Elizabeth Rooney. However David was liked by everyone, and when David introduced Francis, it was with pride and love. He explained that Francis had previously lived in Ireland, not mentioning where or with whom he had lived.

One night after the Nelson, and when Edna had retired for the evening, Francis asked his father, "Dad, have you ever heard from mother again, do you know how she is?"
"No I ain't heard from her lad," David answered in a rough tone, "and it's just as well too, cause if I'd ave got me hands on her after she walked out on you lot, I would have foocking

killed her with me bare hands, and I guess it would have been me in prison instead of her." David paused for a moment, and regarded his son. "Did ya know she ended up in prison for eighteen months son?"

"Yes of course I did, everyone in Ireland knows that, it was in all the papers. I remember getting a real bad time in school over it too."

David looked at his son with pity for a few seconds, and then continued. "I did ear she came over ta London after she got out, but I've never run inta her, and I wouldn't wanna either. I hate the bitch."

"Oh I don't hate her dad, In fact, I often wonder how she is. Although, I often ask myself why she did what she did. I'd like to see her sometime, and ask her to explain what was so important to make her leave us the way she did. I would really like to sort it all out with her someday."

"Son, she left ya cause her lust for sex was more important then her children, and because she's a selfish bitch. If ya want my advice, just stay away from her, she's nowt but trouble. Leave things alone, it's over now, so let things be."

"I just want to see her dad, and ask her why, just to clear my own mind."

"Well I'll not stand in ya way son, you've been through enough, it's about time ya started living life. But I warn ya now, that women brings nowt but heartbreak, and if I were you, I'd stay well clear of her."

Francis listened, and said no more. Neither did David. But Francis had long ago decided that he was going to find his mother again one day. It was an obsession with him now, just like going in the navy was. He had to have it out with her. He still loved her so much, and he needed to know she still loved him. There was nothing he could do at the moment though. He was off to Ireland shortly, but one day, he thought, one day, I'll see her again, and everything will be sorted out. Francis had also decided something else, he didn't like Edna. He had been quite shocked and disappointed when he found Edna living with his father. She wasn't his mother, and she would never take her place. He wouldn't allow her too. But for the time being, he was keeping that to himself. He had to sort things out with his mother first.

The day arrived all too quickly for Francis to go to Ireland. Francis was excited about going, but sad about leaving his father again. David too was sad to see him go. It was like losing him again. Only this time he could see him whenever he wanted too, so it wasn't so bad.

When Francis arrived, Leonard and Bridget were there to meet him and they welcomed him with open arms. Francis settled in without any trouble at all. He loved being with them, and working in the pub. They loved having him too. Bridget cooked and washed for him, as if he were her own son. Francis felt right at home with them, and very much loved.

Francis stayed with Leonard and Bridget for about two years, until he was old enough to join the navy. He wrote to David often and they spoke on the phone frequently. Francis also visted his other aunts and uncle at the farm, and often went to the graveyard to visit his grandma's grave. When David wrote to him at the boy's school, informing him that his grandma had died, he was terribly upset. However Caroline sobbed for days and became quite ill when she found out.

Yes Francis was very happy here, the happiest he had been in many years. He was still very eager to join the navy though, and looked forward to his sixteenth birthday and moving on in life. He spent hours day-dreaming about either what life in the Navy would be like and sailing the seven seas on a big ship, or about planning his great re-union with his mother. He truely believed that she would welcome him with open arms, and would shine with pride when she saw him standing there with his Navy uniform. But then, how could he know that the only reason she would welcome him would be to use him again, not out of any motherly love. Winnie didn't possess motherly love, she still only loved herself.

CHAPTER 21

The authorities finally found a place for us. We were going to be taken care of, but all we wanted was our mother. (Yes our mother, strange isn't it. After her leaving us there to starve, and freeze to death, we still wanted her. She was the only security we had.) It was a very scary time for us. Not knowing what was going to happen to us, whether our mother was coming back, or if grandma, or dad was coming to get us. We didn't know what was going on. Finally they told us we had a new home to go to. A place called "Our Lady of Mercy." It sounded like a lovely place. But there was no mercy there, only rules and cruelty. This was when our nightmare really began, only we didn't know it then. Most of the nuns were wicked. At least that's how we saw it. I'm sure there will be many who disagree with me, but I bet none of them were raised in a convent, as we were. I'm not saying that all nuns are wicked, but ninety per cent of the nuns we grew up with, were. There is a difference between discipline and cruelty, and they always crossed that line.

When we arrived at "Our Lady of Mercy," Caroline was nine, Maureen was four, I was three and Pauline was almost two years old. I can only remember flickers of that first day, but Caroline remembers every little detail. We arrived at about four in the afternoon. We had traveled from Ballinrobe, to Westport to arrive at our new home. We all arrived in tears, we still wanted our mother. The nuns took no notice of our tears though, they showed no compassion at all. We were just more unwanted children to them.

We all walked to a dressing room, except Pauline, who couldn't walk. It seemed like such a long walk too, it was such a large place. To me, it seemed that I had entered a whole new world. There were so many other faces. Children of all ages seem to glare at me from all directions and I just wasn't used to it. The whole time we walked, I cried. I was so scared, and just wanted to go home. Caroline kept telling me to hush up, but I wanted my mum, I needed her for re-assurance. I wanted to be back home, in my own, little, poverty stricken house. All this in-sercurity was making me feel sick in my stomach.

When we finally arrived at the dressing room, we were met by a nun. Her name was Sister Angela. The first thing she did was draw a bath for us. It looked strange, we had never seen a bath before. While the water was running, she placed a large sheet around our necks. One side of this sheet was material, and the other side was rubber. She turned off the water and allowed it to cool. While it cooled she seated us, one by one, and cut our hair. By the time she had finshed we were almost bald. Then she got a small round bowl and filled it with paraffin oil, which she combed through our hair. After that she got out some powder called D.D.T. powder, which was shook all over our heads, and she massaged it in. Next she washed our hair. One by one, we bent over the bath water and she scrubbed our heads, all in the same water. Then she emptied the water, and refilled the bath. This time we were placed in the water, one by one, and our bodies were scrubbed with sope and a scrubbing brush. After we were dried we went through the paraffin oil and D.D.T powder treatment again, only this time the D.D.T. powder was put all over our bodies, as well as our hair.

After we were all clean, we were dressed in a long white gown, and a white rag was placed on our heads, as a scarf. Then we were taken to the infirmary. To us it looked like an extremely large bedroom. There were six beds and two cots in there and everything was white. Sister Angela placed us all in separated beds, and Pauline was put in a cot. Then we were left alone again. Not a word was spoken by Sister Angela while all this had gone on. It was just a lot of shoving and pushing, to get us where she wanted us to be. I began to cry again when she left. I really didn't know what was going to happen next, I was terrified. My crying started Maureen off also. Pauline wasn't crying though, she was happy just lying there, resting. She had no energy at all by this stage, the long journey had totally worn her out. Caroline kept telling Maureen and I to shut up, but we paid no attention to her.

Shortly after, Sister Angela returned with a tray of hot glasses of milk for each of us. She didn't have to tell us to stop crying, we stopped as soon as she came back. She told us to drink up our milk, which we did with pleasure. Sister Angela went over to Pauline, and spoon feed some milk into her mouth. However she wasn't taking it very well, she had almost forgotten how to eat. When we had finished, Sister Angela returned to take our empty glasses, and told us to go to sleep. She informed us that the doctor would be in to examine us the next morning. The lights were turned off, and she was gone again. However, there were no more tears, we all fell asleep instantaneously. The journey, hot bath, warm milk, and all the tears, had totally drained us all.

At nine the next morning, the doctor came to examine us. We never did find out his name. He was the doctor, that's all we ever knew him as. The only words he ever spoke to any of the children, were those of instructions. The only words we ever spoke to him, were "Thank you Doctor". That first morning, he examined us from head to toe and found us to be suffering mainly from malnutrition, amongst other problems. Only

Caroline was found in reasonable health... Well, she was strong enough to remain at the convent. The rest of us were to be sent into various hospitals, around the country.

Maureen was sent to Dublin for further tests. The doctor wasn't happy with her weight. However, after a month of extensive testing, they found that she was healthy enough, but had a high acid level in her body. She was returned to the convent to be with Caroline.

Pauline was sent to the same hosiptal as Maureen. However, she was in a much worse condition. Her stay in the Dublin Hospital was eighteen months. She was later transferred to the hospital where I was going, for a further six months. After several tests, they found her to be suffering from malnutrition, and discovered she was now also a cripple. Within a few months they had her eating again and she regained some strength and weight. However, her limbs needed plenty of attention. They knew that there was nothing physically wrong with them, except for the fact that the muscles had never been allowed to develop. Their main objective was to get the muscles working so that she could walk and have full use of her arms, which at present had no strength at all. She wore splints on her legs for many years after that, but her arms became strong within a short period of time.

As for me, I was nearly blind at this stage. My eyes were full with cysts and sty's which needed to be removed. I was also suffering from blepharitis, which is an infection of the eyes that causes inflamation, and reddness of the eyes. Blepharitis is caused by a bacterical growth, which in turn produced the cysts. By the time I reached the hospital my eyes were barely open at all and I had no tolerance of light what-so-ever. I was sent back to Ballinrobe to the Castlebar Hospital, only this time it was the General Hospital not the Mental Hospital. During my stay there I had several operations, and a lot of eye therapy.

I don't remember a great deal of that hospital though. It's strange, I can remember what happened before but not a great deal during. I was there for a total of two years, but I only remember the last six to eight months clearly. I remember I had an extremely nice doctor though. His name was Dr Mongay. I also remember telling him that I had no parents, that they were both dead. Maybe in my heart they were, I knew I didn't see them anymore. I never had any visitors at all even though I was in my home town.

I also remember that Dr Mongay loved me very much. He would come every day to see me on his rounds in the hospital, and quite often he would bring me a small gift. It's hard to believe now, but he was the only one who showed me any real kindness in my young life. I still have affection for him, even today after so many years. Maybe he felt sorry for me having no parents, I don't know. But I know he really loved me. He would get me up at sunrise each morning and we would go outside. There he would make me look straight at the sun, as part of my therapy. I remember this like it was only yesterday. I'm not sure what kind of a cure it was, but it was done every morning for quite some time. I can still remember how he would hold my hand and how my eyes would water, it didn't matter though, Dr Mongay would hold my hand and that made up for everything. I also had to wear glasses. I can remember them clearly too. They were round, tin rimmed and very ugly.

One day, after I had told him that my parents were dead, Dr

Mongay came in and asked,

"Jospehine, would you like me to be your daddy?"

"What about a mummy?" I asked.

"My wife will be your mummy."

"Oh, I don't know about that"

"What don't you know?"

"I don't know if I'll like her or not. I like you, but I don't know her."

"Well we had better do something about that then, hadn't we. What if I take you out on Sunday, we can all go on a picnic together."

"What's a picnic?" I asked.

Dr Mongay started to laugh "It's when you take food out in a big basket, and eat it on the grass outside."

"Yea," I screamed in excitement, "that sounds like great fun. When's Sunday?"

He laughed again, "Two sleeps away," he told me.

Sunday came around too slow for me, but it was worth the wait. We had a wonderful day, one of the best in my life. The doctor's wife was beautiful. I loved her instantly, and she loved me too.

After the picnic we all went for a walk and then it was time to return to the hospital. I didn't want to go back, but Dr Mongay took one hand, and Mrs Mongay took the other and led me back to the car. I felt loved, and did what they wanted without a fuss. It was nice to be loved and cuddled.

That night it was Dr Mongay who tucked me into bed. He kissed me goodnight, and before leaving he asked,

"Well, how did you like my wife Josesphine?"

"Oh, she's lovely, and I'd love her for my mummy, if she wants to be." I said.

Dr Mongay made some inquiries at the convent, about adopting me. However he was told that my parents were still alive, and living in London. He was broken hearted. The next day when he came to see me, he was very sad, and a little angry at me too.

"Josephine," he said, "you told me a big lie darling. You told me your parents were dead."

"They must be," I answered, "they don't come to see me anymore."

"That's because they live a long way away. They live in London."

He didn't mention that mum had just been released from prison and went to London, or even that they were separated. Maybe he thought I was too young to understand all that.

Telling me they lived in London meant nothing to me. London could have been in the next street for all I knew. But I remember something twigging in my brain as I sat there watching his sad face. I suddenly began to think about my brother and sisters. I had almost forgotten them. It all seemed so long ago. Now it all came rushing back. I began to wonder why Caroline didn't come to see me. In my young mind, I began to think, if Caroline comes to see me, then my mum and dad will know where to find me. Without Caroline they don't know where I am. I suddenly felt very lost and alone.

I looked back at Dr Mongay and said, "I'm sorry, I thought they were dead because they never come to see me anymore."

"That's okay Josephine," he said, but I won't be able to be your daddy anymore I'm afraid."

"But will ya still love me?" I asked.

He grabbed me and hugged me tightly and said,

"Oh, of course I will, with all my heart, and so will Mrs. Mongay, always."

It felt good to be held like this, but I was so confused now. All I could think about was the rest of my family. Why had they left me here.

Later in the evening I remember getting out of bed, and sitting in the middle of the timber floor, crying for my family. As my tears fell they landed in between the cracks of the timber slats turning the dust into little piles of dirt. I remember poking a hairpin, in between the cracks and pulling out the wet dirt. The nurse on duty came to me when she heard me crying.

"What's the matter with ya child?" she snapped.

"I want my sister Caroline." I answered.

"She's at the convent, ya'll be seeing her soon enough."

Suddenly the convent came back to me, I hadn't liked it there, but at least my sisters were there."

I started to cry again, and the nurse said.

"Okay, come with me, I'll bring ya ta see someone from the convent. Maybe ya will remember her."

We went for a walk down some long corridors. It seemed an awful long way. I didn't realise it then, but she was bringing me to the mental Hospital (which was really only another secton of the same hospital, but they had serarate outside entrance's, but were internally linked together as well).

Finally we arrived, and she showed me an old lady (at least she looked very old to me. The truth was she wasn't very old at all). She was very skinny, and sat in a wheel chair, all hunched up.

"Do you know this lady?" the nurse asked me.

"No, who is she?"

"Oh just someone from the convent." she answered.

"When is she going back to the convent?" I asked

"Never, she's too sick to go back."

Then she took me by the hand and led me back to my ward. I didn't realise it at the time but that bitch had brought me to see my Aunt Angela. She was being cruel, (as she was to be again, on several occassions). She thought that recognising my aunt, would be her cruel way of punishing me. However I had never met my aunt, therefore it had no emotional effect on me at all.

CHAPTER 22

A few weeks later Dr Mongay came to see me as usual, but this time he had some good news for me.

"Guess what?" he said, "I've got some really good news for you. I've just been told that your younger sister Pauline is coming down from Dublin Hospital, and will be staying here with you. Not only will she be staying here, but she will be sleeping in the same bed as you, won't that be fun?"

"How come she'll be sleeping in my bed?" I asked.

"Because she still has very bad legs, and you will have to stop her falling out of bed. We will be putting your bed up against the wall, and you will sleep on the outside."

"But my bed's not big enough for two people." I said,

Dr Mongay laughed, "Oh, we'll be giving you a bigger bed don't worry."

I tried hard to remember Pauline. She was the baby in the cot. That's all I could really remember.

"What's wrong with her legs?" I asked.

"Oh the muscles didn't work for a very long time, and now they are getting stronger. She still has splints on them though, and has to do exercises everyday to make them even stronger."

"Will the splints hurt me in bed?"

"No silly, they get taken off at night." he said, tossing my hair at the same time. (I had some hair now, it had grown back again).

A few day's later Pauline arrived. She was nearly four years old. She was so beautiful. Her hair had grown like mine had, but it was snow white, and full of curls. I couldn't believe how pretty she was, her eyes were so big, and vivid blue. I remember being jealous, and scared that Dr Mongay would love her more than me. Everyone else seemed to. She got so much attention from everyone. Even other people's visitors would stop and say hello to her. I'd never had that response from anyone. I wasn't sure if I liked her at first. She was very bossy too, and would throw tantrums all the time, especially if the nurse's didn't do what she wanted, but she always seemed to get away with it. She even got cuddles during her out-bursts. I would have got a slap in the face and told to shut up if I had tried it. However, it's true what they say, blood is thicker then water. It only took me a couple of days to get attached to her, and I too, like everyone else, doted on her. She was so cute, and unfortunate not to have the use of her legs. She was also very affectionate when she wanted to be, and she gave me lovely cuddles all the time.

Pauline would only let two people put on her splints in the morning. One nurse, and myself. If that nurse wasn't on duty, I had to do it. I didn't mind though, it made me feel important. If anyone else tried to put them on, they were likely to get kicked in the face. Pauline could be quite a little brat and very spiteful if she wanted to be.

One night, a few months after Pauline arrived, she wet the bed. She woke me up in the middle of the night and said,

"Josephine, Josephine, wake up."

"What is it?," I asked, still half asleep.

"I've wet the bed."

"So, what can I do?"

"Oh Josephine, I'm gonna get into trouble, can't ya swap sides with me, your bum is much bigger than mine, and ya can dry it for me."

"Get lost, I'll get all wet. Besides, ya might fall outa bed, then we'll both be in trouble."

"I won't fall out of bed, please, Josephine."

"We can swap back later, when the wee has dried."

"Okay." I said, and we swapped sides. When I felt her side, it felt awful.

"Jesus Pauline, this ain't wet, it's soaked." I said.

"Ah, it won't take your fat arse long ta dry it Josephine," Pauline answered.

We both laughed and went back to sleep. I may have dried the bed, but we overslept and got caught on the wrong side of the bed the next morning, and by the nurse that hated me. I got woken up with such a slap in the face, it gave me the shock of my life.

"What the hell do you think your doing child?" She screamed at me.

I awoke stunned and holding my face. "What! what!" I stammered, not realising what hit me, or where I was.

"Why are you on the inside of the bed?" she repeated. "Your a terrible child Josephine, and a wicked sister. You just wait till Dr Mongay arrives, I'll tell him what your really like, you horrible little scally wag."

With that Pauline burst out laughing, she thought it was a great joke. I was nearly in tears with temper. I did it for her and she wasn't even sticking-up for me. She was such a selfish little bitch, I thought. I was so angry with her, I could have killed her.

The nurse stormed off in disgust and I turned to Pauline and said,

"Thanks a lot Pauline, I'm glad you thought it was funny."

"It's when she called you a scally wag, that made me laugh, not cause ya copped a slap Josephine."

"Yea, well ya could have told her what really happened. I got into trouble because of you."

"If I'd told her, we would have both been in trouble, wouldn't we?"

"Yea, that's right, it's okay for me to be in trouble, but not you. Well I'll get ya back Pauline, I'm not puttin on ya splints today, and ya favorite nurse ain't on duty, so ya can spend the day in bed. Then we'll see who laughs."

"You will so put them on," she answered me, "they'll make ya."

"No they won't make me. I don't care what they do to me, I won't put them on."

"I bet ya do."

"I bet I don't."

A little while later, after breakfast was finished, the same nurse who had slapped me returned and said,

"Jospehine, put your sister's splints on for her."

"No, I won't." I answered,

"Yes you will, you little brat."

"No, I won't." I replied in a more stubborn tone.

I got one smack after the other that morning. My face, legs, and arms were all red, but I still didn't put them on. The nurse finally tried putting them on herself. She knew I wasn't going to give in. However, she got back some of what she had given me. Pauline kicked and kicked her and I was really glad. Furthermore, Pauline spent the day without splints and in bed, just like I said she would and that made me happier.

After the nurse had gone, I looked at Pauline and said,

"See, I told ya I wouldn't put them on." Then my tears began to flow, I released all the tears I had stubbornly held back. I was still crying when Dr Mongay came in to see me.

"Why are you crying, Josephine?" he asked, "Don't you realise that your eyes will get sore again with all these tears, then we'll have to get you up early to look at the sun all over again."

I told him what had happened, that I got lots of smacks for not putting on Pauline's splints, but the nurse had already told him that much. Then he asked me nicely,

"Won't you please put them on for her, that's the only way she can exercise, and she needs her exercise Josephine."

"No," I answered bluntly, "and I'll never put them on again. I tried to help her during the night by drying up her wee, because my bum is bigger than hers, and when we got caught on the wrong sides of the bed, she didn't even stick-up for me. In fact she laughed when I got smacked."

"Oh I see," said Dr Mongay, "Well I know why your so upset with her now. Look, I'll arrange for Pauline to have her own bed from now on. That way if she wets the bed, she can dry it herself."

"But she might fall outa bed, if she's by herself"

"No, we can get some safty rails for her, hopefully by tonight. But will you do me a favour now?"

"What?" I asked.

"Put on her splints for her so she can get some exercise."

"No." I said again.

"Okay Josephine, Pauline can spend the day in bed today, and tomorrow her favorite nurse will be back on duty, but I must say, I'm a little disappointed with your stubborness."

He got up to leave, then looked down at my swollen eyes,

"Look at the state of those eyes Josephine," he said, "If I promise to bring you a present tomorrow, will you dry up your eyes and stop those tears."

"Oh yes," I said,

"Well let's see a big smile then."

I smiled up at him.

"That's better," he said, "Now then, what would you like me to bring you?"

"Oh, I'd really love some rosary beads."

"Really, that sounds like a fine gift, I'll go and get them this afternoon."

"Could you bring some for Pauline too."

"But I thought you didn't love her any more."

"Oh of course I love her, she's my sister."

"Well why won't you put on her splints then?"

"Because she said I had to, and I said I didn't, and wouldn't. Then she said that after I was punished, I'd put them on, and I said no way, even if I did get punished, so I'm not putting them on, and that's that."

Dr Mongay laughed, "Okay Jospehine, but it's not good to be this stubborn you know. It make's you feel bad, plus you got smacked, which is even worse."

"I don't care, next time she won't find it so funny when I get into trouble."

"Alright then, I'll bring you some rosary beads each." He kissed me gently on the cheek and left, without saying a word to Pauline.

The next morning, as promised, Dr Mongay came with two sets of Rosary beads. One for me, and one for Pauline. We were both very happy. That morning I put Pauline's splints on without even being asked, and after breakfast we went outside in the courtyard to play with our Rosary beads. But there is only so much you can do with Rosary beads. Mainly look at them. So I came up with a fabulous idea.

"Pauline," I said, "What if I go get some string, and we can make some necklace's out of our Rosary beads. They will look lovely."

Pauline thought it was a great idea too, and I went and got some string of one of the nicer nurses on duty. We had great fun, we broke the wire, that held the Rosary beads together, and giggled as all the beads went flying all over the place, bouncing here, there, and everywhere. After I had collected all the beads, we started to make our necklaces, but we got caught again, by my favorite nurse! Of course it was me who got the blame.

"What on earth do you think you're doing?" she asked me.

"I'm making a necklace" I answered quietly.

"Aren't they the Rosary beads Dr Mongay gave you this morning?"

"Yes," I answered.

"Why, you ungrateful, destructive, little brat," she said, "Just you wait till tomorrow morning. I'm going to put this broken Rosary on the end of your bed, and show Dr Mongay what sort of child you really are."

"But I was just...."

"Oh shut-up, and give me those beads." She snapped, cutting me off.

I handed them over, and lowered my head in shame. I didn't want Dr Mongay to know I'd broken the beads, he mightn't love me any more, I thought.

After the nurse had left, Pauline started to laugh again.

"There you go again, laughing at me when I'm in trouble." I said.

"But, it's funny Josephine, she was so angry."

"Yea, not at you though, only with me. Plus she's gonna show Dr Mongay the broken Rosary tomorrow and he'll be angry at me too."

"Na he won't, he love's ya too much."

"Yes he will." I snapped and got up and went inside leaving Pauline by herself.

I wondered why Pauline never got into trouble. I had learned, (especially since Pauline had arrived,) that I was a very ugly child, but that shouldn't make a difference surely. I often heard the nurses comment to each other, "Can you believe those two are sisters, one's so pretty, and the other so ugly" they would say. Even other peoples visitors came up and talked to Pauline, telling her what a sweet young thing she was, they never did that to me. But Dr Mongay loved me the best, it didn't matter what I looked like to him. I hoped, as I walked back to my bed, that he would still love me when he found out that I had broken the Rosary beads.

The next morning when Dr Mongay arrived, the nurse came with the Rosary beads and placed them on the bed, next to Dr Mongay. I was sitting up, but under the covers. I remember lifting my feet up and down, trying to kick the beads off the bed. He looked up at the nurse and said,
"What's this?"
"This is what's left of the Rosary beads you brought Jospehine yesterday, I found her out in the court yard ripping them to pieces. Maybe you'll realise now that she doesn't deserve anything."
"That's enough, thank-you nurse," he answered in a stern voice, and then added "Leave us alone now, and we'll sort it out."
"Well really," the nurse replied in a hurt manner and then she stormed off.
He looked down at the remaining beads on the bed, (the ones I hadn't managed to kick off yet) and then up at me. "Didn't you like them Josephine?"
I started to cry, and said, "Yes they were lovely, but I got fed up of just looking at them, so I suggested to Pauline, that we make some beautiful necklaces, and she didn't get into trouble, just me."
Dr Mongay had tears running down his face, he tried desperately to hold back the laughter, but he saw the funny side of it all.
I stopped crying, and began to giggle too. "Do you love Pauline more than me now?" I asked.

He hugged me and said, "Oh no Jospehine, I love you the best. I always will. I just wish you could be my daughter, but that's impossible." He pulled away from me and smiled, but it was a sad smile, a smile of loss.

"Everybody else say's I'm ugly, and she's pretty." I said.

"Well don't you believe them. You're very pretty too, and when your eyes are all better, they'll be saying the same thing about you. Besides I think Pauline is very spoilt and selfish. You on the other hand, are a darling, your always thinking about her and other people, and that's the best kind of beauty there is, and don't you ever forget it.

He examined my eyes, and we talked a little more. When he was leaving he asked,

"Now what shall I bring you tomorrow?, and don't say Rosary beads, because you can only look at them." he said with a giggle.

"Could I have a handbag"

"To put your beads in?" He asked with a smirk on his face.

I began to laugh, and said, "Maybe."

"Qkay. I'll bring you a nice handbag tomorrow."

"Can Pauline have one too." I asked.

"Yes," he said, "How could I forget her, with a sister like you."

Pauline and I got along fine most of the time. Yes she was selfish, but she was also my sister, and I loved her dearly. The trouble was, was while she had been in Dublin the nurses had spoilt her rotton, and she was used to it. Even though we got on well most of the time, we still had plenty of fights, but that's common of all brothers and sisters. She was still nicer to me than anyone else, and that at least was something.

CHAPTER 23

One afternoon Pauline and I were out playing in the courtyard minding our own business, when suddenly a young boy came out. He was older than myself, I'd say about seven years old. We didn't take any notice at first and continued playing our game, but then he started to call us names.

"You two are orphan's" he said.

"What's that?" I asked,

"It's what you are" he answered, not knowing what it was either. (he must of over-heard someone talking, and just repeated it).

I didn't know what it was, but from the tone of his voice and expression on his face, I knew it wasn't nice. I knew he was trying to be nasty and I didn't like it.

"Oh go away and leave us alone." I said,

"Orphan's, Orphan's." He kept repeating.

After telling him to shut-up several times and getting no response, I jumped up and slapped him in the face, that soon shut him up, he ran off crying like a big baby.

Pauline and I started to laugh, but not for long, my favourite nurse, (who had since been promoted to Matron) came marching out with the boy and his mother trailing behind her.

"Which one hit you?" she asked the boy.

"That one there, the fat one." he answered.

"I thought as much" she said. (She really hated me and to be honest I really don't know why. Ever since she'd caught me crying and digging the dirt from the floor boards she'd been out to get me. First by bringing me to see my mentally retarded aunt, and by constantly hitting me when ever she got the opportunity. ....However what she was about to do this time was the worst of all. Maybe she didn't hate me, maybe it was just because she could get away with it where I was concerned, like the boy said I was an orphan).

"Why did you hit this little boy Josephine?" she asked.

"Because he was calling us names."

"Well names don't hurt and you had no cause to hit him you spiteful little girl." (She had to use her words carefully, the boy's mother was standing right behind her, which was making me even more nervous).

"But I asked him to stop and to go away, but he wouldn't, so I gave him a slap."

She grabbed my arm and pulled me closer to the boy. "Now say sorry, this instant," she said,

"I'm sorry for hitting you," I said,

"Now give him a kiss and make-up."

"No, I'm not kissing any boy. I said sorry, and I am but I ain't kissing him."

"Now I've had just about enough of your defiance Josephine. You kiss him this instant."

"No" I repeated.

"So help me Josephine, if you don't kiss him right now, I'll lock you outside."

"I don't care, I'm not kissing him."

She tightened her grip on my arm and pushed me outside. Then she wheeled Pauline in and locked the door of the courtyard. It didn't worry me in the slightest, I had been out there anyway. It was a lovely day. It sure beat kissing the boy, even if I was by myself.

About fifteen minutes later she returned. "Are you ready to kiss the boy yet? This is your last chance, because he's going home."

"I'm not kissing no boy," I repeated.

"Okay then, come with me you little brat. I'll teach you how to behave yourself."

I followed her slowly down to the basement and she put me in the morgue and locked the door behind her. It was very cold in there, but I didn't mind, not until I turned around anyway. There was someone lying on the table. At first, I didn't realise she was dead, in fact I don't think that registered until much later. She was very still and was wearing lots of make-up. I walked up to have a closer look. Her make-up was very thick, and she had very long painted nails. I began to imagine that she was a witch, and that she was going to kill me. I was very scared and became over imaginative. I closed my eyes, but things got worse. Suddenly this witch was coming after me with those big, long, nails, her arm's outstretched to claw me to pieces. I began to scream hysterically. I banged and kicked at the door.

"Please, please let me out, the witch is coming to get me. Please, I'll kiss the boy, I'll kiss the boy, but please let me out."

She had been waiting outside the door the whole time, and when I said I'd kiss the boy she opened the door. She had broken my spirit and she was happy. As the door opened I passed out and fell into her arms. She woke me up again by slapping my face, then brought me back to bed. I couldn't sleep though, all I kept seeing was those claws trying to get me. I kept screaming out in horror. The matron returned serveral times to calm me down. She must have been getting worried at the effect the experience was having on me. She told me to shut-up in the end, or I'd find myself back down there again. I was petrified that she would, so I pulled the blankets over my head and tried desperately to stop my crying and my fears. I must have eventually fallen asleep because when I opened my eyes again, Dr Mongay was standing over me. My eyes were red and swollen from the previous nights event, I couldn't even open my eyes properly.

"Wake up sleepy." he said as he stroked my hair away from my forehead.

His fingers reminded me of the claws again. Suddenly I sat up and began screaming on the top of my voice.

"What's wrong Josephine, what's the matter?" Dr. Mongay asked concerned for my well being.

"The witch is going to get me, her nails, stop her, stop her," was all I could say over and over again.

Dr Mongay didn't know what was wrong, at first he thought I had been having a nightmare, but then Pauline spoke up.

"Josephine told me last night that the matron locked her downstairs with the dead people. She said there was a dead witch in there, but she came back to life."

Dr Mongay snapped at Pauline without realising "What are you talking about Pauline?"

Pauline told him all about the little boy, and how I had been punished for not kissing him. He hugged me as he listened to Pauline's story, then he looked down at me and began to rock me to and fro in a effort to console me. Suddenly he yelled out for the matron to come. She must have sensed that I was telling him everything, because she kept herself busy all morning and well out of the way. When he called out to her she came over.

"Yes Dr. Mongay," she said in a sweet tone.

"What kind of a person are you?" he asked, "Locking a young child in the morgue."

"This child was rude, insolent, and defiant, and needed to be taught a lesson. If you ask me she should have been left there far longer."

"Well I'm not asking you. Furthermore I'm going to see to it you don't remain in this hospital, or any other for that matter. You're not fit to be a nurse, you come through pretty poorly as a human being let alone a nurse. Furthermore, I'll do everything in my power to make sure you never practice again. So help me god I will. Now get the hell out of my sight you make me sick."

If looks could kill, I'm sure I would be dead today. She looked at me with such hatred her eyes burned and she stormed off.

Dr Mongay looked back at me and said "There now Josephine, stop those tears, you will never have to worry about her again. I can asure you, she won't be back." Then he tried to explain that the women in the morgue was not a witch, but someone who had died. He told me that the reason she had make-up and nail polish on, was because she was going to be buried, and that people always did that to their loved ones. But he realised by my expression that I was too young to understand it all, so he decided to drop the subject. Maybe it was best forgotten, he thought.

"Look" he said, "tomorrow is Saturday and guess what we are going to do?"

"What?" I said through my sobs.

"Stop your crying and I'll tell you."

I dried my eyes and looked up at him.

"That's better," he said, "tomorrow I'm going to come and take you out. We can go for a drive in the car again."

"With your wife too?" I asked.

"Oh, if she's good she can come too." he joked.

I began to laugh.

"That's the Josephine I like to see." he said.

Before he left he called to another nurse on duty, "You're in charge around here today. I want you to take special care of this little girl, she has had a terrible fright and I don't want her doing too much today."

"Yes doctor." the nurse replied.

Then Dr Mongay opened a plastic bag he was carrying, and

out came two handbags. I had forgotten all about them, but he hadn't.

"Choose one," he said to me.

There was a red one and a blue one, I chose the red, and Pauline got the blue. Then he said,

"Well open it then, have a look inside."

I did as he asked, and I was thrilled with excitement. The bags were filled with all different coloured beads, and some string.

"Now you can make some real necklaces." He laughed as he saw my excitement, and patted my head.

I put my arms around his neck, and said,

"I love you so much."

"Will you still love me, if we can't take Pauline with us tomorrow."

"Yes, but why can't we take her?" I asked, the disappointment showing in my face.

"For two reasons, one, I can only take out one patient at a time, and two, we are going to the beach and she wouldn't be able to cope with the sand."

"Okay." I said and turned to look at Pauline in the next bed.

"Ya don't mind do ya Pauline? It's only one day and then I'll be back," I said.

Pauline looked disappointed, but said,

"Na I don't mind, I'll be glad to be rid of ya."

We all laughed.

Dr Mongay left. The nurse he had left in charge was Pauline's favourite nurse and she was very nice. She liked me as much as Pauline too.

For the first couple of months after the morgue incident, I had nightmares constantly about the witch in the morgue. One day Dr. Mongay came and asked me if I would like some nail polish for a present, and it all came flooding back to me.

"No" I screamed.

When he asked me why, I reminded him about the witch and her long nails. They were painted, I reminded him. Then he told me about how his wife was a lovely lady and not a witch and she wore nail polish. He said all ladies like to have long painted nails. I didn't believe him at the time but he was right. However I still refused the nail polish. With time the nightmares stopped. In fact, I completely wiped it out of my mind. It was locked away in my sub-conscious. As if I was protecting myself from the fear. (However years later, the memory was going to come back quite unexpectedly.)

..... The doctor and his wife took me out many times, in the last few months of my stay in hospital. I loved them so much, we always had such good fun. I often wished that they were my real parents and that we could be a real family. That was something I'd never had and longed for, but that was only a dream.

....Pauline became stronger and stronger. Soon the day arrived, when she was going to the convent to join Caroline and Maureen, leaving me alone again. It was a very sad day for me. She didn't seem so sad though, she seemed excited. Maybe I would have been too if it was me going, but it wasn't, and I cried. I had lost all my family again and I felt alone. When Dr Mongay came in, I asked him why they were sending her away, and begged him to let her stay. He told me he couldn't, but he also told me that I would be going soon too, and I'd have all my sisters again. The trouble was, I didn't realise just how luckly I was being there with him. It was one of the best periods of my life because he really loved me. No one else was going to love me at the convent except my sisters, but they had no control over my welfare.

About six weeks later it was my turn to go. Like Pauline, I was also excited. However I was also very sad to leave the Doctor and his wife. They both came in to see me off. They kissed me goodbye and told me to remember not to cry, because crying made my eyes sore. I asked him if I could take my handbag and beads with me and he told me I could. Then he began to cry, which started his wife crying. They both began hugging me tightly, as if they never wanted to let me go. He gave me something else too, a new set of the most beautiful, white, Rosary beads. "These are to look at and remember me by," he said, "not to make a necklace from". We all laughed at his joke.

He promised to come and see me in my new home, but he never did. Maybe the nuns restricted him from visiting me, or maybe he was just too busy and couldn't find the time, I really don't know. However, I know he never forgot me, like I've never forgotten him. He will always hold a very special place in my heart, till the day I die. I would give anything to see him again, just to let him know how very special he was to me, and still is. Men like him don't come along everyday, so I guess I was a luckly little girl really, to meet such a man.

God bless you DR MONGAY, and your dear wife. I hope life was good to you both.

CHAPTER 24

My return to the convent was just as frightening as my initial experience, even though I was now five and a half years old. However, I was more aware of the surroundings this time. The main entry gates to the convent were huge and constructed from iron. Immediately inside the gates was a house where the watchman and his family lived. His job was to open and shut the gates, he had a little timber watch house where he and his dog (known as the hound) sat during the day.

A long, winding, path lead to the main building. I didn't remember any of this the first time I was there. There were statues of the Virgin Mary everywhere, and lots of flowers. It all looked so calm and beautiful, but somehow over-powering. It made me feel so insignificant.

As we got closer to the convent, the main path branched off into several smaller paths and there was a lot more activity going on. There were people everywhere, all heading in different directions. It was making me feel confused just watching them. This place looked like a Castle. It was so big, powerful and frightening.

I looked up at the nun who was directing me to the dormitory and I asked,
"Where are my sisters, will I see them soon?"
"Yes, you'll see them later, when you're settled."
We finally reached the dormitory. It was a very large room with nine rows of beds. Each row comprised of ten beds, making a total of ninety beds all in the same room. Everything was white and sterile. Suddenly, I remembered the first time I

was here. I became nervous again, but I wasn't sure why. I began to look down at the floor and around the room, to control the fear inside of me. The floor was so shiny you could see your face in it. Down the far end of the room was a small cubicle where the matron stayed at night.

Suddenly the nun turned to me and said,
"Josephine take off your glasses for a moment."
I took them off and handed them to her. She placed them on the window ledge behind a bed, and said,
"Now I want you to remember this. This will be your bed, and your dormitory. Everynight you will place your glasses on this window ledge, and every morning you will put them on again. Now give me your bag."
I handed her my bag and she placed it on my bed.
"Now come with me" she said, "I will unpack your belongings later."
She led me to the dressing room where we were met by Sister Angela, I remembered her from the last time I was there, but it was only a flicker of recognition. Both nuns gave a gentle bow to each other and the nun who had brought me turned and left.

There was a bath ready for me, and I went through the same procedure as my first encounter with the convent, only this time my hair wasn't completely cropped. It was cut with a basin. I was also allowed to wear the clothes I had come in and not a white gown like previously.
Suddenly, the first nun re-appeared, and I was asked to follow her. When we left the room she said,
"We are going to the Dining room now Josephine. You will have some lunch and meet your sisters and the rest of the girls."
I felt so relieved and excited about seeing my sisters again, I

couldn't wait to get there.

"After you have eaten," she continued "you will return straight back to me. I'll be waiting at the door for you. I will take you to get your clothes and give you your number."

I wondered what she was talking about, "Number" what the hell did that mean, but all I answered was

"Yes mam,"

When we arrived at the dining room I noticed Pauline first. I was so happy to see her again. Then I met Caroline and Maureen. They both hugged me tightly and told me that they couldn't talk much now, but they would come and see me later. It all seemed so strange and secretive. I was dissapointed, our re-union wasn't what I had imagined it would be. I imagined that I was going home to be with my family, I wasn't expecting so many people to be around. I felt sad but I didn't know why. I had just expected so much more.

After we had finished lunch everyone quickly scattered in all directions and I returned to the nun who was waiting for me at the door.

"You will have to be quicker than that in the future Josephine, we can't be waiting on you all the time."

"Yes mam," I answered, wondering why she was in such a hurry. I'd come straight back. She led me back to the dormitory and handed me a toothbrush and a hairbrush. (My bag had been removed, but I didn't relise until later.) "Do you see this number, Josephine? This is your number and you must always remember it." (I still remember that number, it was 035.) "Your number will be marked on all your clothes and belongings. So make sure never to forget your number, or you will be in serious trouble."

"Yes mam", I answered again. I wondered what all the fuss

was about. It was only a number, but I memorised it anyway.

"Tomorrow you will be going to school, you will be in the same class as your sister Pauline, so you won't be on your own. She had no one when she came, so count yourself lucky. There will also be the towns children from Westport in your class."

I didn't know if that was good or bad. To tell you the truth I didn't know what difference it made or why she'd told me. I didn't know what she was talking about anyway. I just nodded my head in agreement. Then she said,

"You will get your other things later. You can stay here now and read this book, you will be needing this book at school tomorrow. I will return later and bring you to dinner." Then she turned and left.

I was petrified, why had she left? What do I do here all by myself? How long was dinner? It wasn't long ago we had lunch. How much longer would I be here by myself? All these questions kept crossing my mind, and I began to cry. I cried myself to sleep and was awoken at dinner time.

"Wake up Josephine," she said, "It's time for dinner."

I awoke stunned, but relieved that she was back. After dinner was over I was brought back to the dormitory, and left alone again. I didn't like this place, they left me alone too much. I began to look at my school book and it wasn't long before all the other girls started to come. It was seven in the evening, bed time. At seven thirty Sister Angela came and we all said prayers together. Then the matron came into her cubicle and the lights were put out.

The next morning at six o'clock, Sister Angela arrived again.

"Wake-up everyone." she screamed as she rang a small, brass, bell. I've never seen people move so fast. They all jumped out of bed and stood like soldiers beside the beds. I decided to copy them in case I got into trouble. Then we marched out of the room in single file, row by row. I followed everyone and we went back to the dressing room where I had been yesterday. The dressing room had the same highly polished floors, a row of baths, and a row of basins. There were two shelves going around the entire room. The hair brushes were kept on the lower shelf. On the top shelf were piles of towels. Each sink had a cup, and in each cup were about ten to twelve toothbrushes, all with a little number on, like mine. (I had left mine with my glasses and hairbrush on the ledge behind my bed. I hoped that I wouldn't get into trouble, because I had been told to put my glasses on every morning. I had forgotten with all the excitement going on.) The only thing that didn't have a number were the towels, they were shared and put in a great big bin for washing after each use.

After everyone had washed themselves, we all returned to the dormitory and got dressed. I put on the same clothes as the day before. I felt like a real idiot, I didn't brush my hair, or my teeth. I was just following everyone else around not really knowing what I had to do.

Sister Angela came up to me and said, "Where are your correct clothes young lady?"

I looked down at what I was wearing and then around at everyone else, and answered,

"I don't know, these are all I have."

"Okay" she said, "You can go to mass and breakfast like that, then return here and I'll have some other clothes for you to put on."

"Yes mam" I answered.

In a way I was lucky, I missed out on doing the chores, but I didn't know that then. All I saw, was what the other children were wearing, and I didn't like the idea of having to wear what they were wearing. It was awful. It was all black and you wore black stockings up to the knees, and big boots. I didn't like that idea at all.

I went to mass and breakfast which was the same everyday, a bowl of porridge. Then a girl about my age approached me.

"Hello", she said, "I have to take you back to the dormitory to get your uniform."

I was very shy and just followed her, but she seemed like such a nice person, and I liked her instantly. When we arrived, she said,

"I'll wait here Josephine, I will have to bring you to school too."

"Okay." I said, and went inside to Sister Angela.

"What took you so long" she snapped when she saw me. "You will have to be a lot faster than that child."

"Yes mam,"

"And don't call me mam, my name is Sister Angela and that's what you will call me."

"Yes Sister Angela" I answered.

"That's better child, now come along and put these clothes on."

They felt so stiff and uncomfortable, but I didn't voice any opinion, I just wriggled a lot.

"Will you stop all that movement child, have you got ants in your pants or something?"

I started to giggle, but it was short lived.

"Stop that noise at once," she snapped. "This is no laughing matter." Then she called out to the girl in the hallway. "Linda Mitchell, come here this instant."

Linda came in, walking very fast, but not running.

"Take Josephine, to the kitchen, then you may both get to class."

"Yes Sister Angela." Linda answered.

I liked this girl, and she seemed to like me too. Suddenly, I surprised myself, I spoke to her. I rarely ever spoke to strangers.   "Why do I have to go to the kitchen Linda?" I asked.

She gave a short giggle and said "To have a raw egg. Anyone who comes from a hospital, has to have a raw egg every morning for a week or so."

"A raw egg, yuck, that's terrible, it'll make me sick."

Linda started laughing, but then became more serious.

"You better not get sick Josephine, or you'll get smacked. You won't have to have an egg for very long, so just persevere with it."

"Why will they smack me for being sick?"

"Because that's the way things are around here. You do what they want, or else you get punished. So take the egg and just swallow it quickly. It's not that bad really, and very good for you."

"How long have you been here?" I asked,

"Oh, forever I guess."

"How come?"

"My parents are dead."

"Oh, that's terrible, do you miss them?"

"No, I don't remember them."

"Have you got many friends here?"

"No, not really, I know almost everyone here and get along with them all, but I don't have a special friend."

"Can I be your special friend?"

She turned and studied me for a moment, then said,

"Yea, that would be nice."

"Yea, I think so too." I said.

We walked a little further, then she said,

"Your baby sister is here too, you know?"

"Who, Pauline?'
"No Doreen."
"Who?" I asked, "I don't have a baby sister called Doreen."
"Yes you do, she's only a little baby though, and very cute."
I thought she was mistaken, but didn't want to spoil my new friendship, so I kept quiet.
Suddenly Linda began to walk at a faster pace, "We'd better hurry" She said, "Or we'll be in trouble."
"This place is so big" I said, "It takes forever, to get anywhere."
"You haven't seen anything yet, but it won't take you long to learn your way around."

To get to the kitchen we had to leave the main building and follow a winding path. As soon as we stepped on to the path the gate keepers hound came charging forward.

I saw the dog approaching me, panicked and began to run for my life!!
Linda called out to me, "Don't run, don't run, he won't hurt you if you don't run."
But she was too late with her warning, I was already running for my life. Suddenly the dog jumped up and knocked me over. It pinned me down on the ground and took a big bite out of my thigh, but I didn't feel a thing, I was too hysterical at that stage. Sister Vincent who was close by, came and pulled the hound of me. I didn't even notice, I was too busy screaming, she pulled me up and I continued to scream, so she slapped my face several times.
My screams turned to a softer cry and I asked,
"How come you're hitting me, it's the dog who should be smacked."
She didn't answer, she just led me back inside and told Linda

to go about her duties. Sister Vincent washed the bite and bandaged it up, and then I was sent back to bed to wait for the doctor. I couldn't believe my luck. My first day at school, and this happens. Now I was in bed again. I was beginning to hate this dormitory.

Later in the day Sister Angela appeared with the town doctor. (It was the same doctor who had examined us all the first time we were here however I didn't recognise him. I found out later that he had been attending to the children at the convent for years). He was not a friendly doctor, like my Dr Mongay. In fact, we were instructed never to speak to the doctor, except to thank him.

The doctor instructed me to turn on my side. Then he gave me an unexpected injection in my rear. I cried out in pain. My leg was very sore where the dog had bitten me, and I didn't need any further pain.

Sister Angela came over and stroked my hair,

"Now, now pet, calm down" she said, "The doctor has to give you an injection to stop any infections from the bite. Now I'm going to undo your bandage and let the doctor have a look at what that naughty dog did to you. I promise not to hurt you, so be a big, brave, girl for me okay?"

"Yes Sister Angela" I replied, thinking gee this nun likes me, little did I know it was just an act when the doctor was present. She was a nasty bitch to me most of the time.

The doctor examined the bite and said, "It's nasty alright, she needs stitches" So I was sent back to hospital again, only this time it was the local hospital in Westport, and I was home in time for dinner the same night. Sister Angela served me dinner in bed and told me that I wouldn't be going to school for the next week, that I had to stay in bed and rest my leg. A week seemed like forever to me and I said,

"How come? I can walk and Pauline can't, yet she goes to school, and I can't?"

"Enough of all the questions child," she snapped, "You just eat up all your dinner, and be quick about it." then she walked away.

I looked down at my dinner wondering why she was so nasty tonight, she had been lovely to me earlier in the day. I didn't enjoy my dinner either. It was mainly vegetables and I hated vegetables, but the corned beef was okay, so I ate that. Shortly after Sister Angela returned for my dinner tray and became quite angry when she saw I hadn't eaten all my dinner.

"I thought I told you to eat all your dinner."

"But I don't like vegetables."

"I don't care what you like, you will empty your plate in future. Here at the Convent of Mercy, we waste nothing. It is a terrible sin to waste food, especially when there are so many hungry children in the world." She paused for a moment waiting for a response. When she received none, she continued,

"I'll allow you to leave it today, only because it's cold now, but you will be severely punished for leaving food in the future. Do I make myself understood?"

"Yes mam, I mean Sister Angela." I replied.

She picked up my tray and left. What a terrible first day I've had, I thought. I began to cry feeling terribly sorry for myself. I felt so lost and lonely. What was worse, I would be by myself for a whole week. Alone, in this big, white, sterile, dormitory. I must have fallen asleep again, because I was awoken by the other girls coming to bed. Linda walked past and gave a sly wave and smile, but she didn't talk. I was allowed to stay in bed for prayers that night, instead of kneeling beside the bed but it didn't make me feel any happier.

When the lights went out I began to feel sorry for myself

again, thinking about how I had to spend the whole week here, by myself, in bed. What a drag that was going to be I thought. I tossed and turned for what seemed like hours, when suddenly I heard my name being whispered.

"Josephine, Josephine," I heard the voice saying. At first I thought I was imagining it, and then something touched my arm. I jumped with fright and looked down to see who was touching me. It was Caroline and Maureen, one each side of my bed.

"Shh," they said, "Don't talk too much and whisper. If the matron catches us, we'll be in real trouble," Caroline cautioned.

"How's your leg?" Maureen asked.

"Oh it's okay, I can't really feel anything. How's Pauline?"

"Oh she's fine, but I can't bring her to you, she makes too much noise with those splints of hers."

"How long do we have to stay here Caroline?" I asked

"For a long time, I'm afraid. It's not too bad really, once you learn all the rules, but you have to stop your crying all the time. That will get you in a lot of trouble, they can't stand it. So be brave and don't cry anymore."

"Okay, I'll try not to." I said.

"Another thing, don't answer them back, not for any reason and if they hit you, don't scream. The only time we are allowed to talk to each other is at play time, so don't talk to us at other times. We will come to your bed most nights after lights out, so there will be lots of time together.

"Okay." I said. Then I asked,

"How is Pauline coping with all these rules?"

"You don't have to worry about her, she gets away with murder compared with everyone else. The nuns all love her. We have to go now, in case we get caught. Remember what I said, stop crying all the time."

They both kissed me goodnight and hugged me tightly. It felt so good to have them close again. That's what I expected yesterday in the dining room. But now I realised that talking wasn't permitted during the day. Just before they left I asked,

"Caroline, do you know my friend Linda Mitchell."

"Yes, she's one of my girls."

I didn't know what that meant, but I didn't ask either, instead I said,

"Can you go and ask her to come down here for a minute?"

"Okay, but make it snappy Josephine."

"I will," I answered.

A few minutes later Linda was beside me "Yea" she wispered, "What do you want?"

"I don't want anything, I just wanted to talk to you."

"Well here I am, talk."

"I'm glad we're friends," I said.

"Yea, so am I. I like your sister Caroline too. She's in charge of me and she's never smacked any of her ten girls yet. She's really good to everyone."

I didn't know what she was talking about, but I was soon to find out. I told her that I wouldn't be allowed to go to school for a week, and she told me to relax and enjoy it while I could. Then she said that she had better get back to bed before we got caught and that she would see me at school, and we would be friends forever. Linda left and I went to sleep happy, thinking about my new friend I'd have forever.

The next morning the sound of the bell and all the children jumping out of bed woke me up. I watched them all leave and became sad and lonely again, but I was determined not to cry. Well at least I was going to try hard. After a couple of hours some of the girls came back. They went down on their hands and knees at the far end of the dormitory and in rhythm began working in and out of the beds with a cloth. Rubbing and scrubbing the floor in a circular motion. When they reached the bottom of the dormitory, they all turned at the same time, and started going back the other way. All I could see were these bums in black skirts, going around and around in the same direction as their hands. No one spoke they all just rubbed. It was quite comical to watch. Then the bell rang and they stood up and left the dormitory. They had completely ignored me, as if I wasn't there at all. I didn't realise it then but the bell meant it was time for school.

Stillness came to the dorm so fast I didn't know what hit me. I could feel tears in my eyes, but I struggled with them and held them back. I began counting the beds to keep me occupied. I thought of Dr Mongay who had taught me to read and count, and I became sad again. Then I got out the school book the nun had given me yesterday. By the end of the day, I practically knew it all by heart. I was bored out of my mind.
Suddenly I thought about the bag and beads Dr Mongay had given me. I wondered where they were. Later, when Sister Angela came with my dinner, I asked her.
"Do you know where my red handbag is, and my beads?"
"They have been given away to the poor. You can forget about them, and your other belongings. You'll have no need for them here. Now eat your dinner." she answered.
I did what she said. Dinner wasn't too bad today. It was Irish stew, so I could eat the vegetables without feeling sick.
As I ate I thought to myself, I don't like this place, they took away all my stuff. They had no right to take them. I felt like telling Sister Angela my feelings, but I remembered Caroline's warnings and didn't answer back. I didn't cry either. I missed my belongings though, especially my rosary beads.

CHAPTER 25

My confinement in bed dragged very slowly, but finally the day arrived for me to go to school. It was hard for me to contain my excitement. I was really looking forward to playing with Pauline, and my new friend Linda.

The Convent's uniform was horrid. The material was so stiff, it scratched my skin. As for the boots, I'm sure they were heavier than me, and so clumsy looking. The knickers were made from a mixture of linen and wool, similar to the material jackets are made of. It was a very hard, stiff, black material. Being fat like I was only made it feel worse, because the stiff material rubbed against my thighs as I walked, so it was very uncomfortable.

When I arrived at school and first saw the townfolk children all dressed in lovely clothes and wearing pretty ribbons in their long hair I felt unhappy. I now realise what Sister Angela meant when she said I would be with the town's children. You could tell the difference between us straight away. They had pony tails and plaits in their hair. The convent girls all had basin haircuts, and very short fringes. There was no room for silk ribbons or pretty bows in our hair. It only required a quick brush in the morning and nothing else.

The town children were very mean to us as well. All you heard from them at play time was, "Look at the orphans. Look at their clothes." They would point and laugh continuously till in the end it didn't have any affect on you. You got used to it to avoid being hurt. I didn't like the word orphan though, for some reason I didn't understand it scared me.

On the whole however, I enjoyed school and the learning process. With time, even the daily rountine became bearable. We rose at 6am each morning, and got washed and dressed. At 6.30am we went to mass. At 7.30am we ate breakfast, (Always a bowl of porridge.) Then from 8-9am we did our chores. The basins, taps and toilets were scrubbed. The floors in the dormitory and dressing room was waxed and polished, and the beds were made. We would split up into groups and each perform a different task. These tasks were rotated weekly by the head girl, so that we all had a chance to do our favourite job!

At 9am we would go to school. It was the same routine day in, day out, except Sunday. Sunday was the day of rest. School also had it's routine. Class, lunch, playtime, and class again. At 3.30pm home time, for those who had a home to go to. We just returned to the convent.

At playtime we didn't mix with the town children. They were too special to play with us. At least that's what they thought. They all came from wealthy familys though, and had good up-bringings. It was very expensive to get a convent education by the townsfolk. So only the rich parents sent their children to the convent for schooling. Those who couldn't afford to send their children here, sent their children to a school in the village itself.

Before I started school, I had been looking forward to playing with Pauline. However, now that I was here, I was spending most of my time with Linda and a few other girls from the convent. I still loved Pauline, and I ate lunch with her every day, but she didn't like to play, and she couldn't run around like everyone else. She spend her whole lunch hour sitting on the bench. To me that was boring, so I didn't spend much time with her anymore. Having friends was something new to me, and I liked it very much.

My first teacher was Sister Bridget. She had a bad habit of pinching cheeks, especially mine, which were fatter than most. However, she never pinched the town children's cheeks, only those from the convent. However, if I thought Sister Bridget was mean, I had another thing coming. She was an angel compared to some I was going to encounter.

Saturdays was repair day. We still did the daily chores, but from 9am, instead of going to school we repaired clothes. It was the head girls responsibilty to check which girl's clothing and boots needed repairing. (Caroline was one of these girls. Unfortunaly she wasn't mine. My head girl was called Kitty Kanavin. She also happend to be my sister Maureen's best friend. She wasn't so bad either. She was strict, but fair to her girls. Some head girls abused their authority and were really mean and spiteful to the girls under them, but Kitty wasn't like that so I was luckly really).

If any boots needed repairing the head girl would give them to Sister Angela, who would do the repairs on them. If it was absolutly necessary, she would replace the soles too, but this happened very rarely. The sole would have to be falling to bits and full of holes before it would be replaced. Any clothes that needed repairing would be given to the girls, under the girl in charge, but it was the responsibility of the girl in charge to ensure it was done correctly, so more often then not it was easier for the girl in charge to do the repairs herself, depending on the age of the children below her.

It was also the responsibilty of the girl in charge to make sure all the the washing of uniforms and sheets was done, and new linen was placed on the beds. The Jumpers got washed on a fortnightly basis and the other clothes on the alternative fornight. Each girl had two sets of clothes. If those clothes weren't, washed, dried, and pressed in time for change over, the head girl was strapped.

Another duty of the head girl was to check the heads of her ten girls for lice. She would line us all up in a row and each girl would check the girl in front. Then we would turn and face the other way and do the same thing. We would have to remove any nits or fleas and fine tooth comb each other's head with parafin oil and then shake the D.D.T. powder on their heads. This was done at 4.30 till 5pm every night, then we studied until 6pm followed by supper, play, and the rosary. Then came bed, prayers, and lights out.

On Saturdays the sheets on the beds were changed and washed as well. Each girl would make their own bed, but the head girl would have to check that it was done correctly and make sure the sheets were washed, pressed and put away for the following week.

On Sundays nothing was done except the beds. It was a day of total rest and play. We did drill dancing in the playroom and went for long walks.

I remember one Sunday we went for a walk to Knock Shrine. It was a long way from the convent and my knickers seemed to become tighter and tighter with every step I took. Due to the sweat from the walking and the rough material of my knickers (not to mention my fat) my thighs became raw and began to bleed. With each step I took the pain got worse until I finally collapsed and began to cry. One of the matrons taking us to Knock Shrine called Kathelin Corgoran, came running up to me. (She was the matron of my dormitory and one of the few people that actually liked me. So I was luckly she was one of the matrons taking us today).

"What is it?" she asked, "What's the matter with you?"

"It's my knickers, they're hurting me." I answered.

The girls that were in ear shot of me began to giggle. Which embarressed me and made me cry louder.

Kathlyn Corgoran motioned to one of the other matrons to come down.

"I'm taking her back," she said, "You continue with Sally and the girls. I'll see you later."

The matron walked slowly back to the convent, stopping to rest on several occasions. I think she would have carried me if she was able, but she was a very small lady and she had one bad leg. I was also very fat and heavy, making even a strong person have trouble lifting me.

When we arrived back at the convent she brought me straight to the infirmary to examine my legs. When she saw how bad they were she gasped and said,

"Oh dear Josephine, they really are bad aren't they love. Never mind I'll clean up the bleeding and put a dressing on them for you. There's not much I can do about the knickers though."

"Can't you get me a soft pair?" I asked.

She looked down at me and with a smirk on her face she said,

"What colour would you like, pink or blue."

"Oh! Pink would be lovely," I answered not understanding the sarcasm in her tone.

She laughed and said,

"I was only joking Josephine, but I'll tell you what, I'll make a couple of pairs from softer material, but they'll still have to be black."

She took off the knickers I was wearing and pulled off my number.

"Now who's your girl in charge?" she asked.

"Kitty Kanavin." I answered.

"Okay. I'll make sure she sews your number on your new knickers tonight. Now come with me to the sewing room."

I felt as free as a bird walking to the sewing room. It felt lovely without any knickers on after all the pain I had just gone through. I looked up at the matron and said,

"Oh, this feels so good."

"What does?" She asked,

"Having no knickers on."

She looked down at me and laughed. Then she grabbed my hand and walked faster.

While she was sewing my new knickers we talked quietly together. She asked me if I ever got smacked by my teacher,

"Not smacked very often, but I get my cheeks pinched every day."

"What for?" she asked.

"For everything. If I don't know an answer I get pinched. If I turn my head I get pinched. If I have to go to the toilet I get pinched. I just get pinched for everything."

"Well don't worry too much about it, soon it will be time for summer holidays, after that you will have a new teacher. Maybe she won't pinch your cheeks."

"Oh, I don't mind anymore and it doesn't matter how hard she pinches me or smacks me I don't cry. My sister Caroline told me never to cry, and I don't anymore."

"You're going to be a hard one to break," She said.

"What does that mean?" I asked.

"Oh it doesn't matter," she said, and changed the subject. "I have a niece in your class do you know her?"

"What's her name?"

"Julie Diamond."

"Yes, I know her, but she never plays with me, her friends won't let her cause we're orphans, and she's from the township."

"Oh, I see," she answered.

Before long she had finished and I had two new pairs of knickers. I felt kind of special. No one else had these sort of knickers. I put them on straight away, I was beginning to get a cold bum with none on. Then she suggested that I spend the rest of the afternoon with her in the play room practicing the piano. That sounded like a wonderful idea to me, much better than Knock Shrine.

Sunday was also the day we wrote letters to our families, if you had a family. Four or five letters would be written for us on a large blackboard at the front of the playroom, and we would all copy the same letter. Those who had no family, would also write the letter for practice. There were many in the convent who didn't have families. My best friend Linda was one of those girls. If you had sisters in the convent, like myself, we would each write a different letter from the black board. That way our parents didn't receive the same letters. Our return mail was never forwarded on to us. We were informed that we had received a letter, but never given the letter to read. If we received money, no matter how much, we were only given a shilling from it. With that shilling we had to buy ourselves and a special friend an icecream or some lollies when we went on our Sunday walk. If we were going somewhere special like Knock Shrine for instance, we would have to pay our own entry fee, along with a friends, and go without the icecream. If we had been naughty prior to receiving the money though, we were punished by buying ice-cream for two other girls and going without ourselves.

I was learning the ropes fast, but I had my older sisters teaching me all the tricks, and of course Linda, who seemed to know them all. I never played with my older sisters though, they had their own friends, and I had mine. Caroline and Maureen always stuck together though. Even though there was a big age difference you never saw them apart. Maybe because they had been through so much together. They depended on each other. Plus they had never been separated, un-like Pauline and I.

They were still very close to me and Pauline though. Every night they would creep down to our beds to talk to us. Caroline would teach me things I was having trouble with in school too. It was her that taught me how to read the time. I had no idea at all. It was all too confusing for me and it was getting me into trouble in class all the time.

I wasn't a very intelligent child but Caroline helped me as much as possible to avoid me being punished in school. Pauline was much brighter then me, even though she was younger. The nuns liked her too, and spent more time explaning things to her. They just expected me to know, because I was older. There were no exceptions made for me either because I had been in hospital for so long and had missed my pre-school education.

The time flew by, and before I knew it, school holidays were upon us. When Linda told me that school holidays were coming, I thought we would be going home to mum and dad and was very excited about it. I was quite disappointed when I found out otherwise.

However, the holidays weren't too bad, In fact they were fun.

I had more time to play with Linda, and she brought me to so many new places in the convent, it was like a big adventure. A lot of the nuns went away for the holidays to other convents. I remember we would have to carry their heavy suitcases to the train station for them. Then we would have to carry suitcases back for the nuns arriving from other convents, who were staying with us, for their holidays. Another good thing about the summer holidays was, we got our summer uniform. It was much better then the winter one. We had shoes instead of those big, awful boots. The summer dresses were also black, but lighter in weight. We wore short, black, ankle socks and shoes. Some of the luckier children even received brand new shoes. Linda and I weren't one of those though, but Pauline was. In fact the whole time I was there, eleven years in total, I only ever got one new pair. The rest of the time I got hand me downs. Pauline on the other-hand was always getting new shoes.

During the summer months there were lots of new jobs to be done. The classrooms at the convent, along with the Westport town schools had to be cleaned. The nuns were paid for our services in town by the authorities, which meant extra income for the convent. We never seen any of it though, it was a real case of child labour. The desks, chairs and walls all had to be scrubbed. The floorboards waxed and polished thoroughly. Another job we had to do was clean the matresses on the beds. First we had to remove the matress covers, then we had to hit the mattresses with a big brush, banging them hard so that all the dust would come out. Then we had to flip them and do the same thing, twice or three times, until no more dust came from them. When that was done, we had to repair and wash the covers. If any of the covers were badly soiled from bed wetting etc. they were replaced.

We also had to do "the making of the hay." Apart from the hay fields at the convent, the convent also owned about 800 acres of hay fields in Westport. The making of the hay was a very big chore and very hard work. The hay from the convent fields was kept for the cattle on the grounds and stored in a very large shed. Whereas the hay at the Westport fields was sold to farmers around the country.

One of the better chores, (because you got to nose around) was cleaning the nun's quarters daily. The thing I remember most about the nun's rooms were they all had little bins in their rooms, which was emptied into a larger bin outside and burnt weekly. There was always lots of hair in those tiny bins and it puzzeled me then, and it still does. I still don't know to this day, where all that hair came from.

In our spare time, we had to knit the school jumpers for the following year. These new jumpers were either for new orphans entering the convent, or to replace totally worn out jumpers.

Holiday time was also a time when parents and relatives came to visit. However, I may as well have had no parents, because like Linda no one came to see me. When the other children's parents would come they were taken to what was known as the nun's parlor. One of the nun's present would then go and inform Sister Angela, who would arrange for the child in question to be cleaned, changed into a vistors outfit, and brought to their visitors. While the visitors were there Sister Angela would put on her big act, the one she performed for the doctor. Making them believe that she loved the children dearly. However, when the relatives left the child was ordered to get the special clothes off striaght away and to go about her duties.

Apart from the extra work though, the holidays were fun. Linda showed me lots of new places. Even though I had been at the convent for several months now, I had still seen little of it. You can't imagine how big one place could be. There were even several playgrounds to play in. I had only seen the school playground so far. The main playground was referred to as "the yard". It had swings made of old tyres in it, and a large hole filled with sand. There was also a very large shed with about twelve toilets and a sink to wash your hands in there. The yard was at the back of the convent and much closer to the convent than the school playground. During the holidays we played there most of the time.

Linda and I had great fun exploring new places together. For her they were not new, but having me with her made it exciting anyway. Each day was like a new adventure for us. We went to see the kitchen and Linda told me that Sister Vincent was in charge of the kitchen, but it was the women who worked there who did all the work. Sister Vincent's job was to give the orders and chose the menu. Linda told me that Sister Vincent was very good at her job and that she loved giving orders. I couldn't help but laugh at the expression on her face as she described Sister Vincent with such detail. There was another room close to the kitchen where the convent children learned to cook, wash and iron. This room was in between the kitchen and the wash-house.

We also went to nose around in the nun's quarters, which were completely separated from the convent. They were on the far side of the grounds. During the holidays you could get away with being there, because the cleaning duties were rotated so the nuns didn't know who was so supposed to be there and who wasn't. However, if we had been caught without instrutions to be there, we would have been whipped for sure, but it was so exciting taking the risk and sneaking around like thieves in the night.

It was like another world up there, high on the hill. A clean and fresh world, free from pain and punishment. Each nun had their own pretty, little room. They had their own kitchen with four cooks. They also had their own washroom, and cleaning ladies, who during the holidays went on vacation. They even had their own private chaple and cemetary up higher on the hill. Not to mention their own two orchards full with every kind of fruit and vegertable you could think of. It was quiet up here too. No hustle and bustle of children running around, but I think I would go mad in a place like that if I had to stay there all the time. It was a bit too quiet for my liking.

Another time Linda brought me to see the wash-house which was very close to the kitchen. It was hugh though, one of the largest rooms I have ever seen. There was a very large tub in there which had a fire burning under it all day. This fire supplied the hot water for washing the clothes. There was also two other big baths which were full with starch. Linda explained that the starch was the stuff that mad our clothes so stiff and scratchy. Apart from these main baths, there was also about forty wooden troughs. Each trough had it's on scrubbing board inside.

The duties in the wash-house were performed by the girls who had reached sixteen, but had no where to go, or no family to go to. When Linda told me this I was surprised, and thought to myself, even if I had no where to go, I'd leave this rotten place. Anywhere would be better then here. But I guess if you lived here your whole life, you could become afraid of the outside world a little. Maybe this was the only security they had. Like the old saying goes, "Better the devil you know, than the one you don't."

Some of the other girls who came of age to leave, but didn't have any family were found jobs in Westport. They were the luckly ones. Others would go to work for the priests at the Westport Paraish. They weren't so luckly, at least from what I heard.

After we had a good look around the wash-house, Linda brought me out the back of the wash house, and we walked up a large hill. On the top of the hill, there were rows and rows of clothes and sheets hanging out to dry. A hedge surrounded the clothes, and it to, had clothes placed on it. Anything that was badly stained, was taken of the line, scrubbed with sope, and placed on the hedge to dry. It was then re-washed with the next load of washing. All the clothes had to be snow white without a mark or stain on them. If they weren't, the head girl was in trouble even though she hadn't washed the clothes. It was her responsibility to check them and make sure they were clean. After a few minutes we went back down the hill following a different path. At the end of the path there was a dormitory with about sixty beds inside. Linda told me that this was where the laundry women slept. This dormitory was no-where near as clean as ours. The floorboards weren't even clean, not alone polished. In fact, they were dull and rotting. The beds in there had different covers too. They were made up of all different scrap materials. Our bed covers were snow white sheets.

After seeing the wash-house, and how the girls lived, and how hard they had to work. I hoped that I would never have to work there and was mighty glad I had a family to go to. I voiced these opinions to Linda, and she said that she had worked there several times for punishment. She said it wasn't so bad really, and that it was even fun sometimes. She said that once she had made jelly out of the left over pieces of soap, and had great fun. It did sound like fun too, the way she described it. That was Linda all over though, she always made the best of what she had. She was always smiling and happy. No matter what happened, she saw the funny side of it. She was so much fun to be with, and life in the convent became bearable for me with her around.

In between our chores, Linda brought me to lots of wierd and wonderful places. One day we went to see the orchards and the cattle. In the orchards they grew many different things. There were potatoes, peas, cabbage, beans, luttuce, tomatoes, gooseberries, blackberries, oranges, pears, and every type of apple you could think off. These fruits and vegetables were sold to the towns people, and used for our meals.

After looking around for a while Linda and I climbed a tree, and Linda pointed to another school across the fields. She called it a secondry school and told me you learnt Shorthand, Book-keeping and Typing there. It was a school for the older children who had passed their leaving exam at fifteen. However, she told me it cost extra money, so only those who had parents willing to pay extra money attended the school. She told me that she would love to learn all those things, but for her it was only a dream because she had no parents. It all seemed boring to me though. I wasn't interested at all. Linda laughed when I told her this, and told me that it was really very interesting, that she had known people who attended the school and they loved it. I just took her word for it, but I still wasn't eagar to attend. It was getting late so Linda suggested that we had better get back to the yard before we were missed. She promised to show me more another day.

When we arrived back at the yard we began playing with some of our other friends. Suddenly I saw Pauline. She was just sitting on the bench all by herself and I felt sorry for her. She really doesn't have anyone except me, I thought. Then just as quickly, I had a change of heart. She's so spoilt I thought. All she wants is to be the centre of attention, and if she doesn't get that she sits and broods by herself. She never wants to do anything for herself, she wants it all done for her. I suddenly became very angry with my sister. I wanted her to try harder to walk and without those bloody splints on. She had become extremly lazy since she had been in the convent. She was doing better at the hospital I thought. At least she had been trying there, now she just sat around all day.

Suddenly she looked my way and called out to me.
"Josephine, Josephine, come and play with me, I'm lonely."
I was angry with her and answered rudely, "No I won't. Just look at you, you can't even walk properly. The way you're going you'll never be able to either. You just sit on that bench all day and brood."
I didn't realise it, but the Reverend Mother was standing right behind me listening to every word I screamed at my sister.
I paused for a moment looking at Pauline,
"I'll tell you what", I said, "If you get up and walk all the way over here without stopping, I'll play with you, but I'm not sitting down all day just to please you."
I knelt down and put my arms out to her. She stood up and started walking towards me. She made it too not falling or stopping once, but she literally fell into my arms when she reached me and I hugged her tightly.

All of a sudden, I got such a slap in my face that I saw stars. It was the Reverend Mother.

"What a nasty, nasty child you are," she said. "You are not fit to mix with the other children." Then she grabbed me by the ear and led me to her room.

"Sit down," she ordered when we got there.

"Why did you say such dreadful things to your sweet sister, she's a cripple. Haven't you any compassion at all child."

"Yes," I answered, "I love my sister, but I just became so angry when I saw her just sitting there. She looks like such a dummy, and I know she can walk if she wants to. She just likes everyone doing things for her. She uses being a cripple to get what she wants. She's just getting so lazy, it makes me mad."

I paused for a moment, and then continued.

"I know her, and how she thinks," I said, "If I talk horrible to her, she tries. Just like today. I didn't mean to be terrible, I love my sister, but she'll only walk if I treat her that way."

The Reverend Mother listened intently as I spoke, and after I had finished she said,

"Okay, maybe you're right. I'll tell you what, after breakfast each day, instead of doing the cleaning chores from eight till nine, I'll allow you to spend some time with Pauline, teaching her how to walk. If by two months I haven't seen an improvement, you will be returned to cleaning duties. You will also be punished severely for wasting my time, and for being so nasty today."

"Yes Revenend Mother," I answered.

"Now go back out to the yard and play." she ordered.

I got up and left. I hoped that I was right, that I could really help Pauline. I liked the idea of getting out of cleaning duties, but the idea of being punished, I didn't like at all.

So it began, each morning I spent an hour with Pauline, and

she was really making progress. With time she was walking quite well with the splints. Then I had to teach her to walk without them. It took a couple of years, but I succeeded. It didn't take long before she was actually dancing after that.

The convent took all the credit for it though. It was printed in all the papers around the country. The papers stated that time, effort and perseverence had made the cripple girl walk.

Once Pauline was walking they started to teach her to dance, which she did surprisingly well. They even got in a private dancing teacher every Sunday for her. Soon they were entering her in dancing competitions. These too, were well advertised, bringing more glory to the Convent of Mercy. The advertisments would tell, how the crippled child from THE CONVENT OF MERCY, was taught to walk by the nuns and was now dancing in competitions.

In the beginning Pauline loved all the attention, and won several awards for her dancing efforts. However, as she got older she began to feel like a freak on show, till in the end she actually hated dancing.

CHAPTER 26

The summer holidays were over, but I didn't mind at all. In fact, I was looking forward to having a new teacher. I wouldn't be getting my cheeks pinched anymore. (I was going to get much worse, but I didn't realise that at the time.)

Maureen had additional responsibilities now as well. She was chosen as a girl in charge like Caroline. She wasn't really suitable however, she knew nothing about mending clothes, or darning stockings. In fact she hated sewing. Never-the-less she got the position, which was really quite an honor in the convent. (That's how the nuns portrayed it anyway, to me it was just a lot of extra hard work.)

Like all other girls in charge, Maureen had ten younger children under her. They knew more about sewing then she did. However, because she was so good to her girls they all loved her, and tried to help her as much as possible. Maureen asked them to try hard not to tear their clothes and stockings, so that she wouldn't have to repair them. When they did need mending however, one of her girls would attempt to mend them for her, but because Maureen was still in charge, she always got into trouble when the job wasn't satisfactory.

If one of the girls in the group wet the bed it meant extra work, because the sheets had to be changed daily instead of weekly. Maureen had one such girl. Her name was Maureen McKevily. (She later became a nurse in Dublin.)

As punishment for wetting the bed you had to wear the wet sheet around your head all day, so that everyone else knew what you did. If you pissed your knickers during the day the same thing happened, only you wore the wet knickers on your head. Well poor Maureen McKevily had either a sheet or a pair of knickers on her head everyday. Maureen my sister, used to feel really sorry for her, but there was nothing she could do about it. She couldn't even cover for her because she had to get clean sheets from Sister Angela for the bed.

Luckily for me I never had a bed wetting problem. I would have hated to be forced to wear a sheet or knickers around my head. I can still remember how everyone used to laugh at Maureen and call her "Piss the bed" or "Pissy bum". Kids can be really cruel when they're young. However, it didn't seem to have much affect on Maureen, she just ignored the insults, maybe she was used to it. Besides, at least she got clean knickers everyday, we got them once a fortnight.

My sister Maureen, was a bit like Maureen McKevily in the sense she didn't let insults worry her. She was very small and skinny for her age, but was very proud by nature. She had plenty of friends though, unlike Maureen McKevily. Her best friend was Kitty Kanavin, who also happened to be my girl in charge. Kitty had a sister whose name was Christine and Christine hated my sister Maureen. She couldn't stand her. It was jealously because Kitty preferred to play with Maureen, and not her own sister. Christine would go out of her way to get Maureen into trouble any chance she got.

Maureen loved to act the little lady, and always acted the part. One day she pulled her stockings way above her knee and dress line and tied a piece of string around the top of each stocking so that they wouldn't fall down. Then she paraded around the school yard, posing as the "perfect lady". Kitty and Maureen were in stitches laughing and having a great time but Christine saw them and went to report Maureen to one of the nuns. After receiveing a beating from the nun, Maureen was made wear her winter boots hung round her neck for a week as punishment. I know that the punishment hurt Maureen but she was proud and determined not to cry or show her true feelings. She gave everybody, including the nuns, the impression that it didn't worry her at all. She still walked around with her nose in the clouds. I was really proud of her and admired her attitude.

My first day of school was nothing like I had expected. Not only had Linda been put in a different class with convent girls only, but Pauline and I were the only convent girls left. My new teacher was a total monster too. I thought that Sister Bridget was cruel pinching my cheeks, but this one was far worse. Her name was Sister Colleen and my first encounter with her was terrifying.

The class room was smaller than the last one I had been in. There was a small wood heater to keep us warm, and a cloak-room for the town's children to hang their coats. There was an ajoining classroom next door, where only convent girls were taught by Sister Gill. Linda was in that class now. At the back of the room there was a small broom cupboard. The room actually looked crowded once all the students were seated. We all stood, waiting for our new teacher to arrive. Finally she came in and said,
"Good morning girls, please be seated."
She seemed ever so nice to me at first. She began to give her greeting speech,
"Now then, my name is Sister Colleen. First I will call the register, and I would like each girl to stand as I call their name so that I can see what you look like."
She commenced calling our names, and one by one we stood

up, and then sat down again. When she finished she said,

"Now girls, I expect each and everyone of you to do as your told. For those of you who do not I've got a very good punishment."

Then she called my name.

"Josephine, would you come to the front please. You are going to be my example this morning. You will show the girls what it's like to be locked in the broom cupboard. I remind you that there is no use screaming, because no one can hear you except who is present in this room and the more you scream, the longer you stay in there." She walked me by the hand up to the broom cupboard, but I didn't think she was going to put me in, I hadn't done anything wrong. I thought she was just showing the other girls what would happen, but she opened the door, pushed me inside and locked it. I was only in there about a minute, but it seemed like a lifetime. Panic overwhelmed me. I could never fully describe how scared I was. It was a terrible fear. Balls of sweat began to bead on my forehead, and I began screaming,

"Let me out, I'm sorry, I'll kiss the boy."

I repeated myself over and over again. I could hear everyone laughing, but they seemed so distant. I just had to get out of there. I didn't know, or care what I was saying, I just had to get out. I banged and kicked at that door in an effort to open it. All I could think about was getting out of there. Sister Gill and her students next door heard my screams and she came running in and screamed at Sister Colleen, "Get her out of there, she has parents, she isn't an orphan."

The door was opened and Sister Gill put her arms around me and lead me back to my seat. When I had calmed down she asked me something strange, she asked me,

"What boy will you kiss Josephine?"

"I don't know," I answered,

"But you said in the broom cupboard, that you would kiss the boy."

"I don't feel very well I think I'm going to be sick," I answered.

She didn't question me anymore, it was pointless anyway, I didn't remember a thing, I just remembered I had to get out of that cupboard.

I was allowed to rest at the back of the classroom for half an hour or so and then it was back to my lessons.

I didn't like Sister Collen, in fact I hated her. That was my first bad experience in the Convent of Mercy, but it wasn't my worst. It was only the beginning.

The next few months passed without too many more disasters. Sister Colleen used a ruler to slap you with occasionally, but not very often. I got it the most however. There was only Pauline and I who were from the convent and Pauline was so frail and beautiful. She very rarely got smacked at all. It was always me.

As the months progressed, Pauline and I were informed that if we did well this semester we would be transfered to Sister Gill's class after the Christmas holidays. I worked harder in that semister than I did the whole time I was at the convent. I wanted to get away from this teacher, I always had the fear that she would put me back in the broom cupboard. I also wanted to be away from these snotty towns children, and with my friend Linda.

On the last day of the semester the school guard came into the classroom to discuss some details with Sister Colleen about security during the holidays. As they were talking the girl next to me, Nelly Kearins said, "That's my dad, you know."

Nelly was such a stuck up little bitch and I didn't like her at all. I didn't believe her either, because she was always telling lies.

"No it's not, it's my dad." I answered her.

"It is not," She repeated "I'll prove it to you."

She screamed out to her dad,

"Hi dad, throw me your hat."

Mr Kearins threw his hat to his daughter.

Then I screamed out,

"Hi dad, throw me your keys."

Mr Kearins laughed and threw his keys at me."

Nelly became confused, she was younger then me and had no sense of humour at all.

"You're my dad, aren't you." She said,

"I sure am pumpkin." her father answered her.

Then I said the same thing, and he answered yes to me as well.

With that Nelly began bawling her eyes out.

Her father rushed over to her and hugged her.

"I'm only your dad Nelly. We were only joking with ya honey." He looked at me and winked.

Sister Collen came over and said,

"Josephine, tell Nelly you were only joking."

I looked at Nelly and her father and began to laugh. I just couldn't get any words out of my mouth. The guard started laughing too, but Sister Colleen wasn't laughing, she was furious.

The guard left and I was left to face the music alone. I stopped laughing very quickly, I didn't feel so brave now that Mr Kearins had gone. I was half expecting to go back in the cupboard and became a little nervous. However, I got a beating instead, not with the ruler either. The nuns wore a thick, black belt around their waistline, she removed it and beat me everywhere with it. Where ever it landed it landed. She was in a real rage, because I had defied her in front of everyone. But I was getting stronger, and I didn't shed a tear. After she finished beating me, I defied her again. I looked Nelly straight in the face and said,

"It's not your dad, It's mine, ya big baby."

I got away with it, she didn't hit me again. Maybe she didn't hear me, or maybe she thought she'd kill me if she hit me anymore.

The Christmas holidays were here and I was in my glory. That semister had been terrible. It had stared terrible and ended the same way. I was thankful that Pauline and I were being transfered next semester and we didn't have to stay with Sister Colleen for the full year.

There was plenty to look forward to at Christmas. Caroline told me we would receive money and a parcel from our dad. I didn't care about the money, but I was real excited about the parcel. We actually got to keep the stuff inside, but we had to share them with a friend who didn't have any family. Apart from our families sending us presents the townfolk also sent up gifts. I asked Pauline if she would share hers with our baby sister Doreen, because I wanted to share with Linda and she said she'd think about it. She was really selfish sometimes and I hated that part of her.

My first year at Chirstmas time I learnt a lot. We were all made sit around in a circle in the playroom, and a few nuns would pass out gifts and lollies to eat from the townfolk. Our large knickers used to come in handy when this took place. The nun's would ask who hasn't received something and we would all scream out and raise our hands. If we were passed a small toy or some lollies we would put them in our bloomers and start screamming again. "ME ME," up the knickers, "ME ME" up the knickers. I missed out the first year, but I beat the lot of them every year after that, my knickers were bigger than most!

Along with small gifts the townfolk would send up bags of lollies, chocolates, biscuits, and fruit. I remember my first Christmas there they sent up large boxes of bananas. Everyone got a banana, I'd never tasted one before, nor had Pauline. I loved them, but Pauline wasn't so keen. She took one bite from her banana and then said to Sister Vincent,
"I don't want it, I don't like it very much.
Sister Vincent was angry with her and said,
"You know the rules about wasting Pauline, now you eat that banana right now."
"I can't, it's making me sick, I feel all hot and sweaty."
Sister Vincent snatched the banana from Pauline's hands, and literally shoved it down her throat forcing her mouth shut, so that she had to swallow it. (In a way Pauline was luckly, any other child would have got the belt.)

Pauline was supposed to dance that night. She was making her debut in the Christmas concert for the nuns. She had recently started dancing lessons, even though she was still wearing splints most of the time. However, after she had been made to eat that banana she felt sick. Later on in the evening Sister Angela went to prepare Pauline for the dancing, but Pauline said,
"I don't think I can dance tonight, I feel awful queer in my tummy."
"Now stop that nonsense at once Pauline, you know how you love to dance." (Sister Angela really loved Pauline. She didn't

like many students, but she adored Pauline).

"I know I love dancing, but it's the banana I ate. It made me feel all funny inside and I've got so much pain in my tummy. I can't even walk, let alone dance."

"Now that's enough of this Pauline, you'll be fine."

All of a sudden Pauline threw up all over Sister Angela, and went as white as a ghost.

Sister Angela sat her down on a chair and Pauline passed out falling to the floor. Sister Angela rang for help and one of the laundry workers came and carried Pauline upstairs to bed where she remained. On Christmas day my sister was still unwell in bed. The doctor came in to see her and told Sister Angela that he thought Pauline had a stomach virus. He told Sister Angela to give her plenty of fluids but no dairy products at all. He assured her that she would be fine the next morning, that the virus usually lasted twenty-four hours or so.

Because it was Christmas day my sisters and I were allowed to go and see Pauline one at a time. Because Pauline and I were the closest I was allowed up first and allowed to bring her the parcel from dad. Pauline looked terrible. Her face was swollen and she had red blotchs all over her face and body. Normally Pauline was a very greedy person, but today she was different. When I handed her the parcel she said,

"I don't want it Josephine, you keep it and share it with Doreen. I feel so sick. I think I'm going to die, I really do."

I was shocked at her words. Pauline was very intelligent and she usually knew everything. She might not have had good legs, but she had a fabulous brain. I never even dreamt of dying, it was the last thing in my mind and it scared me that she was thinking like this. Only old people died, not young girls like my sister. The fact that she wasn't excited about her parcel scared me even more. After my visit with her I went straight to Sister Angela and told her what Pauline said, I also told her that her face was badly swollen. Sister Angela left me standing there, and quickly walked away to call the doctor back. Pauline was given an injection and spent two weeks in bed. She did almost die. If I hadn't told Sister Angela about her swollen face, she probably would have. Apparently she was allergic to bananas and was told never to eat one again.

I enjoyed opening my parcel from dad and I shared my gifts with Linda, who was very grateful, and embarrassed that she couldn't share with me. It didn't worry me though, I loved sharing with her. She was my best friend, and a very good one too. We both had great sense of humors and found everything funny.

When Pauline returned to good health she asked for her parcel, but she didn't share it with Doreen, so Doreen received nothing because I'd already shared mine with Linda. Pauline was really back to her normal, greedy self!

The Christmas holidays came and went. Like any other holidays there was a lot of extra chores to be done. But there was also a lot more playing time, or should I say mischief time. Linda always made sure we had new adventures and lots of fun.

Now it was time to return to school. I was looking forward to it really. I had a new teacher, who didn't seem so bad. (At least she had given me a cuddle once when that nasty, old dragon Sister Colleen put me in the broom cupboard.) I was also going to be with Linda again, and no more towns children.

When our teacher Sister Gill first entered the classroom and started her opening speech to welcome new members and welcome back old ones, I wasn't sure if I liked her after all. She began to scream at us all, telling us that she was disgusted at our behaviour on Christmas morning. She began doing the actions of "ME, ME, UP THE KNICKERS." It was quite comical seeing a nun pretending to shove things up her knickers, but she was very angry, so no one was laughing. After a few moments she calmed down and she did turn out to be as nice as I had first thought. She was the nicest nun that taught me while I was at the Convent of Mercy.

CHAPTER 27

Sister Gill was a lovely teacher and I enjoyed being in her class, except there was a girl in there called Rita Donally who wouldn't stop staring at me. She was really quite scary. Every time I looked up she was looking at me. Rita was a couple of years older than me, but a slow learner.

This staring business went on for months. Sometimes I would smile at her when I caught her looking my way, but she would put her head down. She made me feel very uncomfortable. She never spoke, just stared, but then we weren't allowed to speak in class anyway.

It was Sister Gill who taught me my times tables. Caroline and Maureen re-inforced the lessons by my bed at night. I caught on real fast with my tables. It didn't matter which table Sister Gill asked, I knew the answer. Even Pauline didn't know them as well as me, and I felt so proud of myself. Sister Gill was proud of me too, and that made me feel happy. It also made Rita Donally look at me a lot more. If only I knew what she wanted it would have been more confortable. Maybe she was looking for a friend, I didn't know what to expect. Even at playtime she kept her distance, she just stared at me.

Then one day when Linda was sick in bed, Rita approached me in the playground. I was sitting on the bench with Pauline and at first I was scared when I saw her coming, believing that maybe she was going to hit me, I really wasn't sure what she wanted.

"Hello", she said, with a big smile on her face.

It was the first time I had seen her smile, and I was relieved that she wanted to be friendly.

"Hi", I answered, not knowing what else to say.

"Do ya wanna come and play?" she asked.

"No, I should stay with my sister." I answered, still a little wary of her.

"Oh come on, just for a little while."

I looked at Pauline and she smiled at me and said, "Go on, go and play for a while, I'll be here when you get back."

I looked back at Rita and said "Okay, but only for a little while."

We both ran off and played chase. I was enjoying myself too. She had an infectious giggle that made me giggle all the time. Suddenly she stopped running and said,

"I've got to go to the toilet, will ya come with me?"

"No" I answered, "I'll wait here for you."

"Oh, please come, I get a little scared in the shed by myself."

"Oh there's nothing to be afraid of, ya big chicken." I answered,

"Oh please come, I'll only be a minute."

"Okay, cluck cluck," I answered and we both giggled and ran off to the toilet shed.

Going to the toilet with her was a big mistake. She went into the toilet cubicle, and said

"Come in with me."

"Don't be stupid, I'll be right outside."

"Oh, come on, I'll only be a minute."

She sounded desperate so I went in with her. It was the worst thing I could have done. She locked the door and stood with her back against it. Her smile was gone, her expression had changed and I was frightened, but at the same time a little excited.

She pulled down her knickers and lifted her dress. Then she grabbed my hand and put it in between her legs. It felt wet as she massaged my hand around on herself. After a few minutes she released my hand, pulled my knickers down and started to caress me between my legs.

"Do you like that Josephine?" she asked

"Yes, but we shouldn't be doing it." Her words brought me back to my senses. I suddenly felt a loathing inside of me. I yanked myself away and pulled up my knickers.

"Let me out of here". I said.

"Your not going to tell are you?"

"Not this time, but if you ever try and get me in here again, I'll scream it out all over the place."

"If you tell anyone Jospehine, I'll bloody kill ya."

"You'd better not try Rita, because it's you who'll die, not me. I'll tear ya bloody eyes out. Just leave me alone and I'll leave you alone."

"Okay." she said and moved away from the door.

I ran from there, not because I was scared of her, but because I was scared of myself. Scared of the feelings I had experienced in there. Scared because I had liked it, yet I knew it was wrong. I started thinking about my First Holy Communion that was coming up later in the year. I wasn't worthy any more, I wasn't clean. I felt so ashamed. I decided to go to confession on Saturday, and tell the priest what I had done.

That night after Caroline and Maureen left my bedside, I crept down to Linda's bed.

"Linda, Linda." I whispered until she woke-up.

"Hi Josephine." she said in a sleepy voice.

I started to cry, and she sat up with alertness, "What is it Josephine?, What happened?"

"I'm sorry for crying but something terrible happened today and I feel so ashamed."

"Well don't cry, just tell me."

I told her all that had happened, right from the staring in class and at the end of my story she began to giggle hysterically, trying hard to keep quiet at the same time. Tears were running from her eyes as she held her mouth and stomach in a effort to stop laughing. I wondered what the hell she was laughing at. I felt hurt.

"It's not funny Linda," I said.

"I'm sorry, it's just she tried it with me once and I gave her a punch right in the nose. She never tried it again. If you'd only asked me about her when you caught her looking at you all the time, I would have warned you."

I felt even more ashamed now, Linda punched her in the nose, I let her do it and what's worse, enjoyed it. I was glad that I didn't mention that part to Linda, she would have thought I was disgusting.

I pretended to laugh along with her, and answered,

"Well she won't do it to me again, cause I told her I would tell the whole convent if she tried."

"Don't worry about it Jospehine, you learnt something today. Next time you won't be tricked. There's lots of girls in here like that. They make me sick, but as long as they keep their hands of me, I don't care, and nor should you."

I agreed with her verbally, but in my heart I felt no better. In fact, I felt worse and wished I hadn't mentioned it at all. I got back to bed and lay there wishing I could go to sleep and that Saturday would come quickly. I couldn't wait to confess my sins. It was only Wednesday so I still had to wait three more days.

Saturday came and before mass I went to confession. The confession box was small, the priest was in the next room, and we talked through a little hole, which had a black curtain across it. I began with my smaller sins,

"Forgive me father, for I have sinned. I have taken the Lords name in vain, I also didn't polish the floors like I was supposed to, I missed under my bed. I also let another girl play with my private parts."

I didn't get any further, the curtain was pulled back and the priest looked me staight in the face. His eyes were accusing and I looked away.

"Where did the girl touch you?" he asked,

"Down there" I answered as I pointed between my legs.

"Stand up child" he said,

I was scared, but I stood up. It took all my will power not to run out of there. I was so embarrassed and ashamed of myself.

"Now show me where she touched you." he repeated.

I pointed in between my legs again, and said

"There." He started mumbling away but I wasn't listening any more, I was so ashamed. He had never shown his face before. He knew who I was now, and everytime I came to mass he would recognise me and remember what I did. He told me to say twenty Hail Marys and dismissed me. I ran out into the church so quick I thought I was flying. As I said my Hail Mary's, I regretted making confession. I hoped that I could still make my first Holy Communion and that the priest wouldn't tell the nuns. I felt so confused and disillusioned with priests, and the act of confession. It was supposed to make you better, but I felt much worse. As for Rita Donally, I saw her take many other young girls into the toilet. Some of them on several occasions and I knew what they were up to. She would always give me a smile of satisfaction if she saw me nearby, but she never approached me again. (Rita actually became a nun later on, and taught at the CONVENT OF MERCY!)

Like Rita Donally, there were many other senior girls who became nun's while I was at the convent. The girls in the convent used to treat the new nuns a bit like a new boyfriend, and we all got excited when we saw one of our favourite nuns. While I was in the convent I saw many of these ceremonies taking place. Many of the nuns I didn't know, but a few I did. For instance Rita Donally, Margaret Flynn, and Rosarro Blice were all girls I knew. For the first year the new nuns were referred to as the Apostolate's and wore white habits. After the year was up they had a chance to change their minds and leave the convent to find work. If they didn't change their mind they were married to god. It was quite a big event too, just like a real wedding. The parents of the Apostolate's would come to see the ceremony, and watch the cutting of their daughter's hair and the wedding service. During the ceremony the white habits were changed to black ones. The ceremony was followed by a large reception, where everyone rejoiced the marriage of a couple.

My favourite Apostolate was Sister Rosarro, she was so pretty in her white habit. I wasn't the only one who liked her either. Many of the other girls did too. She was a kind girl and never tried to hurt you in any way. Even later when she was ordained and became a teacher she remained the same and all her students loved her. There was another girl in the convent who also liked Sister Rosarro. In fact I think she was in love with her. Her name was Grace Gawley. Grace was a lovely girl by nature, and would also go out of her way to help others. She had a brilliant mind and if we had a test she would be finished by the time the rest of us had barely answered a couple of questions. She never had to study hard either. She heard or read it once and knew it. I remember one day Grace and I were in the courtyard during recess and she was eating some bread and jam, and Sister Rosarro came down the stairs. Grace turned to me and said,

"Oh look Josephine, here comes Sister Rosarro."

"Yes" I answered wondering why Grace was getting so excited.

"Oh Josephine look at me, here take my bread, I have to get my handkerchief out to clean myself. I can't let her see me like this. I have to see her close up, I just have to."

With that she fell in a heap. I jumped up dropping her peice of bread, and bent down beside her.

"What's the matter, Grace?" I asked, worried in case I would be in trouble, while at the same time concerned for the poor girl.

As I turned her over I saw froth bubbling out of her mouth. It reminded me of the hound when it pinned me down and I felt scared. She was having spasms too. Her hands and legs were going up and down in sharp rigid movements. I became very frightened and began screaming.

Within seconds Sister Angela was at my side, slapping me and telling me to stop my screaming. When she had me under control she shoved her hand in Grace's mouth and pulled at her tongue. It looked revolting and was making me feel sick. (I didn't realise it then, but she was stopping Grace from choking on her own tongue.) Then she grabbed the handkerchief that Grace was cleaning herself with, and shoved it in her mouth. She instructed some of the older girls standing close by to take Grace up to her bed. Then she looked at me and said,

"Come with me Jospehine, I want to talk to you."

I started to get nervous. I knew I didn't do anything wrong, but Sister Angela and I didn't get along too well, and her tone gave me the impression that I was in trouble.

When we arrived at her room she phoned the doctor straight away for Grace, then she turned to me and said,

"What exactly happened out there Josephine?"

"I'm not sure Sister Angela. She was fine one minute, then she saw Sister Rosarro coming and she got all excited. Then she collapsed and went all funny, throwing her arms around and frothing at the mouth."

"Look, what happened to Grace is called an epileptic attack. It is caused by a disturbance in the normal electrical rhythm of the brain cells and a deficiency of glutamic acid in the brain." (I didn't know what she was talking about as my interpretation of her words was that Grace had brain damage.) "Grace has been on medication for these attacks since she was a young girl and hasn't had a fit for many years now. It must have been the excitement or maybe she forgot to take her medication. I won't know for sure until the doctor comes. However, regardless of the cause you must not tell her what happened. If she does ask you, just tell her she became dizzy and passed out. Do not tell her that she was having spasms, Okay?"

"Yes Sister Angela." I answered, wondering what all the fuss was about.

"Okay, you can go back to play now," she said, "but remember, don't tell Grace what happened to her, she will have no memory of it."

"Yes" I repeated and left the room thankful that I didn't get punished like I assumed I would be.

Sure enough, the next day Grace asked me what happened, and I told her that she had fainted, just like Sister Angela told me.

The day arrived when I and the girls who were old enough, made their First Holy Communion. Pauline wasn't one of us, because she was too young. Like the senior girls becoming nuns, this was also a very celebrated occasion and we all looked forward to it. It was so exciting, we all got to wear a white dress and veil. It wasn't a new dress, it had been worn by hundreds before us and probably a few more hundred would wear it after us, but it was so pretty and it made us feel good wearing it.

There were twelve of us making our First Holy Communion, and I stood out the most. Not because I was the prettiest, or had the nicest dress, but because I was the ugly duckling of the group. I still had my lovely tin rimmed glasses, and was still extremely fat. However, there must have been fat girls before me, because they still had a fat dress for me to wear!
We wore our beautiful, white dresses all day and paraded around in them like queens. Then, when it was time for our party we had to take them off so that they wouldn't get dirty.

I remember thinking at the end of my very special day, "Well that's over, the next thing to look forward to is the holidays." I also remember feeling very guilty about what had happened with Rita Donnelly, and hoped that God had forgiven me. I promised him that day that it would never happen again, and it never did.

CHAPTER 28

Children seemed to come and go in the convent. As fast as the bigger girls left, new ones came in. The girls in charge never changed, just new ones were appointed to look after the new girls that came in. My sister Maureen probably wished they did change, she didn't like the job at all. It was always getting her into trouble. She was still quite young really, only one year older then myself. She was expected to act like an adult, and I was still treated like a child. It didn't matter how old you were, it depended on the nuns, and if they felt you were capable or not.

At first Maureen felt proud of her position as head girl, but now she agreed with me, it was just a lot of hard work and brought trouble to her every day. I felt so sorry for her at times, like when the other head girls criticized her ability, and told her how slow she was. Even the nun's chastised her for not doing a good job. They even straped her sometimes for no reason. My heart would break for my big sister, as she stood there definitely holding back her tears, standing straight and tall, but there was absolutely nothing I could do for her. The funny thing was, you didn't ask for the job in the first place, you were allocated it, so you shouldn't be punished for not doing it well. But in convent you were punished and beaten all the time for no reason. They didn't need a reason, they were in control!

I can remember many of the new girls that came into my class, and how exciting it was finding out all about them and their backgrounds. All the new girls that entered the convent, went through the same initiation that my sisters and I had been through. They were all bathed and had their hair cut so short they were almost bald. I can understand this procedure if you had fleas, like we did when we first arrived, but it seems pointless and cruel otherwise. Maybe the nuns just wanted everyone to look the same, but we believed that they only cut our hair because they had all theirs cut off when they became nuns.

I remember once, two sisters that came to the convent, they had lovely hair when they first came. However, when they were in full custody of the nuns, their hair was cut off immediately. The sisters were known as the McClick sisters. There was about eleven months between them in age, and they were extremely close and fond of each other. Their mother was an English protestant, but she was married to an Irish Catholic. Apparently, they had to go to England, to take care of some sick relatives, and since the girls were being taught at the convent, they decided to leave them in the nun's care, until they returned, so as not to disrupt the children's education. However, the nuns wouldn't accept the girls, unless the mother became a Catholic through baptism, even though she was married in a Catholic church and the girls were baptised Catholics. We were all invited to the baptism which was performed in the Convent's chapel. I remember thinking how strange it was to see a fully grown women baptised. We had previously witnessed only babies being baptised. (The Catholic's sure have some strange ideas sometimes.)

The McClick sisters were treated just like Towns school children at first, but when their parent's went to England things changed. Their lovely blonde hair was cut, and their clothes discarded for the dull grey uniform the rest of us wore. They were luckly though, they were only in the convent for about six months not like most of us.

Another girl I remember was a girl called Marion Kennedy. She had no parents, I'm not sure what happened to them, maybe they died, but she was about eight when she arrived. She had really funny skin and we nick-named her Turkey Skin. Incidently, we all had nick-names of some sort. Mine was Dumplin, (cute wasn't it, I'm glad I still don't get called that.) Pauline was called Cripple, even though she wasn't anymore. In fact not only could she walk, she was a fabulous dancer, thanks to me. Not that the nuns would agree to that, they took all the glory for her recovery.

Anyway, getting back to Turkey skin, she was a lovely girl and well liked by everyone, but she came to a tragic end. Years later when she turned sixteen, the nuns got her a postion working for the Priests in Westport. When she left the convent she was a strong young women. In fact I don't ever remember her being sick, apart from the odd cold. She had always been strong and healthy. On her day's off, Marion would often come and visit us at the convent. I remember her telling us that she didn't like her new job, but there wasn't anything else available. She told me and a few other people that the priest worked her very hard. She had to cut wood and do everything else that needed doing, no matter how hard. Marion Kennedy became thinner and thinner each time we saw her and finally we heard that she had died. We never did find out the true cause of death, but I believe that she was exhausted from the work load and underfed by her employers. Marion was only eigthteen years old when she died.

Since the nuns had become so highly regarded for curing Pauline and teaching her to dance, a lot of parents started to put their disabled children into the convent for care. They believed that god and the nuns had helped Pauline, and could help their children too. One such girl was Patrica McCormick, she was a deaf-mute, but she could lip read. Her parents believed that the famous Convent of Mercy could cure her. Of course they didn't. Patricia's parents were very wealthy and were prepared to pay extremely well for her recovery. She didn't get her hair cut off either, but she still had to wear the convents uniform. Her parents came to see her every Sunday, and always showered her with gifts and affection. Patrica was a spoilt, spiteful, little brat. Everyone hated her, but we were all ordered to treat her nicely. Furthermore, guess who had to try and teach her to talk. Yes me, a child of nine years old. It was also me who was being punished when she wasn't making any progress. When my efforts failed, they began rotating her speech lessons. Each day a different girl would try and teach her something during class recess. So I was only with her once a fortnight, but even that was too much for me. I really hated her. I would say a word, which she would lip read, and then try and repeat, but all that would ever come from her mouth was "BA BA", it was really hopeless. There was one good thing though, her mother would bring grapes to all the girls that were helping her, so I got plenty of grapes, which I shared with Linda and my sisters. But we were also punished for not achieving results, so it would have been better to go without the grapes.

I still can't believe how spiteful Patricia was, she really had a nasty streak. She would scratch at your eyes, and bite you for no reason at all, and not feel a bit bad about it. I remember one day, another girl in our class tapped her on the shoulder to get her attention. What the girl wanted was to ask Patricia to pass her a rubber, but she had to face her so that Patricia could read her lips. However, Patricia didn't turn and look at the girl, she turned and stabbed the girl in the hand with the nib of her ink pen. It wasn't so much the stabbing, it was the hate in her eyes when she did it that was terrifying. Her face was all distorted and evil looking, I can still remember the expression on her face as clear as if it were yesterday it was that frightening.

The teacher abused the poor the girl who had wanted the rubber, for frightening poor Patricia. I saw the whole thing and Patricia wasn't frightened, she was just a spiteful bitch. However, I didn't say anything for fear of being strapped myself, for not minding my own business.

All the teacher said to Patricia was, we mustn't hurt other people darling. It made me sick, the victim was the victim twice. It was always the same in that place, no justice and certainly no MERCY.

With time, Patricia's parents took her out of the convent realizing that nothing could be done for their deaf daughter. I think everyone was glad to see her go, I know I was. The nuns wouldn't have been too thrilled though, they would miss the lovely income Patrica was bringing them. That's why we were being punished for not making any progress with her, they didn't want to lose her, or should I say the money!

There was another girl that came to the convent for treatment. She was about twelve when she arrived, it was a few years after Patricia McCormick. Her name was Elizabeth Doyle. She suffered very badly from Asthma attacks. Like Marion Kennedy, Elizabeth came to a tragic end. The thing I remember most about Elizabeth, apart from her death, was that she was terrified of mice. When she first came to the convent she saw a small field mice in the classroom. Well you never saw anyone move so fast. She jumped up on her desk, lifted her skirt and started screaming un-controllably. After the initial shock of her screams the whole class started laughing at her. In the end we were making more racket than she was. She became very sick because of it though. They had to put her on a ventilation machine, which was all very new to us, and we were a little scared that she was going to die there and then.

As I got to know Elizabeth I found her to be a lovely girl. She was quiet, and considerate, and fun to be with. Linda and I played with her often in the yard. Elizabeth and her parents were very religous people. I think she would probably have become a nun later in life, if she had lived.

When she first arrived at the convent, her parents warned the nun's that she couldn't be kept in crowded areas, because she would have a severe attack. The trouble was the nuns didn't care enough to remember the warnings. All they cared about was the money that the child brought in. Several months after Elizabeth arrived, the convent got the opportunity of showing a movie at the convent. The O'Brien's, who owned a theater in Westport, had a daughter attending school at the convent. They got a religious film called St. Joan of Arc, and thought that the convent would appreciate a private showing. The O'Briens delivered the movie, and the necessary equipment to show it, and we were all seated on the floor of the playroom to watch the film. The playroom was a large room, but not large enough to hold two or three hundred girls at one time. So we were all crammed up like sardines. Along with us, was Elizabeth Doyle.

For the first half an hour of the film nothing happened, then there was some screaming from the girls sitting near Elizabeth, she was having an attack. Everyone started standing up to look at what was going on, which made it impossible for the nuns to get to her side and help her. It took about fifteen minutes to get us all out of the room to help Elizabeth. However, it was too late, Elizabeth died that night.

Elizabeth's mother knew the O'Brien's had had a screening of the movie at the convent, but she assumed that after her warnings her daughter would have been excluded from the showing but she must have had her doubts because the next day when Mrs Doyle came to pick-up the last of her daughter's belongings, she didn't report to the nun's parlour as was customary. Instead she walked straight towards me and some of the other children playing in the yard and asked if her daughter had seen the movie the previous day. We told her she did, and told her what had happened. At that stage none of us knew that Elizabeth had died, or what story her mother had been told, but Elizabeth's mother seemed very distraught.

Suddenly Sister Angela came over and said in a subdued tone, "Hello, Mrs Doyle, if you'll come with me, I'll get Elizabeth's clothes for you."
We all gathered around to see and hear what was going on, it was unusual to see a parent in the yard and from Sister Angela's tone we knew something was wrong.
Mrs Doyle began screaming at Sister Angela,
"Clothes, what good are my daughter's clothes. I want my daughter, but she's dead and you killed her."
"Won't you please come inside, and we can talk about this," Sister Angela said.
"What's to talk about, I told you that she couldn't cope with crowds, yet you let her see that movie. You killed her, that's what you did, you killed my daughter."
Mrs Doyle was now in tears and Sister Angela took her gently by the arm and lead her up the stairs and inside, but we could still hear Mrs Doyle's screams and accusations.
"Why did you kill my daughter? You were supposed to cure

her, not kill her. I told you about the crowds, why did you kill my only daughter." she accused.

About an hour later there was a general meeting called and everyone in the convent gathered in the playroom. We were told that Elizabeth died during the night and that we were to forget any incidents that we may have over heard in the yard. We were also informed that we would be severely punished if we were caught talking about Elizabeth in the future.
There was an enquiry into Elizabeth's death by the authorities, and some of the children were called up to be questioned by the police. However, the convent was not held responsible for the death, and no further action was taken. The matter was closed and forgotten about.

Lots of girls came and went in the convent, but when some of them left they left in a wooden box just like Elizabeth. So I was a lucky one I guess, although there were many a times that I would have given anything to die. As if death held some sort of freedom, or escape. An escape that I wanted more than life itself a lot of times.

CHAPTER 29

From time to time gypsies would pass by the convent. They often came with babies in their arms and waited by the gates of the yard until they caught one of the nun's attention. Then they would offer to sell their babies to the nuns, and most times the nuns would take them.

On one particular occasion a gypsy came up holding the smallest baby I had ever seen. It looked almost like a kitten wrapped in a tartan blanket. It was sister Gill who approached the gypsy.

"Be off with you gypsy," Sister Gill said, "We've got no room for your gypsy child."

"Please mam, take this small child off me hands, I'm only asking a shilling for em. The poor wee thing will starve if ya don't take em."

"What do you mean em, is the child a boy then?"

"Yes mam, and a good strong un too. It breaks me heart ta let em go, but I can't afford ta be feeding the young mite."

"God has given you the means to feed your child, with your own breasts. Now be off with you and your lies."

"I'm not lying mam, the lad will grow and for sure he'll starve. If ya take em off me hands now, he'll have a fighting chance at life."

"We don't take boy's here, this is an all girl's convent, so be off with you."

"What's the difference? They are all children of the lord. Boy, girl, what's the diffenence?"

"We don't take boys and that's final. Now be on your way before I call the authorities."

The gypsy fled with haste. The sound of the authorities seemed to scare the life out of her. As I watched her go, I wondered what was the difference between a boy and a girl. Like the gypsy said, we are all children of the lord. The only difference that I could see was that boys wore trousers, and girls wore dresses. But if you swapped the clothes around there wasn't any difference.

Why didn't Sister Gill take the baby then, I wondered. They took babies from the gypsies all the time. Why was it so bad to have a boy.

This question played on my mind for weeks, until finally I decided to ask Sister Gill what the difference between a boy and a girl was.

One day a few weeks later we were doing our times table and everyone had their hands up, including me, to answer the table being asked. Sister Gill finally called my name to answer the sum, but I didn't answer, I asked a question.

"Sister Gill, you know a few weeks ago when that gypsy came with the small baby."

"Yes Josephine, I remember, but that's not what we are talking about now."

"Yes I know that, but I need to know something. How come we can't take boys in the convent."

"Because this is a girls convent."

"What's the difference?"

"The difference is you are all girls here, and he was a boy."

"No, I mean what's the difference between a boy and a girl, except what clothes they wear. I mean we could put the boy in a dress too, couldn't we?"

Everyone started to laugh when I said that, but I wasn't trying to be funny, I was really confused.

"Look it has nothing to do with what clothes we wear Josephine. God made boy a boy, and girl a girl, and that's all there is to it."

I still wasn't satisfied and went to tell her so, but she cut me off, and told me to get on with the class. Then she asked someone else to answer the table she had orginally asked me.

I was no better off now, than before I had asked the question. In fact I was worse off, because all the class had laughed at me when I said we could put a dress on the boy. The worst thing was that I still wanted to find out the difference and I didn't know who to ask next.

Later in the evening while we were having dinner, I saw the night matron going into the kitchen to have her meal and it suddenly dawned on me to ask her. I knew she liked me and wouldn't tell me off. It was she who made me my lovely knickers. I might even get an honest answer from her I thought. I was suddenly looking forward to lights out, which was unsual for me, I hated going to bed. The only good thing about going to bed was Caroline and Maureen would come to see me. However, today I was eager to go because I wanted to find out the difference between a boy and a girl.

It's typical, but the rest of the day dragged and when lights out finally came, I couldn't wait for Caroline and Maureen to come and go. I was getting tired and I didn't want to fall asleep before talking to the matron.
As soon as my sisters left my bedside I snuck out of bed and went up to the matron's cubical. I opened the door and walked inside to find her reading a magazine. She looked up as I entered and said,
"What is it Josephine, are you ill?"
"No, I'm fine, I just couldn't sleep."
I had left the door to the cubical open and when the matron realised that there was nothing wrong with me she asked,
"Josephine, doesn't your father have a door in his house?" she

was being sarcastic again, but I was still too dumb to realise, so I answered,

"I don't know, I don't remember my father's house."

She laughed at me and asked me to close the door of the cubical so as not to wake the other children. Looking back on it now, I wonder if she thought that I was being sarcastic back, or whether she realised that sarcasm went straight over my head. She liked me either way, so I guess it didn't matter.

"So if you're not ill Josephine, why are you out of bed?"

"Well I have this question, and it's been bugging me for a long time now. I asked Sister Gill today, but I still don't know the answer."

"Well what's the question?"

I explained all about the gypsy and her baby boy, and then I asked her,

"So what I want to know is what's the difference between a boy and a girl?"

Suddenly she started laughing and said,

"Oh, Josephine did you really ask sister Gill that question?"

"Yes, but I didn't get an answer."

"What did she say?"

"She said, that god made a boy a boy, and a girl a girl, but I knew that much, I wanted to know the difference between the two, and why a girl could stay but the baby boy couldn't?"

She was still laughing and through her laughter she said,

"Look Josephine, I'm afraid I can't answer that question either."

"Why not?" I asked

"Because it's not my place."

"Well can I ask Caroline to ask dad, when she writes to him."

"No you can't. You have to copy the letters off the board. You would be in serious trouble if you wrote your own letter. Don't you realise the nun's read your letters before posting them."

"Oh" I said, thankful that she hadn't fallen in. Caroline had been sending off sly letters to dad for a year or so now, getting ex-convent girls to post them for her when they came to visit, or posting it without a stamp when we were out on our Sunday walks. Trust my big mouth, I had nearly let the cat out of the bag and got Caroline a big beating.

"Well how am I going to find out the difference then, if you won't tell me?"

"You will find out the difference when you're older."

"Why, is there something wrong with boys?"

"Oh Josephine, you are too inquisitive for your age. No there is nothing wrong with boys. However, you must never ask that question again. There is a difference, but you are too young to know about it yet. You will find out about all that when you're older. Now promise me you will forget about boy's and girl's for the time being. If you ask Sister Gill again, you might be in trouble, so just forget about it, okay."

"Yes." I answered in a sulking manner. I still didn't know the difference, but from her tone of voice I decided to drop the subject. Like she said, I'd find out when I got older. I just couldn't wait to get older now.

"Now don't sulk," she said, "come here and give me a cuddle."

I went closer and hugged her and suddenly I thought about Dr Mongay. He used to give me lovely cuddles like this and I missed him and his cuddles. I wondered why he hadn't been to see me, but I didn't have that answer either.

Suddenly the matron patted my behind, and said,

"Now young lady, back to bed before we're both in trouble."

I giggled and ran back to bed, closing the door of the cubical behind me.

She just smiled and put her head back down to read her magazine.

CHAPTER 30

Francis lay in bed reading a letter he had just received from his father. It confirmed that he would be leaving Ballinrobe to return to London and that David and Edna had decided to have a holiday and pick him up at the same time. Francis couldn't believe what he was reading. How on earth did his father expect to bring Edna back to Ballinrobe, she wasn't his wife. Everyone would be talking about them. The fact that she was English made matters even worse. Francis decided he would go downstairs and ring his father. He didn't want to offend his Uncle Leonard by having a English woman staying here. He had to set his father straight.

It was Edna that answered the phone,

"Hello Francis, what a pleasent surprise" she said,

"Hello Edna, is my father there?" he asked, not entering into a conversation with her.

"Yes lad, I'll go call him for you. she said wondering why Francis was always so cold towards her. She never did the lad any harm. Still he had had a very unpleasent life, maybe that was just his way she thought, and went to call David.

David came to the phone and said, "Hello Francis, did ya get me letter lad?"

"Yes I did. As a matter of fact that's why I'm ringing."

"What's the problem lad?, David asked noting the concern in his son's voice.

"Well, I'm not sure it's such a good idea bringing Edna to Ballinrobe, that's all dad."

"Well don't concern yaself Francis," David said in a hurt tone, "I'm not bringing her to Ballinrobe. We're going ta Dublin for our holiday, and I'll travel by meself ta Ballinrobe ta pick ya up, then we'll both go back ta Dublin, pick up Edna and return ta London."

"Oh, I see" said Francis a little embarrassed and ashamed of himself. "Well how have you both been then?"

David was short with him and answered, "We're both fine Francis, and I'd best be getting off the phone, Edna and I were just going over to the Nelson for a couple of drinks."

Francis noticed the change in his father's tone and said,

"Okay dad, I'll see you both in a couple of weeks then. I'll look forward to it."

"Yea, yea," David said and hung up the receiver leaving Francis on the other end listening to a dead line.

Francis regretted making the phone call, he should have known better. Now he had offended his father, but there wasn't much he could do about it. He just got so jealous of Edna sometimes even though he didn't want to be. He felt that Edna was becoming the most important person in his father's life. Plus he didn't want Edna replacing his mother in any way.

Francis went back up to bed looking forward to seeing his father again. It had been nearly two years since he saw him last. He couldn't believe that he would soon be going in the Navy either, and he went to sleep happy with this last thought, forgetting about how he had just upset his father. Instead he was thinking about how grand life was going be in the Navy.

David and Edna ventured off on their holiday. Edna was in her glory. She had never been away before and she was having the time of her life. Dublin was a beautiful place and very friendly. David even brought her a ruby ring while they were there, which added to her happiness. It wasn't anything elaborate, but to Edna it was worth millions. David didn't often buy anything for her and he had never bought her jewellery before. He didn't need to, she loved him dearly without the gifts. In fact, that's an under-statement, she worshiped the ground he walked on and would have died for him.

After two weeks in Dublin David left Edna and went to Ballinrobe to pick up Francis and spend a week with his family. It was good seeing Francis and his family again and David felt at ease wtih them this time. He also went to visit his parent's graves while he was there, and made his peace with his mother. (He didn't come and visit us though.)

The week flew by and David and Francis returned to Dublin to pick up Edna. David and Edna had previously planned to only stay in Dublin for one night with Francis before returning to London. However, Francis wanted to stay a couple of days to have a look around and do some shopping, so David changed their travelling arrangements.

Francis had saved most of the wages Leonard had paid him over the last two years, but he went on a real spending spree in Dublin. Amongst other things, he bought himself a very expensive, white wool jacket.

When David saw the jacket he thought it looked sissy and commented

"Why on earth did ya buy a white jacket Francis, don't ya realise it will be as black as the ace of spades in just a few days?"

"No it won't dad, I'll look after it."

"It don't matter how much ya look after it lad, with all the smog in London, just wearing it will make it filthy."

"Oh don't exaggerate dad, besides I'll need it for the interview at the Navy offices."

"What interview, ya just fill in some forms and send em off. They'll write and tell ya if ya accepted or not."

"Oh, I didn't realise that. Oh well it doesn't matter, I can keep it for best, don't you think it's kind of swell?"

"No, I think it's kinda poofie meself." David said, looking at the jacket and laughing.

"Oh dad, you haven't any style at all. You're too old fashioned, that's your problem."

David didn't say any more, he realised that Francis was taking offence and decided to change the subject."

"Well what do ya think about Dublin lad, have ya enjoyed ya stay ere?"

"Yes I have dad, it's been really swell. I couldn't live here though, I much prefer Ballinrobe."

"Yea, it's quiter there, but the people are so set in their ways, they make me sick sometimes."

"Oh they're alright dad, just a little old fashioned, a bit like you." Francis said with a laugh, as he admired his jacket again.

The following day all three left on a ferry for London. Francis loved the boat. He spent the whole trip talking to the crew and looking out to sea. When David finally caught up with him he asked,

"Where on earth have ya been lad, I've not seen hide nor hair of ya since we got on the ferry."

"Oh dad, it's just so exciting and there's so much to see. I can't wait to join the Navy, I just can't wait. You know when I ran away from the Christian Brothers School and was hiding on the boat, it took all my strength not to look around. If I hadn't have been so scared of getting caught I would have investigated every nook and cranny, but this trip has really made up for it."

They arrived home at 8.45pm and Edna made some tea for them all. It had been a long day and they were all tired from the journey. The tea relaxed them, and they all went to bed.

The next morning David got up before the others and went to get the application forms for the Navy. When Francis got up he found Edna in the kitchen preparing breakfast,

"Where's my father?" he inquired.

"Oh he'll be back soon lad, he's just gone out to pick up your Navy applications. Now sit down here and have some breakfast."

Francis sat down and ate in silence. Edna felt uncomfortable with the silence, but couldn't think of anything to say to Francis, he was so hard to talk to when his father wasn't around.

After he finished eating, he excused himself by saying,

"I'll just go and tidy up my room Edna."

"Don't be silly lad, you relax, I'll clean it up later for you."

"No, that's fine, I'm used to cleaning up after myself."

"Well you don't have to in this house. You deserve a rest before you go off to the Navy."

Francis became short tempered and snapped back at Edna,

"Look, I'm old enough to clean up after myself. Besides, I don't want anyone in my room, I like my privacy, so stay out of there, understand."

"I'm sorry Francis, I wasn't trying to be nosey luv, I was only trying to help."

"Well I don't need your help, I'll clean up after myself."

"That's fine, if that's what you want."

"That's what I want," Francis said pushing his chair in and walking out of the kitchen.

Edna was dumbfounded, what is the matter with that boy she thought. The more I try to help him, the worse he treats me. She decided not to mention it to David, it was best for everyone if it was just forgotten about.

David returned with the forms shortly after. He ate breakfast and then he and Francis filled in the forms together and went out to post them.

Later that evening after tea, David relaxed in his favorite chair and dozed off to sleep. Edna came in from the kitchen, and seeing David taking a nap, decided to begin a fire. When she lit the paper she threw the match in the fire place. However it didn't go right in, and some of the ashes from the fire came out on to the outer bricks.

Francis got up from his chair and immediately grabbed a dustbin and handbush and began sweeping up the few ashes.

Edna watching him, said,

"Don't worry about that Francis, I'll clean it all tomorrow morning, when the ashes have cooled."

"That's alright, I can't stand seeing it there."

"Seeing what there?"

"This match and ashes."

"That's nothing, don't worry yourself."

"Well it get's on my nerves. I like a tidy, clean house. That's what I'm used to." (He had obviously forgotten what our house was like in Ballinrobe, or maybe that's why he was so fastidious now. Maybe he had a psychological problem.)

Edna decided not to argue with him and said,

"Okay Francis if it bothers you I'll clean it."

"Don't worry about it, I'll clean it myself." he said in a angry tone which woke David up.

"What's going on ere?" David asked.

"Nothing David luv," Edna answered, not wanting to cause a fuss, "Francis was just cleaning up a mess I made when I was lighting the fire, that's all."

"Oh," he said believing that he must have imagined the harshness in his son's tone due to being half asleep.

About two weeks later Francis got a letter of acceptance from the Navy. The letter also informed him that the ship he had been stationed to left at the end of the month and would be away for four months. Francis was over the moon with joy. His life long dream had suddenly come true.

David and Edna went to see him off and reminded him to write to both themselves, and his sisters. He promised he would and he did. It was nice hearing from him after so long. He hadn't bothered with us at all when he was in Ireland, so it was a real treat hearing from him now. His letters made Caroline especially happy, because it represented the freedom that would soon be hers.

About three weeks after Francis had left, David received a letter from him, it read:

Dear dad,
Life on the ship is very exciting and fulfilling and although I miss you, I'm extremely happy. I've meet someone wonderful on board called Michael Sheppard. Like myself, he's a sailor. He has been a wonderful friend to me and has helped me in many ways. I hope you don't mind, but I have invited him to stay with us in London when we get back and I'm writing to get your permission. I'm sure you will not mind, as he really is a lovely person and I'm sure you will get along just fine.
He will pay his own way of course, and don't worry about where he will sleep because he can share my room, the same as we do aboard ship. I hope you will not mind, as it will make me very happy having him with me.
Your loving son,
Francis.

David was shocked and ashamed at his son's letter. It was

blunt and demanding and hadn't even menditioned Edna at all, not even at the top of the page. David didn't even show the letter to Edna, not wanting to hurt her feelings. Francis hadn't even asked how they both were. David read the letter again and wondered how Francis could be so selfish sometimes, and hoped that he wouldn't turn out just like his mother. That night David answered his son's letter. He opened the letter by saying that Edna and he were fine, and that he didn't have any objections to having his friend stay at the house, as long as they both respected Edna and himself, and he underlined the word Edna. Francis got his fathers message loud and clear and every letter that came after that, was addressed to both Edna and David.

The time soon arrived for Francis to return home. David was looking forward to seeing his son again, but he wasn't looking forward to meeting his friend Michael. He was a bit worried about having someone else in the house. As it happened Michael turned out to be a lovely young lad, and very polite. David and Edna took to him straight away. However, Francis became very secretive and put a lock on his bedroom door, which David didn't like at all. This was his house and he didn't like locked doors. He began to wonder why his son and Micheal went to bed so early and why they locked the door. He wondered if they were lovers, but rejected the idea as nonsense. No son of his was a poof. However, he never confronted him with it, but he did question the lock on the door. Francis told David that ever since the Christian Brothers Home, that he had a phobia of someone coming in his room at night and David accepted that without question. The truth was he didn't want to pursue it, because he didn't want to know the truth about his son. In fact his son was a homosexual and was having a sexual relationship with Michael.

About a month after they came home, Francis and Micheal received instructions to leave again, only this time it was for nine months, much to David's dissappointment. Francis cleaned his room, changed his sheets, and locked his bedroom door before leaving, even though he knew his father hated locked doors and secrets.

CHAPTER 31

Winnie sat knitting in the lounge with Richard snoozing in the arm chair beside her. Things hadn't been so great between them lately, and Winnie was growing tiresome of the relationship.

Since she told Richard about her six children back in Ireland, there was a certain tension in the air, even though she made Richard believe that her husband had run off with another woman and left her with five children, pregnant and no money to feed them, and that the authorities consequently took the children and put them in a home until they reached the age of sixteen. She hadn't mentioned Dr Flannery or her stay in prison, which was just as well, the news of the children had made him withdrawn enough for her liking.

The reason she told Richard about the children, was because she knew that Francis was out now, and probably with David which she resented. The truth was, she realised that she still loved David and wanted him back. Richard was becoming a bore. All Richard thought about was his work. He worked irregular hours and a lot of shift work, which got on her nerves because they had no social life at all. He was a timid person, more like a pet than a man, and their lovemaking was non-existent. At least David had been a good lover, and Winnie actually missed all the excitement of their firey arguements.

Winnie began writing to Francis, just before he was supposed to get out of the home. Her first letter gave details of her address, her new name and phone number and details of the story she conveyed to Richard, but she received no reply. Her second letter was returned saying not known at this address.

Winnie gathered that Francis had left the convent, and was living with David. She didn't want to contact the Christian Brothers School personally, because she didn't want them knowing who she was, but she needed to contact Francis. She hoped that Francis could re-unite her with David. She also hoped that Francis had forgiven her and would come to stay with her. That was the only way she could get David back, through the kids. Even then she only had a slim chance. That's why she had told Richard about the children, she couldn't tell him after Francis was living with them. She still needed Richard's support, at least until she was back with David.

She was pretending to be very understanding towards his moods since she had told him about the children, but he was beginning to aggravate her. He was always complaining about his health and this pain and that. He was like an over grown baby, he was even bald like one. He looked quite attractive when he had his police hat on, but awful without it. However, he paid the bills so she was stuck with him until such time as she got back with David.

Winnie was determined to get her way, she decided to get David back by using the kids. She knew how he adored them, and if they were with her, he would follow too. She knew that he must have Francis living with him, and cursed herself for not contacting Francis a few months earlier. (Little did she know, that Francis had been out for nearly three years.) Winnie looked up the phone number of the hostel where David was supposedly staying, and dialed the number.

Winnie had a plan, first she was going to abuse him for stealing her son, then she was going to inform him that she was on her way to Scotland to collect Francis. However, when she got through to the hostel she was told that David moved out about three years ago, and was now living in London, as far as they knew.

Winnie couldn't believe her luck, this was going to be easier than she thought, and less expensive. She looked through the London Telephone directories and there it was, David's name, address and phone number. She decided not to confront him on the phone now, she would just show up on his doorstep and really take him by surprise.

She knew what she was going to tell Francis, the same story that Richard had been told. That it was David who had been having an affair, and that he wrote and told her that he was leaving her and the kids, and that she felt desparate, and because of a sense of insecurity she had left with Doctor Flannery, who had been there to comfort her in her time of need. Then she was going to explain how she believed that David's mother would take care of him and his sisters, and that she never would have left if she thought that the authorities would take them.

Winnie's main objective was to portray David and his family as being selfish and totally un-caring for the children. She knew Francis would believe her, he loved her. He always had loved her the best. Then she would play the part of the forgiving wife and make-up with David. First she would get Francis on her side, then she would seduce David back into her bed.

A couple of weeks later, Richard was on night duty at the police station. Winnie knew that he always rang at about 8pm to see how she was and to inform her that he had arrived safely. So this night she waited for his call and when it came, she told Richard that she was feeling poorly and was going to have an early night. This ensured her that he wouldn't call again, which gave her six hours to do what she had to do. As soon as Winnie hung up on Richard she put on her coat and left the house.

"Edna, will ya hurry up luv, it's already eight thirty, the Nelson will be closed if ya don't hurry yaself up."

"Oh David don't be so impatient, I'll be down a in minute."

"Well hurry up, I don't know what takes ya so long, it's only accross the road we're going, not ta a ball ya know."

"Yes I know, but I still like to look my best. Besides I'm finished now."

David went to the hallway cupboard to get their coats as Edna walked down the stairs.

"About time" he mumbled, more to himself than Edna.

As Edna approached the bottom of the stairs there was a loud banging at the front door.

"I'll get it David," Edna said.

"Okay luv.,"

The banging got louder and louder and Edna yelled out,

"Hold on, hold on, I'm coming."

Edna opened the door just as David came back down the hallway with the coats.

"Yes." Edna asked when she saw a stranger standing at the door, "Can I help you."

"Yea, you can help me you foocking home wrecker. Where's my husband and son?"

Edna was shocked. She didn't know who Winnie was. At first she thought that this angry women was at the wrong house. She was just about to tell her this when David marched up and pulled the half closed door fully open, taking a long look at Winnie.

"What the foocking hell are ya doing ere tramp. Haven't ya caused enough trouble. Foock off away from me door before I foocking kill ya."

Edna, now realising who it was backed away from the door. This was something David and Winnie had to sort out. It really wasn't any of her business, but what a cheek she had coming here Edna thought.

"Where's my son?" Winnie spat at David.

"He's not your son anymore, you gave him up six years ago for ya foocking doctor friend."

"I never gave him up and I want him back. It was me that reared him all those years by meself while you were galavanting in Scotland."

"Galavanting, that's a foocking joke, don't ya mean paying the bills, while you were galvanting with ya foocking doctor. Ya nowt but a foocking tramp Winnie."

"Well this tramp is a mother, and I want me son back. I'll wait here all night if I have ta, and I'll take him with me when he comes home."

"Well he's not here."

"Don't give me that, he's past sixteen so I know he's ere."

"Look women, I've had the lad since he was fourteen, but he ain't ere now, he left about three weeks ago, and he won't be back for nine months, so you'll have a bloody long wait out there." David said with a short laugh.

"What are you talking about, nine months?"

"He's joined the Navy and his ship left, and won't be back for nine months."

"Well you mark my words David Lynch, I'll be back, and I'll take my son off you next time I'm ere."

"There won't be a next time Winnie, I don't want ya calling round ere again, I've got me own life now and I don't want ya round messing it up. So stay away, or you'll be getting what ya deserve, and I'll be giving it to ya."

"Oh, I'll be back David, ya better believe it. I want my son, you can go to hell, but I'll get Francis off you."

"Look Winnie me and my lady friend were just going out, so why don't ya leave ya number and address and I'll be sure ta pass it on ta Francis. Now foock off ta what ever man ya with now."

"Lady friend, that's a joke. I must say ya standards have lowered David, are ya struggling ta find a decent women for yaself, old man."

"Look bitch, it's all I can do ta stop meself hitting ya one. You leave Enda out of this, you're not bloodly good enough ta lick her shoes, not alone talk about her. Now piss off before I make ya sorry ya came."

Winnie backed off, she still knew that David's temper was terrible, and from the tone of his voice he was just about to lose it, so she said.

"I'll go David, but I'll be back and don't think about running away, cause I'll find ya and I will get me boy back."

"Me, run, ya must be foocking joking. I'll never run from the likes of you, or any women. I'll still be ere, but ya better not let me catch ya at me door again Winnie. I want no more ta do with ya, now foock off."

Winnie turned and left. He hasn't seen the last of me she thought, I'll be back, maybe next time I'll have the police with me she thought, thinking about Richard. He might come in handy after all. Furthermore, I'll get David back too, that ugly bitch he's with doesn't stand a chance against me, she's like a dried up old prune Winnie thought, and laughed to herself about David's new woman, and the remark she had made to David about her.

That night in bed, Winnie started planning how she was going to get David back. Little did she realise that she had no chance, no matter what she did. Edna may not have been as attactive as Winnie, but she was an honest, genuine person. Everything that Winnie could never be, and everything that David wanted in a partner.

CHAPTER 32

St Patrick's day was close and the whole convent was looking forward to it. It was a very special day in Ireland and like Christmas and Easter was a day of celebration in the convent. There was no chores to be done, and no school on St Patrick's day. It was treated like a Sunday, a recreational day with traditional folk dancing during the evening. This particular St Patricks day was going to be a special one for us all. It was also one we would never forget.

Caroline was coming up to her sixteenth birthday and I was nine years old. Caroline had completed and passed her leaving exam, which was surprising because none of us were very bright. I guess out of all of us though Caroline and Pauline were the smartest.

We were all sitting in the playroom doing different activties. Some were practicing for their dance routines that evening, some were sewing costumes, some playing paino, and some like me, just happy doing nothing and laughing with our friends. Today I was playing with our baby sister Doreen. She was four years old now and a sweet natured child. She wasn't a very pretty child, in fact she was very fat like myself, but she was cute. Sister Angela loved her dearly and didn't let her mix with the rest of us Lynches very much. In fact, if she saw one of us playing with her, she usually called her away and Doreen always went. Sister Angela was the closest thing Doreen had to a mother. She had cared for her since she was only four days old, so I guess they had a strong bonding.

However, Sister Angela and I didn't get along very well and if she was around I always stayed clear of Doreen. Sister

Angela's hands were very free when I was around. Suddenly the loud speaker bell rang and a message came through.

"Would all the Lynch girls except Doreen Lynch, please report to Sister Angela's quarters immediately."

The four of us made our way to the door, and as we gathered in a group we looked at each other wondering what was going on. This was something new to us all, and to be quite honest we were all worried. Even Caroline our leader looked disturbed. When we got outside the room, I asked,

"Caroline what's going on, are we in trouble?"

"I'm not sure Josephine, let's hurry up and get there and find out."

"But I'm scared, they've never called us over the load speaker before."

"That's because they've never wanted us all at the same time. My guess is, that someone has died in the family. It couldn't be visitors because we don't get visitors, so someone must have died."

"Who could have died?"

"Oh Josephine how the hell do I know, I might even be wrong, let's just get there and find out, okay."

I was shocked by Caroline's tone. She never got angry. Maybe she was worried too I thought, and decided to take her advice and shut-up for a change.

When we arrived at Sister Angela's quarters she had visiting clothes layed out for us along with a bowl of water, a flannel and a hairbursh. We were ordered to clean and dress ourselves on the double and told we had vistirs.

I, like the rest of us was excited. Imagine our very own visitors, but who could they be I wondered. Curiosity got the better of me and I asked,

"Sister Angela, who are our visitors?"

She grabbed me by the hair and shock my head taking me by surprise, because usually she gave a slap in the face or accross the ear'ole, but this hurt just as much.

"You're too nosey Josephine and very impatient. A lady should have patience, when are you going to learn that?"

"I'm sorry Sister Angela, I just got excited."

"Please control yourself in the future, now hurry up and you will find out who your visitors are."

I finished brushing my hair (for the second time) and the four of us were lead out to our waiting visitors. There were two ladies and one man waiting there, who I didn't know from a bar of soap. However Caroline and Maureen remembered them and ran over to hug them. I felt kind of left out as did Pauline because I felt her small hand encircle mine, and I looked at her in pity. She pretented to be so tough our Pauline, but she was just as lost and lonely as the rest of us. I squeezed her hand and edged her forward.

"Hello," I said, "this is Pauline and I'm Josephine, who are you?"

"This is ya aunty Phyllis and ya aunty Kathleen, and I'm ya uncle Shamous. We're ya pa's brother and sisters."

"Well where's our dad?" I asked.

"Oh he's in a different country lovie, but when ya sixteen, ya will be going ta live with him."

"Caroline's sixteen, how come she's still here?"

"She's not quite sixteen yet, but as soon as she is, she'll be going ta live with him. In fact ya brother Francis is living with em already. Well he was anyway, till he joined the Navy. When Caroline turns sixteen Francis will come pick her up and take her ta London. By the way Caroline," he said changing the subject, "did ya pass ya leaving exam last year?"

"Yes I did, I did quite well."

"That's great news lass, well done. I want the rest of ya ta do the same too, ya must all study hard."

I was having great trouble understanding them. They talked fast and cut off the end of all their words, but I wanted the conversation back again, so I asked,

"Where do you live, and why haven't you been here to see us before?"

"We live in Ballinrobe dear and have a farm ta run, which keeps us mighty busy with just one man. It's quite a long journey too." my aunt Kathleen answered me.

"Well if it's such a long journey why didn't you want to see Doreen while you here?"

"Doreen ain't our neice luv, and she ain't ya sister either."

"Yes she is, the nun's say her name is Doreen Lynch and she's our sister."

"Well she has the same ma, but a different pa, so she's not our neice, because we're on ya pa's side, not ya ma's side, and she's only ya half sister."

"How can someone be a half sister, that's stupid?"

My aunt Kathleen was getting a bit short for answers for me so she decided to change the subject (just like my uncle had done).

"Josephine, could ya bring me ta the toilet please."

"Yes." I said, realising she didn't want to talk any more. I began to wonder why they had bothered coming if they didn't want to talk to us. It was nice to have our very own visitors though, and I was glad that they came really.

However after aunt Kathleen had finished in the toilet I wasn't so sure if I was so glad they had come anymore. In fact I was speechless. She had shit everywhere except in the toilet bowl. There was shit down each side of the bowl, loads on the rim, and a big lump on the floor just in front of the toilet. I felt so ashamed of her and wondered how she could be so stupid.

I grabbed some toilet paper and picked up the lump on the floor first, and threw it down the toilet heaving as I did so. Then I began cleaning the bowl itself. It stunk and was making me quite ill. She looked at me as I cleaned up her mess, and said,

"What's the matter Josephine?"

"You left poo everywhere." I answered,

"I'm sorry luv, I'm not used ta these toilet things ya know. Back at the farm we use the same place as the cows, the field." She said with a giggle. I didn't find it amusing though, in fact I was quite ashamed of her, but I didn't voice my opinions but she must have noticed it in my expression, because her face went red and she said,

"Come on then, let's get back ta the others."

As she walked off in front of me I saw another lump of shit pressed into the bottom of her long, wool coat. I heaved at the sight of it and said,

"Wait up aunty, there's some more poo on your coat, I'll clean it with some paper."

I wet some paper and cleaned the bottom of her coat real fast. I was hoping that no one would come in and catch us. I didn't want my day of visitors spoiled by the other kids calling them shit bum. I wanted my visitors to be special, but I felt embarrassed by them.

When we got back to the others they were all talking merrily amongst themselves. I soon forgot about the toilet episode and the rest of the visit went quite well. They couldn't believe how quiet Caroline had become. They told us how she had been such a tomboy as a child and always had something to say. Now she was quiet, shy and conservative. Quite a different person.

Uncle Shamous asked her,

"How come ya so quiet now Caroline?"

Caroline shrugged her shoulders without answering. So I answered for her,

"She hates it here, that's why. We all do. It's better to stay quiet because you get hit less. We get smacked every day here for nothing. Especially Caroline, she's got Sister Martha and she's the worst nun here. I'll have her after the next holidays and Caroline said I had better learn to keep my mouth shut all day or I'll always be getting the strap."

"Is that true Caroline?" Uncle Shamous asked.

"Yes it's true, but the more you complain about it or cry, the worse it becomes, so please don't make a fuss with the nun's because we will all be in serious trouble when you leave."

"Why don't ya tell ya pa about it?"

"Because there's nothing he can do anyway. If I told him in one of my sneaky letters, he would answer it showing concern and then the nun's would read it and I'd really be in trouble. I've learnt the best way is to keep your mouth shut, say nothing, and hope the time passes quickly. My time is nearly up. I'm just trying to get Jospehine to understand. Maureen and Pauline aren't too bad, but Jospehine just can't keep her mouth shut. I think she'll be learning the hard way next semester though when she has my nun teaching her."

Everyone just listened to Caroline especially me, I was getting very nervous about Sister Martha. I knew from now I wasn't going to like her. (However I didn't know just how bad she was, but I was going to find out that very same evening.)

"Well at least they taught Pauline ta walk, that's one good thing on their part." Aunty Phyllis said, "Did it take em very long ta teach ya Pauline?"

"They didn't teach me how to walk. They did teach me how

to dance though after I could walk."

"Well who taught ya how ta walk then?"

"Josephine did."

"Josephine, but it was in all the papers that the nun's did."

"Well it was all lies, it was Jospehine who taught me how to walk, we had lessons every morning."

"Oh!" she said in a surprised tone then dropped the subject.

When the end of the visit came, our aunties and uncle gave us some fruit, lollies and some St Patrick's day badges and ribbons. We were allowed to keep the ribbons and badges ourselves, but the fruit was shared with everyone. Before they left I asked them if they would call more often, and they said they would. However, often must have different definitions for different people, because it had taken them six years for their first visit, and they never came again!

After they left we changed back into our uniforms and were quizzed by Sister Angela about the visit and what was said. We told her everything, except the fact that Francis was coming to get Caroline. In our minds, we thought that they might try to stop her going if they knew. We didn't realise that we could all legally go at age sixteen until after Caroline left. After we had changed our clothes we were told to return to the playroom. Pauline was told to start preparing for the dance routines later on in the evening. The rest of us were free to do what we wanted.

I couldn't wait to tell Linda all about our visitors. I wasn't going to tell her about the shit though, that was too embarrassing even for Linda to know. I told her how our older brother Francis was going to come and collect Caroline on her birthday, and take her to another country to live with our dad.

She asked me if she could come with me when I left, and I promised her I'd ask my father to take her too when the time came for me to leave.

Later on in the evening the dancing began and as usual it was Pauline who opened up the dance. I have to admit though she was good and had come a long way from being a cripple. She was now eight years old and still beautiful and intelligent. You would never believe that she was once lame. She had the most beautiful pair of legs you could imagine, even for a child. (They only improved with age, not like mine. I always had big fat ones, until I was about eighteen or so.)

Several other folk dances were performed in the middle of this large room, with all the girls who were watching sitting in a big circle around them. There was actually three sessions of dancing so that there was plenty of room. Everybody had a clear view of what was going on and the time passed quickly. Sister Martha was organizing the dance festivities and she sat on the sideline announcing the dancers before they danced. However, she must have got bored with the tradional dancers during the last session (which we were at) because she started to call some of the older girls who couldn't dance or were too shy, to the floor. First she called a couple of fatties and laughed as they stumbled over their own feet and of course the rest of the children laughed too. It was so embarrassing for the ones dancing, but great fun for everyone else.

Then she called Janette Motten and my sister Caroline to perform a duo. Both of these girls were very conservative children, who never gave any trouble at all. They just liked to be left alone. However, Sister Martha who taught them hated their demure natures and took every chance she could to show them up. She really was a cruel nun. Both girls came to the middle of the floor when they were called but they just stood there.

"Well, we're waiting." Sister Martha said,

Both girls continued just standing there. Sister Martha rose from her chair and released the strap around her waist. Then she began strapping both girls across the back of the legs.

"Maybe this will get you warmed up." she said as she lashed out at them.

My heart was in my mouth and I kept praying for Caroline to just move one foot to keep Sister Martha happy. I begged her silently not to be so stubborn, but Caroline didn't hear my silent plea and she didn't move either.

Eventually Caroline's legs began to bleed from the whacks she was getting, and my heart began to bust. I felt like running up and punching Sister Martha in the face, but I was too scared. Caroline had told me that Sister Martha was cruel and always strapped her girls in class, but this was the first time I saw her in action and she really was a monster. Much worse than I could have imagined anyone to be.

Sister Martha was getting very annoyed by this stage, but when she saw the blood on Caroline's legs she stopped the strapping. Caroline had parents to answer to!

She decided to change her tactics. She grabbed a pair of scissors that someone had been using for their costume and unfortunately for Caroline, had left on the piano and she said,

"Well if you two won't do as your told I'll make an example of you both."

She pulled Janette Motten closer to her, and cropped off all her hair. By the time she had finished Janette had hardly any hair left at all and the little she did have was sticking up all over the place. She looked a total mess.

The whole room was quite now. No one was laughing any more. Least of all me. My insides were totally knotted up. I kept wishing that they would both just move a few steps and finally Janette did. She jumped up and down a few times and was allowed to sit down straight away.

Sister Martha turned to Caroline with the scissors still in her hand and said,

"Okay Lynch now it's your turn. Are you going to dance, or am I going to cut your hair off too?"

Caroline just stood there. She didn't say a word, cry a tear, or move a muscle. Sister Martha got closer to her as if to cut of her hair and Caroline raised her hands to protect the little hair she had. However, instead of trying to move her hands and cut the hair, Sister Martha began hitting her repeatedly with the scissors across the back of the hands. I wanted to scream and run out there to protect my sister, but there was nothing I could do except get a beating along with her. Each blow seemed to be harder then the one before. I looked over at Maureen and Linda and they were both crying silent tears like myself, but still Caroline wouldn't give in. Not one sound came from her, and not one dance step did she do. She just stood there frozen, taking the beating without even a murmur coming from her.

Sister Martha, becoming very frustrated began to use another tactic.

"Look Lynch, we can stay here all night and you'll not eat, but you will do a dance. Even if it's only one step. You will do it."

Caroline didn't answer, she didn't move, she just looked straight ahead.

"Okay let's go out by ourselves to the play ground, and you can do a dance by yourself with no one looking." Sister Martha said. She was becoming desperate now and willing to compromise, just to get Caroline to give in to her demands.

When Caroline still stood there not moving a muscle she dragged her outside, but once in the playground Caroline just stood there frozen again.

"Now then," Sister Martha said, "We're by ourselves. I just want you to put one foot in front of the other for me, and we'll forget the whole affair."

Caroline didn't answer, she just stood there staring out at the yard. Suddenly Sister Martha gave her such a slap across the face she knocked Caroline down. It was more of a punch than a slap. Caroline lay on the ground stunned, still not moving.

"You're a stubborn little girl Lynch and you will be punished severely in life by god. Now pick yourself up and get to dinner." She walked back inside leaving Caroline lying on the ground. When she came back inside she dismissed us all for dinner.

I wanted to run outside and see how Caroline was, but just as the bell went for dinner Caroline walked in.

She looked as white as a ghost. She didn't eat any dinner either and Sister Angela sent her to bed for not eating her meal. I believe that Caroline was actually thankful for this punishment and smiled gently at me as she left the dining room.

Our St Patricks day that year started out lovely with our visitors but ended terribly. Later that night I crept up to Caroline's bed to see how she was.

"Hi Caroline, how are you feeling?" I asked

"Not very well Josephine I feel quite ill and very shaken, but I'll be okay."

"Did you do the dance outside for the old bag?"

"No I didn't?"

"Did you cry outside?"

"No I didn't, I wouldn't give her the satisfaction of seeing me cry. Besides it just gives them another excuse to hit you. They must get pleasure out of it."

"I felt so sorry for you, I cried myself." I said.

"Well you shouldn't. You have to be strong in this place Josephine. I keep telling you that. Besides I haven't got much longer here, just a few more months. I'm more worried about the rest of you when I leave. Which reminds me, your friend Linda is lovely, but you two get into too much trouble together. Next term you will have Sister Martha, so you will have to stay out of trouble. Please Josephine, promise me you will. You saw how bad she was today and she's like that all the time, so please be careful."

"I will" I promised, but it wasn't a sincere promise. It was a promise to stop my big sister from nagging me.

"Look you better get back to bed," she said. "We've been in enough trouble for one day. Go past Maureen and Pauline and let them know I'm alright. Also tell Maureen that I need her strength now and to stop crying because I'll be going soon and she will have to look out for the rest of you, including Doreen."

"Okay." I said and told her not to worry, that we would be fine when she left. I went past Maureen first and she felt better knowing Caroline was okay. Then I went to Pauline. That bitch was sitting in bed admiring the new shoes that she received for St Patricks day. I never received new shoes and it didn't worry me in the slightest. She got them all the time and yet she was so excited about them. She was a greedy, selfish cow and at that moment I hated her. When I told her that Caroline still wasn't feeling well she answered.

"What are you telling me for, I'm not a doctor."

"You have a heart of stone Pauline, you think about no one but yourself. You just wait till one of the older girls pick on you again, I'll start looking at my old shoes and you can look after yourself." I said and stormed off to bed.

The next morning, it was back to school and the normal routine. However, at breakfast Caroline still wasn't feeling the best. She was weak and still in shock from the night before. Because she hadn't allowed herself to cry and kept all the tension inside, she had made herself ill.

She sat looking at her breakfast for what seemed the longest time, then she took a mouthful of porrdige and heaved on it.

Caroline decided to just sit there and wait for the next bell to ring but Sister Angela walked past and noticed she wasn't eating again.

"Why aren't you eating Lynch?" she asked.

"I don't feel very hungry Sister Angela."

"Well that's too bad because you're going to have it anyway."

Sister Angela picked up a spoonful of porridge and started shoving it down Caroline's throat. It was even making me feel sick watching it. Suddenly Caroline heaved and pushed the spoon away from her mouth in an effort to breath, but the spoonful of porridge flung up and hit Sister Angela right in the face. The whole dining room started to laugh, which made it worse for poor Caroline. Sister Angela quickly wiped her face and told us all to shut up. Then she turned to Carolne and said,

"Stand up Lynch."

Caroline stood up and was about to turn and face Sister Angela but she didn't get the chance. She was knocked right back down again. As she fell she knocked her head on the table and landed in a heap on the floor.

"Get up" Sister Angela ordered but Caroline didn't move.

"Get up I say," she said as she nudged her with her foot, but still Caroline didn't move. Then someone screamed,

"She's bleeding, her head's bleeding."

Everyone stood up trying to get a better view of Caroline, but only those closest could see. As I looked down at her, I honestly thought she was dead. I kept thinking they've killed my sister, my sisters dead, but no words would come out I was totally shocked.

Caroline wasn't dead. She had taken a hard blow to the head which had knocked her out cold and she was suffering from concussion. The doctor was called, but they told him that she fell down the stairs and Caroline didn't argue the point. If it were me, I'm sure I would have done, I would have made sure the doctor knew the truth.

Caroline was still alive in body, but they had finally managed to kill her spirit. She wasn't the same child that had come into this home, but then I guess none of us were, or ever would be again.

It took a few weeks for Caroline to go back to school, but she was never really well again. The doctor was called in frequently for her during her last months at the convent because she was constantly ill. She sunk even deeper into herself and was even more reserved then she had ever been. In fact she very rarely spoke at all, even to us.

Caroline didn't really pick up until about two weeks before she was to leave with Francis. Then she seemed to get a new lease on life. Maybe she could see a light at the end of the tunnel. She told us years later that she worried for us continuously those last few months. She worried that without her the nuns would kill us all. She worried about Linda and myself getting into trouble and being in Sister Martha's class. But most of all she worried about not having us with her anymore. She still depended on us, even though none of us knew it at the time. I was just as worried about her as she was about us. She got sick so often those last few months, I was getting worried that she wouldn't be going at all. I felt worried that if she didn't leave our father wouldn't want any of us. One night I remember telling Caroline this and I gave her an old cruifix that I had swapped for a holy picture with one of the other girls. It was broken but for some reason I cherished it. I told Caroline that the cross would make her well and that she had to go because our dad wouldn't want any of us if she didn't go. She assured me that she would be fine and our dad would always want us, no matter what.

CHAPTER 33

The holidays came around again. Normally I was in my glory when the holidays came, because Linda and I had so much fun. Apart from the extra chores like knitting and turning the mattresses etc, there wasn't much to do, but have fun. However these holidays were different. I didn't really want them to come around so fast, because it meant that we would have Sister Martha next semester, and it also meant that Caroline would be leaving us. I was looking forward to seeing my brother again, even though I didn't really know him. It was seven years since I last saw Francis, and I had been so young then only three years old. I had no idea what he looked like. I didn't remember him at all. However, he was my brother, and I couldn't wait to see him.

The holidays were still fun. Linda and I went everywhere together. We were closer then sisters at times, because we never argued. Within the first couple of days of the holidays Linda and I were in trouble again. The day came for turning and beating the mattresses on the bed and Linda came up with a fabulous idea.

"I've got a great idea, Josephine", she said.

"What is it?"

"Well, after we have spanked the lives out of these mattresses and turned them over, why don't we take off these horrible petticoats and hide them under my mattress. They won't be found, because the beds won't be touched again until tomorrow. Then we can take a nice cool walk to the orchards after lunch."

"That sounds great Linda. It will give my fat legs a chance to cool down." I giggled.

However, we must have been overheard or followed because we got caught. We finished doing the beds and pulled off our flannelette petticoats and hid them under Linda's mattress. Then after lunch we went over to the orchard. It felt so good having only underpants on and we ran all the way up the hill to the orchards killing ourselves laughing. We were in a world of our own and had no idea that we were being followed.

At the top of the hill there was a fence dividing one paddock from another. On our side of the fence was a tin shed and on the other side of the fence was a large apple tree. When we arrived Linda said,

"Come on let's try and get on top of the shed, then we can steal the apples on that tree."

I looked around at all the other apple trees on our side of the fence and said, "There's loads of apples here."

"Yea, but it will be more fun getting those ones up there, just look how red they are."

I started laughing and Linda followed suit. "Alright you go first" I said,

Linda got up on the shed with ease, but when I tried I didn't find it so easy. We were both killing ourselves laughing at me trying to get up on the shed. As I climbed in a very awkward fashion, she attempted to pull me up. It was all she could do to stay up there with my weight hanging of the end of her, but finally I made it. We both lay down on the top of the shed for ages trying to catch our breath, which was almost impossible because we couldn't stop laughing. Eventually we calmed down and began picking the apples. I was sitting on a branch of the apple tree, with Linda holding on to my skirt. As I reached out and got the apples, I passed them back to her. Suddenly we heard someone below coughing. I looked down at Linda hoping it was her, then we both looked down at the ground. We had been followed by Sister Angela and what was worse, she was holding our underwear in her hands. I was so scared I nearly died right there in the tree.

"Josephine Lynch, you come down here this instant and be very careful not to fall." she warned.

"Will you hit us if we come down?"

"No, I will not hit you but just be very careful coming down." (She was worried I'd fall because I had parents, but she didn't care about Linda falling. There was no one to report any broken bones to in her case.)

"Do you promise not to smack us?" I repeated.

"I promise, now get down here this instant."

We both came down and when we were safely on the ground she beat the living day lights out of us, right there on the hill. We got so many slaps across the face, I was starting to believe that she would never stop, but she did eventually. Then she produced our underwear for us to see again.

"What is the meaning of this?" she demanded.

"We wanted to stay cool." Linda said.

"And who's idea was this, might I ask?"

Both of us answered together,

"It was mine."

"Oh you two will never learn" she said rolling her eyes. Then she gave us both back our underwear, only she placed it on our heads not in our hands.

"Now you can both wear these on your heads for the rest of the day, including in the playroom after tea."

Linda and I looked at each other and it was all we could do to stop ourselves from laughing. We looked really stupid. It reminded me of a black wedding veil, but I couldn't say anything until later. Not without getting into trouble again. We also got another punishment, we were told that the next day we would have to stay in bed all day and do knitting by ourselves. One each end of the room. We didn't mind though, in fact it turned out to be good fun. These petticoats weren't good fun though, everyone laughed at us all afternoon. They thought we had pissed the bed and wouldn't believe us when we told them what really happened.

The next day Linda was in her bed and I was in mine. For the first hour or so we were good, and got on with our knitting without talking. We couldn't talk, because we would have had to scream at each other, because of the distance between us. However I became very bored having to keep my mouth shut for so long. So I snuck out of bed and ran down to Linda's bed as quickly as I could.

"Why don't you come and sit on my bed then we can do our knitting together" I said.

"You come and sit on mine."

"No I'm closer to the toilets, and the door, so we can hear if someone is coming, and if we do you can hide your knitting under the covers, and say you were going to the toilet. If I get caught up here there's no excuse."

Linda saw my point of view, and packed her knitting up and followed me down to my bed. As it happened no-one came to check on us anyway. So we spent the day merrily chatting away to each other and racing each other along the rows of knitting. We seemed to find fun in everything we did. Just being together was fun for us.

The holidays went fine for the next couple of days and we didn't get caught doing anything naughty or mischievous. I think half the fun was knowing that we could be caught and we felt so clever getting away with things. One day during dinner Linda whispered,

"Look at the rubbish they feed us. Always vegetables and sliced meat. The nuns and matrons get lovely thick chops and steaks and we have to eat this rubbish."

"It's not that bad." I said.

"Yes it is, it's terrible. The cats get better than us."

"How do you know?"

"Because I've seen them being fed. They get the nuns left overs, and it sure beats this rubbish."

"Really, well why don't we go and take the cats food tonight."
Linda started giggling quietly and said, "What a great idea Josephine, you really are smart sometimes."

So after tea instead of going to the playroom, Linda and I snuck out back and waited behind the rubbish bins until the nuns came to feed the cats. That fifteen minutes seemed like a couple of years and I was starting to wonder if we would be missed, but finally out came a nun, it was Sister Martha of all people. We waited for her to go back inside, then Linda shooed away all the cats and the pair of us sat down to enjoy our dinner of real meat.

However, what had once been juicy lamb chops, were now only bones and fat, but we still dug in. We sucked and picked at those old bones like we had never been fed before. They were so tasty. We didn't even speak to each other. Suddenly the door flew open again and Sister Martha stood there with another plate of bones for the cats. I don't know who was more horrified, her or us. We must have looked pretty revolting sitting there. I was so scared, I nearly wet my pants. I couldn't even get up, I just sat there looking up into her face.

"Get up" she screamed,

That made me move, we both jumped up dropping the bones we had been eating with relish.

"You, dirty, filthy, little beasts." she said as she shook the pair of us by the ears.

"You two are about to get the hiding of your lives, get up against that wall."

We did as we were told. I was so scared my knees felt like

- 276 -

jelly, I saw the way she had treated Caroline for not dancing, so I thought she would kill us for what we just did. She pulled off her belt and doubled it over. Then she commenced strapping the back of our legs with all her might. We received six lashes each and the pain was so severe I nearly passed out. What was worse she took our names and said she would remember them. When she realised I was Caroline's sister she said,

"Ah, you will be in my class next semester and I'll be watching you carefully, both of you. Now get out of my sight, you both make me sick to the stomach."

We didn't need to be told twice, we ran for our lives. I wished with all my heart that this hadn't happened. Now she had it in for both of us even before we were in her class. So I made a suggestion to Linda.

"Oh Linda, now we've really done it. She's going to give us hell next term, I just know she will. I think we had better run away now."

"Oh, don't be silly Josephine, where will we go?"

"I've got my aunts address in Ballinrobe, maybe we could find our way there somehow."

"No, they would catch us, and then we would really be in trouble."

"Oh Linda, I'm really scared about next semester, she's going to make life terrible for us. I really think we should run away tonight."

"We can't run away, we have no money or anything and we would be caught for sure. Besides even if we got to your aunties she might send us back. Can you imagine what trouble we would be in then. They would kill us. The best thing we can do is sneak back inside and hope she forgets us by the time school starts."

I agreed, but I wasn't totally convinced. I knew she would remember us, and I knew she would make things hard.

During the last two weeks of the holidays Linda and I were assigned to Sister Carmel in the orchards to help pick the fruit for selling. We couldn't believe our luck. That was the best duty to get, because you got to eat all the fruit you wanted, without getting into trouble. Our luck was short lived though, Christine Kanavin, my sister Maureen's enemy caught hold of us on our second day at breakfast and threatened us. She said that if we didn't bring her back four red apples each she would beat our brains out.

Sister Carmel was very happy with our work and she was one of the few nun's that was actually nice to us. She allowed us to eat as much fruit as we wanted, and didn't tell us off the whole day. Just before we were about to leave we both stole four red apples, and put them down our knickers. However unlike the first day, today Sister Carmel checked us. She reached down and felt the apples, and then she asked us to remove them. She told us that we were very dirty to put food down there, and that she was very disappointed that we had stolen the fruit when we could eat as much as we wanted anyway. She said that we were very greedy little girls and that she would report us, which she did. However, she reported us to Kathleen Corgorgan, the matron in our dormitory, which wasn't so bad, because she liked me. She also told us that we were not welcome in her orchards again, but we weren't punished. That was the worse punishment we could have got though. It had been fun in the orchards.

Later at dinner Caroline asked me why I was so sad, and when I told her she was furious with me. She reminded me about my promise of staying out of trouble, and told me that I was disgusting. However, when I told her why I did it she said,
"That bitch Christine has gone too far this time. I'll get her

back somehow, just leave it to me."

Later that same night while we were in the playroom and the girls in charge were mending damaged clothes for the next semester, the matron approached them. Not knowing that Caroline already knew, informed her about the apples that I'd stolen. Everyone in the room laughed including Christine Kanavin. Caroline looked at her straight in the face, and said,

"What are you laughing at, they stole the apples for you."

"They did no such thing, I knew nothing about it until now."

"Liar, you threatened to beat them up if they didn't get four red apples each, they told me this afternoon."

"That's a bare face lie Caroline, and you know it."

The matron looked from one to the other, and finally said,

"Well there's only one way to find out, we'll call Josephine and Linda up here and sort this out."

The matron came and got us both from the playroom. We wondered what we had done now, but followed without asking. When we arrived at the dormitory, I was told to wait outside for a moment, while Linda and the Matron went inside. Linda was questioned about the apples and decided to tell the truth, then I was brought inside. When the matron asked me why I had stolen the apples, I knew what was going on. I knew that Linda had been questioned, but I didn't know what she said. It was more important to me that I didn't get Linda into trouble, rather than getting Christine into trouble, so I just stood there and said nothing. The Matron asked me again, and again, but I stood there too afraid of getting Linda into trouble to say a word. Then the Matron said,

"Look Josephine, just tell the truth, it's always the best." I trusted her and told her why we had stolen the apples. As luck would have it our stories were the same, they had to be, it was the truth.

We were sent back to the orchards the next morning,

promising to apologise to Sister Carmel and ask for her forgiveness. She did forgive us and we spent the rest of our holidays in the orchards having great fun, and eating plenty of fresh fruit.

As for Christine, she was given laundry duties for one month, and that was a hell of a job. Caroline had come through for me again as she always did.

CHAPTER 34

The last two weeks of the holidays flew by. We were having so much fun in the orchards we couldn't wait to get there each day. However when the last week of the holidays arrived, I realised that it was Caroline's birthday in a couple of days, and became very depressed. I started hanging around her at nights at dinner and in the playroom. In fact, I spent as much time with her as I was permitted. Maureen did too, but Pauline couldn't have cared less. All she cared about was herself. She had no friends either, because any girl who became close to her got into trouble, so everyone wanted to stay well clear of her. Pauline spent most of her time with our step-sister Doreen. She couldn't get her into trouble, because Sister Angela loved her. In fact, she loved them both, so they made a good pair.

Doreen was five years old now. She was going to school and was very happy. She knew that we were her sisters, but she also knew that she didn't get any parcels sent to her. She was confused by this fact, but she didn't seem to mind. At least she never spoke about it. If Pauline was feeling generous she would give her something out of her parcel, but you can bet it was something she really didn't want herself. I always shared mine with Linda, but would sometimes save something for Doreen. Maureen shared hers with Kitty Kanavin and Doreen. So Doreen didn't really miss out. Caroline would share with one of her friends. She was too old to share with Doreen, there was eleven years difference between them, so the stuff that Caroline received was of no interest to Doreen.

Caroline's birthday arrived and so did our brother Francis. We were all called to Sister Angela's quarters and cleaned up for our visitor. I didn't ask who it was this time, we already knew.

Caroline was packed and ready to leave. Not that she had many belongings to take, but it was still all ready. Caroline had changed the last two weeks. She got a new burst of life and looked radiant. All the nun's were being extremely nice to her too, especially Sister Angela. Since St Patricks day Caroline had been continuously sick. She hardly ate and the doctor was always being called for her. But these last two weeks she was back to her former self. She even laughed a lot lately, she seemed really happy for once in her life. In fact, she was happier than I'd ever seen her. I remember thinking to myself, maybe this is the Caroline my Uncle was talking about. She seemed so carefree and happy.

As we entered the visiting parlour I saw this man dressed in a suit and tie. He was gorgeous. He was just so handsome and his eyes were like magnets, so blue you couldn't help but look at them.

Because it was Caroline's birthday and her last day at the convent, we were allowed to have a special visit. We went to the playroom and all our friends were allowed to come in. Pauline was allowed to do a dance for him and all the girls were making a fuss of him. I felt so proud, this was my brother and he had come to take our sister back to our father, where we would all go one day. I don't think Francis felt so at ease though. I think he was down right uncomfortable with all these girls hanging around. He would have felt much more comfortable if it were a room full of boys I think. He really didn't enjoy the company of girls.

After Pauline danced, Sister Angela did something very strange, she made everyone present sing happy birthday to Caroline. Then she came up and kissed her on the cheek. She was putting on her usual visitor act for Francis. I stood there dumbfounded, I just couldn't believe it. She hated Caroline as much as she hated me, and here she was pretending that she loved her. Then she dismissed the other girls and we were allowed some private time before Francis and Caroline left.

When we were alone Francis showed more affection and hugged us all tightly, he seemed to like me the most for some reason. We just clicked straight away. Maybe it was because we were the only two with black hair. Caroline and Maureen were red heads, and Pauline had white hair, so did Doreen, but Francis didn't know that. Francis suddenly turned to Pauline and said,

"You're a very good dancer Pauline, and to think you couldn't even walk a few years ago. You should be very proud of yourself."

"I know, everyone tells me." she answered in a stuck up tone. She made me sick sometimes, she was so snobby and bossy, but looked like butter wouldn't melt in her mouth. Francis didn't seem to like her very much either and turned his conversation to me.

"Who's this Linda someone?" he asked.

"Linda Mitchell you mean, she's my best friend."

"From what I hear, she's a trouble maker and you two are always getting into trouble. Did you know dad gets a letter nearly every week about the two of you?"

"She's not a trouble maker and she doesn't get me into trouble. We do fun things together that's all. But you can't breath in this place without getting smacked. I really hate it here Francis. I wish it was me that was leaving."

"Well according to the letters, it's Linda doing all the wrong and making you do it too."

"Well that's not true and dad shouldn't believe everything he reads. They only blame her because she's got no parents. We are not naughty anyway, we just like to have fun, but you get smacked for nothing in this place. You can tell dad to send some stuff for her in my parcel too, because she never gets any parcels."

Francis laughed and told me he would pass on my message to dad. Then he turned to Maureen and asked,

"How have you been Maureen?, you're still as thin as ever."

"Oh I'm fine, I just wish Caroline wasn't going, I'm going to miss her so much." Then she burst into tears and I joined in.

Caroline stood up and said, "Now you promised me you wouldn't cry, so don't you start."

But we couldn't help it and soon she started too. I had never seen Caroline cry before. It seemed strange, she came closer to us and hugged us fiercely. She told us she would write to us often, and not to worry. Pauline just sat there in a world of her own looking down at her shoes. It was as if we weren't there. Francis came over and joined in the hugging, telling us all to stop crying and reminding us that one day we would all be together and never separated against our wills again. Then in an effort to produce a happy atmosphere again, he told us that dad had arranged for us to do a typing and shorthand course the last year of our stay, so the time would go faster. He told us that he had to pay extra for that, but he only found out about it when he made arrangements for Caroline to leave and that's why she missed out.

Francis changing the subject seemed to calm us all down and we all sat down again. He made us even happier still when he gave us a pound each. "This is too much Francis, it's better to just give us enough for an icecream because they take it from us anyway." I said.

"Well hide the rest of it and buy some stamps for sly letters."

"We don't need stamps, we just pop them in the box without any. They always get there, cause I always get what I ask for in my parcels. Besides we could never get a chance to buy stamps, we are watched too closely."

Francis laughed and said, "You're very straight to the point aren't you Josephine. You call a spade a spade alright."

Caroline butted in and said, "Yea, that's what gets her in so much trouble. I keep telling her to keep her big mouth shut, but she doesn't seem to understand."

"Caroline's right Josephine, the less you say the less trouble you'll be in."

"But I like to know why I'm in trouble, so I ask."

"Well don't, take your sister's advice and learn to button your mouth. Things will go a lot smoother for you if you can learn to keep quiet."

"I'll try" I said, more to shut them both up than anything else.

Suddenly Francis stood up and said, "Come on Caroline, let's get your stuff and get out of here. This place is starting to give me the creeps. It brings back too many bad memories for me. I'm beginning to get short of breath just being here."

But I didn't want them to leave, so I said, "Oh stay a while longer, it will be so long till we see you again."

He hugged me close and said,

"We have to go luv, we have to catch the ferry over to London."

"What's the ferry?"

"Oh it's like a ship, but smaller."

Just then, Sister Angela re-appeared, as if she had been waiting outside the whole time listening in on the conversation.

"Hello children," she said, "I've brought Caroline's things down for her. It's about time she made a move now."

Francis stood up and said,

"I was just saying the same thing Sister."

"How have you been anyway lad, and how are your parents?" (She knew full well that they were separated, but she asked anyway).

"Oh, they're fine thank-you sister."

"Are you working now?"

"Yes, I'm in the Merchant Navy as a matter of fact, and very happy."

"That's good lad, that's very good."

She went over to Caroline and said,

"Well you take care of yourself lass, it's been a pleasure having you here, and you'll be missed very much."

Caroline turned and gave her a cold stare, and for the first time she answered her back,

"Oh I don't think I'll be missed." She said with an icy tone.

Sister Angela ignored her and said,

"Now you keep that lovely hair short. Long hair doesn't suit you, you know."

"I don't know about that, I've never had it long, have I. I think I'll grow it now and see how I like it."

Sister Angela ignored her again, and put her arm around Caroline's shoulder to lead her outside, but Caroline shrugged it off and walked forward with her head held high. We all went to the gate and said our goodbyes. I asked Francis to write more often and to tell our dad to come visit us and he promised he would. I felt so empty and angry inside. Suddenly, as if on impluse, I wanted to help Caroline disgrace Sister Angela some more in front of Francis, so I said,

"Francis tell dad to take good care of Caroline, she has been very sick and in bed most of the time since February.

Sister Angela contradicted me, "Oh Josephine, don't exaggerate. She hasn't been that bad." She had daggers in her eyes as she spoke, which made me hold my tongue. I had to stay here and I knew from her look that I was already in big trouble when Francis and Caroline left.

We all hugged each other and cried some more, even Pauline cried at the gate. Caroline was sobbing and it hurt so much to see it. Caroline never cried, and her tears were making me feel terrible. Sister Angela shut the gate and I felt like she was trying to punish me for my words. They were on one side and we were on the other. I reached through the bars to touch her one more time, but I was pulled away by Sister Angela and brought inside. Caroline was gone. I felt so lost and lonely I wanted to die. Maureen hugged me and Pauline walked off crying with Sister Angela, she had an adult to comfort her, Maureen and I had no one except each other.

Strangely enough though I didn't get into trouble about my remark at the gate, maybe she forgot about it, or maybe she just felt some compassion that day, who knows for sure. Later in the evening everyone crowded us to ask about Francis, and that sort of took the sting out of Caroline leaving. We felt so proud of our big brother. We got caught up with all the excitement of everyone telling us how handsome he was. Linda thought he was gorgeous. I hoped that they would both come visit us, but I had a feeling they wouldn't. Maybe it was just too hard for them to say goodbye all the time. It was just easier for all of us if they stayed away.

CHAPTER 35

The night that Caroline left was one of the loneliest nights of my life. I lay in bed wondering why I spent most of my life losing the one's I loved. I asked god what I did to deserve all this. What I had ever done that was so wrong, to make him keep taking my loved one's away from me. I really couldn't think of anything. Maureen came to my bedside that night and like me she was very depressed, but somehow we managed to cheer each other up. She warned me that Sister Martha was very wicked too, and told me to study hard from now on, or I'd be getting the strap everyday. I asked her if she got the strap very often and she told me that she got it daily. When I asked her how come she never complained she said,

"What's the use, I'm the class dummy and she makes an example out of me. I don't care though, it only hurts for a few minutes. The names she calls me are much worse. They hurt for much longer."

Maureen had the Lynch pride, it didn't matter what happened to her, she kept her head high. I guess we all had a little of it, but she was the proudest. All she ever wanted was to be a lady and dress in fine clothes and speak with dignity.

Maureen left my bedside and I was alone again to think. I cried a little after she left, but then reminded myself how Caroline would want me to be brave, and I stopped. Instead I began thinking about going back to school. Not that it was something to look forward to, it wasn't. I was thinking that it was only two days away now, and how much I was dreading it, especially after what Maureen had just told me. I didn't realise that Maureen was the class dummy, I thought it was just me who was stupid. I thought about Maureen, and how I should try to be more like her. She wasn't in the least ashamed about being dumb, infact she was as proud as a peacock. I told myself that I would try and be like her in the future.

The day arrived when we started school and faced Sister Martha. From this day forward until we left the convent, Sister Martha would be referred to as our homing nun. This basically meant that she would teach us all our main lessons, for instance, English, maths, history etc, but we would have different teachers for home economics, sewing and singing. It didn't take us long to realize that any class away from Sister Martha was a joy, a real blessing. This lady should never have become a nun. She had a very nasty nature, and was very cruel. She was also very vain. She had a habit of pushing her bust up and out when she was addressing the class. There she would stand giving us a lecture and up would come the hands under her bust pushing them up. Then she would throw back her shoulders and push the huge things out. She did this a least fifty times a day. It seemed disgusting to us, because any girl that was developing a bustline in the convent, was made to feel disgusting. From the age of eleven you were made wear a binder around your breasts. Sometimes even earlier, if you were an early developer. If the binder didn't flatten your bust, you were given a bigger jumper to hide them, as though it was a big sin to have breasts. Yet here was this big, fat cow, parading them off for all the world to see. Everyone thought it was quite revolting.

On the first day of school it was just like any other first day, with a new teacher, except we were all made to stand at the back of the class and had to step forward when our names were called by Sister Martha. In previous classes we were allowed to choose our own seat and stand up when our name was called. However, in Sister Martha's class she allocated the seats, as she called our name on the register.

When she came to my name she said, "Oh, I remember you. You and Mitchell are the cat food eaters, go and sit down there." As she pointed to the seat at the very front of the class. The whole class laughed at her statement about us being cat food eaters, but I doubt that any of them knew what she was talking about, which I was very thankful for. Linda's name was next on the register, and she placed her directly behind me, telling us both that she would be watching out for us, and she did, like a hawk. When we were all seated in our designated seats, she called out my name again,

"Stand up Lynch," she ordered.

I did as she asked and stood looking at her, wondering what was going to happen now, and a memory came rushing back to me. A memory of my very first day of school, when I was locked in the cupboard, and I had a gut feeling something bad was about to happen.

"I teach your sister Maureen, you know?"

"Yes Sister Martha," I answered wondering why she was telling me something I already knew.

"Do you know that she is very stupid?"

Suddenly my fear turned to anger. I could feel my blood starting to boil, and my first reaction was to ask her who was more stupid, her or my sister, but I curbed my initial reaction and said,

"I don't think she is."

"Well she is, and I think you are going to be just as thick as her," She said walking towards my desk and standing over me, like a big mass of fat.

"I'll try to be clever" I said getting nervous again with her closeness.

"Sit down" she said poking me in the shoulder pushing me back into my seat. Then she fixed up her bust and returned to her seat.

She sat and looked around at each girls face in silence, and after a few moments she opened a draw beside her and pulled our her weapon. It was six pieces of thick leather. Each piece had a hole in the top, and twining held them together. She slapped it down on her desk hard and smiled as she looked up and around at all the scared faces staring back at her.

"This is my friend called "Discipline". If anyone does not achieve my standards in class, or act the way I expect they will meet "Discipline" first hand. I must warn you he isn't very nice, so don't be eagar to meet him." She placed the strap back in the drawer before continuing her lecture.

"Now then, let's begin our lessons." she said standing up. Then she prepared her breast's for action and walked to the black board.

I hated her already and wondered why she had tried to embarrass me by telling me Maureen was dumb. I couldn't believe how horrible she was. She's a witch not a nun I thought to myself, a horrible witch.

Later I told Maureen what happened and she told me not to worry about it. She told me that I shouldn't have answered back and in future to just agree with everything she said. She knew all about "Discipline" too. She said he came out most days to say hello to someone and to be very careful.

On the whole we settled in quite well, and for the first couple of weeks, Linda or myself didn't get acquainted with the famous "Discipline", but it didn't take long before we got a little too confident for our own good.

One day Sister Martha gave us all a ruler, and told us to rule a line down the page's of our new exercise books. She was making her way around to each one of us, and doing the first line for us. My turn came and as she stood beside me about to rule the first page, Linda kicked me up the bum, through the desk chair, warning me she was about to do something stupid. "Oh no", I thought, "What's she going to do now." I moved slightly forward and put my fingers over my lips and squeezed them together to stop myself from laughing. I was preparing myself for what ever she was going to do. I didn't want to laugh. I didn't want to be in trouble.

Sister Martha was standing beside me ruling my line, when suddenly Linda made a noise with her mouth that sounded exactly like a fart, coming from my rear end. I couldn't hold the laughter any more, it just escaped my pursed lips. Sister Martha didn't find it so funny though, I got my own ruler across the face. All I could do was let out another roar of laughter. What Linda did just kept flashing across my mind and I couldn't stop laughing. The whole class was laughing too, but at me, not with me. They all believed that I had farted just like Sister Martha.

Sister Martha became very impatient with the giggles, and she grabbed me by the ear and draged me to the front of the class room. Out came "Discipline", and boy did he hurt. She belted me everywhere and anywhere. I soon stopped laughing and so did the rest of the class. It took her ages to stop belting me. It was as if she was enjoying it, or maybe she was just waiting for me to cry which I didn't do anyway.

Linda felt terrible about the whole thing and couldn't stop apologizing after class. However, even after class the pair of us couldn't help laughing at the expression on Sister Martha's face when she thought I farted in her royal presence.

Maureen heard about the episode and that night she told me off. She said that I would end up dead if I didn't stop my messing around, but when I told her the whole story she saw the funny side of it too. We sat on my bed with our faces buried in my pillow in and effort to surpress the roars of laughter and we had tears rolling down our faces as I retold the story. Maureen still had Sister Martha teaching her which like the rest of us she hated. It was harder on her than me though, because she was in her exam year, but she endured it better than I. Maureen was given a new duty this semester as well, but it was one she liked. She had to clean the parlour, in the nun's quarters every saturday morning. Occasionally, while she was doing this she would see the parish priest from Westport, who just happened to be very good looking. (This was why she liked her new duties so much.)

Kitty was still Maureen's best friend and confident and Maureen told Kitty about the priest and how attractive he was, and how she could easily fall for him. Somehow Kitty's sister Christine found out what Maureen had said. Kitty couldn't remember telling her, but said that maybe she had in passing. Christine who still hated Maureen repeated Maureen's words to Sister Gertrude.

Maureen and Kitty were called to see Sister Gertrude, where she questioned them both separately starting with Maureen.
"Maureen, did you say that the priest was good looking, and that you could fall for him?"
"No Sister Gertrude why would I fall for someone, I'd hurt myself." Maureen answered, playing the dumb and innocent.
"No, what I meant is did you say you loved him?"
"No, I don't remember saying that, I've never spoken to him."
"Okay Maureen, wait outside a minute and send Kitty in

please." Sister Gertrude said, quite tired of this conversation which seemed to be going around in circles and getting nowhere.

Maureen went outside and tried to warn Kitty with actions, shaking her head with a frown. She hoped that Kitty understood and as luck would have it she did. They knew each other instinctively, they didn't need to speak their actions were sufficient to communicate each others thoughts.

When Kitty was seated, Sister Gertrude asked,

"Now then Kitty, I want to know if Maureen ever mentioned any private feelings that she may have for the Parish priest in your presence?"

"No, Sister Gertrude."

"Well that's very strange, because your sister Christine said you told her that she had."

"Christine must be making it up, she doesn't like Maureen very much."

"But why would she say you told her that Maureen said it?"

"I don't know, maybe because I'm Maureen's friend. Plus Maureen's sister Caroline got her into trouble, because she made Josephine and Linda Michell steal the apples for her. Maybe Christine's trying to get revenge."

"It seem's strange that she would get her own sister into trouble, doesn't it, especially since it's not Caroline that will be in trouble."

"Maybe she didn't think. I really don't know why she would tell a lie, except to get back at Maureen's sister Caroline."

"Okay, you and Marueen can go back to class now. Tell your sister I want to see her on your way through please."

"Yes Sister Martha," Kitty said thankful it was all over. She felt a bit sorry for her sister though, she knew she was going to get in big trouble this time.

Christine was the one who got punished for supposedly telling lies. She got another month of laundry duties. Her story didn't make sense to Sister Gertrude, especially since her own sister Kitty had defended Maureen. So no matter how much Christine insisted she was telling the truth, Sister Gertrude wouldn't believe her. Christine was furious with Kitty and didn't speak to her weeks. I was glad that Christine had been punished. It taught her a very important lesson, which was not to tell stories to the nuns, even if they were true. The chances were you wouldn't be believed anyway and would end up with a punishment yourself. Kitty and Maureen were like Linda and I, as close as sisters, and I guess Christie, Kitty's sister was a bit like our sister Pauline, a trouble maker. Not that I really knew Christine that well, but I know I would have defended Linda before Pauline any day, and I guess Kitty felt the same way about Maureen.

Kitty was still my girl in charge and I liked her very much. I knew how close she was to Maureen as well, so I always did the best I could for her. Along with liking the girl, I also knew Maureen would be angry with me if I didn't do all I could to help her. One evening Kitty had her ten girls standing in a straight line looking for nits in each others hair. This chore was supposed to be done in silence and it was the heads girl's responsibility to ensure this happened. Well on this particular occasion, I found a big, black flea in the head of the girl I was checking and jumped when I saw it running through her head. It was the first one I had seen. We didn't often find them because each girl was cleaned on entering the convent. After the initial shock I found it quite amusing and whispered to the girl,
"There's one. Hold on I'll catch it for you", and giggled knowing she would be embarrassed.

Kitty heard me laughing and came up and told me to be quiet, but I started laughing remembering what I had just said to the girl, so Kitty gave me a back hander in the nose. I put my head down, a little embarrassed myself now and my nose began to bleed. Instead of telling Kitty my nose was bleeding I became scared and said nothing. It wasn't long before I was standing in a pool of my own blood. A few minutes later Kathleen Corgoran walked past and when she saw the blood, she came over to me and turned me to face her.

"What on earth happened Josephine?"

"I was talking and Kitty gave me a smack in the face and my nose started to bleed."

"Did you do this Kitty?" The Matron asked in an angry tone.

"Yes mam I must have without realising, you see she was talking and...,"

Kitty didn't get a chance to finish, she got a slap in the face and was told to wait in the matron's cubical.

"Oh," I said, "It wasn't her fault, I wouldn't listen to her. She told me twice to...."

I didn't get a chance to finish either,

"Be quiet and lie down flat on your back Jospehine," the matron said. Then she put her keys down my back and told me to lie on them. (This must have been the Irish remedy for a nose bleed, and it seemed pretty strange to me, but it worked, my nose stopped bleeding. When I think back on it, it was proberly going to stop anyway, it was bleeding for a good ten minutes before the matron walked past.) However, my nose wasn't of any concern to me right now. My concern was that Kitty would bash me up later for getting her into trouble. Furthermore, I knew Maureen was going to be mad at me.

When I saw Kitty later I apologized, and she apologized as well. She told me she didn't mean to hit me that hard, and I explained that she hadn't hit me hard at all, and I had no idea why my nose bleed so much. Maureen wasn't as forgiving though. She came to my bed that night and really told me off. She said that the head girls had a hard enough time without brats like me getting them into trouble. She told me in future to do what Kitty asked instead of what I wanted. I promised I would, but she still didn't talk to me for a couple of days and that broke my heart, because she had never reacted this way before, and apart from Linda she was all I had in this dreadful place.

As for Sister Martha's class I hated it. I had more run-ins with that strap named "Discipline" than I can count. Linda got her fair share too, but I got more because I was so stupid, as if that were my fault. Linda was a bright child and helped me as much as possible at nights, but I just couldn't get facts through my head. My only ability was sewing. I was fantastic at that because I loved it. I also enjoyed home economics, although I wasn't very good in the kitchen I'm afraid. The truth of it all was. any class away from the 'beast' was heaven. She really was a terrible human being. She seemed to get great pleasure out of abusing and hurting others. She would get a certain grin on her mouth as she inflicted her pain. It was a grin of pure satisfaction. She was evil and I hated her. I hated the convent too, and longed for my sixteenth birthday. To me, my remaining six years seemed like a life sentence of pain and misery, and I wasn't sure I was going to go the distance.

CHAPTER 36

Winter came and with it came the snow. It was very cold in Ireland in winter, but it was great fun. My sister Pauline hated it though. She suffered from frostbite in the winter and would be in agony. Sometimes her fingers would swell up, then crack and peel. When this happened the nuns would take extra care of her hands for fear of gangrene setting in. Pauline often cried with pain and my heart would go out to her no matter how mean she was to me. It didn't matter how selfish Pauline was, she was my sister and she looked so sad when she was crying, that I would often cry along with her. The truth was we all loved her no matter how she treated us.

I, on the other hand loved the snow. We all had great fun throwing snow balls at each other and rolling in it. When the snow melted all the girls would polish it, the way we did the dormitory floors and when it dried it became an ice slide to slide along. We would all be absolutely freezing and soaking wet, but would endure the uncomfortable feeling, because we were having so much fun. On one particular occasion whilst we were sliding on our snow slide, Sister Martha came out of the class room. She walked out as proud as a peacock, pushed up her bust and threw back her shoulders in her usual fashion and began to clap her hands, calling us back into class. She took a step forward straight onto our slide and down she went, flat on her back. It was hysterical and everyone started to laugh, not one or two of us, but everyone who saw her fall. She stood up, regained her posture and straightened her bust once again. Her face was flushed and angry and she screamed at us,
"Who made this slide?"
No one was laughing anymore, and since everyone made the slide no one answered her. However, she had to blame someone

and guess who it was.

"Lynch, Mitchell, come here. It was you two who built this slide wasn't it?"

Linda did the wise thing and bowed her head ready to take the blame, but not me, I had to speak up.

"No Sister Martha, we all built the slide not just us two."

"Really Lynch, but it was you two who laughed when I fell down."

"No it was everyone, not just us," I contradicted again.

"Well you shouldn't have laughed at all. How dare you laugh at a holy nun you dreadful child."

As she spoke her words I thought, you're not a holy nun, you're a wicked witch, but I didn't voice my opinion aloud. Suddenly I thought about her falling again and I let out another skite of laughter, which started Linda laughing, and before long everyone else joined in. It was like a chain reaction.

"Get down on your knees the lot of you," She screamed in disbelief at our outburst.

We all knelt on the freezing ground and she walked by each and everyone of us and gave us an almighty slap in the face, which stung more than usual, because we were all so cold. It was the strangest day though, because as soon as we received the slap someone else in the line laughed. It was as if we had no control. It didn't matter that we were getting slapped, we couldn't stop laughing. Due the lack of control of the situation Sister Martha began to verbally abuse us in an effort to regain some control. She said to one girl who had a very sly eye and always looked at you under her eyes,

"You, sheep's eyes Moran, stand up," but as she was about to vitcimize her Linda took into another fit of laughter.

Sister Martha left Annie Moran standing where she was and walked over to Linda. She gave Linda such a hard slap in the face it made my eyes water, but instead of feeling sorry for my friend and keeping quiet, I also laughed uncontrollably. She left Linda and stormed back to me. She grabbed me by the hair and pulled me up to a standing position and slapped me several times screaming at me the whole time.

"How dare you laugh at someone's misfortune Lynch, especially a holy nun. You above all people. Do you not know that you and your sisters are nothing but dirty tinkers from Ballinrobe. You came into this convent filthy, with your heads crawling with lice and nobody wanting you. It was us holy nuns that gave you a home, and this is how you repay us."

She had hit a raw nerve now. I wasn't laughing anymore. I was completely embarrassed by her telling all these lies in front of my friends. None of this was true, it couldn't be, our father loved us. My anger flared and again I answered her defiantly, "That's not true and you know it. If it were true, how come my brother came just a few months ago to bring our Caroline home to our father. If we were tinkers from Ballinrobe, he wouldn't have come, would he?"

She slapped me again with all her might and said,

"How dare you question me you little brat. It is true, all of it. You weren't wanted, you were dumped."

I felt so embarrassed, this was the first I knew about all this. I didn't remember coming into the convent. I felt ashamed standing there and wanted to get my own back, so I said,

"Well I'll have to write and ask my father if it is true then, won't I?"

Again I received a slap, but this one knocked me down.

"The only letter you'll be writing is the one on the black board."

The last blow had been hard, and made me realize I was fighting a losing battle so I decided to shut up for the time being. However, it wasn't the last of it, I was going to find out if she was telling the truth and I was going to write to my father and tell him what happened here today. I didn't care if I got found out either. In fact, I wanted dad to write and tell them off and I was going to tell him that when I wrote. When Sister Martha saw that I was holding my tongue and no one else was laughing anymore, she lead us back inside triumphantly.

Later in the playroom all the children were talking about Sister Martha's accusations and asking me if it was true, but I denied it. To tell you the truth, I wasn't sure if it was true or not at that stage, but I still would have deined it, even if I had known the truth. Pauline came up to me later having heard the news on the grape vine to find out if it were all true. I told her that it wasn't true and not to worry about it. To just ignore anyone who called her names. I couldn't believe how it got around so quickly. The few people who didn't like us Lynch's had already started calling us terrible names:
"TINKERS FROM BALLINROBE, TINKERS FROM BALLINROBE." they shouted out and it hurt so much I felt like dying. I was going to tell my father, and that bitch was going to pay for what she did, if it was the last thing I did.

That night when Maureen came to my bed I asked, "Maureen is it true what Sister Martha said today."
"No it's not, she was just trying to shame you because you shamed her. Now don't be thinking about it anymore."
"Yea that's what I told Pauline, but it was only to keep her from worrying, is that what your doing for me?"
"No, of course not. Why would dad bother sending us parcels for our birthday if he had dumped us. It's just not true Josephine."

"Well why are we here then?"

"To get a good education. We live too far away from him to go home everynight, that's all."

"Well he's wasting his money. I'd much rather be with him anyway."

"Well we can't until we're sixteen, so make the best of it."

"Do you think it could be true, that he didn't want us and we were filthy and full of fleas."

"No of course not. Like I said before why would he bother now if that were the case."

"Yea, that's what I told Sister Martha."

"You never."

"Oh yes I did. I hate her so much Maureen."

Maureen started laughing and said, "You're so cheeky Josephine, how did you have the guts to say such a thing. What did she do to you when you said it."

"She kept slapping me everytime I opened my mouth. I also told her I was going to write and ask dad if it was true. I will too, you better believe it."

"No Josephine you mustn't, you might get caught. You'll really be in trouble then."

"I don't care, he has to know what she did and I need to know if it's true."

"It's not true, just take my word for it. Please don't write Jospehine. I couldn't bare you to get in trouble over this again, and it's really not true, believe me."

"I have to find out for sure. I just can't help myself, besides don't you care when the other kids say bad things about you?"

"No, why should I care. It's not just you Sister Martha gives a hard time to anyway, it's everyone. The difference is we just shut-up and accept it without making a fuss."

"Well I can't do that. Damn her, I hate her guts." I said frustrated and angry. "I'll make dad write back to them too and stop them from doing it again. I'm going to tell him not to donate the records and music any more. That'll fix em up."

"Oh do what you want, but don't expect me to be around when you get into trouble, because I won't be." Maureen snapped back at me. Then she stormed off to bed leaving me alone again. I knew that she was only trying to stop me writing the letter though, and I knew that she would always be there for me. I also knew that she would talk to me again tomorrow, because she had promised me never to stay unfriendly again, after the flee epiosode and getting Kitty into trouble.

Over the next few days I wrote my letter to dad. I did it in the toilet, in the playground and anywhere else I got a few minutes to myself and that weekend I posted it. This is how the letter went.

Dear dad,

Although I do not really know you, as I was too small when I got put into this hell hole, love seems to have grown between us. Whether it is because you send me parcels, or whether it is because I just want to be loved and wanted by someone, I don't really know. But one thing I know for sure is, it feels very good to be wanted.

As you know I'm a very big girl now, nearly eleven years old, and I've got feelings. That's why I'm writing this letter, I want you to tell me if we're tinkers from Ballinrobe, and if nobody wanted us, and that's why we're here. I want to know if only the Convent of Mercy would take us, when nobody else wanted us, and if our heads were crawling with fleas. You're the only one who can answer these questions for me dad.

I don't know why mum never writes to us. I do keep writing to her, but she never answers, and your parcels never say from mum and dad, just always from dad, could you please tell me why.

The reason I am asking, is because a nun told me all this. Her name is Sister Martha and she said all those things out loud in front of all my friends and I felt very ashamed. I kept wishing that I'd never been born. I told all my friends that it wasn't true, but I don't think they believed me. I don't even believe me.

Dad if you love me, even a little, I'm begging you to do something about this. I want you to make me feel clean again and not ashamed of my family. In my past sly letters I've only asked for things, so this time I'm going to tell you a little about myself.

I know that the Reverend Mother keeps writing to you about me and Linda Mitchell, because Francis told me. Well let me tell you the Reverend Mother doens't even know me. She doesn't know one girl's name here. You could tell her your name today and tomorrow she wouldn't know who you were. She is half blind, and very old and the only time we see her is at church. So what ever she writes, she is told to say from the other nuns. Linda and I are not bad, we are very good, but we always get caught having fun. And they call that naughty. You can't do anything here. I am kinda cheeky in the sense I ask questions I'm not supposed to, but that's all.

I am a very fat person and I get reminded of it every day. I also get told that I'm very ugly everyday. Maureen gets told she is ugly too. Pauline and Doreen are supposed to be very pretty. To tell you the truth though I don't know what pretty and ugly is. To me we are all people and should be treated like people. In here you get punished for being fat, having glasses, being ugly and any other disability you may have. I really hate it here and wish I could come home immediately.

Dad, I'm going to stop writing now. It has taken me three days to write this much. I have to sit on the toilet and pretend I have a pain in my stomach all the time. I think I love you very much, and look forward to the day I come home to you. I hope you still want me, even though you know I'm ugly now. Please do something about my letter. Make them stop being cruel. In the past I have asked you not to answer my sly letters, but this time I want you too. Even if I get into trouble.

God bless,
from your Daughter Josephine.

P.S. Please stop sending the music and records too, they don't deserve it.

Three weeks passed and one day Maureen was called to the Reverend Mother's room. As soon as I heard her name over the loud speaker I knew what was going on.
When she arrived and was seated the Reverend Mother asked, "Maureen, have you written a sly letter to your father?"
"No, Reverend Mother. The only letter's I ever write are the ones on the black board mam." Maureen answered as innocent as they come. She knew who had written the letter but she couldn't tell the Reverend Mother that either.
"Okay. Who is your next sister Maureen?"
"Josephine, Reverend Mother."
"Okay, go and ask her to come to my office please."
"Yes Reverend mother," Maureen said leaving the room.
When she came to call me she whispered, "Look dad answered your letter, but just deny the whole thing okay. The Reverend

Mother will believe you, she believe's everyone. Just say you didn't do it."

I nodded, but I only half understood what she said, because she had spoken so quietly.

When I arrived at the Reverend Mother's office I was told to sit down and then she asked, "Did you write a letter to your father Josephine,"

I was shaken up and very scared so instead of answering yes or no to her question, I asked "Why?"

She looked at me dumbfounded and said, "Because one of the Lynch's did and told your father a bunch of lies. Your father is deeply hurt and wants an explanation as to why a thing like this was said to one of his daughters. He is refusing to send anymore music or donations to the convent as well. He states that he would love to take all his girls away from the convent right now and that they are not unwanted. In fact, he says he has plenty of love to give them. He said that any nun who could state such things to a child must be very cruel." She stopped talking for a moment, looked up from the letter, then she went on,

"I don't know why I'm telling you the contents of the letter anyway. I'm the one asking the questions. Did you, or did you not, write these things, these terrible lies to your father?"

"Yes I did write the letter, but if it were lies I was telling, why did Sister Martha say them in front of the whole class."

The Reverend Mother stood up and leaned over her desk, pushing her fists into the top of the desk in an effort to control her temper.

"What was that you said?" She asked in a low dangerous voice that frightened me much more than if she had yelled at me.

I repeated myself and this time she roared at me, "You wicked little child. Sister Martha would never say such cruel things."

"But she did Reverend Mother, I wouldn't lie. She kept slapping me and calling me a Tinker from Ballinrobe in front of everyone."

"Stop telling lies Josephine. You are sinning in the presence of god."

I'm not lying, it's Sister Martha who's been telling the lies. She told me all those things that you said aren't true, I just repeated them to my father."

"Oh shut-up girl, you're confusing me." Suddenly she turned to the microphone on her desk and called Sister Martha to her office. Reverend Mother and I waited until Sister Martha arrived.

"Good morning Reverend Mother, good morning Josephine. How are you both this fine morning?" She said in the sweetest of tones, a tone that I'd never heard from her before, which only served to confuse me more.

I was pretty shaken up. Her sweet tone made me very nervous, and I began to tremble as I sat there in front of these two women. I knew that I had asked my father to reply to my letter, but now I was beginning to think that was a big mistake. In fact, I wished that I had taken Maureen's advice and not written the blasted letter at all.

"Yes, good morning Sister Martha." The Reverend Mother replied, "Look, I'm sorry to have to do this to you Sister Martha, but this girl has written a very distressing letter to her father and he is most upset with the convent."

"Yes Reverend Mother, you read the letter out at breakfast this morning." Sister Martha replied,

"Yes, Yes, that's right. Well do you teach this child."

"Yes Reverend Mother." The confused Sister Martha replied. (The old lady was going quite daft in her old age. She was very forgetful and became confused quite easily. I guess she was a little senile, but she was still the Reverend Mother and still in charge of the convent and very much respected by everyone.)

"Oh yes, of course. Now where were we," the Reverend Mother continued, "Oh yes, did you say those dreadful things to the girl Sister Martha?"

"No Reverend Mother, I did not." Sister Martha said with such shock in her tone it made me sick.

"Liar" I accused. "You, me, and god all know you said those things." I screamed out at her.

Sister Martha marched straight over to me and began slapping me continuously. I got so many slaps across the face I felt dizzy, but for some reason I couldn't shut up.

"Liar, liar" I kept repeating. "You know you're lying, and god knows it too."

Suddenly she stopped slapping me and I stopped crying and screaming out my accusations. The room went suddenly quiet and the Reverend Mother walked over to me slowly and asked,

"Jospehine, how old are you?"

"I'm nearly eleven Reverend Mother, I'll be eleven in March."

"Oh, so you will be making your confirmation in a few months then."

"Yes, in about five months."

She raised her voice at me again, and said,

"Well how can you stand there and tell all these lies just before a holy sacrament. It's disgusting."

"I'm not telling lies Reverend Mother. You can ask anyone in my class and they will tell you what happened."

Sister Martha tensed outwardly, I was saying the right things and she couldn't take the risk of being found out herself, so she interruped me,

"I think we have heard enough of your lies today Josephine." Then she looked at the Reverend Mother and said,

"We've wasted enough of your time Reverend Mother. Leave this to me. I will teach this little liar a lesson or two. I will also ensure she writes to her father withdrawing her lies and telling him the truth."

The tired Reverend Mother, who wasn't used to such excitement, nodded and apologized for putting Sister Martha though all the questions.

It made me sick. Sister Martha was the one lying and I was the one being punished. I knew that this cow wasn't finished with me either.

As soon as we got out of the room she said,

"Get back to class Lynch." I did as she asked with her walking so close behind me I could hear her breathing. I knew I was going to get a terrible hiding when we got back to class, so I walked slowly, and every now and then she would thump me in the back pushing me forward and tell me to hurry up. The only good thing about the whole affair, was I knew my father loved me and that made me very happy.

When we were back in class I was ordered to take my seat. The rest of the class hadn't arrived back from lunch yet and I wished they would hurry up. This punishment wouldn't be dragged out so long if they were here. The first thing she did was go to her draw and take out "Discipline". When I saw it coming out I thought I was really going to cop it. Only she didn't hit me. Instead she walked to the black board and with "Discipline" in her hand, began writing a letter for me to copy. It went like this.

Dear Father,

I am so sorry for all the trouble I have caused you. Everything I said in my last letter was a lie. I made the whole thing up. I was only looking for attention and the nuns are very good to us here. We are all well taken care of.

I will be making my confirmation soon and I am looking

forward to that. This is why I'm telling the truth now, because I want to be forgiven by god before this very special sacrament.

Would you please also reconsider your donations to the convent, as they are very needy and need all the help they can get from loving people like yourself.

Signed your Daughter,

Josephine

As I copied the the letter Sister Martha and "Discipline" walked up and down the aisle of the chairs and each time they passed I got a strike from the strap accross my face, hands, or anywhere else she felt like hitting me, so I didn't know which part of my body to protect. I was trying to rush the letter, thinking to myself, if I hurry up she won't walk by so often, but I was crying so much from the lashes I was getting it just slowed me down. I was really sobbing by the end of it all and my writing paper had big blobs of tears on it, so I copped a few more blows for being messy after my letter was finished.

When I completed the letter she made me stand up and apologize to her for writing a sly letter. I submitted to her wishes, but I thought to myself you teach us not to lie, yet you are the biggest liar I've ever met. I wondered how I expected the Reverend Mother to believe me. She had to believe the holy nun. Nobody in the world would believe me against the word of a nun. I knew my sisters believed me and more importantly my dad believed me. This last thought made me strong again and I stopped my tears, knowing that he loved me.

Sister Martha broke into my thoughts and said, "Well Lynch, have you learnt your lesson?"

"Yes Sister Martha," I answered, but I was thinking I've learnt you're a liar, and I don't stand a chance in this place against the likes of you.

"You won't be writing any more sly letters home, I take it."

"No, Sister Martha." (Not much I thought).

"Okay, you may sit down and wait for the rest of the class to arrive. You will miss out on lunch today but that won't hurt you, you can afford to lose some of that fat, child." she said.,

So could you I thought, but just bowed my head in silence.

A few days later I wrote a sly letter again. However something told me not to hang on to it. I knew I couldn't give it to Pauline, as she was likely to turn me in just for the fun of it. I learnt long ago never to trust her even though she was my sister. I finally gave it to Kitty Kanavan. It was the best thing I could have done, because before we went for our Sunday Walk, Sister Angela called Maureen, Pauline and myself to her office, where we were strip searched. I sort of guessed that they would check me, but I didn't expect them to check my sisters too.

After we were all checked she called Linda Mitchell. Then I did begin to sweat, they were getting too close for comfort. Thankfully they didn't call Maureen's best friend, only mine. But I was really starting to think they would after calling Linda. This random checking went on for a long time, nearly a year in fact. They were trying to catch us off gaurd. Kitty was never suspected though, and consequently she was never checked. However, we warned her to discard any letter that she may be holding if she was ever called at any time, for any reason. They obviously felt that Linda was the only one daring enough to be involved in sly letters, Kitty was such a good girl!

CHAPTER 37

A few weeks after my run-in with the Reverend Mother, Kathleen Corgoran came to my bed after lights out and asked me to come down to her cubicle to talk to her. I had grown to love this old woman. She must have been in her fifties at least and she worked very hard. She had a limp and the other girls in the convent would sometimes copy the way she walked and have a good laugh at her expense. They used to call her hop-a-long Annie, or peg-leg. I never made fun of her, I felt sorry for her. She spent her whole day except Sunday making all our clothes including our thick, black coats for our Sunday walks. She would sit on her machine from morning till night and then she would watch over us while we slept. I never found out if she was paid, or if she had once been a orphan in the convent. I often wondered what happened to her leg, but never had the opportunity, or the nerve to ask her.

None of the other girls liked the matron except myself. They were all scared of her, but I really liked her. For some reason she had taken a liking to me, maybe I reminded her, of herself as a child. I used to have these daydreams that she was brought up in the convent and that the nun's had given her the bad leg by beating her once too often but it was only my imagination. Not that I thought it was beyond imagination, after what I and many others went through in there.

I followed the matron to her cubicle and felt proud that she called me to talk to her. I had no fear of being in trouble where she was concerned so had no hesitation in going, although I was curious by her calling me so late at night. Apparently, she had heard about my sly letter and wanted to know more about it. She had only heard the nun's story and wanted to know mine. I think she just used to get lonely down there by herself sometimes and wanted someone to talk to and was only using this as an excuse. I didn't mind though it made me feel kind of special.

"Sit down Josephine," she said, "I want to talk to you. Well I want to find out if Sister Martha really said all those things to you."

"Yes Matron she did. I wouldn't lie about something like that."

"Yes I know, you are too honest for your own good."

"Well that's what they teach you, but Sister Martha tells lies. She told so many yet I was the one who got the smack, and nun's aren't supposed to lie."

"No one's supposed to lie Josephine, especially nuns. Did you get smacked very much for writing the letter?"

"Yes, but it was worth it."

"Oh, how come?"

"Because the Reverend Mother said that we weren't tinkers, and that made me feel good because I knew Sister Martha lied to me."

The matron laughed at my answer, but then became serious again and said, "Josephine, I'm going to ask you another question."

"Yes, what?" I asked.

"Are you still writing sly letters to your family?"

I hesitated for a moment wondering if I was being set up. I mean the matron was on the nun's side, she was one of them. Everyone hated her except me. She could be quite nasty when she wanted to be. It was just that she liked me. God knows why, but I needed as many people to like me as possible. I turned and looked her in the eyes. I trusted this old woman. I didn't care what the others thought. She had always been kind and loving to me. The same as Sister Angela was lovely to

Pauline and Doreen, but hated the rest of us. Finally I answered her question.

"Yes I am still writing sly letters. I hope you won't turn me in as I have trusted you and I hate telling lies to you."

"Well it is my duty to report you Jospehine."

My heart sank, she had double crossed me and it made me feel sick inside, but then she added, "Don't look so frightened, I said it was my duty, but I won't report it, don't worry."

She pulled me closer to her and wrapped her arms around my fat, little waist and said, "Just be extremely careful, because if you get caught again I hate to think what they will do to you."

"I will" I assured her and gave her a kiss on the cheek. It was so nice to be cuddled like this. It made me feel all warm inside.

The matron changed the subject and asked, "How is your school work coming along?"

"Not very well I'm afraid. I'm very stupid at everything except sewing. I'm like you, I'm very good at that."

"That's great, but try and study your other subjects too. They are very important for you when you leave this place, plus you will make your dad very happy if you do well at school."

It was my turn to change the subject. School wasn't my favourite subject so I began to tell her about other things that I enjoyed.

"You know how Linda and I clean the chapel and throw the holy water on the graves?" I said.

"Yes" she answered.

"Well for fun we usually try and jump the wall of the grave yard. Linda always gets over, but because I'm fat I rarely make it. Sometimes I even fall when I running to make the jump, I slip on the mud and go for a sixer, gee we laugh when that happens."

"You mustn't do it any more, you could be seriously injured, then it wouldn't be fun. Besides ladies should use the gate and you're a young lady now Josephine."

"Okay," I half promised, "I'll try and remember."

"Come on, back to bed, enough of this chit chat." She said to my disappointment. I was really enjoying our friendly chat.

"Well actually there is something else I want to tell you."

"And what's that," she said in an amused tone.

"Well, when I was kneeling in the chapel today, my knee became very sore and now it's hurting much more."

"Did you bang it jumping over the wall?"

"No, I didn't bang it at all. It just became sore when I stood up."

"Oh well, let's take a look at it while you're here."

I lifted my nightie to let her see my leg, but there wasn't that much to see. My knee was swollen, but I was so fat anyway you could hardly tell.

"There doesn't seem to be much wrong with it," she said. "Did you mention it to Sister Angela after mass this morning?"

"No, she would have said that I was faking it to get out of school, but it really is quite sore when I stand on it now."

"Well, let's get you back to bed then and I'll check it out in front of Sister Angela first thing tomorrow morning."

"Okay." I said, feeling safer that she would be with me when I told Sister Angela.

She walked me back to bed and as I was limping like her, I found it amusing and said "Now we both have to hop Matron."

After I had said it I regreted my words instantly, thinking that may be offended, but laughing she said, "You cheeky young pup. Enough of that lip, before I spank you."

Her light tone made me feel at ease again, and thankful that I hadn't hurt her feelings. I felt pretty special when she tucked me back into bed and gave me a small peck on the forehead. No one else got to stay up late with the matron, only me, and I felt wonderful, even if my knee was sore.

When the morning whistle blew I awoke and my leg was even worse than the night before. I saw the matron approach Sister Angela and when they turned and looked my way I knew what they were discussing. Then the pair of them came over to me. By this stage I was standing beside my bed, but my leg was extremely painful.

"Lift your nightdress Josephine" Sister Angela ordered.

As I did, she asked me to lift my leg as well.

"I can't," I answered, "It's too sore."

She gave me a slap in the face and yanked my leg up. I began to cry. I wasn't sure from what, the slap in the face or the pain in my knee. She dropped my leg back to the ground and ordered me back to bed. The matron stood there helpless to help me, but I knew she was feeling my pain, it showed in her face.

The dormitory was empty and I lay alone on my bed. I buried my head in my pillow and sobbed my heart out. I began talking to myself, I did this often lately, it seemed to comfort me.

"Why am I always getting smacked" I asked myself aloud. "I wish Caroline was here. I miss you Caroline especially at times like this. Please come back." I cried out, and then began sobbing.

About an hour later Sister Angela returned to find me still crying.

"What are you crying for Lynch?" She snapped.

"My leg is very sore," I replied.

"Well that's what happens to girls who tell lies on nuns and write sly letters, they get punished by God."

"I didn't tell any lies."

"How dare you answer me back, you liar." she said as she slapped me across the face.

I couldn't hold back my words, she was so wrong and I was

·so angry. I answered back again.

"Why do you keep slapping me. I'm telling the truth. I told the truth when the Reverend Mother asked me if I wrote the sly letter, and I'm telling the truth now."

"Shut up" she said slapping me again.

But I couldn't shut up, "God knows I'm telling the truth, and so does my father." I answered with a vengence.

"How do you know your father believes you?"

"Because he hasn't sent any more records and because Caroline's out now and she knows the truth about this place." I answered in a spiteful tone.

"You brat" she said giving me another slap in the face. "I suppose you have told your father everything?"

"Yes, I used to, but I don't any more. I told him about Sister Martha forcing Caroline to dance and how sick she became after. I also told him to answer my last sly letter and tell the Reverend Mother what Sister Martha said about us."

"You did what? Why would you do that when you knew you would be punished for it?"

"Because I wanted to know the truth and that was the only way to find out."

"So have you learnt your lesson now or are you still writing sneeky letters?"

I remembered my conversation with the matron last night and half wondered if Sister Angela knew I was, but I answered,

"No, I don't write them any more. I've learnt my lesson alright."

"My, my, we are brave" she said in a sarcastic tone. Then she deliberately pulled my leg up stretching the knee out.

I cried out. The pain was unbearable. She smirked and said,

"Not so brave after all, are you? You have caused a lot of trouble to this convent Josephine, and mark my words you are going to pay dearly for it."

"But I'm not writing sly letters anymore."

"Too bad, the damage is already done." She paused before going on, "How come your are not frightened to tell me all that you have written to your father in the past."

"Because I'm trying to prove a point."

"And what point is that?"

"That I'm not lying. I'm telling you the truth and I told you the truth about what Sister Martha said too."

"Liar" she snarled, and slapped me yet again.

"Oh why won't you believe me?" I wimpered, worn out from the slaps, and all the crying.

"Because you're a liar, that's why. Who taught you how to write the sly letters anyway?"

"Caroline" I answered knowing there was nothing she could do about it anyway.

"Yes, it's always the quiet dog that bites." she said,

"Pardon"

"Never mind" she said looking at my leg more closely.

"Why didn't you show me your leg yesterday when it first got sore?"

"Because you couldn't see anything then and I thought you would think I was faking to get out of school and I'd be punished."

"I think you didn't show me yesterday because you wanted it to get worse, so you could have lots of time off school."

"That's not true."

"Yes it is, but I'm going to bring your books up here for you to study, so it didn't work."

"Good, it will give me something to do."

"Shut up, you defiant little brat." she said hitting me in the shoulder.

She turned to leave and told me she was going to get my school books and phone the doctor to check my knee.

Normally I hated being alone. It made me very frightened for some reason. Maybe because my mother had left me alone when I was so young, not that I remembered, but being alone was the worst thing in the world to me. Today however, I was glad. My face was flushed and stinging from all the slaps I received, and as I lay back on my bed I remember thinking I hope you fall down the stairs you old cow, and the feeling of guilt that overwhelmed me immediately after for having such bad thoughts about another human being and I prayed to god for forgiveness.

The books came straight away, but the doctor didn't come until the next morning, by which time I was in agony. I can't describe the pain I was feeling. Even to walk to the toilet which was very close to my bed was hell itself. When the doctor finally arrived Sister Angela performed her usual act as a kind, loving and concerned nun. She was very convincing too. The doctor packed my leg with ice and then stepped outside with Sister Angela to explain what was wrong with me. About fifteen minutes later he returned. He removed the ice pack dried my leg and then rubbed some cream on to it. Then he bandaged it up tightly and left the room with Sister Angela following right behind him.

I don't know what that cream was, but it made my leg feel very hot and the pain was much worse. I was longing for Sister Angela to return even though I hated her. I couldn't wait for her to return with my lunch. When she finally got back I was sobbing. I tried to go to the toilet, but I was unable to go because of the pain in my knee.
"What's the matter with you now Lynch," She yelled when she saw me crying.

"I have to go to the toilet."

"Well go."

"I can't, I tried. My leg hurts too much."

She yanked my legs around and over the side of the bed and pulled me out. The pain went right through my whole body as the blood rushed down into my leg and the knee bent. I screamed out in pain. Then I collapsed and passed out.

When I awoke a few moments later, I was back in bed with a potty beside me. The doctor returned about an hour later and gave me an injection. I didn't eat dinner that night. In fact I slept through the night. I didn't even wake up when the rest of the girls came to bed. The next morning I awoke with the sound of Sister Angela and her brass bell. I felt lifeless and unaware. It must have been the injection I'd received the day before. I was still tired now and my leg wasn't hurting so much anymore.

However, a couple of hours later when everybody was at school, the pain returned in full force. My knee felt like it was on fire and it was throbbing very badly. I started to imagine that my leg was going to catch fire and I'd only have one leg.

"Oh no," I said to myself, "I'm all by myself and my leg is going to drop off. Somebody help me." I started screaming out. "Please help me."

I panicked and picked up the potty and began beating it against the wall with all my might. I didn't care who came or how much I got smacked. I just had to have some help. The thought of being here alone for a moment longer was scaring the hell out of me. Luckly for me it was the Matron who heard my banging first. She ran into the room and said,

"What's the matter Josephine?" and started yanking the potty out of my tight gripped hands.

I sat up and hugged her with all the strength I had, "My leg's falling off. It's jumping all the time and having spasms. It's burning like crazy too, and I'm so scared by myself."

"Hush hush" she said as she rocked me to and fro. "Your leg isn't falling off. The jumping feeling is called throbing and generally means that there is a healing process going on. You are not going to lose your leg darling, it is getting better."

"Why is it burning so much then?"

"Because of the cream on it, and the infection inside."

"What's wrong with my leg? Why is this happening?"

"Well you have what they call "Housemaids Knee", the medical term is called Bursitis, which means inflamation of the bursa in front of the knee."

"What's a bursa"

"It's a small sack like structure filled with a thick fluid that is found in different areas of the body, but mainly around the joints. Like the knee, or elbow."

"Oh" I answered not really understanding at all.

"In simple terms" she added, noting the confusion on my face, it means that you have fluid in the knee caused from kneeling too much, and because you are also overweight it is more likely to happen to you. That's why they call it "housemaids knee" because housemaids are always on their knees."

"Oh I said, and started to laugh thinking of the name.

The matron smiled, happy to see be in good sprits again and said,

"It also means that you should never go down on your knees in the future Josephine, you have to be very careful not to stay on your knees for too long."

"That's good, no more scrubbing the floors."

"Don't be too sure of that," she said frowning and then added, "Look I have to get back to my machine. You be a brave girl for me now and no more crying. Sister Angela will be up soon with your lunch, and I believe the doctor will be back to give you a pain killer again tonight.

"Okay." I said. I was feeling better now since I knew my leg wasn't going to fall off and people were just a scream away. My leg was still very sore, but now that I felt safe it was bearable at least.

I lay back down on my bed and thanked my lucky stars that it was the matron who had come to my aid and not Sister Angela. I dozed of to sleep again thinking about how lucky I had been.

CHAPTER 38

My knee got better and I returned thankfully to school. Only it didn't take a week like they told me. It took three weeks, and they were the longest three weeks of my life. It wasn't that I liked school, I hated it and I hated Sister Martha with a passion, but I hated being alone more. Now, years later, I realise that it was a phobia I had caused by being left alone by my mother at such a tender age, and by being locked in the morgue at the hospital. Although I had no memory of either of these events at that stage, I still hated being alone. It was a fear undescribable, but very strong. To me being left alone was the biggest punishment they could give me. Much worse than anything Sister Martha could dish out.

There was one good thing about my bad knee, I wasn't allowed to clean or polish the floors anymore. This delighted me as I hated waxing the floors. It was very hard work. The bad thing though was I had a lot of catching up at school.

I seemed to emotionally grow up in those few weeks though, and I was ready to pay attention and apply myself to catch up on what I had missed. Linda was a great help too, so it wasn't so bad. Sister Martha gave me a week to catch up with the work, giving me extra study time during lunch hours. She also allowed Linda to stay in the classroom with me to help. I don't know why she trusted the two of us alone, but she did. Maybe she sensed that I was eagar to catch up and was giving me the opportunity to do so.

Maureen also tried to help at nights, but the funny thing was she was more stupid than me. Even though she was a year older, most of the time I knew more than she did, but she found that amusing and would kill herself laughing. It didn't matter to her that she knew hardly anything, all she wanted was to be a "Real Lady".

One night after correcting her several times when she was trying to teach me, I said,

"I bet you get the strap a hundred times a day Maureen."

"You're not far wrong Josephine, I am a bit of a dummy you know. The only thing I'm good at is Gaelic, but who cares." she answered letting out a roar of laughter.

I looked at my sister with admiration and wished I could be more like her. She was so grown up and independant. She didn't need anybody. She was secure in herself. I, on the other hand was very self consious and had a low self esteem. The truth was I didn't like myself very much at all. Sister Martha had a nick name for Maureen which was, "Cock of the Walk". She called her this because Maureen always had her head held high. Maureen was very slim and very short, but she had a fighting spirit, that not even Sister Martha could break. As I sat studying Maureen I felt proud she was my sister, no matter how dumb she was and I reached over and hugged her tightly.

Maureen didn't cry very often, but when she did it made everyone around her want to cry as well. It was such a pitiful, sad cry. She shed silent tears, and never pulled ugly faces like I did. It was really pitiful to watch. Sometimes I used to practice crying like her, without distorting my mouth. It worked during practice but when the real tears came I had no control at all over my mouth. As though it had a mind of it's own! Even at a very young age Maureen was a very gentle, kind and loving person, and I loved her dearly for it. She was also very clean and tidy and the smallest undesirable event, like someone eating with their mouth open could make her stomach turn upside down.

Maureen's trademark was her small, black comb, which she hid in her stockings. Every chance Maureen got to comb her hair she took advantage of it. She was so vain. As for me I couldn't have cared less. Once a day was plenty for my hair to be brushed. I remember asking Maureen once why she walked with her head stuck in the air and she told me, it helped make her taller because she was so short. Then she added, if I don't hold my head up tall no one would be able to see me. I can remember her laughing at her own statement so much tears ran down her face. Those things are nice to remember because they were the nice times, and hard to hang onto sometimes when so many bad things were happening.

Well the extra studying worked wonders, and with Linda's help and my promise to myself to try harder, I succeeded. Success was sweet too. For once in my life I was really proud of myself and it was such a good feeling.

During my second week back at school when all my studies were completed, Linda got into trouble again. It was over me really. She had been so busy helping me that she neglected her own homework. To save time, Linda copied another girls homework. It wasn't that she was stupid, just rushed and too lazy to look up the answers herself. However, it back-fired on her. She got caught by Sister Angela who reported her to Sister Martha. Sister Martha went mad and after giving her six lashes with "Discipline", gave her an extra punishment. Linda was made to wear an ankle length, tight, black cotton dress for a week. Most children would have cried their eyes out over this punishment, but not my Linda. Her sense of humour was like mine, crazy! When she walked into the classroom on the Monday morning she walked down the aisle swaying her hips from side to side and batting her eyelids, saying,

"I'm the queen of the ball. Don't I look just fine in my long, party dress."

The whole class was in stitches laughing at her. She looked so funny parading the dress. When she reached her desk she jumped up on it and started to mimic Sister Martha. She pushed out her bum, lifted her bust and threw back her shoulders, and said,

"Look Josephine, I'm Sister Martha." Then she started to clap her hands and mimic Sister Martha's voice,

"Sit down girls, sit down girls."

The whole class was in an up-roar, but suddenly the room went dead quiet, you could have heard a pin drop. Linda and I turned slowly and looked at the classroom door. There she was, standing like a statue watching us. God only knows how long she had been there and how much she saw and heard. She was earlier than usual this morning.

Linda and I stood frozen, me on the floor and Linda still on her desk. Finally Sister Martha spoke.

"Mitchell, Lynch, outside."

Linda jumped down from her desk and led the way outside. I wondered why I was being sent out too. I hadn't done anything the rest of the class didn't do. I was only laughing like everyone else. It took a lot of self control to stop myself from asking Sister Martha this question. I kept telling myself it would only get me into more trouble. Sister Martha followed us outside the room and when we were out of earshot from the other children, she said,

"You two are disgusting. You are both very bad children with no respect for your elders at all. Well this time you are going to pay dearly for trying to humiliate me, 'a Holy Nun', now follow me."

She loved to call herself a holy nun. She used that expression nearly as much as she pushed out her bust and both made me feel sick. We followed her to the Music room and we were told to wait outside. She entered the room and approched Sister Marie inside. Sister Marie was the nun who taught piano and singing. She also organized all the Christmas plays and concerts.

Until we reached Sister Martha's class we had had little to do with her, but now we saw her all the time during our music lessons. She didn't mind Linda, but seemed to detest me. I had never been punished by her, but she was always insulting me in class, calling me names in reference to my large size. She seemed to have a dislike for children with a bust too, embarrassing them at every opportunity. Sister Martha and Sister Marie were best friends. They were always together. They ate, drank and propably slept together. The only time they were separated was during school hours, even then they would have their breaks together. Sister Martha finally came back outside and said,

"Go to the dressing room both of you. Strip down and just wait there. Sister Marie will be up in a few moments to give you your punishment. When she is done with you I want you both to return to class on the double." She walked off leaving us standing there dumbfounded.

"Why do we have to strip down Linda?"

"I'm not sure, but we better hurry before Sister Marie comes out and finds us still standing here."

"But why do we have to take off our clothes?" I asked nervously. "We don't have to be searched surely."

"I really don't know, but it sounds rude to me. I guess we'll find out soon enough though."

We went to the dressing room and took of our clothes, but we both decided to leave on our bust-binders and knickers, knowing how much Sister Marie hated girls with breasts like myself. Linda was as flat as a pancake, but she left hers on in sympathy for me. Sister Marie came up about ten minutes later. She was puffed and panting from walking up the stairs. When she walked into the room we saw that she was carrying a thick piece of leather, and we knew what was going to happen next. We just didn't know how bad it was going to be.

"You were told to strip down, why are you still wearing your underwear?" she asked.

"We thought it was rude to stand naked in front of each other." I answered.

She grabbed me by the hair and shook my head hard. "It's rude to try and belittle a nun too, but it didn't stop you. Now take all your clothes off this instant." she snapped, releasing my hair with a forward jolt. Our faces were flushed with embaressment. All the girls dressed in this room every morning together, but this was different. There was only three people here, and we were aware of each others nudity, and embaressed by it.

Sister Marie started with me, while Linda just stood there naked, embarressed and horrified. Sister Marie circled me several times, eyeing me up and down and hitting out with the strap now and then. Then she went into a frenzy and began hitting me harder and faster. She hit me across the back of my legs and every part of my body, but mainly my breasts. I tried to protect them with my hands, but she would scream for me to put my hands down and would hit harder. It wasn't so much the strapping that was hurting. It was the sheer shame of it all. It was the way she looked at my breasts and lower parts. Her eyes seemed to penetrate and burn my flesh. She made me feel so un-clean and disgraceful. I knew nothing about sexual relationships then, nor about men, but the way she made me feel that morning was like a whore. The pain she was inflicting seemed to excite her. She was looking at my body the way a man would. With a satisfaction that shone from her eyes as she observed my nakeness, and submission to her pain. She was enjoying seeing my tears and hearing my cries. I had welts all over my body and began bleeding in several places before she finally decided to stop. I ran to put my clothes back on straight away, I needed to hide myself and protect myself from her eyes, but she stopped me. I was made stand there naked, watching her as she whipped Linda.

I was only eleven years old but that women made me feel like dying. I just wanted to crawl away and hide. I felt so ashamed. I remembered Rita Donnally and what had happened in the toilet. I felt ashamed then, especially when I confessed my sin to the priest, but this shame was far worse. Maybe because I was older I don't know, but I was feeling really bad inside. My heart was crying out for my friend now too. I knew what she was going through, and how she felt.

Like me, Linda tried to protect herself, but to no avail. When Sister Marie had finished, had satisfied her lust. She instructed us to get dressed and return to class. She stood watching us putting our clothes back on, and gave us a warning before we left.

"If you two ever try to embarrass a nun again, you will be very sorry you did. Your punishment will be much worst next time. Now get back to class."

We left without saying another word. When we were outside, Linda apologized for getting me into trouble and we hugged each to console each others pain and humiliation, and within a few minutes we had nutured each others needs and were ready to carry on again. As we were walking back to class after our terrible punishment we walked past Kathleen Corgoran's sewing room. Linda was walking directly in front of me, still wearing her long, silly dress. She looked so comical from behind. You could see every movement she made, because the dress was so tight. While behind her, I started to swing my arms and hips in the same way and keep in time with her steps. Then I said, "Left right, left right."

Linda turned to look at me and let out a roar of laughter, but when she turned to face the front again she was greeted with a slap in the face which knocked her off balance, because it was so unexpected. It was the matron. She had heard us laughing.

I spoke up telling her it was my fault and explaining what had happened.

"I'll talk to you later Josephine." was all she said to me. Then she asked

"Why are you two out of class?"

"Because we were sent to Sister Marie for punishment." I answered,

"Well, it doesn't seem to have done any good, does it." She said smiling down at me. Then she said,

"Well don't go back to class laughing, because you will be punished again. Now get going and quietly please."

"Yes matron," we both answered, bowing our heads as we walked away.

Just before we went back into class Linda and I put spit on our eyes to make believe we were still crying and upset, then we entered with our heads bowed, and sat in our seats quietly.

Sister Martha wasn't finished with me yet though. Linda was okay, even though it was her who had mimiced Sister Martha. However since my sly letter to dad Sister Martha had been out for revenge any way she could. I was really surprised she gave me time to catch up on my work when I was away with my knee. Maybe she had no choice in that decision, maybe the order came from the Reverend Mother.

"Lynch" she said when I was seated, "I want you to write and tell your father how you tried to disgrace me this morning."

"Yes Sister Martha, are you going to write it on the black board for me?"

"No, I'm not, you can write it yourself. You're good at that, aren't you Lynch?"

"Yes, I mean No, Sister Martha". I wasn't sure what I meant, and more importantly, what was the right answer. She came over to me and handed me one sheet of paper advising me not to make any mistakes or I'd be in real trouble. I started my letter. I felt confused and angry and this is what I said,

Dear Father,
Sister Martha has asked me to write this letter to you. My friend made a joke in class and EVERY GIRL in the class laughed, but only my friend and I got punished. We were sent to the dressing room, told to take all our clothes off, then we were strapped until we had welts all over our bodies. Now I ask you father, do you think that is fair? I don't have anymore to tell you, but please come and get me soon or I'll die in here.

Signed your daughter,
Josephine.

When I finished my letter I read through it. Then I wished somehow I could change the letter and write what I knew she wanted me to. However, it was too late now. I only had one peice of paper. I was shivering in my skin as I put my hand up.
"Yes Lynch,"

"I've finished Sister Martha." I said in a nervous voice. I was almost stuttering I was so scared.

"Well bring it here to me."

I was so frightened as I walked up to her desk. My legs turned to jelly and I thought they would collapse from under me. I got to her desk and handed her the letter. I stood in front of her as she read the letter, tembeling all over. I felt sick, and my whole body began to sweat. I thought I was going to faint right in front of her. Suddenly her face turned scarlet with temper and she jumped up from her seat and began slapping me continously. Then she shoved me backwards, ordering me back to my seat. She folded my letter neatly and placed it in her pocket. What worried me most was the suspicious grin on her face. At playtime I explained to Linda what I had written and she said,

"Oh, Josephine, weren't you scared?"

"Not when I was writing it, not one little bit, I was angry, but after I was finished and realised I couldn't change it, I was shaking like jelly"

Linda laughed, but I was still scared. It was puzzling me why Sister Martha put the letter in her pocket. Why didn't she tear it up and make me do it again I wondered. Why was she keeping it. I think it was the smirk on her face that told me to be aware that she had bad intentions.

After worrying about it all day I finally told myself there was no use worrying, only time would tell what was going to happen. Maybe she just wanted to show it to Sister Marie later I told myself. It didn't matter anyway, I couldn't do anything about it. I was at their mercy.

CHAPTER 39

It was a week before my Confirmation and I was really looking forward to it. We had spent most of the last semester studying our catisgism in preparation for our holy sacrament. I was surprisinly good at religious educaction too and enjoyed it immensely. Even after all that had happened in my life, I still loved god and wanted to be closer to him. I chatted away to him when things went wrong in my life. Sometimes at night I would mumble away for ages in a world of my own, asking his forgiveness and asking him to stop punishing me. At this time of my life I was very happy and looking forward to my Confirmation with all my heart.

This Sunday however was the day that all last years Confirmation dresses came out for sizing. Everyone was excited about having a special dress for the day, especially me. The matron and Sister Angela were fitting and altering the dresses together. The matron pulled out a large dress and with a smile on her face, said
"Josephine, this one should fit you."
I tried the dress on and it fitted like a glove. There weren't any alterations required at all. I felt like a queen turning for the matron. I felt so beautiful and special inside, but not for long. Suddenly I was robbed of these feelings when Sister Angela called out,
"Lynch",
"Yes Sister Angela."
"Take that dress off this instant."
I looked at the matron for some support, but her face went sad as she said, "Take the dress off Josephine."
I did as she asked and handed the dress back to her. I wondered what was going on, maybe they have to fix it I

thought, and looked at Sister Angela in hope of an explanation. I got one too, but not the one I expected.

"You are going to have your special day in black." she said, with a smile on her mouth, that went from one side of her face to the other.

I was choked up, but fought back my tears. I occupied myself with putting on my uniform again bowing my head to hide the hurt. I began to talk away to myself in my head, asking myself what I did so wrong, and why I was in trouble again. Sister Angela was still rattling on but I couldn't hear her anymore. I can't wear a black dress, I was telling myself. It would be shameful to god. I thought about running away again. I began making a plan. I would have to leave it till the last minute, that way even if I got caught everyone would have made their Confirmation and it wouldn't matter. I would leave next Sunday morning straight after breakfast. I would climb over the fence and keep running until the afternoon.

"Lynch." Sister Angela snapped, refocusing my attention to what was going on around me, "Are you listening to me." she said, realising I was in a world of my own.

"Ah, yes Sister Angela."

"You're not thinking about writing another sly letter home are you Lynch?"

I didn't answer, I was still drifting back from my thoughts and my get away plans, and only half listening to what she was saying.

"Well it won't do you any good," she continued, "Because it would never leave this convent, remember we are still checking you."

"Yes Sister Angela." I said, still not paying attention.

"Now", she said, "I think I'll make a long black dress for you."

I looked at her and she was beaming all over as if she was really enjoying my hurt and I decided then and there I wasn't going to let her get the better of me. Suddenly I stood up straight and as tall as I could. I don't care I thought, I won't be here anyway.

"Bad girls must be punished," she rammbled on.

Oh shut up I thought but smiled back at her. I don't care any more and you're not going to make me cry or know how much you're hurting me.

As if reading my thoughts she went silent. She wasn't getting the response she wanted so she turned back to her alterations. As she did so she spitefully said, "Go away now child, go and watch the other girls trying on their beautiful, white dresses."

I walked over to Linda, she looked lovely in her dress. She smiled sadly at me and said, "I'm so sorry Josephine, if I could give you my dress you know I would."

"Yes I know, but I don't care about the stupid dress." I lied, and forced a smile back at my dear friend.

Sister Angela turned and saw me talking to Linda. She was keeping a very watchful eye on me.

"Lynch, what did you say to Mitchell." she snapped.

"I told her she looked pretty, and she said thanks. That's all."

"It's a pity you won't look pretty in your long black dress, isn't it?"

She really was a bitch but I was determined not to show her my true feelings. Instead I smiled at her and turned back to Linda saying,

"I'd better go, before you get into trouble too." and walked away.

I began walking around looking at the other girls telling them how lovely they looked when suddenly something happened and I felt light hearted again and I truly didn't care anymore. It was as if god had come into my heart to comfort me. I had this thought flash through my mind telling me it didn't matter what

I wore. The important thing was that my heart was clean and pure and that god loved me. It was like a miracle. I felt so peaceful and safe inside and ready to make Confirmation even if it were in black.

Realising that I was walking around aimlessley the matron called out to me.

"Joesphine, come here for a moment I need some help." she said.

I went over, but she didn't need any help.

"Do you realise you are going to be wearing black for your special day?" she asked in a low voice.

"Yes."

"Don't you care?" she whispered.

"No, I did at first and felt like running away, but just now, well, I can't explain it, but a feeling came over me and I felt that it didn't matter what I was wearing, because I know I am pure inside and I know that god loves me. Besides, I'll be different to everyone else so in a way I'll be special." I said smiling up at the matron.

Sister Angela called out to me again when she saw that I was happy. I think she was becoming annoyed at my attitude, and the positive way I was handling her punishment.

"Lynch you seem to be doing a lot of smiling for someone wearing black for their Confirmation." she said.

I turned to face her and replied, "Sister Angela, it doesn't matter to god what colour you wear so long as you're clean on the inside."

"But you are far from that Lynch," She growled. Then she got up from her machine and left the room. Her words were like a knife, but I had won the battle of wits and that made me feel great.

The whole week prior to our Confirmation dragged. I spent the whole time thinking about my black dress and wondering if the other girls would laugh and make fun of me. Then I would convince myself that it didn't matter, but deep down I knew it would and I knew that no matter how hard I tried to look happy, my insides were in a knot and I was really very unhappy.

When the morning of our Confirmation finally arrived we didn't attend early mass with the rest of the convent, because we had to prepare ourselves for our special day. All the girls making their Confirmation had their dresses hanging at the end of their beds. Everyone except me that is. I watched them putting on their beautiful, white gowns and since I had no dress, black or white, at the end of my bed, I put on my black school uniform. Linda came over to me when she was dressed. I knew she was feeling sorry for me, but couldn't find the words to console me, so I helped her by saying,

"Linda I don't really mind, there must be plenty of poor children in the world that don't have special clothes for their Confirmation and it truly doesn't worry me.

Sister Angela, un-aware to either of us, was standing behind us listening to our conversation. Suddenly she broke in and said, "Lynch, get those clothes off."

I turned to face her half expecting her to be holding my black dress, but she stood there holding a white dress, the same one I had tried on last Sunday.

"I've decided to give you one more chance." she said,

I felt like telling her not to bother, that I didn't feel like wearing it anymore, but I knew that would make things more difficult for me so in my nicest tone of voice I said, "Thank-you Sister Angela, you're so kind," and took the dress off her gracefully.

I put on the white dress, but I didn't feel good in it now. All the excitement had complety vanished from me. Even after my Confirmation, I was solemn and didn't smile for any of the photos. When the group photo came back I was the only girl not smiling.

We had a special breakfast together after the mass and sacrament. Each girl got a holy picture and a plastic bag with four lollies in it. When Sister Angela gave me my bag of lollies she said, "Your bag is special Lynch, you have four black liquorice lollies in it."
Little did she know I loved liquorice, but I wasn't about to tell her that. She probably would have snatched them right back off me leaving me with none at all.

Later in the day when we were changing back into our uniforms I said to Linda, "I don't think I'll ever forget my Confirmation day Linda."
"No, me neither. It was good, wasn't it?"
"No, it was terrible. I will always remember my black dress, and black lollies."
"But you didn't wear the black dress."
"Yea I know, but all week I thought I would be so all the excitement was gone for me. I'm just glad it's all over."
She hugged me and said, "Never mind Josephine, It's a new day tomorrow."
Yea I thought, and another five years of hell before I get out of here.

CHAPTER 40

A few months later we were having our music lesson with Sister Marie. Sister Marie sat with her back to us playing notes on the panio and at the same time nominating different girls to tell her what note she had played. I loved music in general but I hated piano because I never knew what note she was playing. To me they sounded the same. It was all guess work where I was concerned. As for reading a music sheet, that was a sheer impossibility.

The music room had four rows of benches, situated one behind the other, each bench a little higher then the next, similar to a football staduim. The smaller girls sat in the front row, whilst the taller girls sat progressively further back. On this particular day, I was sitting beside Linda and I had another girl called Margaret Delayne who was a couple of years my senior, sitting directly behind me on the last row. Margaret was another weirdo, who was prone to epileptic attacks. However, unlike Grace Gawley who looked perfectly normal in appearance, Margaret had a strange look about her. She didn't walk normally either, she dragged herself around. She was a big, solid girl who had a strange stare. She was really quite scary to be around. I for one stayed away from her as much as possible. In fact, she had no friends at all due to the fact that she was very bad tempered, rude and quite abrupt.

Margaret must have recently been assigned to kitchen duties because she had a raw chicken's leg, which she kept rubbing up against my face and neck. I elbowed her away a few times then I turned around and whispered,
"Do it to someone else, I don't like it."
Unfortunately she had made up her mind that it was me she

was going to torment. The more I pushed her away the more persistent she became. I looked at Linda in a plea for help and she produced something from under her jumper. I saw her taking out a brown paper bag very carefully, in case it rustled and Sister Marie heard it. At first I thought it may have been a raw egg because she was being so gentle. She quietly opened the bag and pulled out an apple. However, the apple was so old it was completely brown. It was even beginning to grow it's own winter fur coat.

"What's that" I whispered, not really recognising it as an apple because only it's shape was familar.

"It's an apple, I was saving it for a rainy day, but I think I kept it too long," she whispered with a low giggle, "Here throw it at Margaret."

"I can't, I'll get into trouble."

"So will she, when you tell Sister Marie why you did it."

I took the furry looking thing from Linda and wimpered as I felt it's sogginess. Then I turned around to Margaret and showed her the apple.

"If you don't stop touching me with that chicken leg, I'm going to throw this at you." I whispered.

She didn't stop like I had hoped she would. She did it more frequently in fact.

Finally I lost my temper. Between holding this rotten apple and feeling that cold, yukky chicken leg across my neck and face, I had goose bumps all over me. I turned in my seat, aimed the apple at her face and threw it at her as hard as I could. The only trouble was I forgot what a lousy shot I was. I couldn't catch or throw anything so instead of hitting Margaret's face, which was only five inches away from me, I hit the wall behind her.

It made a splatting sound on the wall which made everyone look around, except me. I turned and faced the front. I felt flushed and I'm sure I gave myself away instantly. Everyone in the room gasped which made Sister Marie, who was at the front of the room, look up towards the mess on the wall. I caught Pauline's eyes and the expression on my face must have given me away but she only smiled and bowed her head. I turned to look at the apple on the wall again copying everyone else and the sight of the apple reminded me of soft shit running down the wall. It looked quite disgusting. Sister Marie stood up and in a demanding tone said,

"Who threw that?"

No one answered.

"If the person who did it doesn't own up immediately, I'll punish every girl here. Now who threw it?"

I was waiting for Margaret to speak up and report me, but no one answered again. Sister Marie was becoming furious by this stage, and this time she screamed at us.

"I want to know who threw it, and I want to know now" she demanded.

Then something unusual happened, Linda stood up and said, "It was me Sister Marie.

Then another girl beside Linda stood up and said, "It was me Sister Marie."

Then I stood up and said, "It wasn't them, Sister Marie, it was me."

Two more girls stood up and said it was them. Suddenly, Margaret became very excited. She stood up and began clapping her hands,

"It was me, It was me," she mumbled and began to jump up and down on the spot. We all turned and looked at her, then suddenly she dropped to her knees and began banging her head on the bench I had been sitting on. She was frothing at the mouth, and drooling all over my seat. I began to scream and the other girls looking at her followed my reaction. Sister Marie yelled at us all to shut up and made her way up to Margaret. She told one of the older girls to go fetch Sister Angela, who came and took Margaret off to bed. The whole room was quiet now and Sister Marie told us all to sit down. I was hesitent to sit down again though because of the saliva which had been all over my seat. Even though it had been cleaned now, the thought of it still made my stomach queasy.

After all the commotion we went through, Sister Marie had calmed down about the apple, however she hadn't forgotten it. How could she, it was still plastered on the wall.

"Who made that mess on the wall," she repeated in a quieter tone.

Out of the blue Pauline, my own sister stood up, and said,

"It was Josephine who threw the apple Sister Marie."

Linda jumped to my defence and said, "She's lying Sister Marie, she couldn't even see who threw it from the front row. It was me who threw the apple, not Josephine."

"You two again," Sister Marie said, "Alright, both of you down here now, and you too Pauline." she said in a harsh voice.

Pauline began crying, she hated being in any trouble. She loved being the "teacher's pet" so to speak.

"I haven't done anything wrong" Pauline whimpered in a pityful voice, which made me sick right now.

"Oh shut-up child" Sister Marie answered, obviously annoyed with her whimpering as well.

The three of us stood in front of her like soliders, while she marched up and down in front of us like the general. After a few minutes she said,

"Who threw the apple?"

"I did" I said, and told her the whole story. When I had finished she left the room. She returned a few moments later with two buckets of water, and 'Discipline'.

While she was gone I gave Pauline a good thumping in the back and said, "I'll get you for this."

That was the worse thing I could have done and I regretted it immediately, because she began screaming louder as though someone was trying to kill her making me nervous in case I would be further punished for the apple. Linda and I received six lashes each across the back of the legs. Margaret Delany was safe in bed and received no punishement for her part in this scenario. As for Pauline she was verbally reprimanded and told to mind her own business in the future.

Apart from our lashes, Linda and I were made wash down the wall while the rest of the class continued with the music lesson. When we had finished cleaning the wall to perfection, we assumed the punishment was over. However we were in for another surprise. When we returned to Sister Martha's class we were greeted by a slap in the face from her. Sister Marie had obviously told her about the incident when she came to get 'Discipline' from her. There was also a letter ready and waiting for me to copy on the blackboard. It was addressed to my father and it went like this,

Dear father,

Today I threw a rotten apple at a girl and missed her, hitting the wall instead. I am writing to ask you to send some money for paint, as the wall now needs repainting.

Love from your daughter
Josephine Lynch.

I copied the letter with disgust, knowing there was nothing wrong with that wall after we cleaned it. It was snow white again. They were just using me as an excuse to get money out of dad and there was nothing I could say, or do about it. Even if I sent a sly letter and told him the truth, they would know I did it, because he wouldn't send the money. I just had to let him pay for nothing and forget about it. It was safer that way.

As for Pauline I didn't beat her up as I threatened. I decided to just stay away from her. Every time she approached me I told her to get back to the nuns and tell them some tales, and that she couldn't be trusted. Sometimes I felt cruel doing this and my heart would cry out for her, but I just reminded myself of what a traitor she was and how many times she had double crossed me in my young life.

I was as soft as butter and she was made of stone. She didn't need love or companionship, I lived for it. We were two totally different people. I often thanked god for finding Linda when I first arrived here, because she got me through so many bad times. Looking back on it now, I doubt that I would have survived the years in there without her friendship and loyalty. I'm sure I would have found some way to end my own life without her. Where ever you are now Linda, I thank you with all my heart.

CHAPTER 41

One Saturday morning Kitty Kanavin instructed me to pull all the sheets off the beds. I was busy doing this but when I came to about the fourth bed I pulled down the top covers and the sheets were full of blood. At first I was startled and images flashed across my mind about the time I took a razor blade from the matron's sewing room, and cut an ugly wart off my knee. I stood there remembering how much blood gushed from it, and how I was slapped by Sister Angela for being both stupid, and vain.

I returned from my thoughts and viewed the bed in front of me again, it must have been her leg like mine I thought. It couldn't have been a nose bleed because the blood was in the middle of the bed. I gazed around the dormitory for the girl who slept in this bed but she wasn't in the room. I called Linda to come over and have a look at all the blood in the bed, and before I knew it there was a crowd around the bed looking at the stained sheets.

Kitty saw the commotion and came over to investigate it's cause. When she realized what we were looking at she shooed us all away, telling us to go about our chores before she reported us. She gave me a filthy look and told me to finish off the other beds that she would finish this one.

I went on to the next bed wondering why she had been so short tempered with me, then I shrugged my shoulders discarding my negative thoughts and went about my business.

Later in the afternoon Sister Angela approached me in the playroom. She tapped me, or should I say poked me in the shoulder and said,

"Outside Lynch,"

I looked at Linda and with my eyes asked her what this was all about, before following Sister Angela outside. As I followed her I searched my brain for something I had done wrong but nothing came to mind. I was one hundred per cent sure I'd been good, so what was this all about. As soon as we were outside the playroom she slapped me throwing me off balance because it was so unexpected.

"What did I do?" I asked holding my face from the blow.

"You're a filthy little cow Lynch, and not fit to mix with other children."

I scanned my brain again for an explation to her anger, but like before came up blank.

"I don't understand."

"I don't understand," she mimiced, "well I have a surprise for you tomorrow regarding next Sunday, which I'm sure you will understand. Now get out of my sight."

I went back inside the playroom to the comfort of my friend Linda, and told her what happened.

"What do you thing I did Linda?"

"I've got no idea. Maybe your dad answered the letter you wrote about being stripped and beaten by Sister Marie."

"No, I begged him not to. He wouldn't do that to me because he knows I'd get punished and he loves me too much."

"Well I don't know then."

"No, neither do I. Ah well maybe I'll find out tomorrow, the old bag said she had a surprise for me, but the smirk on her face tells me it's another punishement of some sort, not a surprise." I said pulling a crooked mouth.

Linda started laughing at my expression and I joined in. For the time being Sister Angela and next Sunday were forgotten about.

However, later in bed when I was by myself, it all came back. I tossed and turned most of the night racking my brains for what I had done wrong, not to mention what was going to happen tomorrow and next Sunday. Finally I got up, not able to stand the uncertainty anymore and I marched down to the matron's cubicle, but after going in I regretted being there. It must have been later than I thought because the matron was fast asleep. I turned around ready to sneak back to bed, but I had already disturbed her and she whispered my name sitting up in her bed.

"Josephine, it's 2am, what are you doing up?" she asked looking at her watch.

"I can't sleep, but I'm sorry for waking you, I'll just go back to bed."

"No, I'm awake now tell me what's bothering you."

"Well Sister Angela slapped me today for no reason, well no reason I can think of, and I was wondering if you knew what I'm supposed to have done?"

"No, I have no idea."

"Well I don't think I did anything wrong. I think she was just being mean to me. I wish I could just run away or disappear some how. I can't stand this place any more. I'm always getting strapped and slapped for no reason. When is it going to stop?" I said, breaking down into tears.

"When you're sixteen and leave here I'm afraid. You should be used to it by now Josephine."

"Well I'm not, and it's nearly four years before I leave."

"Three and a half".

"Three and a half, four, what's the difference, it's still years away," I said getting all boiled up inside and angry with my predicament.

"Now now love, calm down. Listen, I know what will make it easier on you."

"Yea, what?" I asked, thinking she was going to give me some great solution to keep me out of trouble.

"Stay away from Linda Mitchell."

I sat on the end of her bed staring at her for a few moments, too shocked at her suggestion to move.

"I could never do that. Linda's my very best friend. She's what makes it bearable in here. I'd much rather take any punishment than lose her as a friend."

"Look love, Linda has no parents so they punish her more frequently and because you're always with her, you cop it too."

"I don't care, besides I've asked my dad to take her so in a way she has got parents."

She studied me for a moment with affection, then she smiled and said,

"You're a very loyal and loving friend Josephine. Linda's a very lucky little girl."

"No, it's me that's lucky. She's also very loyal to me. She would take my punishments for me a hundred times over, and laugh about it later."

"Yes, I'm sure she would." the matron answered with the gentlest of smiles on her face.

We sat in silence for a few moments just holding hands. Then I remembered my surprise for next Sunday and said,

"Matron, what's happening next Sunday?"

"Sister Angela will be announcing it tomorrow at breakfast."

"Oh, but can't you tell me now?"

"Okay, but act surprised in the morning okay."

"Yes, I will." I promised.

"Well apparently when your father sent the money to repaint the wall of the music room, he also sent extra money to take all the girls at the convent to Knock-Shrine."

"Why? Is my father religious?"

"I don't know" she answered me, laughing at the same time. "You are a trick Josephine, you come out with the funniest things sometimes."

I giggled too, but didn't know what was so funny.

"Here's the bad news though. Sister Angela isn't going to let you or Linda go."

"Why not?"

"She said that there wasn't enough money for everyone."

"But it was my dad who sent the money."

"Yes I know love, but never mind you can go next time, and you have been there a few times before anyway."

"Not with my father's money. I'm going to write a sly letter and tell my dad never to send money again and tell him that Sister Angela wouldn't let me go."

"Don't you dare Josephine. They'll crucify you if they find out."

"I don't care. I get punished for nothing anyway, so I may as well get punished for something."

"Come on love you'd best get back to bed, you're getting yourself all upset. Besides, it's nearly 3am and you look exhausted."

I stood up. Then I bent over and kissed her cheek affectionately, and marched back to bed. She was right, I was exhausted, too exhausted to even hold on to my anger.

The next morning my eyes stung from lack of sleep and it was hard to pull myself out of bed, not only because I was exhausted but I was also dreading the announcement at breakfast. I went about my chores like everyone else and at breakfast the announcement was made. First Sister Angela asked everyone to give thanks to my father, then she announced that Linda and I wouldn't be going. I sat there battling to hold back my tears. They were not tears of self pity for not being allowed to go to Knock-Shrine. They were tears of fury. I was angry at the un-fairness of it all. My father's money and I couldn't go. It just wasn't fair. After breakfast Maureen came over to me and put her arm around my shoulders,

"I'm sorry," she said and the tears that I was holding back just flowed from my eyes.

"Oh Maureen I hate this place." I said as I hugged my sister. Maureen started to cry as well. "Don't cry Josephine", she comforted, "we haven't got much longer in here. It's nearly over, so be strong for a while longer."

"But I don't even know why I got punished, it just doesn't make sense."

"I know why you were punished."

"You do. How come you know when the matron doesn't."

"Because Kitty told me. When you saw the blood in the bed you showed it to everyone. It's supposed to be a secret, never to be spoken about."

"What's a secret that Julie hurt herself?" I asked, feeling even more confused.

"Julie didn't hurt herself. It happens to all young girls at about twelve or thirteen years old."

"What does?"

"Oh never mind Josephine, you'll get us both in trouble if we're caught discussing it. Just drop it for now, okay."

"Okay." I answered wondering why Maureen was so nervous all of a sudden. I was so confused. I wanted to find out how Sister Angela had heard about it as well, but for Maureen's sake I dropped the subject. I had never seen her so nervous.

Sunday came and everyone was in the yard ready to go to Knock-Shrine. Sister Angela came up to me and Linda and with her big grin intact on her prune face, she said, "Don't get too lonely girls."

I couldn't hold my tongue, "Sister Angela why am I being punished, what did I do that was so wrong?"

She slapped my face and said, "You're a filthy little girl

Jospehine. Just get out of my sight."

I turned and walked back inside quickly fearful of receiving another slap. Linda followed closely behind. We walked silently to the playroom and watched everyone leaving through the window, wondering what Sister Martha had planned for us to do.

When everyone was gone we looked at each other and as if we were siamese twins attached by the brain, we both burst out laughing.

"I'm sorry you got punished along with me Linda."

"Don't be, it's not your fault."

"Yes it is. If you wasn't my friend you would have been allowed to go. I know why I got punished, but you were punished for just being my friend."

"Why did you get punished?"

"Because I showed the blood in the bed."

"If you knew why you were punished why did you ask Sister Angela before and get another smack for nothing?"

"Because I wanted her to tell me herself. Maureen said it was a secret and shouldn't be spoken about, so I wanted Sister Angela to tell me all about it."

"Why is it a secret, what's wrong with it? There's no difference between a bed full of blood and a bed full of vomit and we're allowed to talk about the vomit."

"Oh Linda that's revolting," I said giggling, "but you're right, I don't know what the difference is either. One thing though, I'm going to write and tell my dad about this, that's for sure. I'll make sure he never sends any money again."

"You can do that today there's no one around."

"No they'll be watching, expecting me to do it. I'll leave it for a couple of weeks, when they think I've forgotten about it."

"I wonder what "Proud Tit's" Martha has planned for us

today?" Linda asked, making us both laugh again.

"I guess studying, who knows until she comes in. Hopefully she never will." I said with a giggle.

A few moments later the matron entered the playroom, "Get lost you two, go for a walk up the hill. Sister Martha asked me to keep a watch on you, but I've got work to do, so stay out of trouble."

I looked at her and smiled, "We will" I said, "and thanks."

She patted me on the head and winked at me as I left the room. "Be good," she reminded us.

Linda and I walked up the hill and over to the nun's private cemetary. When we arrived we started reading the names of the dead nuns from the tombstones, killing ourselves laughing when we came across a strange name. When we were bored with that Linda suggested we go to the laundry and play with the soap and water. Shorty after getting to the laundry we began playing with the baths of starch, stirring them around with a big stick. Suddenly a tom cat ran past from behind one of the troughs making us both jump with fright. Then Linda decided to coax the cat towards her. When it came she picked it up and gently stroked it.

"It's all dirty" I said, "No one loves the poor thing." Then I got an idea,

"Why don't we give it a bath in the starch and it will come out lovely and crispy fresh."

"That's a great idea." Linda said with glee.

Neither of us were being cruel. We just didn't know any better. In our hearts we were being kind to this poor deserted cat. Neither of us had a vicious bone in our body. We put the cat in the bath of starch and began washing it. Somehow I don't think it liked it very much, because it began screeching and scratching at us, but at the time we figured it just wasn't used to being washed and held a firm grip on it while we gave it a good cleaning.

Suddenly our names were called out, "Lynch, Mitchell, what on earth do you think you're doing?"

We both looked towards the laundry room door instantly releasing the cat and standing up-right like soldiers. The cat jumped to freedom and fled past Sister Vincent running for it's life.

"We were only trying to make it clean" I answered. "We weren't hurting it."

"Tomorrow morning when the furnace has been lit and the water is boiling, I'm going to put you two in the hot water for a bath and see if you like it."

"But the starch is cold, we wouldn't put the cat in the starch if it was hot, that would be cruel."

"It was cruel, hot or cold. Cats hate water, it's a wonder it didn't die with fright, the poor thing."

"We didn't know that."

"Oh shut-up and go and play somewhere else you idiots. I'll inform Sister Martha about this later and let her deal with the pair of you."

Both of us ran out thankful we weren't going to be put in the boiling water. We still had Sister Martha to deal with, but not until tomorrow. Today we could have fun.

When we were well away from Sister Vincent, I suggested that we go to the chapel and say a prayer that we wouldn't get into too much trouble tomorrow over the cat and Linda said, "Do you think that will really help us Josephine?"

I laughed at her expression and answered, "Well it won't hurt, will it?"

"I guess not" she said and the pair of us went off to pray for a light punishment. When we left the chapel we decided to go back to the convent for lunch before Sister Martha came looking for us, otherwise the matron would get into trouble.

Later in the evening when the girls returned from Knock-Shrine, they told us what a lovely day they had, but we didn't mind. We had great fun by ourselves, without all that walking, not to mention the bossy nuns. That night I lay in bed wondering what was going to happen with Sister Martha the next day. I hated night time because that's when I seemed to do all my worring. During the day I had Linda there to help me forget the bad things, but at night I was by myself, left alone to think about everything that happened. I knew Sister Martha was going to punish us, I just didn't know how. I was always so scared in that place. Always wondering what punishment I would receive next. It really was hell on earth. I finally fell into a restless sleep and Monday came around all too soon. I awoke with a terrilbe feeling of fear inside me. However it was an unjustified fear because apart from being called a dirty or filthy child all day, I received no phyical punishment. So I had worried restlessly all night for nothing.

CHAPTER 42

Eventually the blood filled bed dilemma was forgotten about and life went along as usual, very slowly! One day Sister Martha informed us that the Health Inspector was coming from Dublin, and she instructed us not to talk to this doctor. In fact we had to strip down to our underwear and stand in single file, silently waiting our turn. This procedure only happened once before that I could remember, which was when I first arrived at the convent.

A few days later the doctors arrived, one male and one female. I was third in line from Sister Martha's class and I stood there in just my vest and knickers. Our bust binders were removed and it felt quite nice being free from them. There was about six other girls standing in the row after me and two had already been seen.

We all stood there in dead silence when suddenly Sister Marie said,
"Lynch take off your underwear."
"But Sister Martha told us to leave them on Sister Marie."
"Get them off" she growled, annoyed that I had answered her back.
I took off my underwear but I felt like hiding. I was so embarrassed and ashamed of my appearence. I had a dark brown mole on my backside and I was exceptionally large, but that was no reason to embarass me like this. Looking back on it now, I'm sure Sister Marie was just a rotten pervert who got her kicks out of seeing us children in the raw.

Sister Martha and Sister Marie stood there sniggering, as they commented on my obvious faults. I wanted to die, right there on the spot. I felt so trapped, like a tiger in a cage with nowhere to run. All my friends watched on, as the sniggering remarks were being made. However none of them joined in or laughed. Maybe they felt sorry for me or maybe they were scared in case they got the same treatment. However their silence didn't make me feel any better, they were still there and they were still watching me in my embarrasment.

My name was finally called and I went into the visiting room. As I entered I burst into tears through sheer frustration and embarrassment, over what I just experienced. Maybe it was my way of seeking help from these strangers. Sister Angela put her arms around me, acting concerned to the doctors and said, "What's the matter Josephine, are you afraid of the doctors?"

"No" I answered, pulling myself away from her,

"I was the only one who had to take their clothes off and Sister Martha and Sister Marie were laughing at my brown spot and my shape in front of everyone."

Both doctors looked at Sister Angela for an explantion. She in turn looked back at them dumbfounded. That was the last thing she had expected me to say.

Finally she found her tongue and said, "All the little girls took off their underwear."

"I'm not little, I'm nearly thirteen."

"I'm sorry love you look little, I mean short" she corrected herself. "Maybe Sister Marie was confused, she is getting old now Josephine, and can't remember all the girls ages."

The women doctor cut into the conversation, "Sister Angela, would you go and get the child her underwear please," she said, smiling my way.

As soon as Sister Angela went to the door, the female doctor said,

"Do you like it here in the convent Josephine?"

But before I could answer Sister Angela was back, so I hesitated.

"Well?" the doctor asked in an encouraging tone.

"No, I hate it here" I answered bravely, thinking that just maybe this woman could help me.

The doctor reached out and took my underwear from the very nervous Sister Angela and said, "This is cruelty you know, and I will be reporting it to the authorities and her family."

"The girl's exaggerating because she got embarrassed. It was a genuine mistake on the part of an elderly nun. I just asked Sister Marie myself and no one was laughing at her, she must have imagined that part. Surely we would have heard them from here if they were laughing, it's only in the next room."

How well she lied, I thought. She was so convincing, but I could tell by the doctor's face that she wasn't totally convinced by Sister Angela's explanation, even though she was staying quiet. My examination began and afterwards the female doctor took out a card and handed it to me.

"Take this Josephine and if you ever need something or someone to talk to, I'll come to you okay."

I looked at the card which had her name and phone number on it, and gave a short laugh. It was more of a noise of disbelief than a laugh though.

"What's so funny?" she asked.

"Nothing really, it's just that I would never be able to contact you." I said handing her back the card. "We even have to copy our letters from the blackboard. To tell you the truth, even if you came back here I wouldn't be allowed to talk to you." Then I looked up at Sister Angela and added,

"I'm probably in big trouble already."

"Oh, I don't think so," she said looking at Sister Angela with a threatening gleam in her eyes."

Then she changed the subject, "What would you like to be when you grow up."

"Well my dad wants me to be a secretary, but I want to be a dressmaker." I said with confidence.

I looked at Sister Angela again and the spirit I had just displayed when I was talking to the doctor died instantly as I saw the anger in her eyes. In fact I felt quite sick inside, wondering what I had let myself in for. I decided to shut-up and not say another word. The doctor dismissed me and I left the room to go back to class where the previous two girls were waiting. Sister Martha and Sister Marie marched in a few minutes after the last girl returned to class. They weren't laughing any more, they were deadly serious and I knew by their expressions that I was in big trouble.

"Stand up Lynch" Sister Martha snapped.

I stood up, shaking from head to toe.

"Why were you crying and carrying on in front of the doctors."

"Because you were laughing at me." I answered, but my voice was trembling as I spoke.

"We were not laughing at you."

"Yes you were, everyone heard you as well."

"We were laughing at something else."

"You were pointing at me and laughing at me too." I contradicted defiantly.

Sister Martha walked down from the front of the room and slapped my face hard, "You're nothing but trouble Lynch and you have a very big mouth."

She grabbed my ear and began shaking me to and fro.

"You will pay dearly for your lies. You mark my words. Now sit down before I knock you down."

As usual I began to worry. I felt terrible. The anticipation of a punishment was far worse than the punishment itself and I knew it would come. The nuns did that a lot. They were always frightening us to keep us under control, until in the end you were a nervous wreck. I decided that this was a good time to write a sly letter home and tell dad everything that had happened since Knock-Shrine. The nuns would believe the doctors had written to him because she took notes as we spoke. She even told Sister Angela that she would be reporting it to my family as well as the authorities.

Sister Martha never forgave me for telling the doctor that she was laughing at me. I did write a sly letter to dad which he answered to the Reverend Mother revealing his fury with the situation. He didn't mention Knock Shrine because I told him not to, but he made it quite clear that he wouldn't be offering any futher support to the convent and that he was disgusted with the news he had received from the Dublin Health Department.

Sister Martha set out to repay me for the trouble she got into over it. She was out to get me anyway she could and it stood out like a sore thumb. She constantly called me stupid, and would tell me that Margaret Delayne, the retarded girl, had more brains and common sense then I did. One day we were standing around the black board looking at a map, and as she walked past me she punched me extremely hard in the stomach. "You weren't paying attention Lynch" she said and smirked as I moaned in pain.
I became very depressed and solemn with the constant torment. I was afraid of my own shadow. Alone in bed each night I begged god to make her stop punishing me but it didn't seem to help. This went on for several months and I began to live a life of harrasment, always expecting something bad to happen. I was only thirteen years old, a time where life should be happy and carefree. My life was misery and imprisonment.

One day Sister Angela came into the classroom and began whispering to Sister Martha and the pair of them looked my way. My heart began beating faster, Oh no I thought, what are they going to do to me now. I can't take anymore of this I thought, feeling extremely sorry for myself, and I broke down into tears. Tears I had held back for the past several months.

"What on earth are you crying for Lynch?" Sister Angela asked.

"I'm scared"

"Don't be silly child, dry up those tears now and come along with me."

This can't be happening I thought. Why is she being so kind to me. I felt confused and hesitant to follow her. I felt unsafe and my imagination ran wild. Images of horror flashed through my mind. I trusted no one, including my sister Pauline. Maureen, Linda and the Matron were the only people I had any faith in now.

"Come on child," she repeated, "Sister Gertrude would like to see you." What does she want I asked myself. I haven't done anything wrong, then for a brief moment I had a hopeful thought. Maybe they were going to send me back to dad because I was too much trouble, but I discarded the thought instantly as wishful thinking.

When I arrived Sister Gertrude was sitting in the Reverend Mother's Chair, which seemed extremely strange to me.

"Come in Josephine." she said.

I went in and after Sister Angela left, Sister Gertrude began to speak.

"The Reverend Mother is getting too old now to handle the mail and the problems of the convent so I have been assigned to take over." She paused briefly looking up at me from her desk, "I was just going over a back log of mail and there is a letter from your father along with a copy of the Health Departments Report. Now I want you to tell me what exactly happened the day the doctors were here."

I sat there in silence, scared to open my mouth.

"Well come on dear."

"Will I get into trouble again, if I tell you?"

"No, not if you tell me the truth."

"Well I am big and not in the baby class anymore, but Sister Marie told me to take off my clothes like the babies. Then she and Sister Martha started making fun of me and I just burst out crying because I was so ashamed."

"Yes dear, I would have felt the same way." She paused again, then added, "Look, I will talk to them both about this for you."

"Oh no, please don't do that" I said, beginning to panic. "You promised I wouldn't be in trouble if I told the truth. I've been in trouble everyday since then. I can't stand any more punishment." I said, bursting into tears yet again.

"Now now, stop those tears. No one is going to punish you, I promise. Is that why you told the doctors that you hated the convent?"

"Yes, I get punished nearly every day and half the time it's for nothing."

"Okay. I'll look into that too. Now will you do something for me?"

"Yes"

"I am going to get Sister Martha to draft a letter, in answer to your father's angry letter, and I want you to copy it."

"Yes" I answered wondering why I was being asked to do it rather than ordered, like usual. Especially since dad's letter came months ago.

"Okay, you may leave now. Sister Angela is outside to take you back to class."

When I opened the door Sister Angela was sitting there

waiting for me, and as she stood up to take me back to class the Reverend Mother called out, "Oh Sister Angela,"

"Yes Sister Gertrude"

"Could you ask Sister Martha and Sister Marie to come up for a moment please."

"Yes of course Sister Gertrude."

I was expecting the third degree from Sister Angela on the way back to class, but she didn't speak a word. I was totally confused with this change in her and wondered why everyone was being so nice to me today. Maybe they were trying to send me mad or trick me into trusting them I thought. I would have to be on my gaurd, nothing good lasted long around here. I returned back to class and Sister Martha left. She returned about fifteen minutes later and avoided me totally for the rest of the afternoon. Although I didn't understand this change in her, I was in my glory about the situation.

That night at dinner I was talking to Linda quietly, telling her all about my meeting with Sister Gertrude. Afterwards I said, "Linda before I die I'm going to write a book and tell the world about this place. I'm going to write about how cruel most of the nuns were. I know I'll need help doing it, but by christ, I'll do it somehow."

"That's a great idea and I know you will get it done Josephine. You are very determined, but I want to ask you something."

"Yes, What?"

"I want you to do this one special thing for me."

"Yes anything, What is it?"

"I want you to stay away from me."

My face dropped, I couldn't believe my ears.

"Why, what's the matter?"

"I'm the cause of all your problems in here. They only pick on you because you're my friend."

"No way, I couldn't stay away from you. You mean too much to me Linda."

She hugged me right at the dinner table regardless of getting into trouble and tears rolled down her face.

"You mean too much to me too." She said, "I was hoping you would say that Josephine, I just wanted to give you the opportunity to stay away from me, if you wanted too. You haven't been very happy lately, and I thought it was because I got you into trouble all the time."

I smiled affectionately and squeezed her hand.

"I've asked my father to take you with me when I leave here and you ask me to stay away from you. You're completely mad Linda Mitchell."

We both laughed and the bell went for play time. We left the dinner room happy for a change.

The next day we were doing our maths class with Sister Martha, when suddenly Sister Gertrude entered the room. As usual lately, I became frightened and the first thing that came to mind was I hadn't written the letter to dad, but Sister Martha hadn't drafted it yet, but I still thought I was in trouble. However Sister Gertrude left the room without speaking to me, making me relax again. Sister Martha immediately announced that we were to put away our books and that there would be no school for three days because the Reverend Mother had just passed away.

To be honest, at the time I can't say I was sorry for the old woman. I did pray that she would go to heaven with sincerity, but in all truth, her death meant nothing more to me than three days off school. A pretty selfish attitude looking back on it now, but that's how I felt. The funny thing was, I did like the Reverend Mother, everyone did. I knew she wrote to my father constantly telling him how naughty Linda and I were, but she only wrote what she was told, so I never held any ill feelings towards her. In the end she wasn't even writing the letters, she was only putting her signature to them. She had a favourite saying as she walked through the yard if we were being rowdy.

"Quiet girls," she would say, "young ladies should be seen and not heard."

(That saying has stuck with me through the years, and I often used it on my "TOMBOY" daughter, who has now grown into a fine women, and is now the one helping me transcribe my life story.)

Sometimes a nun would threaten to report us to the Reverend Mother if we did something wrong, but it had no affect on us. The Reverend Mother never held a grudge like some of the other nuns, in fact she wouldn't even remember you the next day. Her slaps were so soft they fell off your face. She never showed violence or cruelty to anyone. So it was no punishment being sent to her. She was the kind of person I would regard as a "Holy Nun". She was strict with words but gentle and kind in actions. Not vicious and spiteful like some of the other nuns.

On the third day of her death she was buried. The gateman and his sons carried the coffin from the church to the grave yard and the nuns and children followed. We walked up the hill to the nun's cemetery in pouring rain. The Westport parish priest gave his sermon. I didn't understand a word he was saying, but he made all the nuns cry. Then the Reverend Mother was layed to rest.

As we walked back down the hill I overheard one of the nuns saying,

"She had a great day, it's pouring with rain."

"Yes," her companion answered, "a very good sign that god was pleased with her."

It seemed like a strange comment to me at the time but I've never forgotten it. When ever I see a funeral and it's raining, I think to myself, god must have been pleased with that person. As for the three days holiday, well it was three days of praying and saying the rosary. We had to go to the chapel four times a day. Even when we returned to school we continued praying for her for the next four weeks. She was a very important person in the convent and acted as the mother of all the nuns, so it's not surprising that her death was treated with such high regard.

Sister Gertrude became the new Reverend Mother and I was thankful that it wasn't Sister Marie, Sister Martha or Sister Angela. Sister Gertrude never strapped me and seemed fair in her descisions. She punished us accordingly and without vindictiveness.

The day after the Funeral we returned back to school, picking up where we had left off with maths! I hated maths, it always got me into trouble. I was lucky to get three out of ten sums right most of the time, so I was always being verbally and physically abused during maths. Today however, we got our sheet of ten sums and I found them surprisingly easy. So easy I thought I must be doing them wrong. I had no confidence in my abilities at all, which wasn't surprising because any confidence we had was continuously stripped from us. We were never praised for our efforts or achievements either.

"Lynch are you finished?" Sister Martha asked when she saw me sitting doing nothing.

"Yes Sister Martha."

"Bring them here and let me see." she said with disbelief.

I walked up to her with my work sheet and she checked my answers, and ticked them all correct. Then she got out "Discipline" and began beating me.

"Who did you copy from" she yelled in an accusing tone.

"No one Sister Martha" I said, trying to duck the blows being lashed out.

"Stop your lying Lynch and tell me the truth." she screamed, as she continued beating me.

"No one," I assured her, "Give me ten more and I'll do them up here, Please stop hitting me, I didn't copy, I promise."

She stopped for a moment and studied me.

"Okay." she said, "I'll give you ten more, but if you get even one wrong, god help you."

I sat on the floor at the front of the room doing my ten sums. They were a little more difficult this time and I began to worry. When I finished I stood up to show her but my legs felt weak beneath me. I was so scared in case it had been pure luck the first time and these were all wrong. Sister Martha corrected them and with amazement they were all correct, which surprised me more than her I think. However, there was no praise given. In fact, she said in a scarcastic tone, "Your baby sister Pauline must have been showing you how to do them." Then she sent me back to my seat. I didn't mind the lack of praise, I was just thankful that I wasn't going to be punished.

Each day we got an hour study time, but because of the funeral and the three days off school Sister Martha fell behind in her schedule, so she decided to teach her younger class their maths during study time which she generally supervised anyway. She gave out the work sheets and she was correcting them immediately as the girls fininshed. Pauline sat there trying to complete the work sheet she had been given. She had no difficulties with maths. She was excellent at maths far better than Maureen and I put together. However it was winter and very cold and she was suffering from frostbite again. Her hands were red raw, dry and swollen. They were very tender to touch so writing was an awkward and painful experience for her.

I felt sorry for her seeing the obvious pain in her eyes as she sat at her desk writing. When she finished she raised her hand and Sister Martha called her up. She marched up as proud as punch knowing that all her sums were correct. They always were. Sister Martha began correcting them and when she finished she said, "Pauline you got two wrong."
A few of the younger girls in Pauline's class started to laugh, not many people liked, or trusted Pauline.
Pauline shocked and embarressed answered. "No I did not."
"Are you arguing with me Pauline."
"No"
"Well it sounds like it to me. Now go back and do those two sums again." Sister Martha said, handing her back the old worksheet along with a new one. Pauline stormed off, more marching then walking. She hated being wrong. She was angry and embarressed because she had been ridiculed by Sister Martha. When she got back to the desk she ripped up the old work sheet and threw it on the floor in temper. Sister Martha saw her do it and became angry. She stood up, picked up "Discipline" and marched over to her and really gave her a hiding. The strap came down straight across Pauline's two swollen hands. Several chillblanes broke and began to weep and bleed. Pauline screamed, "My hands, my hands." but it didn't do her any good. Sister Martha kept striking again and again.

My heart cried out for Pauline. I began wishing it was me being punished instead of her. It didn't matter about our past differences, she was still my sister and I loved her and seeing her in pain like this was killing me. Sister Martha gave her six lashes across each hand and when she had finished she sent her to Sister Angela to clean and bandage her hands. Sister Martha was more concerned about the mess that Pauline may make on the desk with the blood, rather than the pain Pauline was suffering.

I hated Sister Martha more at than moment, than any other time before. To me she was worse than the devil, and much more dangerous.

The next day at playtime I saw Pauline sitting on the bench in the yard, with her bandaged hands stuck under her armpits in an effort to keep them warm, and again my heart melted for her. I walked over and sat beside her.

"Do they hurt very much?" I asked looking at her hands.

"Yes, the cold makes them very sore, and the strapping has made them worse."

I wanted to abuse Sister Martha to Pauline and tell her I thought she was a wicked, cruel person but I held my tongue. I didn't trust my sister enough to speak my mind to her. She was very likely to use it against me later on. So I said, "Why don't you sit inside the door. You can hear the bell from there and if Sister Angela catches you, you won't be punished, she likes you too much."

"Yea, I think I will," she answered and got up and walked away, her hands still under her armpits. My insides were in knots for her. I sat on the bench and asked god why we had to suffer so much. I knew Pauline was a bit cocky but she didn't need this kind of treatment, no one did. I thought about Maureen who never hurt anyone. She too went through hell everyday, even more than me because she was studing for her final exam. Which reminded me that it would be my turn next year. Maureen said it was the worse year so far, but I couldn't imagine things could get any worse, but they did! I had hoped that when Sister Gertrude became Reverend Mother she would have abolished the strap forever but that didn't happen unfortunately.

CHAPTER 43

Christmas was with us again and as usual everyone was very excited, especially those with parents because they received parcels. This particular Chrismas, Margaret Delanye got over excited and had a severe fit, propably her worst, and she just wouldn't stop banging her head. Her face turned grey and her lips purple. I truly thought she was going to drop dead in front of us. That was the last fit she ever had at the convent and the last time we ever saw her. The convent sent her away to a Mental Institution where I believe she still remains. At the time I was relieved she was gone because she was crazy and you never knew what she would do, like the time with the raw chicken leg in the music room. However, looking back on it now, she wasn't a bad person, just not in full control of her actions or emotions. She was someone to be pitied, not hated.

The best thing about Christmas besides the parcels, was getting away from Sister Martha. Although the last few weeks hadn't been so bad, because we had a new nun teaching us. The reason we had a new nun was because Sister Martha was very busy, and the convent decided to get her a relieving nun from another convent, to take over some of her general classes, while she concentrated on the exam students. The new nun's name was Sister Rosa, and it was as if god had answered my constant prayers and sent her to me. She had only taken us for a few lessons prior to Christmas, but would be taking most of the classes after the holidays, because the older children, like Maureen, would be studing for their final exam.

Sister Rosa was lovely. She always took time to talk about our personel problems during lessons. I remember on her first day there some photos that Caroline sent in my birthday parcel fell out of my book, where I had them hidden. (I still remember the day I recevied the photos and how that night I lay studying them in the darkness. There was one of Francis in his Navy uniform, one of dad and one of Caroline. She looked so healthy and beautiful now. Her hair had grown past her shoulders. I remember Sister Angela saying that she looked dreadful when she saw the photos, but I knew different. I lay there wondering if I would turn out even a little like her, but I was doubtful. I thought about myself, fat legs, fat body, four eyes, and doubted that I could ever be beautiful. Then I remembered Caroline the day she left. She was so sick and frail, and a ghostly pale colour. Her hair was short and dead straight like my own, yet she was gorgeous now. I went to sleep that night happy and with a small amount of hope that I too would turn out beautiful when I left this place.)

As my photos slid across the classroom floor, I panicked thinking I would be in trouble. I sat there frozen just looking at Sister Rosa. She looked back at me and smiled. Then she bent down and picked up all three photos and looked at them.
"Josephine who are these photos of?" she asked
"My family."
She looked at me as if I were crazy and said, "Josephine you are an orphan."
"No I'm not." I answered offended. (I still hated that term 'orphan'.) She looked at the photos again and said "Who are they?"
I pointed out Francis, Caroline and my father and told her who they were and their names. I told her that Caroline had been in the convent and that dad took her out at the age of sixteen. Then I added that he would take Maureen and myself out when we reached sixteen too.
"Josephine, you have a great imagination darling." she

answered me, but her gentle voice gave me confidence to contradict her, so I said,

"No really, it's true, you can check with the Reverend Mother if you like."

"Okay Josephine, put the photos away now and let's get on with our studies." she said. She still didn't believe me, but she was too nice to make an issue out of it.

Christmas morning came and so did all the parcels from our families. I got three parcels this year, one from Francis, one from Caroline and one from dad. Dad didn't send any money this year though, he obviously got wise with Caroline there. There was also the townfolk's presents to share around, and we played "ME, ME, UP THE KNICKERS, like every other year. It was more fun than greed though, as we often gave back some of the things we got to children who weren't fast enough to get anything, or to those without parents. Linda and I had great fun comparing who got the most up our knickers. I always beat her because my bloomers were far bigger than hers so there was a lot more storage space!

On Christmas morning as I sat looking through all my gifts, Sister Rosa approached me, and said, "Josephine, you do have a family. I'm very sorry for doubting you."

"That's okay." I said, feeling very proud of myself.

"May I see the photos again?" she asked kindly.

"Yes of course" I said, producing the photos for her to look at and we sat talking merrily about my family. She told me how nice they all looked and that made me very happy and proud. I really liked Sister Rosa, she was such a genuine person and the only nun that ever apologised to me. The other nuns were mightier then thou and far too important to apologise to a child, even if they were wrong.

Maureen and Pauline also received three parcels from home, but Pauline got an extra present. A special present all wrapped up in pretty paper, from Sister Angela. It was another new pair of shoes. That night when we went to bed, Pauline's head girl, Nelly Grady, grabbed a wooden hairbursh and began beating Pauline over the head with it. She was jealous because Pauline received a special present from Sister Angela. As she hit her over and over again, she yelled,

"You think you're pretty special, don't you. Sister's Angela's little pet. The rest of us don't get special presents. We don't even get new shoes. You're a spoilt little brat Pauline."

After she had finished hitting Pauline and had her in tears, she said,

"Shut-up before you cop some more, and if you tell Maureen I'll bloody kill you."

I had seen and heard the whole thing and when Nelly left, I went over and cried along with Pauline, cuddling her in an effort to make her stop crying. Not only did I feel extremely sorry for her I also felt like a coward for not trying to help her, but that would have got all three of us into trouble. I had to get Nelly some other way. I turned to the still crying Pauline and said,

"Don't cry Pauline, I promise you I'll get her back somehow."

However Pauline didn't stop crying. In fact, she only sobbed harder and said,

"It's not my fault if Sister Angela gave me new shoes, I didn't ask for them."

"I know you didn't. Come on, stop your crying."

Finally she calmed down and I went back to bed, thankful I hadn't been caught near Pauline's bed by Sister Angela. It didn't matter for what reason I was out of bed, I knew she would take the opportunity to punish me. When I was safely back in my own bed, I said to myself "You'll pay for this

Nelly. I don't care what happen's, but you won't get away with beating my sister up."

A little later, when Sister Angela came up to say the night prayers, I pretended to be crying.
"Okay Lynch, what's the matter with you now?" she asked, annoyed with me.
"Nelly Grady was hitting my sister Pauline on the head with a hair brush because you gave her new shoes for Christmas."
"What!" she answered, and then angerily called out to Nelly.
"Grady get here this instant."
As Nelly walked past my bed she looked at me with daggers in her eyes. I, in turn, looked her straight in the face and smiled at her with great satisfaction.
"Is what Josephine said true Grady?" Sister Angela asked, when Nelly was standing in front of her.
"Yes Sister Angela."
"Why you jealous little animal," she yelled, slapping her across the face and head continuously as she spoke, "Don't you know that Pauline has very bad legs and needs decent shoes to wear. You're not fit to mix with other human beings, as from tomorrow you can start work in the laundry, you're too stupid for school anyway. Now get back to bed and if I ever hear of anyone beating Pauline again they will answer to me. Is that understood?"
Everyone nodded their heads with agreement and answered "Yes Sister Angela."
The next morning Pauline was allowed to stay in bed for the day. She was examined by the doctor for any signs of serious injuries, but apart from her frostbite she was fine.

The holidays flew by very fast as they always did and on the last night of the holidays some of us were playing on the verandah. The Reverend Mother was in a nearby classroom preparing for the following day. When she came out it was dark, although not late. It was only about five thirty in the evening. The Reverend Mother was a heavy set women and when she came out of her room someone shouted, "Look, there's a man coming out of that classroom."

With that everyone panicked and began to run inside like a herd of cattle. Because of my size and my lack of balance I stumbled and fell down. The herd of cattle with their big winter boots on ran right over the top of me, stamping me into the ground. There was no way I could get back up. When they had all passed, I sat up dazed and sore. There was someone standing over me and I became scared thinking it was the man we had all been running from, but when I looked up it was the Reverend Mother standing there.

"What on earth happened?" she asked as she saw the blood caused by the studded boots all over my head and hands.

"I don't know. One minute we were playing, then someone said there was a man coming and everyone ran, but I fell and they all stomped all over me."

"Come on. Can you walk?"

"I think so." I said as she helped me up.

"We will sort out who did this to you when we get inside." she said helping me walk back inside.

"Oh it wasn't anyone's fault" I said in an effort to defend my friends. I was just too fat to keep up with them, and we were all scared of the man."

"There was no man, it was me." she said,

"Oh", I answered laughing and feeling very silly.

We went into the playroom where all the other girls were watching out the window. As soon as she had me settled in a chair she looked around the room at all the other girls in disgust. Then she gazed at Linda.

"Mitchell were you outside with the others?" she asked,
"Yes Reverend Mother."
"Isn't Josephine supposed to be your best friend?"
"Yes Reverend Mother."
"Well why did you run off and leave her, if you thought she was in danger?"
"I thought Josephine was running too, I didn't realize she had fallen, otherwise I would have stopped to help her."
"Look what you have all done to Josephine through pure panic and stupidity. You are like animals. I want you all to grow up into ladies, gentle, caring, and above all level headed. You mustn't panic the way you just did. Panic causes accidents like tonight. Do I make myself understood?"
"Yes Reverend Mother," everyone answered.
"Okay. Well goodnight ladies. You come with me Josephine, I'll take you to Sister Angela, she will get these cuts cleaned up."

After the Reverend Mother left me in the care of Sister Angela, Sister Angela said,
"How come you're always in the midst of things Josephine?"
"I don't know, it just happens that way I guess."
"Ha" she answered and began cleaning up the cuts for me. When she was finished she said,
"You'll live, get back to the playroom."
"But my back is very sore too Sister Angela, couldn't I lie here and rest for a little while?"
"No you can't. Your back is fine, now go about your business. I've got work to do. You've already wasted enough of my time."

About half an hour later we were all doing the rosary with the matron. I was sitting with my legs stretched out in front of me, whilst everyone else was kneeling. Suddenly I felt strange. I began to see stars all around and felt very nauseous. Then, without warning, I fell forward landing between my own two legs.

Kitty Kanavan who was sitting beside me said, "Josephine, what is it?", but I didn't hear her, I was out cold.

The matron came over and I awoke to her slight tapping of my face.

"What happened Josephine?" she asked when I came to.

"I don't know, I just felt dizzy all of a sudden and really sick."

"Come on, off to bed with you. Kitty bring her upstairs please, here are the keys."

"Yes Matron." Kitty answered.

Kitty brought me up to bed and shortly later Sister Angela came up.

"What happend this time?" she asked, annoyed with tending to me yet again.

"I fainted."

"Are you okay now?" she said in a gentler tone.

"I guess so. You told me earlier that there was nothing wrong, so I guess there's nothing wrong."

"Don't get cheeky with me Lynch, just answer my question. Is there anything wrong?" she asked in a more abrupt tone.

"My legs, arms and back are very sore, but I'll be okay I think."

"That's better, I'll be on my way then." she said and left me on my own not giving me a chance to complain anymore, or giving me any sympathy!

I began to cry when she went. I felt so sore and I had an awful empty feeling inside of me. I felt so unloved and unwanted. No one seemed to care about me, especially Sister Angela.

However to my amazement Sister Angela returned about half an hour later to find me still crying.

"Here you are Lynch, I've brought you a hot drink, she said in a gentle voice, totally ignoring my tears. Usually I would have been abused for crying, but I think she actually felt sorry for me for a change. However, I didn't have the trust in her to feel comfortable with this change in mood.

"Why are you crying?" She finally asked gently.

"I don't know, I'm just so sore everywhere. Every part of my body is aching."

"Well drink this lemon drink and have a good nights rest. I'm sure you will be fine tomorrow."

"Okay." I said enjoying the attention.

"Good night Josephine." she said as she left.

"Good night Sister Angela." I answered. I couldn't believe the change in her. She was actually nice to me, with just the two of us present. It wasn't an act for someones benefit. It was me she was being nice to and I found myself liking her and realized why Pauline liked her so much. She could be quite nice when she wanted to be. I went to sleep that night, hoping that our relationship would grow into a friendship, but it didn't!

CHAPTER 44

I felt quite stiff the next day but I returned to school regardless. I didn't really mind though because Sister Rosa was teaching us, so that was all the incentive I needed. Besides I still hated being alone all day. It wasn't just me who adored Sister Rosa, all the girls in the convent did and everyone tried extremely hard to please her. The first week back at school, I was quite sore. I had these aching cramps around my back which I put down to the fall I had taken. On the Saturday Linda and I were cleaning the chapel as usual. I dusted whilst she did all the hard work, because I wasn't allowed to kneal. Linda didn't mind though and never complained about it. She was only too happy to do it for me. Before we left we threw the holy water on the graves, this was part of our duty as chapel maids. I could have done this chore alone while Linda finished the floors, Lord knows, I always finished my chores before her but I was too scared in the graveyard by myself.

Today my back felt really sore, ten times worse than it had been all week. I also had these dreadful stomach pains which seemed to be spreading from my back. As we walked out of the chapel to the graveyard I felt something dripping between my legs, so I said, "Linda, let's hurry up, I have to go to the toilet."
"Sure" she said, and we finished our chores quickly and ran back to the toilet yard.
My knickers were wet, but because they were black I didn't realise that it was blood. I pulled them back up thinking it was urine and that they would dry on me. I certainly didn't want them on my head for the rest of the day and had no intentions of reporting it, it was far better to be a little uncomfortable.
The pains in my abdmomen and back seemed to become worse after using the toilet. I had a constant dull ache with an

occasional sharp pain in my stomach which felt like I was being stabbed. I left the toilet and returned to Linda who was waiting outside, but about fifteen minutes later, I felt some more dripping and said to Linda, "I have to go again. You go and play, I'll catch up with you later."

When I was in the toilet I pulled down my knickers and there was a vile smell coming from them, so after I had finished going to the toilet I took them off and rinsed them out in the hand basin, which was actually a long trough with several taps along it. As I wrung them out I saw blood coming from them which shocked and frightened me. I panicked and put the knickers back on quickly but they were still very wet. I ran outside confused and in pain not knowing what to do or where to go. I wanted to sit down and rest, but I knew that if I sat my skirt would get wet from the knickers and everyone would think I had pissed myself. Instead, I leaned up against the wall with my shoulders only pushing my lower back forward so that my lower skirt wouldn't get wet. However with just my shoulders supporting me that became very uncomfortable, so I began to walk around.

I had to return to the toilet every ten minutes or so, because the blood kept dripping from me. I spent most of the morning just walking around, worried sick about what was happening to me. I thought about going to see Sister Angela who tended the sick or injured, but I was too embarrassed to show her where I was bleeding. I had no idea how or where I hurt myself and the strange thing was that my back and tummy were most painful and down below didn't hurt at all, yet that's where I was bleeding from. I started to imagine that I was bleeding from the inside and it had no-where else to come out, except my vagina. Then I thought, maybe it was the other way round.

Maybe I cut myself down there without realising and the infection was causing the stomach pains and that I was going to die. I contemplated going to Sister Angela again, but embarrassment won over fear and I discarded the idea.

Linda saw me and came running over, "Where have you been?" she asked.

"In the toilet most of the time, I've got terrible cramps in my stomach and back."

"Are you alright?" she asked concerned, "You look awfully pale."

"I don't feel too good?" I said as some more blood dripped between my legs.

"I have to go to the toilet again" I said running off "Sorry Linda."

"That's alright. I'll wait here."

"No don't worry, I may be a while. You go and play." I said, too embarrassed to tell her the truth and not wanting her wasting her day waiting around for me.

My head was pounding by this stage and I was freezing cold. I thought the headache was from worrying, as I had been wondering all day how on earth I cut myself down below. It was all very frightening to me at the time. I was still sitting on the toilet when I heard the lunch bell, so I got up quickly and went to go inside, but then remembered my wet knickers. How on earth can I sit down, I thought. My dress will get all wet. I decided to stay where I was. I was feeling bad enough without being punished and ridiculed as well, so I pulled my knickers back down again and sat on the toilet with my head on my knees and cried. I wasn't hungry anyway, I just hoped I wouldn't be missed.

About half an hour later I heard Kitty Kanavin calling my

name, Linda must have told her where I was and I knew I must have been missed for her to come get me.

"Josephine, are you in here?" she called.

"Yes, I'm in the second toilet. I've got pains in my tummy."

"Sister Angela told me to come get you for lunch."

"I don't want lunch, I don't feel very well."

"You'll feel better after you eat."

"No I won't."

"Look you must come out Josephine, they sent me looking for you. We'll both be in trouble if you don't come back with me."

"Please Kitty, could you just go and ask the matron to come and see me" I said, thinking she would know what to do to get me out of trouble.

"Josephine, please come out. The matron is having her lunch, I can't disturbe her, she'll kill me."

"Please, she won't tell you off, I promise. Just tell her that I'm sick and have very bad pains in my tummy and back."

"Okay Josephine, but if I get into trouble god help you."

A few minutes later the matron was knocking on the toilet door calling my name.

I started sobbing when I heard her and opened the door looking for some comfort.

"What's the matter Josephine?"

"I didn't jump the fence," I said, thinking that maybe she would think I had cut myself that way, when she had already asked me not to do that anymore."

"What?" she asked confused.

"I've cut myself down there somehow," I said pointing to my private area and I have a terrible headache and tummy pains and my back's worse than it was last Sunday," I mumbled through my tears.

"I'm scared to show Sister Angela in case she calls me dirty," I added.

"Stop your crying Josephine," matron said, realising what was happening to me. "There's nothing to worry about. Really love, it's quite normal. Now dry up your tears and come along with me."

As we walked back inside she said, "You look flushed Josephine, are you feeling alright?"
"No, I feel quite sick and my back and stomach are really hurting."
"I think you may be running a high temperature you feel very hot." she said as she felt my forehead with concern.
"We had best get you cleaned up and into bed."
"I don't want to go to bed, it's Saturday."
The matron laughed and answered, "You have to Josephine, you've got a temperature and you need some rest."
"But Sister Angela will probably get upset with me and slap me again when I tell her what's wrong with me."
"No Josephine, you don't tell her anything. I'll do all the explaning. You must never talk to anyone about this, especially a holy nun. It is very private. I'll explain it all to you myself when you're feeling better. You should have told Kitty, if anyone, she's your head girl and has been through all this. She would have told me but it doesn't matter now."
"I was too embarrassed to tell Kitty."
"Yes love, I know you were. Let's just get you into bed, I'll explain it all to you when your feeling better, okay."
"Okay." I said. I was relieved that I didn't have to face Sister Angela and another punishment, and if that meant spending another day in bed it was worth it.

After cleaning me up and giving me a towel to put between my legs and some clean underwear, the matron led me to my dormitory. When we got there she lay me on my stomach with a hot water bottle and left the room. She returned shortly after with some hot milk which I drank. Then I fell into a deep, peaceful sleep almost straight away.

The next day I felt much better, but Sister Angela told me to stay in bed. The matron came up later in the morning to explain what was happening to my body.

"Hi Josephine."

"Hi Matron."

"How are you feeling today?"

"A lot better thankyou."

"Good, that's nice to hear. Now what has happened to you is quite normal. You are becoming a young woman and once a month you will bleed like you are at the moment."

"This will happen every month" I interrupted, with disbelief and dismay.

"Yes I'm afraid so," she said smiling, "but you probably won't be as sore or as sick in the future. You will still get pains in the tummy of course, but I doubt that they will be as severe."

She hesitated for a moment, and then continued on a more serious note."You mustn't complain about the pain though. It is very private and should never be spoken about."

"Now then, I'll give you three towels which will be kept in your locker. It will be your responsibility to keep them as white as snow and never have a stain or mark on them. Your number is on them already for you." "Josephine, remember they will be checked from time to time and there will be hell to pay if there is even a faint stain to be found on them, so keep them clean."

I studied the towels in front of me. They were white, and made of terri-toweling. They were actually four pieces of towling stitched together, with a loop on each end.

"What are these for?" I asked pointing at the loops.

She handed me a thin, elastic belt, with a small hook on each side,

"You put this around your waist and the hooks go to the front and back. Each hook goes onto one of these loops to keep the towel in place, because when you walk around the towel sometimes moves and it can become uncomfortable."

"Oh, I see" I said, thinking that it must be awfully uncomfortable wearing the elastic around your waist, especially a big waist like mine!

"Okay," she said, "I better go now and leave you to rest, it's back to school for you tomorrow. And remember Josephine, keep those towels spotless."

"I will, I promise." I answered. I lay back down in bed feeling very grown up, but wondering why a strange thing like bleeding had to happen just to be grown up. It didn't make much sense to me and I considered it an awful nuisance.

The rest of that year passed surprisingly quickly, I can hardly remember any of it. Sister Rosa made life a lot more pleasant and the convent more bearable, so I guess that's why it wasn't so dramatic, at least not for me anyway. Maureen, on the other hand, was going through hell, studying for her final exam with Sister Martha. I knew next year would be hell for me. Maureen had given me plenty of warning. I just didn't know how bad 'bad' could be!

CHAPTER 45

Maureen's exam was in a few weeks, and while I had enjoyed Sister Rosa teaching us most of the time, Maureen painfully endured Sister Martha's class. I asked her one night what she would do if she failed her exam and she answered,

"Well apart from having to sit the exam again next year and missing out on my secretarial studies and of course putting up with "Proud Tits" for another year, I will get the strap and a lovely "Dunce Hat" for a week, while everyone else has a big party."

"Are you looking forward to the secretarial course?"

"Oh yes, I can't wait, that's why I want to pass so much. The other punishments wouldn't be too bad, but I'd hate to miss out on the course. It brings me that much closer to being a lady."

"You're mad Maureen," I said laughing, and then added, "Do you think you will pass?"

"Yes, I think so. Well, I hope so, I couldn't stand another year of Sister Martha and her famous "Discipline". This has been my hardest and longest year so far Josephine. If you think she is mean to you now, just you wait until next year. It's really terrible, you have no idea." she said with dismay.

"Thanks" I said sarcastically, "that's all I needed to know."

"Oh don't worry about it. If I got through it, you will, you're much tougher then me you know."

I didn't agree with her, I regarded myself as a bit of a cry baby and I had a very high impression of my her. I really looked up to her, and she was the strong one as far as I was concerned. However, I was glad she said it. It made me feel good knowing she admired me too.

"I better get to bed, I've got another big day of study tomorrow," she said, and left, laughing as she went.

"She is mad" I thought as I went to sleep, she doesn't care

about anything. Just being a so called lady.

Maureen's exam day finally arrived. It was referred to as the leaving exam, even though it was taken at fifteen, not sixteen when we left the convent. This gave those who failed, a second chance to pass. I guess if you failed a second time, there was no hope for you anyway.

The exam started at 9am sharp and finished at 4pm. There was a special room where the exams took place. The exam room was huge, with about twenty long benches about five feet apart. Three girls sat on each bench, one either end of it and one in the middle, leaving no opportunity to cheat or copy. The Dublin examiner and a nun from the convent sat on high pews at the front of the room. The exam papers were prepared in Dublin as well and arrived in sealed envelopes. The girl taking the exam was the one who opened it. This seemed strange because all our mail was opened and read by the nuns, so you were made to feel pretty important knowing you were the only one to open the envelope. A fifteen minute break was given between each subject to have some refreshments or use the toilet. Plus a half an hour break for lunch. The worst part of the exams was the waiting for the resuts which were posted from Dublin. This usual took four to six weeks, although each girl usually had a pretty good idea of their results before they came from Dublin.

The next few weeks went by very slowly for Maureen. One night she told me that the waiting was even worse then the exam. She had a pretty good idea that she had passed, but was so anxious to find out for sure. I felt really sorry for her. It was the first time that she seemed worried about anything. About three weeks into the summer hoildays the results came, which was only four weeks after the exam. One girl who had taken the exam failed, but it wasn't Maureen thankfully. It was Ilean

Kerry which was unfortunate because she had no parents, so she was more severely punished by Sister Martha than, say, Maureen would have been. For instance she was made wear the "Dunce Hat" for three weeks instead of one, even though it was summer holidays. She wasn't allowed to repeat the year either. Instead, she was put in the laundry and told that all she was good for was washing.

Maureen was very excited that she had passed, but she felt very sorry for Ilean Kerry, especially since she had been thrown in the laundry. Maureen told me that Ilean was really nice, and that she had always got along with her, and she thought Sister Martha was dreadful for being so hard on her.
For those who passed there was a big party. Well, what I mean by a big party is, there were cake and biscuits, which was a real treat for us, and very exciting. As for me, I was happy for Maureen, but even more excited about the summer holidays!

I was about fourteen now and still had the intellect of a ten year old. I could read and write basic words, but anything with more than five letters in it left me baffled. The standards for leaving the convent were equivalent to primary school standards, yet at fifteen it was a major accomplishment for us. Even Sister Martha was happy for about five minutes when we passed.

One day as Linda and I sat knitting, Linda turned to me and said,
"You'll be out of here in two years Josephine."
"I wish I was leaving next year with Maureen." I answered.
"Will you be doing secretarial studies like Maureen in your last year?" she asked,
"Well dad wants me to and has paid for it, but I'm not all that

keen. I'd like to learn dressmaking instead. I have to pass my exam first though, before thinking about anything else. I think Maureen just got lucky when she passed," I said with a skite of laughter.

"What's so funny?"

"Oh nothing, I was just thinking about Maureen a few months ago, when Sister Marie caught her pulling her stockings above her knees and how she made her carry the clothes horse tied to her back for a week. The clothes horse was bigger than she was the poor thing."

"Oh yes, that was funny," Linda said laughing along with me. "It wasn't so funny at the time though."

"No, I felt really sorry for her. The funny thing was she did the same thing a few weeks later."

"Yea I know, she's crazy sometimes," Linda said as we laughed at poor Maureen.

As usual the holidays came and went like lightning. We still had Sister Rosa some of the time, but not very often worse luck. We knew it wouldn't be long now before we had "Proud Tits' all the time, so we enjoyed Sister Rosa as much as possible for the time being. Doreen was now being taught by Sister Martha as well but only occassionally. Doreen was nine years old and no longer pretty as she was as a young child. In fact, she was quite ugly. She had turned very fat, even bigger than myself, and that's saying something. The only thing she had going for her was her blond curly hair, like Pauline. It didn't matter how much they cut it, the curls grew back. Doreen had big grey eyes that bulged like a cows. In fact Sister Martha gave her the nickname of Bulls eyes. Even Sister Angela didn't take much notice of her anymore. She didn't turn against her, she just wasn't as friendly towards her as she was when Doreen was smaller. In fact, she didn't have much contact with her at all now.

In a way it was harder on Doreen than the rest of the Lynchs. She never received any parcels at Christmas or her birthdays. To be honest, I didn't even know when her birthday was until years later. However, the rest of us shared our Chirstmas parcels with her, well at least Maureen and I did. Pauline only shared hers if she felt like it. Doreen knew that dad was taking the rest of us out at the age of sixteen, but she had no idea who was going to claim her, or if she would ever get out and we didn't know either. Her father, Dr Flannery never contacted her, nor did our mother. Mum hadn't bothered with any of us. Doreen's loneliness must have been more devastating than mine, at least I had my sisters and my dear friend Linda. Even though we knew Doreen was our step-sister we never, even as youngsters, regarded her as part of the family. We treated her as someone who had no one, with pity.

A few weeks after Maureen's exam results, Sister Martha told us that we would be having a long weekend, because on Monday we would be going to Westport for a "FESH", which she explained was a carnival type atmosphere with entertainment and singers and dancers from all around the country who performed folk songs and dances. We were also told that Pauline would be dancing there, and that we all had to clap loud when she came on stage to give her encouragement. This seemed strange to me, because Pauline didn't need encouragement as she was a cocky little brat who loved all the attention, or so I thought. The truth was she hated dancing in public, she felt like a freak and told the nun's that she didn't want to do it, but was forced to anyway. I didn't find out all this until years after we left the convent.

Sister Martha instructed everyone not to talk to anyone, or make a nuisance of themselves, and above all we were not allowed to accept anything. She told us that anyone caught disobeying the rules woud be severely punished. We travelled by bus to the Fesh, which was, in itself very exciting since we had never been on one before. When we first arrived we walked around looking at all the different attractions of the Fesh. There were food stands, and rides. (Not that we were allowed on any rides.) There was ice-cream, popcorn and all different sorts of lollies. There were clowns, ballons, but most of all people, more people than I imagined were alive. At the time I thought that the whole world must have come to see the dancing and singing. I was truely amazed by it all.

After about two hours, the dance performances were announced and everyone gathered around a huge stage. We were given a nominated meeting place by Sister Martha and told to sit wherever we could find a seat.

Linda and I ran off together amazed at the freedom we were given. We found some vacant seats beside a women, and quietly watched the different acts being performed. Finally it was Pauline's turn to dance and I became strangely nervous for her, even though I knew she wouldn't be. Pauline came out on stage and the women sitting beside me said to her male companion, who I thought was her husband,

"Oh look, it's the orphan girl. Can you imagine, she was once a cripple and the nuns taught her to walk."

"No love, it's just unbelievable isn't it." the man answered.

I looked at Linda and she knew I was angry by the womans words.

Then I turned and looked at the women, and said,

"That's my sister up there and we are not orphans, we have parents. Please don't call us orphans because we hate that word.

It wasn't the nuns who taught her to walk either it was me. They only taught her to dance afterwards."

"Oh," she said, "I'm sorry darling, I didn't mean to offend you or your sister."

Then her husband bent over and smiling he said, "Would you both like an ice-cream?"

"No thank-you we're not allowed to take from strangers." I answered

"But a stranger's just a friend you don't know and it's so hot today. Besides, if any of the nun's walk by you can just drop it and we'll watch out for you." he said.

I looked at Linda and we both nodded to the man in agreement. We managed to eat the ice-cream without getting caught and we thoroughly enjoyed it. While we ate our ice-cream the couple asked us many questions, which we answered gladly, forgetting all the rules Sister Martha had stipulated. I still don't know if they thought I was imagining my parents, but it didn't matter they were awfully nice to us.

Pauline danced several routines that day and won quite a number of medals. The nuns were there to take all the glory for her and they were extremely pleased with her efforts. After all the winners were announced, they showered her with ice-cream, lollies and drinks. However, we probably enjoyed our ice-cream much more, because we weren't supposed to have it! As for Pauline, I think she was just glad it was all over. All she heard all day was the orphan, or the cripple and it got on her nerves as much as mine.

We returned to the convent late that night and went straight to bed, having eaten packed dinners on the bus. Maureen was looking forward to getting back, because tomorrow she was starting her commercial classes. However she was greatly disappointed because she believed that it would occupy the whole day, but as it turned out they were only one and half hours lessons per day. Half an hour typing, half an hour book-keeping and half an hour shorthand. The rest of the time she helped the exam students with their studies, which meant she would spend some of her time with me, which was great as far as I was concerned. However, she still loved the course and worked very hard at it. She was surprisingly good too, even with the book-keeping and figure work.

As for me I wasn't so eager and defintely wasn't enjoying my time. I was buckling down studying for my final exam, but was finding it very difficult. This year made last year look like kindergarten. Pauline was now at the level I was last year. She had Sister Rosa teaching her most of the time, but Sister Martha taught her Gaelic, the Irish language, amongst a few other subjects. One day during her Irish lesson, Pauline said to the girl seated next to her,
"What good is this subject to me, I'll be going to live in England when I get out of here."
Sister Martha overheard her talking and approached her.
"What was that, Miss Cocky?" she asked.
"I was just saying that the people in England speak English not Irish, so Irish is of no use to me because I will be living in England when I leave here."
"How dare you speak about your own language like that you cheeky brat." Then she slapped her several times across the head and arms.
"If you've got no respect for your own country how can you have respect for yourself, you stupid child?"
Pauline burst into tears. She wasn't used to such harsh treatment. She had always be handled with kid-gloves. Later, when she told me about it all, I said,

"Pauline you have to learn not to speak your mind, especially with Sister Martha. Otherwise you'll get a hiding everyday, or worse, the strap."

"I'll try to remember," she said. "I didn't realise she was so mean."

"You haven't seen anything yet. She's much worse when you're studying for your leaving exam."

Pauline finally learned how tough things were going to be. As for me, I was trying desperately hard to pay attention, study hard and keep out of trouble. However I wasn't very intelligent and I was finding it all extremely difficult.

There were only five off us taking the exam from the convent this year. Sister Martha announced the five of us as follows:-
"MITCHELL, SHEEP EYES, SMELLY, GRACE GALWAY & LYNCH". They were our names, as far as Sister Martha was concerned.

Grace always got called Grace, she was the "Teachers Pet", and the brains of the class. She was also very nice to her friends and always ready to help us with our work during study time, so we held no grudges, because she got along with "Proud Tits." Smelly, was Maureen McKevily, who had always wet her knickers and bed, and was still doing it occasionally at fifteen years of age. Sheep eyes was Sandra Moore. She had very sly eyes, small and thin, and had a habit of looking at you from under the eyelid, or sidewards with one eye only, while the other eye focused in front. Linda and I were the other two. Out of the five, Linda was the only one who didn't have parents.

Occasionally Sister Rosa took one of our classes and those classes were extremely enjoyable, but it was very seldom now since the exams were slowly approaching and we had a lot of work to complete. It appeared that we were expected to remember all our education in the final year. Surprisingly enough though, unlike what Maureen said, the year passed quicker than I had expected and one day I came to the realization that Maureen would be gone before I even got my results of my exam. For the first time since I had been in the convent, I began wishing that time would slow down. I just dreaded Maureen leaving. That would leave me as the oldest, with no one to turn to except Linda. Pauline was a dead loss. I couldn't even trust her, let alone turn to her for help or comfort and Doreen was only a step sister, not really part of the family.

I cheered myself up by reminding myself that I'd be seeing Caroline again soon, which I was really looking forward to. I took out my photos and after studying her for a few moments, I gave her a kiss and put her back feeling happy again.

That evening I went to dinner feeling happy for a change, and looking forward to Caroline coming, even though it was still several months away. However my happiness was short lived because they were serving parsnips for dinner and I hated parsnips. I tried them once before and they made be feel ill. Just the texture alone turned my stomach. Kitty usually took them off me and ate them herself, she found them quite nice. Tonight though, Sister Angela was hanging around us like a bad smell. It was as if she knew what we had been up to in the past. Maybe she did, maybe someone reported us, because she never stayed in one spot at dinner time, she walked around the whole room but tonight she appeared to be staying really close to me.

I ate everything else on the plate apart from the parsnips and as soon as Sister Angela saw them just sitting on my plate, she approached me and said, "Lynch, what about the parsnips?"

"I can't eat them Sister Angela, they make me very sick."

"Nonsense, you eat them right now," she snapped

"Please, I really can't." I pleaded, nearly in tears with just the thought of putting them in my mouth.

"Okay Lynch," she said with malice, "you can carry your plate around with you all night, unless you eat them. Every last one of them."

I didn't mind this punishment at all and when I left the dinning room to go to the playroom, I carried my plate with me. In the playroom, I put my plate on a bench and began playing with Linda, but Sister Martha came in shortly after to supervise us and when she saw the dirty plate with parsnips on it just sitting on the bench she yelled.

"What pig left their dinner plate here?"

"It's mine." I said. "Sister Angela said I have to carry it with me all night."

"Well what's it doing on the bench?"

"I was playing."

With that she walked over and slapped me in the face, then said,

"You play after you've finished eating, not before. Now eat those parsnips this instant."

"I can't, they make me sick."

"How dare you. Who are you to say I can't or won't. You don't know how lucky you are to have good food. Now eat them before I shove them down your throat."

"I can't" I repeated.

"We'll soon see about that young lady." she said, and started pushing the cold parsnips in my mouth and forcing my mouth shut, to make sure I swallowed them. I began heaving. They felt like lumps of fat in my mouth. I became sticky all over and begged to go to the toilet after the first mouthful. She let me go fortunately, but I never made it. I threw up all over the yard. I became nervous. Worried about how I was going to clean up the mess, which was making me even sicker just looking at it. Suddenly a sticky feeling overwhelmed me and everything in front of me began to spin. I tried hard to fight it and attemped to walk back inside, but everything went black.

When I awoke I was in bed with Sister Angela standing over me.
"Lynch, Lynch, are you okay?"
I felt terrible but was too scared to tell her. I began rubbing my face in an effort to wake up and than I mummbled.
"Yes, I'm fine."
"Will you be okay for school tomorrow?"
I was un-sure of what answer to give. If I said no, she would say I was acting to try and avoid school. If I said yes, she would say that I had caused a fuss for nothing to avoid eating the parsnips, so I answered,
"I don't know, it's up to you. You tell me if I'm well enough?"
That was the wrong answer I think because I got a slap in the face,
"You'll be fine," she said. "If you can still give cheek like that, there's not a thing wrong with you. Now get to sleep."
I couldn't win with this woman, there was just no pleasing her. Nothing was right where she was concerned, but I felt too ill to worry about it, and went straight to sleep.
During the night I had a dream that there was loads of fat in my mouth and the fat was stopping me breathing and I began throwing up in my sleep. I awoke to find myself lying in vomit. My nose was bleeding and I was freezing cold.
I climbed out of bed and ran down to the matron's cubicle

holding my vomit stained nightgown up and my head back to avoid making a mess on the floor.

The matron jumped up concerned for me, and got me cleaned up as best she could in her room. She removed my nightdress replacing it with one of hers, which was miles too big. She told me that she would clean up the bed in the morning and sent me back to bed.

I was disappointed because I had expected more tender loving care from her, but I guess she was exhausted after her hard days work not to mention being woken up in the middle of the night. I went back to bed and removed the dirty sheets and blanket, and threw them on the floor. Then I jumped onto the bed laying on the bare mattress, with only one thin blanket covering me. I couldn't get warm no matter how hard I tried, I lay there shivering until the morning not able to get any rest at all.

When Sister Angela came she was shocked at the mess beside my bed.

"Josephine Lynch what on earth is this mess?. What happened here?" she asked, looking at the sheets on the floor and the terrible smell coming from both me and my surroundings. I jumped out of bed assuming by her tone that I was in trouble again. I was still freezing cold and pale looking and the sudden rise made me dizzy.

"You look awful. Come, get back to bed." she said gently.

I went to jump back into my own bed, but she put me in the bed next to mine.

"I'll get your's cleaned up later. You can stay in this one for the time being."

She tucked me in but I was still freezing and my teeth chattered away wildly, even with the extra blankets. She pulled off my clean blanket and put that on top of me too, but it still didn't stop my teeth chattering.

"I'll be back later with the doctor" she said, "Try and get some sleep in the meantime."

About an hour later she returned with the doctor.

"What's wrong?" he asked. "It's the parsnips, they made me sick." I answered

"Oh, I don't think so", he said laughing slightly, "I think it's more than that. Let's take a look shall we?"

I couldn't believe he was actually talking to me, not alone laughing. I had never even seen him smile before, but I did appreciate his friendliness. I was really feeling quite lousy and needed all the friends I could get.

He examined my ears and throat, then he turned to Sister Angela who was standing beside him and said,

"She has a bad case of tonsillitis. I'll give her a shot of penicillin tonight, and check her again tomorrow."

For the next four days the doctor came back daily, but I hadn't improved during that time, the injections didn't appear to be having any effect. On the fourth day he turned to Sister Angela and said,

"It's no use, they have to go."

At the time I had no idea what he was talking about and I was too sick to care, but I soon found out what "They have to go" meant!

CHAPTER 46

I stayed in bed for the next two weeks, my only company being Linda and Maureen and only after lights out. I still hated being alone and I was dying to get back to school. I had felt well enough for the past week, but they insisted I stay in bed to recuperate. In the end I was convinced they were only punishing me for some unknown reason.

One night Sister Angela came to my bed and asked,

"How are you feeling Josephine?"

"Good."

"Are you sure?"

"Yes" I answered, hopefully believing that I was finally going back to school after two weeks.

"Okay, I'm going to get you a drink and you must drink it all. You won't be having tea tonight, so make sure you finish the drink." I wondered why I was missing out on tea, and again thought it was some sort of punishment. (Being alone was making me paranoid!)

Later that night when all the girls were in the dormitory, Sister Angela came back and called out four names and I was one of them. At first I became frightened, wondering what she wanted with the four of us, but I got out of bed and went to stand in front of her and she said,

"Lynch, you can stay in your nightgown, just grab a blanket and wrap it around yourself, then the four of you follow me. The rest of you to bed, I'll be back shortly."

She led the four of us to the infirmary and put us into bed.

"You will stay here tonight," she said, handing us nice clean underwear.

"Tomorrow morning an ambulance will come and take you to the Westport Hospital, where they will remove your tonsils.

You will stay at the hospital for three nights, and then return to the convent. While you are there remember your manners and behave yourselves, otherwise you will be severly punished when you return."

After Sister Angela left we talked amongst ourselves. Apparently, the doctor did a rountine check of all the girls in the convent after he had examined me, and decided that the four of us should have our tonsils removed, even though the other girls weren't sick like I had been. We were all a little scared, but more excited about sleeping away from the convent and going in the ambulance. Our lives were so dull, that even hospital was a treat for us. Finally we fell asleep, but during the night I had a severe nose bleed. I was lucky because I was sleeping on my side and the blood dripped freely to the floor. I'm sure I would have choked to death if I were on my back. The bleeding didn't awaken me or even disturb my sleep. It was no ordinary nose bleed either, the floor was a massive pool of blood.

The next morning Sister Angela woke me from a deep sleep.
"Josephine, Josephine, wake-up" she said, the panic evident in her voice. I wonder now if she thought I was actually lying there dead. I awoke startled by her tone,
"What, what" I stammered still drowsy.
"What happened to you?" she asked looking down at the blood.
I followed her gaze and was shocked and frightened by what I saw.
"I don't know" I said, "I was sleeping."
"Look just stay there. I'll get some clean linen and phone the doctor. You may not be able to go to hospital after this. It must have been a nose bleed." She added, as she looked the large amount of blood again. Then she asked for the second time,

"Are you positive you didn't fall out of bed Josephine?"

"No, I don't think so. If I did I didn't feel anything."

"Okay." she said, seeming really flustered and nervous. Then she went back to the dormitory, to get some clean linen, calling the matron as she did so. They both came down together and the matron examined my nose.

"It looks clean to me," she said to Sister Angela, in a surprised tone. Then she turned back to me and said, "Are you sure you didn't hurt yourself Jospehine?"

"Yes I'm sure. If I'd hurt myself that much I would have felt it."

She turned back to Sister Angela, "Well it's a wonder she didn't choke to death if it was a nose bleed and there doesn't seem to be any other explanation."

"Yes, she's a very lucky little girl," Sister Angela answered. "Well, I'd better phone the doctor, would you mind cleaning up the floor Kathleen?"

"No, not at all Sister," the matron answered.

About half an hour later the doctor arrived to examine me.

"It was her nose," he concluded, "She's very lucky, it could have been fatal. It puzzles me how she didn't wake up." he said to Sister Angela.

"I agree," she answered.

The doctor turned back to me and asked,

"Do you have many nose bleeds?"

"No, I've only had a couple before this. Once when I was punched in the nose and another a couple of weeks ago when I was sick."

"Who punched you in the nose?" he asked in an amused tone.

"My girl in charge for talking and laughing when I shouldn't have been."

"Oh, I see. Well do you still want to have your tonsils out with the other girls or wait a few days and have them removed on your own?"

I wondered why he was asking me, I was only a kid, but I didn't hesitate in answering,

"Now please, with the other girls."

He turned back to Sister Angela,

"I think it will be okay. There doesn't seem to be much wrong with her now. I can't see why we can't go ahead as planned."

"Fine, I'll get her ready. Thank-you for coming doctor, I know how very busy you are." Sister Angela said.

The ambulance arrived and in a short time we were at the hospital. We all got undressed, put on our nightgowns and within a few minutes they were wheeling me into another room. Then they placed a mask over my face and asked me to count to ten. I never made it, I was out cold on the count of three!

The next thing I remember was waking up to the sound of spitting noises. When I opened my eyes I saw that it was the girls from the convent, spitting out blood into a bowl. My eyes opened wider at the sight and I realised that it was going everywhere except in the bowl. It was in their hair and all over their faces. It was making me feel quite sick. I tried to sit up and as soon as I did, I began to spit too. A nurse ran up and passed me a bowl from beside my bed and I joined the other three girls. My throat was very sore and dry. I was extremely thirsty but all I could taste was blood. There was a woman facing me peeling an orange, god know's how she could stomach it with us four facing her, but my eyes became glued to it and I savoured it in my mind. I could almost taste the lovely juice that would be in that orange. The woman looked over and saw my pleading eyes, and asked,

"Would you like some?"

"Oh yes please," I said, dying for some of that lovely juice.

However the nurse on duty wouldn't allow it, explaining to the woman that it was too soon for us to eat or drink. That we would be violently ill if we attempted to. I felt like dying I was so sore and so very thirsty. The nurse gave us some clean bowls and took away the dirty ones. When she left I looked around the room and I saw a tap that the doctors and nurses were using to wash their hands and I was very tempted to run down and get a drink right then, but the nurse re-appeared much to my disappointment. I thought about the situation for a moment and came up with a good idea, and called to the nurse,

"Excuse me nurse, may I please wash my face and hands I have blood everywhere and I feel awful."

"Okay, but make it quick."

I wasn't the least bit worried about cleaning up and when I turned on the water it went straight into my mouth.

The nurse came running and pulled me away, long before I quenched my thirst. In fact I barely got my throat wet before she yanked me away,

"What do you think you're doing?" she asked,

"I'm thirsty, please let me have a drink." I pleaded,

"Well I'm very sorry about that, but you can't drink now. You will get something later. You will get very sick if you drink now."

"I'll be sicker if I don't. My throat is really sore and dry," I said, and began to cry.

"Oh stop your crying and get back to bed. You won't die, I assure you." she said in a stern voice, which made me do what she wanted quick smart.

I went back to bed feeling very sorry for myself, but a couple of hours later they brought us all some ice-cream. As I ate it I savoured the soothing effect it was having on my throat.

That night I cursed myself. If I'd known it was going to be so sore, I would never have come, I thought. What an idiot I am.

I didn't like hospitals and I was stupid to want to come. They tricked me, making it all sound so exciting, like one big adventure, but it all happened so fast there was no excitment at all. I told myself that I wouldn't be so eager to go to hospital in the future no matter how sick I was. The next day we all felt much better and on the fourth day we returned safely to the convent. We stayed in bed for a few extra days and then we returned to school.

I was really happy to be with Linda again and during study time she helped me catch up on the school work I had missed the past three weeks.

It wasn't that I was interested in knowing what I missed. I was just scared stiff of getting strapped for not knowing the work. There was no allowances made for absences, well very rarely anyway. In all the years I was there I had only once got an allowance and extra study time, which was when I had my knee problem, never before and never after. However, I was really putting my efforts into studying now, even if it was for the wrong reasons and the time flew by quickly for me. One day in the playroom, Linda and I were just sitting around talking and I asked her what she wanted to be when she grew up and she said a nurse,

"You a nurse, I answered sarcastically, "You would send all your patients crazy."

"No I wouldn't, I'd make them all laugh and they would be happy. I really love helping people you know."

"Yea that's true. I think you would make a wonderful nurse really."

"What would you like to be when you grow up?" she asked,

"I would like to make dresses and clothes."

"What about a secretary?"

"No way, I'd hate that. Dad's wasting his money on me, he

really is. Any chance I get I'm on the matron's machine. I just love it. I don't think my dad will let me do it though, worse luck."

"What will be, will be." Linda answered, and how right she was.

We continued with our studies and endured Sister Martha. If we weren't scared of her before, we certainly were now. She gave the five of us hell.

I remember her as a very evil person. It didn't matter how happy you were, somehow she managed to make you miserable. After being around old "Proud Tits", our personalities changed, we became nervous, insecure and frightened human beings. She took away our dignity and made a jack ass out of us everyday. All self esteem and confidence was ripped away from our very souls until in the end we were just empty, shallow human beings. What's more, she took pleasure in doing it.

We spend ninety per cent of our young lives worrying about what punishment or ridicule we would endure next. There was never any love or encouragement from her, only insults and hate. We were like obedient dogs, just following instructions. Sit, walk, talk, and eat. Just one order after another. Don't laugh, or play, or even be a child, because "Discipline" would get you. Sister Martha had no feelings at all, she was just evil. One thing she never managed to take away from Linda or I was our sense of humor. But believe me, that's all I had when I left the convent. I remember one day, another nun came into our classroom. Her name was Sister Margaret (another dragon) and she occasionally helped Sister Martha with the exam preparations. She came in and spoke to Sister Martha first, and I heard her say,

"Lynch has to pass no matter what, otherwise we won't get the money for the course next year. He definetely wants to take her when she's sixteen."

Then she sniggered and making sure I could hear, she added "She'll be able to go to work for him then, and earn her keep,"

Then she looked at me and said,

"Isn't that right Lynch?"

I looked at her, but I made no response.

"Stand up when I'm talking to you."

I stood up, but froze on the spot. I was in trouble again and as usual I didn't know why.

"Isn't that correct?" she repeated. I still stood frozen, fear making me unable to answer her. To be honest I didn't think she really wanted an answer.

"Answer me child" she snapped

"I don't know the answer Sister Margaret. I don't know my father or what he wants."

She walked down to me and shook me by the hair of my head.

"You insolent child. I asked you if it's true that your father wants you to earn money for his keep." she said slowly, emphasising each and every word to make sure I understood.

"Maybe," I said, as I began to cry from the pain of my hair being pulled so tightly, "I don't know him."

She shook my head again saying, "Not maybe, the answer is yes. Now say, yes Sister Margaret."

"Yes Sister Margaret, I answered with obediance.

"Good girl." she said releasing my hair.

I looked at her with hate, wishing that I could kill myself, just to be free of this place. I couldn't wait another year and a half. I didn't think I could make it through another day. That night as I lay in bed I wondered why Sister Margaret had been so cruel and again wished I was dead and free from this terrible torture that I endured every day of my life. My wish nearly came true, or so I thought that night!

There was a shoe factory in Westport and it caught fire. Sister Angela appeared suddenly during the night getting everyone out of bed. As we looked out of the window we could see the flames and smoke roaring high. The whole sky seemed to be alight. We went through a fire drill, and we were instructed not to hold the hand railings of the stairs and to walk slowly without pushing. We were then returned to the dormitory and told to pray that the surrounding trees and the convent wouldn't catch alight.

A few minutes later the matron came over and said to Sister Angela, "The children will have to be evacuated, the fire is getting closer."
When I heard that, I began to pray like crazy. "Please god, keep us safe, I don't really want to die." I started thinking about my exam, which was only three weeks away, which I had suffered and worked so hard for. Then I began thinking about my dad and sisters and truly believed that if we were evacuated that they would never find me again and I really began to panic. Suddenly I stopped thinking and began praying with all my heart for everyone's safety.

Then Sister Angela stood up and walked across to the Matron who was standing beside the window and the pair of them looked out, as we continued praying. Then she came back telling us we were all to go down stairs to the playroom quietly and slowly. When we were all there she said,
"We shall wait here for a while and hope and pray the fire dies down."
We prayed hard for another hour or so. I knelt and prayed that night, even though I wasn't supposed to kneel. In my heart I believed that god would listen more if I was kneeling. Even when my knees became sore and swollen I remained there

praying my little heart out. Eventually our prayers were successful. In the early hours of the morning the fire was extinguished and we were sent back to bed. We had got very little sleep that night but we were still woken up at 6am to get ready for school. However it was a relatively easy day because we spoke mainly about the importance of praying and how we were blessed by god who protected us from harm. No one was punished by Sister Martha that day either and that, to me was a bigger miracle than the convent not burning down! In fact she didn't hit us much at all for the next three weeks leading up to the exam and for that we were all grateful, especially myself and poor sheeps eyes who she hated the most.

CHAPTER 47

A few days before our main exam we were tested for home economics, which included cooking, sewing and laundry subjects. These were nothing to worry about because they had no bearing on whether you passed the leaving exam. These exams were even less important and stressful to me than most other people, because I was good at them, especially sewing.

First came the sewing test. We had to complete a French Seam and a button hole, amongst other trivial things. The Examiner from Westport had a very posh accent which was quite comical to listen to. It also added a more relaxed atmosphere because we giggled a few times when she was speaking and she laughed along with us. When we had all finished our set tasks she came around to examine our work. When she came to me she was surprised and said,
"Oh, what a beautiful button hole. Your sewing is much better than most others I've seen. Well done!"
I felt as proud as punch. It was the first compliment I had ever received for my work and it made me happy.
Then she asked us some general questions and when ever I put my hand up to answer them, she would say, "Yes, the girl with the nice button hole."
I can't explain how good she made me feel. It was so easy to make me happy really, just a little praise and I was over the moon with joy. Needless to say I passed my sewing exam with flying colours!

Next came cookery which wasn't quite so easy. Linda had to make lentil soup, and I had to make a swiss roll. Linda completed her soup without a problem, but I wasn't quite so lucky. First I cut the sides of my swiss roll and sampled the piece's I had cut off which Sister Marie always allowed us to do, telling us "Waste not, want not." However, the Examiner screamed out to me, "Good cooks do not eat in the kitchen while preparing."

"Oh no," I thought, "I've just failed." but I carried on regardless and spread the jam and cream. But when I went to roll it, I kept putting holes in the sponge. The Examiner came down and helped me finish it, realising I was having difficulties. I saw Sister Marie frowning at me and I knew I was in trouble later, but not while the Examiner was still in the convent. With a bit of luck, I told myself, she would forget about it which was doubtful, but I was always full of hope, usually a false hope!

Finally came the laundry test. This was a verbal exam which we found relatively easy. We all passed that one. After it was over and the Examiner returned to Westport, Sister Marie got hold of me and slapped me for the swiss roll. She didn't bother to congratulate me for my perfect botton hole or sewing efforts though. The Nuns were very quick to punish in that place, but never took the time to praise our accomplishments.

It was Thursday night and I lay in bed thinking about my exam the following morning. I just couldn't go to sleep. I had mixed emotions going through me. Feelings of fear, anxiety and excitement all rolled into one. I tossed, turned and prayed that I'd pass. I compared myself with Maureen and figured that if she passed than so should I, but then thought that maybe she passed purely out of luck and I didn't consider myself very lucky. In fact quite the opposite, I was very unlucky.

Finally I fell into a restless sleep and when Sister Angela woke us the next morning, I felt like I'd just fallen asleep ten minutes ago. I was still extremely tired. We went straight to breakfast after dressing, without doing our daily chores. At breakfast Sister Martha met the five of us and told us to take our time eating our extra large bowl of porridge and to relax as much as possible. She was in a surprisingly happy mood this morning which made her seem almost human. I remember thinking to myself,"Maybe I could have liked you, if you were like this everyday", but she wasn't. The truth was that I wanted to like everyone, because it made me feel good. When I hated people, I felt bad inside and I didn't like that feeling, so I always tried to like people. Sometimes however, that was impossible!

After breakfast Sister Martha escorted us to the exam room and told us to do our best. Then she wished us all good luck and took us inside to seat us. When she placed me in my seat, she whispered, "Good luck Jospehine, I hope you pass."
I looked at her and smiled. I felt happy inside as if being called by my first name was important. Then I thought to myself "Don't be happy Josphine, because every time you're happy something goes wrong." Happy was bad, I reminded myself. You were only here to be punished and you were punished everyday just for being happy.

At 9am, Sister Martha left and the Examiners and Sister Collette arrived.
We were handed out the first envelope, which was an English Composition. I opened it and lay it flat on my desk to examine the contents. Suddenly all these ink spots came through and I panicked. I stood up quickly and Sister Collette who was supervising said,
"Yes girl. What is it?"
I knew that we were only allowed forty minutes for the paper and that you lost plenty of marks for untidy work, so in a

strained voice I said,

"My ink well has overflowed and has spilled on the desk and exam paper. I haven't even lifted my pen yet, I was merely reading the topics we could choose from."

"Everybody, please put down your pens. We will clean up this mess and continue afterwards," Sister Collette said.

She picked up my exam paper and cleaned my desk for me and blew on my ink stained paper in an effort to dry it.

"May I have a new exam paper?" I asked,

"No you may not. There are no spare papers, only one per person."

"But I'll lose marks for messy work."

"Don't worry, I'll write a signed note and attach it to your work sheet, explaining the circumstances."

"Okay,." I said "and thankyou."

"That's okay. Now girls we have thrity five minutes remaining. Let's start again shall we. Hopefully with no further disruptions." she said, looking at me.

Everyone picked up their pens and began writing. I wrote a composition on the time I went on a picnic. It was easy, because I just recalled Dr Mongay and his wife, and how lovely our picnic was. When I was finished, I was extremely happy with my work. It was very neat, apart from the ink blobs and I had finished in plenty of time. "So far, so good", I thought proudly.

When we went out Sister Martha was waiting for us wondering why we had been an extra seven minutes in there. "Come on" she said, "We have lost seven minutes of our fifteen minute break due to Josephine's mishap, let's hurry up." However she didn't strike me, which I was concerned about when I was telling her why we were late coming out. During the break she asked us all how we went as we drank the milk she had waiting for us. She was pleased to know that we all thought we did well. After our refreshments we returned to the exam room. This time we had to write an Irish composition followed by Irish and English grammar. This exam would take us up to lunchtime. I found this a lot harder but when I was finished and read it through, I felt confident that I had passed and was really pleased with myself.

The Examiner called for everyone to put down their pens. (If we did not respond immediately we were disqualified. Even if we were just finishing off a word, the pens had to go down.) Then Sister Collette began collecting our exam papers. When she was half way through there was a very loud knock at the door. I was sure it was Sister Martha. However, when Sister Collette opened the door, it wasn't Sister Martha it was a very tall man who entered the room.

"Carry on Sister" he said, "I'll talk to the girls when you're finished."

The man walked to the front of the room and looked around then he looked at his watch impatiently several times. I wondered why he was doing that when there was a big clock on the wall for everyone to see. When Sister Collette had finished collecting all the papers, she made her way over to this tall, fascinating man (that I couldn't take my eyes off) and they talked quietly for a few moments. Then he addressed the rest of us.

"Hello" he said in a posh voice, "I'm the head inspector from Dublin. I know you must all be very hungry and I will allow you to leave for lunch in just a few moments." Then he paused and looked at us individually and said,

"I will be with you for the rest of the day to keep an eye on things and ensure that no cheating takes place, which I'm sure it won't." he said eyeing us all separately again. "Now then, congratulations on your efforts so far. You are free to leave and enjoy your lunch."

He hadn't said very much at all and as I left the room I wondered why he said anything at all. From the way he looked, I expected him to say something special! Sister Martha was outside waiting for us, ready to escort us to the dining room. She couldn't wait to ask her questions again either.

"How do you think you went Josphine?"

"I think I went well"

"What about you Linda?"

"I'm sure I passed everything I've done so far" Linda answered with confidence.

"That's good girls," she said after quizzing us all, "Now make sure you eat up all your lunch, you need your strength for the rest of the day."

However, no one took her advice. We couldn't eat, we just didn't feel hungry. None of us were repremanded for leaving the meal either which was even more surprising.

After lunch the five of us went into the yard and quizzed each other about the exam and what answers we had given. We talked and laughed amongst ourselves feeling happy and vibrant. It was a strange atmosphere that surrounded us, well unusual anyway. In the afternoon we had arithmatic which I personally dreaded. Just as I was thinking about it, Maureen came up to see how I was doing so far.

"I've done well so far Maureen, but I'm really worried about the next exam."

"Oh don't worry. You're far better than I am and I passed. Look, even if you think you've failed when you finish the exam, tell Sister Martha you did well."

"Why?"

"Because she'll give you hell otherwise, until the results come. Why suffer all that extra time. Anyway you have nothing to worry about, I'm sure you'll do fine. Just do your best."

"I will" I said

She wished us all good luck and left. I was glad that she had taken the time to come and give me some encouragement and suddenly wondered if Pauline would come and wish me luck. But she didn't! Just before we were about to go back in to my surprise my step sister came over and wished me good luck. I was really shocked since we had little to do with each other. I loved her in my own way and never liked seeing her hurt or upset, but I never played with her. She seemed much happier with girls her own age anyway, and we had nothing in common. Today however, my heart melted for her and I pitied the year she would have to go through all the beatings with Sister Martha. I thanked her for coming and asked her if Pauline was going to come and see me.

"I don't think so," she replied, "she's too busy playing."

I immediately regretted asking. I knew Pauline didn't care about anyone except herself and cursed myself for even entertaining the idea, let alone speaking it aloud. Just then the matron and Sister Angela approached us and Doreen ran off, which was good timing because I was very embarrassed and at a loss for words.

"Come inside girls and have some milk. You have ten minutes before the next exam starts." Sister Angela said.

As we walked inside the matron asked me,

"How are you going so far?"

"So far, so good," I said with a big smile, "but I hate the next one."

"Oh don't worry, you'll be fine. I'll be praying for you."

"Thanks, I need all the prayers I can get."

"That's alright, but what ever you do don't get caught talking or cheating or they will disqualify you. Plus you will never be allowed to sit for the exam again."

I laughed and said, "I know, I don't cheat."

Sister Angela who was leading the five of us turned when she heard my giggles.

"I don't know why you're laughing Lynch, you have no hope of passing. You'll be sitting it again next year, and more than likely you'll fail again."

"Oh no Sister Angela I'm going to pass today. I know that for a fact." I answered. Her spitefulness making me more determined to succeed.

Sister Angela sniggered at my confidence and said, "We'll see, won't we?"

After we drank our milk and were on our way back to the exam room, Linda said,

"I heard what Sister Angela said, but don't worry about it Josephine you will pass, I just know you will."

"Yea I know, but why does she hate me so much. She likes my other sisters, even Doreen. What have I ever done to her. She's always trying to spoil my special days, even today she's at me."

Linda didn't get a chance to answer me. Sister Martha arrived to escort us inside the exam room.

"Good luck" she said patting each of us on the shoulder, "and try hard. This is the last part of your exam and it will go for two hours, so stay calm, you have plenty of time."

This was the hardest part of the leaving exam for me and I was dreading it. I was so nervous and ill at ease that my stomach was in knots. The exam envelopes were handed out and as I opened it my hands were trembling. I felt sick and suddenly very hungry and sat there wishing I had taken Sister Martha's advice and eaten lunch.

"You may start" Sister Collette announced and we all picked

up our pens. I said a little prayer before starting and then looked at the man walking around the room.

It was so quiet in the room and his shoes seemed to echo with each step he took. It was making me even more nervous than I already was. I told myself to buckle down and concentrate on the exam, and began to study the first sum. It was easy and I answered it. I answered the next ten with ease as well, but when I came to question twelve I was stuck for about ten minutes. I decided to leave it and complete the others and go back to it if there was time. The rest of them I breezed through, like the first eleven. In fact I thought I must have done them all wrong because they were so easy. I decided to check them all again in case they were trick questions, but again I came up with the same answers. I looked up at the clock and I still had fifteen minutes to go. "Boy that went quick" I thought and went back to question twelve. I studied it and studied it and finally put down 0.1 as the answer. I doubted it was correct but it was the best I could do. The more I looked at it the more confused I became. I put my pen down and waited for Sister Collette to collect the papers wondering why I had finished before time, but as I looked around the room I noticed that everybody had. In fact I was the last to finish and for some reason that gave me more confidence that I had passed. Before we were dismissed the Head Inspector stood before us again and congratulated us on our fine efforts. He told us to thank Sister Collette for her time, which we did, and then we were allowed to leave.

When we went outside there was a crowd waiting for us. Sister Martha, The Matron, Sister Angela, my sister Mauren, (who had been given special permission from Sister Martha to join us since she had completed her studies for the day.) Even the Reverend Mother was there. Everyone was congratulating us and swarming around us as we went to the playroom. When we got there, the Reverend Mother addressed us all and said,

"I want to congratulate you all and I hope that you all pass. It has been a very long, and worrying day for Sister Martha. She has worked very hard to get you through today, so let's all thank her."

We clapped and said thankyou and she seemed pleased with us all. I was standing next to Maureen McKevilly at the time and she stunk of urine. With my nerves and empty stomach, the smell was making me feel sick. All of a sudden I spoke up, not able to stand it anymore,

"I think smelly has wet herself" I said,

Everyone laughed, even Sister Martha, but the Reverend Mother didn't think it was so funny, she was shocked.

"Josephine Lynch, that's not very nice."

"I didn't mean it to be nasty. It's just she must be shy to say something, and she must be very uncomfortable."

"Yes that may be so but you shouldn't call her smelly, regardless of your intentions."

"Sorry Reverend Mother, it's a habit. That's what everyone calls her, even Sister Martha."

The Reverend Mother looked at Sister Martha who in turn stared at me, making me very nervous, so in an effort to correct my last statement and get myself out of trouble, I said,

"But she only calls her that when she wet's her knickers in class (which was a bare face lie) and Maureen doesn't mind the name. We all have nicknames."

"Oh I see," the Reverend Mother said, smiling at Sister Martha, "Well let's try and call her Maureen in the future, shall we?"

"Yes Reverend Mother." I answered

"Now Maureen, you go with the matron and change your underwear.

"Yes Reverend Mother," Smelly answered!

The rest of us were seated and given some milk. Then we were told to relax and play in the yard until tea time. I was starving by this stage but I knew the milk would have to sustain me for the next hour or so. The matron returned with Smelly a few moments later. Then she came and sat beside me,

"How did you go in the last exam Josephine?" she asked,

"Much better than I thought I would, I think I passed."

"Oh Josephine that's great. I'm so happy for you. I've been praying for you all day and last night too."

Sister Angela who had been there the whole time supervising us, over-heard the matron's words and couldn't help sticking her long skinny nose in. In a mocking tone, she said,

"Sure it will take more than prayers for her to pass."

I looked up at her and shrugged my shoulders, in an attempt to show I didn't care and answered,

"I've already passed, I know I have. It was very easy." I exaggerated.

"Time will tell. Only the final results will tell us if you passed, not your opinion, she answered me and walked away.

I was trying hard to make her believe that I didn't care what she said, but the truth of the matter was I cared very much. I would have begged my father not to let me go through another year with Sister Martha. I would have rather killed myself than take any more of her beatings. There wasn't one subject that Sister Martha taught where I hadn't been either beaten, punched, or pinched at least ten times in every hour of the day, till in the end I was so nervous that I was jumping every time she walked by.

I knew I couldn't take another year of that terrible feeling of fear. The whole year I had been on edge, frightened of my own shadow, and I knew I wouldn't survive it again. I came back from my anxious thoughts when the matron spoke,

"You must be very happy Josphine."

"I am, but I'll be happier when the results come back."

"Oh don't worry I'll be proud of you, whether you pass or fail and I'm sure you did pass. The worst is over for you now love. In a week you will be breaking up for your summer holidays and just think, this time next year you will be with your family."

"Yes" I said, and realized that Maureen would be leaving me in just a few short weeks.

As if reading my thoughts Maureen came up and hugged me.

"Well done sis" she said, and tears rolled down my face. They were tears of happiness and relief, but mainly sorrow. I wouldn't be getting many more hugs from Maureen and I hugged her with all my might, while crying onto her shoulder. I just hated her going.

"I love you" I said,

"And I love you." she repeated, and tears ran down her face too. The matron kissed me on the head, stood up and left us alone. I was grateful for this time alone with Maureen.

For the rest of the weekend the five exam students were allowed to relax and do what ever we wanted. It was wonderful, we were like real grown-ups that weekend. It was the best weekend that I ever spent in the convent. It was the only time I felt at ease and not scared of physical abuse!

CHAPTER 48

We returned to school on the Monday morning to find that Sister Martha had a copy of the exam papers. So we spent the whole week before the holidays revising our answers to each question and topic. It was like sitting the exams again, but this was taking much longer! When we were summarising the maths exam we individually gave our answers to each question. When it came to question twelve which was the one that I had the most trouble with, I told sister Martha that I gave 0.1, as the answer. Grace, who was regarded the brains of the group, gave 0.2, whilst the other three girls gave 0.0. To everyones surprise I was the only one who had given the correct answer. I couldn't believe it. I felt so proud I'm sure I must have been shining all over.

"How did you know the answer Josephine," Sister Martha asked obviously as shocked as I was.

"Well it was a lucky guess really. I studied it over and over again and that's the answer I kept coming up with."

"Well done" was all she answered, but I knew that was something special, coming from her.

"Will they give me a hundred out of a hundred?" I asked feeling as though I had earned the right to speak freely to her.

"No they won't."

"How come?"

"Because they never do, they mark you down for neatness."

"But my work was very neat."

"Oh shut-up Jospehine and let me carry on with the work." she snappd.

I kept quiet very quickly realising that getting the correct answer didn't give me the right to speak to her openly after all! Her harsh words didn't matter too much. I was still happy knowing that I was the only one to get them all right. Not to mention the fact that Sister Martha had actually called me Josephine and said "well done", a sure sign that she was pleased with me.

I drifted off into a daydream filled with happiness. I was thinking about Sister Martha being pleased with my results. She had also praised me for my English Composition which made me ever so happy. Suddenly Sister Martha brought me back from my contented thoughts when she yelled,

"Lynch, what are you day-dreaming about?"

"Sorry Sister Martha."

"I want to know what you were dreaming about?"

"I was thinking about my English Composition and how you said yesterday that it was very good and that I would pass. Then I began to wonder why you never told me that I was good during the year?"

"Because you are a very bad speller and I think you were just lucky the day of the exam. You will never get anywhere with your writing abilities, so I've never given you false hope." she answered in a nasty tone.

She was doing it again, telling me I was hopeless. I sat there wishing that I'd never told her what I was thinking about, but it was too late now.

Sister Martha changed the subject by saying,

"Well girls, I can safely say that you have all passed if you have told me the truth this week, that is. I dare say that as soon as we get the results from Dublin, you will all be enjoying a party."

She started to clap and we all joined in and once again I was happy. It was so easy to make me happy, yet she seemed to go out of her way to do the opposite.

On the way to the dinning room, Sister Martha walked beside me down the long corridor. Out of the blue she asked,

"Did Pauline come and congratulate you for passing your exam Lynch?"

"No," I answered wondering why she was taking time to talk to me in this fashion, as she never had before. "But Marueen and Doreen did. Pauline only thinks about herself. I don't care though, it will be her turn next year and thank-god I won't be here when she's sitting for her exam."

"Why won't you be here?"

"Because I'll be sixteen about six weeks before Pauline sits for her exam."

"Oh that's right, but why does that make you so happy?"

"Because if I was here I know for sure I would wish her good luck and I don't want to."

"Why not?"

"Because she hurt me a lot when she didn't wish me good luck. She didn't even bother to congratulate me afterwards, that's why."

"Oh I see and are you doing your commercial classes."

"I guess so. Dad want's me to but I know I won't enjoy it."

"Why not?"

I couldn't believe she was asking me all these questions. She even appeared to be interested in my answers. It was as if I was talking to the matron, not Sister Martha. I hesitated, becoming strangely suspicious of her motives, and thought that maybe she was going to get me into trouble later. I really wasn't sure with this woman. I looked up into her face as if her expression could help me to decide whether to trust her or not, but I couldn't read her expression so I answered with caution.

"Well I really want to do dressmaking."

"You can forget about that, your father would never hear of it."

"I know, but that's what I love doing."

"Well there's no use thinking about anything until you get

your results back, but I do know that Maureen really loves the Commercial classes and she's doing very well at them too."

"Yea, but she's cut out for it, I'm not."

"How so?"

"Well she's lady like."

"I don't understand. What do you mean 'lady like'?"

"Well she walks with her head stuck up in the air."

"That doesn't mean she's a lady."

"Yes I know, but it's just that she wants to be a lady and work in an office when she leaves here. I don't."

"Well if you don't do the course you may end up cleaning toilets and washing floors when you leave here."

"No way, I'd never do that. I only do it here because I have to. I'll never do it again when I get out."

She looked at me and suddenly she turned back to her own nasty self,

"Yes you Lynch's are all very proud aren't you, even though you have nothing to be proud of."

"Pardon?" I answered, looking at her straight in the face, sensing her change of mood.

"Oh I've tried to knock it out of each and everyone of you, but it seems I've failed." she added,

"What?" I asked, "I don't understand what you mean."

"Nothing Lynch, forget I said it." She said and changed the subject returning to the nice person.

"Who's picking Maureen up?"

"I'm not sure, I think Caroline, but maybe my father if I'm lucky."

"No chance of that."

"Why?" I asked.

"Because he's too ashamed to show his face, that's why."

"Why would my father be ashamed, he's a good person isn't he?"

"Yes he is, please forget I said that Jospehine. There is a very good chance that your father will come."

I stood there gaping at her. It was as if I was talking to two different people, one nice person and one horrible person. Now the nice person was actually saying please in a sincere voice. I was shocked, well astounded really.

"Go and eat" she said and walked off in front of me leaving me staring after her with disbelief. The whole conversation had left me confused. She had spoken to me like an adult, something I just wasn't used to. Even though I was fifteen I was always treated like a child and a servant. She just asked me to "Please forget her nasty words," and I was dumbfounded, but on the same token I felt good inside. It was like I was a real human being for a change, and not some stray dog in the gutter.

I went into the dinning room and sat beside Linda. I was filled with a feeling of being, of just pure exsistence, and with a strange promise of tomorrow. Linda was also light hearted and happy, but none of us spoke. We just sat there eating in peaceful silence. After lunch we played outside just laughing and joking quietly together, when suddenly Linda brought up the subject of the book that I had long ago talked about writing.

"Josephine, do you remember last year when you said you were going to write a book about this place?"

I laughed as I remembered and said, "Yes I remember. Why?"

"Oh nothing, I was just wondering if you are still going to do it?"

"I doubt it Linda, I haven't got the confidence."

"Rubbish, didn't you hear what Sister Martha said. She said that your composition sounded great. She didn't say that about anyone else's."

"Yea, she also said that my spelling was lousy, and that I was propably just lucky the day of the exam."

"Oh, you know what she's like. Always trying to be-little us, and steal our pride. Don't let her worry you."

"But she does worry me. Besides, I don't think I could do it anyway."

"Of course you could. You can do anything you want to, if you put your heart into it."

I was getting embarrassed with her confidence in me, and my lack of it, so I said,

"Well maybe I will some day, who knows. I know I'd love to. I have so much to tell about this place and I'm sure most people would want to know the truth."

"You bet they would and you're just the person to tell them."

I was just about to tell her that I would write the book one day and thank her for her encouragement, but Pauline came over to us accompanied by a few of her friends. (Who all happened to be much younger than her. The truth was Pauline didn't have any friends her own age because they didn't want to have anything to do with her. She could manipulate the smaller children and they still came to her, because she was older than they were and it made them feel good playing with someone bigger than themselves.)

"Hi Jospehine, I've come over to say congratulations."

"That's nice. A bit late but thank-you anyway."

"Well I've been scared to say it before because you've probably failed anyway," she said. Then she burst out laughing and all her so called friends joined in like a choir.

"Pauline, you and Sister Angela are very much alike you know. You know what, it's a pity she's not your sister because I don't consider you a sister anymore. In fact I hate you. Now get lost and go tell Sister Angela what I said if you like I really don't care anymore. Then you can go to hell Pauline because I want no more to do with you."

I stamped my foot, with a threatening look on my face, as if

I was going to chase her and give her a hiding. Pauline ran like a scared mouse, with her group of friends running behind her. My screaming had drawn a small crowd and they joined Linda and myself laughing as we all watched Pauline running for her life.

When we calmed down Linda said, "She'll go straight to Sister Angela and report you, you know."

"If she does Linda I really will beat her up this time. I'm sick of her betraying me all the time." I meant every word I said too. She had never stood by me, or anyone else for that matter. She needed to be taught a lesson, and I sort of hoped she would report me, so I could be the one to give her that lesson.

The bell rang so Linda and I made our way inside. Suddenly I got the fright of my life and stopped dead in my tracks as I saw Sister Angela and Pauline standing on the top step waiting for me. Linda and I looked at each other. My heart began beating so hard I thought everyone could hear it. It was absolutely throbbing in my ears. I looked at Pauline with such hate and disgust that she turned away from me. Sister Martha came along and Sister Angela spoke to her quietly for a few moments, then Sister Martha said,

"Lynch, in the playroom."

I walked towards the playroom with the three villans close behind. I saw the tears of pity in Linda's eyes and I smiled a reassuring smile her way and carried on walking to the playroom.

When we got there, Sister Martha said,

"Lynch, what did you say to your sister outside,"

"She was laughing at me and said that I'd probably failed my exam and because Sister Angela said the same thing last week, I told Pauline that she should be Sister Angela's sister, instead of mine."

"Yes, and what else did you say?"

"I told her I hated her and that she could report me to Sister Angela if she wanted to and then she could go to hell."

"Did you tell her that she could go to hell along with Sister Angela?"

"No, I never said any such thing."

Sister Martha looked at Pauline and said, "Well one of you is lying, which one is it?"

"It's not me," I said, "Ask everyone who heard us fighting, then we'll see who's lying." I added, looking at Pauline with hate in my eyes again.

Sister Martha agreed to my suggestion and after questioning all the girls who heard the argument, all of them vouched that I was telling the truth, including Pauline's so called friends.

Sister Martha returned to the playroom some fifteen minutes later. She stormed in slamming the door behind her and grabbed Pauline by the ear, yanking her away from Sister Angela who was holding her hand lovingly, while Pauline lapped up the attention. The whole time that Sister Martha was out of the room, I stood there watching the pair of them and hating them both. They were making me feel like the villain, when in all truth it was them that were the bad ones, especially Pauline. She was my sister, my own blood!

"Come here you little liar" Sister Martha said, "You're going to say hello to "Discipline" for your terrible lies."

"Oh give her a second chance, maybe she was confused because she was frightened," Sister Angela said, stepping forward to protect her darling Pauline.

I stood there dumbfounded, I couldn't believe my ears.

Sister Martha looked from Sister Angela to Pauline and then she said,

"Okay Pauline, I'll let you off this time but don't ever let me hear of you telling lies again. Is that understood?"

"Yes Sister Martha" Pauline said, running back to the comfort of Sister Angela's waiting arms.

Well I'm not letting you off with it. I thought, still wondering why she hadn't been punished. I sure as hell would have been. I'm going to bloody kill you. You just wait till I get my hands on you later.

Sister Martha turned my way and in a harsh voice she said, "Lynch, get back to class.

"Yes Sister Martha" I said, thinking to myself as I walked swiftly out of the room. "You bitch, you're yelling at me, when I wasn't the one who lied, I was innocent."

When I got back to class I knew Sister Martha would be right behind me so I only briefly told Linda what had happened. But I did manage to tell her that I intended to kill Pauline for this and nothing was going to stop me.

It was the first time in my life that I didn't feel any remorse for Pauline. I think I just had too much anger inside me to release and Pauline was going to feel the full strength of that anger.

Dinner time came and I was still just as angry. As we ate I said to Linda,

"I'll let her have her dinner in peace and enjoy it, but after dinner when we're playing, I'm going to grab that curly head of hers and shake the living daylights out of her."

"Oh forget it Jospehine, she's not worth it. You're the one who will end up in trouble, not her."

"No I won't forget it, not this time. I'll put some manners and loyalty into her if it's the last thing I do." I said with determination.

Linda didn't answer me. She had never seen me so worked up. In fact, I had never felt so much anger for anyone in my life.

I think Linda was a bit scared of me right now and decided to stay out of it.

When we went out into the yard I spotted Pauline and I began walking towards her. She saw me coming and began running back inside to the safety of Sister Angela. She ran like lightning and because of my size I couldn't catch her, so I yelled out to Linda,

"Linda catch her, she's running to her new sister, Sister Angela."

Linda laughed at what I said and began running after Pauline. She caught her before she could get inside and held her around the waist till I got there.

I walked up to them very slowly quite puffed from my hopeless chase. Then I grabbed Pauline by the hair and pulled and shook her in every direction giving her an occasional slap in the face at the same time.

"Listen to me, you have to learn who to be good to. I've done everything for you. I've looked after you, I've stood up for you, and what's more I've really loved you. But I hate you now Pauline. You're nothing but a dirty liar and a traitor, who just loves getting me into trouble. You have dirty, filthy ways, and I'm not taking anymore from you." I screamed as I continued shaking her all over the place like a rag doll.

"You've got me into trouble for the last time, because everytime you tell on me from now on I'll beat you up, and every time the beatings will get harder and harder." I said, giving her another punch. "And that applies for reporting any of my friends too." I added looking at Linda. "You're disgusting and very selfish and I'm glad I'm not like you Pauline."

"At least I'm pretty and not like you. You're an ugly beast Josephine." she snarled back at me defiantly.

Her words fueled my anger even more and I tightened my grip

on her hair, slapping her face at the same time,

"You're pretty on the outside Pauline, but it's you who's the ugly beast on the inside and I'd much rather be like me any day. At least people like me, no one likes you."

"Who cares?"

"You will one day, " I said and threw her away from me in disgust.

"Just you remember, every time you get me or my friends into trouble from now on you'll get another hiding like this. Now get out of my sight before I kill you altogether."

I stood watching her run away and I suddenly realized where she was going. I just couldn't believe my eyes. After everything I had just said and done to her she was going straight inside to tell Sister Angela. At first I thought she was bluffing, but when I saw her walking back out a few moments later I nearly died. The pair of them just standing there holding hands, waiting for me, their prey!!

"Lynch, Mitchell, inside this instant." The angry Sister Angela growled.

We followed her to the playroom and when we were inside she asked,

"Lynch, did you pull Pauline's hair and slap and punch her?"

"Yes I did" I answered with pride and standing as tall as I could.

"What about you Mitchell, did you slap her too?"

"No, I did not."

"Well Pauline said you did."

"Well Pauline's lying again," I answered, "it was only me who hit her, no one else."

"I wasn't talking to you Lynch, I was talking to Mitchell. Did you slap her face Mitchell?" she repeated

"No Sister Angela, I did not."

Just then the door opened and Sister Martha walked in, holding

"Discipline" in her hands. Sister Angela must have told her that we beat up Pauline before calling us in and she was here to teach us a lesson. Little did any of us know it was going to back fire on both Pauline and Sister Angela. I knew Sister Martha hated Pauline but she never strapped her in class because Pauline was so intelligent and didn't warrant any punishment. However, I think Sister Martha had just been waiting for a chance.

"Well, what's going on here?" Sister Martha asked,

Again it was me who spoke up first when in fact I should have let Sister Angela explain the situation, but I didn't want to give Sister Angela the chance to distort the truth so I said,

"Pauline's been telling lies again."

"Be quiet, you little brat." Sister Angela said in defence of Pauline. "No one was talking to you. Besides we are here because you beat-up Pauline, not because of any lies Pauline told."

To my amazement Sister Martha ingnored Sister Angela totally and grabbed Pauline by the hair.

"You are going to get it this time young lady. You had a chance to stop lying, but you abused it. Now not even Sister Angela can save you. You are too cocky and tell too many lies for your own good. I'm going to make it my business to knock it out of you."

"I'll leave it in your hands then Sister," The offended Sister Angela said. The truth was she didn't want to see Pauline being punished, and had been put out by Sister Martha over-riding her decision. As she walked out she brushed by me and looked at me with a vengence which made me go cold all over so that I actually shivered inwardly, but I looked at her and smiled as if to imply, I won this time, and I silently vowed that Pauline was going to get another hiding later. I was determined not to give in to her.

However, as I watched her getting strapped I began to feel sorry for her again. It took all my strength not to comfort her when it was all over, but then I came back to my senses, telling myself that I couldn't let her get away with it. Not after the threats I made in the yard. I had been punished too often because of her, for too many years and it had to stop. I had always given in to her in the past and I was determined that she wouldn't get away with it anymore.

I finally realized that she wasn't worth the love I had given her in the past. She had no love or respect for me. In fact she treated me like an idiot most of the time. She was a cruel, senseless bitch, who just laughed at other peoples misfortunes, even if they were her own flesh and blood and it sickened me.

I vowed again that by the time I was finished with her she would be so scared of me she would never report me, or any of my friends, again.

Linda tried to persuade me not to hit her any more but the more she tried the more determined I became. It wasn't that she felt sorry for Pauline, she just didn't want me to get into trouble. I knew as well as Linda that I was lucky to get away with it the first time and I knew I might not be so lucky next time, but I didn't care. Pauline was going to pay come rain or shine. Besides, any punishment I received would be worth it if I could knock Pauline's bad habits out of her.

The next day after lunch I stayed away from Pauline for the first fifteen minutes or so to give her a false sense of security. Then I saw my chance. She was playing near the shed so I walked over to her very casually and when I was close enough I grabbed her and pushed her into the shed. Once inside, I began hitting her and pulling her hair wildly trying to inflict as much pain as possible and the whole time I couldn't stop yelling at her.

"Why do you insist on getting me into trouble." I yelled, "I'm your sister. What the hell are you made of anyway. If we don't stand by each other, we may as well be dead." I said half in tears myself. Eventually, I released her hair giving her a chance to answer me, but I didn't like her answer,

"You can die if you want Jospehine, but I won't. Besides, you would be better off dead because you're far too ugly to walk on the face of the earth and no one will ever love you."

The anger flared up in me once again. I grabbed hold of her roughly and began punching and slapping her with all my might. I pushed and pulled with all the power I possessed. I actually had the urge to kill her but she broke my uncontrollable rage with her pleas.

"I'm sorry Josephine, please stop. I'm sorry. I'll never tell on you again." She began crying like I'd never seen her cry before. "Please stop, you're hurting me." she begged.

I gave her one final thump and pushed her away from me looking down at her with revulsion.

"You better not report me again Pauline," I threatened, "Because next time I'll bloody kill you." Then I walked out of the shed leaving her crying on the ground. I was shaking all over as I left, not from fright, but from pure rage and hate for her.

Pauline did change a little after that. She never reported me for anything again, so in a sense I won but that was all that changed. She still remained selfish and an uncaring brat. She appeared to enjoy hurting people, and that never changed. However, I knew that was one of her charactaristics I couldn't change. It was just her nature and I was lumbered with her for a sister. As they say, you can choose your friends, but you can't choose your family!

Maureen came to me later in the week and asked me what I did to Pauline. At first I thought she was angry with me and answered her defensively.

"I got fed up with her betraying me and telling stories all the time, so I nearly killed her."

"Well good for you." She said to my surprise. "But weren't you scared she would tell on you?"

"A little, but I would have got her again and she knew it."

"Well you'll never win with her that's for sure Jospehine. Don't get too confident and make sure to be very careful of her. She's very clever and has a rotten nature. She might just get you back when you least expect it. The funny thing is she's so pretty she will probably go far in life, regardless of her nature."

"Are you saying I'm ugly" I teased.

"No of course not." She laughed, "What I'm really trying to say is watch Pauline. I'm sure she'll try to get you back somehow, so just be careful."

"I will." I said, then changing the subject, I asked, "Are you looking forward to leaving?"

"Yes, but I'll miss you a lot."

I hugged her and tears pricked the corner of my eyes and I said.

"I hate you going. I'll only have Linda when you go. Pauline's a dead loss and I hardly know Doreen."

"I know, but next year you'll be coming. Your over the worst of it all now Jospehine. The last year here is only helping the younger students, except when you're doing your commmercial classes and they're really fun."

"I'm glad you think so. I don't think I'll enjoy them."

"Ah yes you will, you'll see, it's a breeze."

I decided to change the subject again. I was dreading the

commercial classes, no matter what Maureen said.

"Do you know who's picking you up next week?" I asked.

"Yes, Caroline is."

"Oh good, I'm longing to see her. Do you think she's changed much?"

"Oh yes. I bet she's a real lady now Josephine."

"Oh you and your real lady, you're bloody mad, I'm sure of it Maureen."

We both laughed for a few minutes, but then her mood changed and she became sad. She looked into my face slowly and said,

"You won't cry the day I'm leaving will you. I just couldn't bear it.

"I'll try not too." I answered.

"Thanks" she said. "There's something else too."

"What?" I asked, wondering what other impossible task she was going to ask me to perform.

"I want you to promise me that no matter how nasty Pauline is, you remember that she's still your sister and stand by her, and Doreen too?"

"I'll try, but I just don't trust Pauline at all. Doreen is okay, but I have so little to do with her."

"Please Jospehine, you still have to look after them both. We are still sisters."

"I will," I said, then added, "I feel so sorry for Doreen, she's so ugly and she still has such a long time before she gets out of here." I paused momentarily looking at Maureen. Then I asked,

"Maureen, how come when we get visitors they never want to see Doreen? She's our sister, but she's always left out of everything."

"I don't really know. I'll ask dad when I see him. I want to find out why mum never writes to us either. We haven't heard from her once since we've been here."

"Yes that bothers me too. I've written a few sly letters to her and dad begging them to come and visit us, but neither of them came. At least dad wrote back to us, she didn't even do that."

"Me too. I gave up in the end and now I only write to dad. I wouldn't waste your energy on her any more Jospehine. She obviously doesn't care about us. So why should we worry about her. I can't wait to see her though and find out why she never bothered."

After Maureen's last statement we both just sat there in our own private worlds, thinking about our family and Maureen's forthcoming freedom until the bell rang. Then we went inside holding hands without saying another word to each other. Our touch was speaking much louder than all the words in the world could ever do.

CHAPTER 49

The next week flew by quickly. Maureen and I spent every spare minute together, usually with Kitty and Linda tagging along behind us. Finally the day arrived for Maureen to leave and I had to let go. The previous night I cried all night and when I awoke my eyes were red raw and badly swollen, due to lack of sleep as well as all the tears. When Maureen saw me her first words were, "You promised Josephine"
"I know but I think I've cried them all. I don't think I'll cry again today." I said, putting on a brave smile.

Later in the morning Caroline arrived and I couldn't wait to get to the playroom to see her. She looked stunning too, she was wearing a black jumper, with a white cotton skirt. She had high heels on and was wearing just a touch of make-up. Her hair hung loose down her back and she looked radiant and happy. She looked and smelled just like a freshly picked flower, I thought.
The first thing Maureen said was, "Wow, you're a lady" and the pair of us burst out laughing, but Caroline just managed a bashful smile.
Caroline addressed me first by saying,
"Josephine, dad wants to know if you passed your exams."
"Well we haven't received the results yet, but I'm almost sure I did thanks to you and all your help with my times tables. They really made the difference in the maths exam, it just made it so much faster to get the answers."
"How have you all been?" she asked,
"Oh fine," Maureen answered, "but Josephine still makes a lot of jokes and gets in the dog house all the time."
I looked at Maureen sidewards as if to say "Big Mouth," and reading my thoughts she burst out laughing again. We all did

except Pauline. I suddenly turned and looked at Pauline. She was just sitting down quietly by herself. The only thing she had managed to say so far was "hello". She showed no excitement about seeing Caroline and no sorrow because of Maureen leaving. She really was made of ice I thought as I eyed her closely.

Caroline broke into my thoughts,

"Josephine you have to stop getting into trouble. It breaks my heart when I think of you being strapped in here while I'm out enjoying life. I spend a lot of time worrying about you all."

"I'll be fine don't worry about me. I can't help it if I find things funny." I answered.

"Well at least you will be doing the commmercial classes after the holidays, that should keep you out of trouble!!"

"Rubbish, it will bore me to tears. You should tell dad not to waste his money. I want to learn dressmaking not secretarial skills."

"You don't know dad, he's very strict. He has sent me back to night school for real secretarial qualifications, which I really didn't want to do. I would have preferred to enjoy my evenings going out, but he doesn't give you a choice. Maureen has already been enrolled for the next semester, whether she wants to do it or not."

"Oh that's great." Maureen responded, the happiness gleaming in her eyes. "I don't mind at all. In fact I can't wait, I'm exceptionally good at it too." She added without any modesty.

"I don't think you're as good as you think," Caroline said mocking her slightly, "they don't teach you anything at the convent. You'll find out when you go to the London college that you know very little. The standard in London is so much higher."

Caroline's last statement put me off the course even more and I said,

"If you learn nothing here tell dad not to waste his money. I can learn dressmaking here and do the course in London."

"You're very smart Josephine, but the convent course is a good foundation for what you will learn in London, and you'll not get out of it that easily."

I laughed at Caroline's accurate account of me and I was still laughing when Sister Martha and Sister Angela entered the room. The main purspose of them being here was to look Caroline over and maybe discredit her if they could. They had overheard what I said too, (They were probably listening through the door) because as soon as they walked through the door Sister Martha said,

"What was that you said about the commercial classes Josephine?"

"I told Caroline to tell our father not to waste his money on commercial classes for me," I answered with confidence. (I'm sure this burst of confidence came only from the fact that Caroline was here.)

Instead of acknowledging my answer Sister Martha turned to Caroline and said,

"Don't bother telling your father that Caroline, the child just doesn't know what's good for her." she said smiling, "I'm sure she will love the course once she starts."

"Yes I'm sure she will." Caroline answered politely.

Sister Angela stood behind Caroline looking her up and down during the whole conversation, not saying a word. Although Caroline was talking to Sister Martha she could sense Sister Angela staring at her, but she stood there tall and proud pretending not to notice.

Suddenly Sister Angela directed a question at Caroline,

"Your hair looks terrible Caroline, when are you going to cut it?" she asked.

"I'm not Sister Angela, I like it just the way it is." Caroline answered in a sweet tone with a wide smile on her face.

Sister Angela turned to Maureen and asked,

"I bet you'll let your's grow this messy too won't you Maureen?"

"Oh no Sister Angela." The chicken Maureen answered in a cute voice.

I bit down on my lip holding back the laughter. I knew very well that Maureen would grow her hair the moment she left the convent. She would love to be able to grow it long. I decided to get into the conversation not able to hold back my tongue.

"Oh I'll grow mine when I get out of here." I said feeling quite brave while Caroline was still with us.

Everyone looked my way. Sister Angela with angry eyes and Caroline with eyes pleading for me to shut-up.

"Nothing you could do, could be an improvement Josephine," Sister Angela announced, degrading me as usual. I knew she was trying to tell me I was ugly but I just looked at Maureen and the pair of us burst out laughing at her nasty remark.

Caroline looked from Maureen to me and back again in disgust, thinking we had both gone quite mad. She didn't even manage a smile at our outburst of laughter.

"You two are quite mad." She finally managed to say which caught the attention of Sister Angela, who had been staring at us as well.

"I agree with you dear." Sister Angela said, "They really are quite silly aren't they?"

Caroline ignored her totally as if she hadn't spoken at all. She didn't even look at her.

Sister Angela relizing she wasn't getting an answer from Caroline, decided to change the subject altogether,

"Now then," she said, "Pauline and some other girls have agreed to dance for you. A few of the nuns will come down to see the activities as well. Our own mini concert, won't that be fun Caroline?"

That was the last thing Caroline wanted, she just wanted some quite time with her family. The truth was, that the nuns all wanted a sticky-beak at Caroline and this was a good excuse to do so and Caroline knew what they were up to. However, Caroline agreed politely.

"Come along Pauline let's get you ready." Sister Angela said, holding out her hand to Pauline.

Pauline rose and without a word left with Sister Angela.

They returned shortly after with a few of the other girls and began dancing. However, the nuns present didn't take any notice of the dancing, they were all too busy watching Caroline and whispering to each other.

Finally, Caroline had enough of their nods and whispers and turned to Kathleen Corcorgan who was seated beside me and asked if she may go to the toilet.

"Of course, use the one in the dormitory." the Matron answered, and then added, "Josephine here's the keys. Don't forget to lock up after yourselves."

"No mam, I won't." I answered feeling very grown up by her giving me the keys.

When we got to the dormitory, instead of going to the toilet Caroline lit a cigarette.

"What are you doing?" I asked, shocked at the open flame of the lighter. I had never seen anyone smoke before.

"Smoking, silly. Everyone does it in London."

"Does dad know?"

"Yes of course he does, he doesn't mind."

"Why do you do it, it looks so stupid."

"You won't think so later." she answered grinning at me. "I'm sure when you see everyone else doing it you'll change your mind." Then she changed the subject and said,

"Josephine I want you to promise me something."

"What?"

"Promise me you won't cry when Maureen and I leave. We will be picking you up next year so please don't make it hard on us today. It makes us feel guilty for going."

"I'll try," I said and decided to change the subject myself.

"How come you look so beautiful now?" I asked.

She smiled at me gently as she answered,

"Darling it's the clothes,the make-up and most of all, the freedom. You will be beautiful too when you get out of here. We'll go shopping together and I'll buy you some nice clothes and make-up and you'll be stunning, just wait and see." she said. Then she paused for a moment studing me, and asked,

"Did you understand what Sister Angela meant down stairs, when she said nothing would improve you?"

"Yes of course I did, she meant I was ugly."

"Well why did you laugh?"

"Because I don't let her see me upset anymore. I hide it by laughing or smiling. That gets her even more angry because she's not getting any satisfaction from her insults."

"Well good for you, I'm proud of you. She's very wrong about you anyway."

"What do you mean?"

"You're not ugly. In fact you have very pretty eyes and features and when you lose some weight you will be very beautiful, you mark my words."

I smiled not really believing her words. My whole life I had been told I was ugly, now I was being told I would be beautiful some day and I found it very hard to believe, but it was nice hearing it anyway,

"I hope so." I answered.

"Did Linda pass her exam?" Caroline asked to change the subject realising I was a little embarrassed by her statement.

"Yes she thinks so, we all did as far as we know."

"Oh good, congratulate her for me. Are you both staying out of trouble?"

"Yes we are" I said mimmicking her bossy voice.

"Good" she said pinching my chubby cheeks lovingly. Then she said,

"Come on love we better go back before they come looking for us and smell the cigarette. I just had to get away for a few minutes. I couldn't stand them staring at me any longer."

She put her lighter back in her bag as I watched on fascinated by it.

"That's beautiful." I said.

"Yes it is, isn't it? Dad gave it to me, it's called a lighter."

"Aren't you scared of it?"

"At first I was, but dad showed me how to use it safely. Come on let's go" She ordered, "You talk too much."

When we returned to the playroom the dancing had finished and all eyes turned to Caroline as she glided gently across the floor and back to her seat. Sister Martha approached her immediately and began some general chit chat, which appeared to be more of an interegation than a conversation. She asked her how life was at home, was she working, and where, and how was her father, and a load of other personal questions, which Caroline answered with dignity and pride, but very briefly. The bell rang for the rest of the students to leave for morning recess, but Sister Martha didn't budge, she stood there and continued chatting to Caroline, so I decided to go and get Linda.

"I'll go and get Linda" I said interrupting them, and ran from the room before anyone could stop me. When Linda and I returned Caroline turned away from Sister Martha and smiled at Linda.

"Hello Linda," she said, "I'm happy to hear you both did well in your exams."

"Thank-you" Linda answered shyly, not sure of the new sophisticated Caroline.

Sister Martha realised that she was getting the brush off and walked away, which pleased us all. Especially Caroline who just wanted a little privacy. As soon as Sister Martha was out of earshot Caroline's smile dropped and in a serious voice she said,

"Linda, I want you to stay out of trouble please and keep Josephine out of trouble too. She only has you to watch out for her now and I'm afraid, you're as bad as she is."

Linda was a little surprised by Caroline's request and the urgencey of her voice, and she responded,

"I'll try." But when she looked back at me I gave her a sly grin as if to say, you keep me out of trouble, fat chance, and the pair of us burst out laughing into Caroline's face.

"You really are mad" Caroline said through pursed lips. She wasn't in the least amused with the situation.

Our laughing soon brought Sister Martha back to spoil things.

"Caroline, what is going to happen to Doreen?" Sister Martha asked abruptly.

Caroline stiffened and replied in a very stern voice,

"I have no idea and it's not my concern. You can take that up with her mother."

I couldn't believe how sharp Caroline's words seemed to be and how angry she suddenly appeared when asked about Doreen.

"Okay dear, I was just enquiring." Sister Martha answered in a sharp tone herself. Then she walked away. I'm sure she felt like slapping Caroline's face and had to walk away to calm down because she couldn't lay a finger on her now.

I looked up at Caroline's red angry face. I noticed that she was actually shaking from sheer temper and it surprised me because she was always so calm.

"What's the matter, what did Sister Martha mean?" I asked

"Nothing love. I told you before you ask too many questions." She said smiling, trying to give the situation little importance. I looked at Maureen who had just sat listening since we returned from the toilet. I hoped she could give me some sort of explanation but she simply shrugged her shoulders. However I sensed she knew more than she was letting on, but I wasn't going to persue it. It was upsetting Caroline too much and that's the last thing I wanted. Suddenly Pauline decided to join in the conversation and for some strange reason that made me happy and I spoke to her immediately in hopes of making her feel welcomed.

"Just think Pauline one day I'll be coming back here just like Caroline, to collect you."

"Yes, but you won't look like Caroline does." she answered in a bitchy tone, which hurt like hell. Here I was trying to make her feel comfortable, only to be slapped in the face with one of her insults.

"Oh shut-up" I snapped, "With a bit of luck I'll convince dad to leave you here forever. Then I won't have to come back for you."

"Stop that you two," Caroline snapped.

"Well she started it." I argued.

"Well she beat me up a few weeks ago." Pauline said, trying to get me in trouble with Caroline.

"You've had it coming for a long time Pauline." Caroline answered, which made me giggle.

Caroline felt sorry for Pauline, because of the expression on her face, and she added,

"You have to try and love other people Pauline and be nice to them. You mustn't always be so spiteful, especially to your sisters."

Pauline didn't answer, instead she began looking up at the roof with her hands behind her back swaying from side to side. She didn't like being reprimanded by Caroline not one little bit. Suddenly as if getting tired of the situation, Caroline said,

"Come on Maureen let's get out of here, I can't bear it any longer."

"Okay, I'll get me stuff" Maureen said running out of the room in a great hurry to leave.

As Maureen re-entered the room with her few belongings my heart began to pound. This was it, they were actually leaving. I knew that saying goodbye to both of them was going to be terrible, I just didn't know how terrible. It was like a nightmare! We all walked to the gate together and with every step I took, I began to panic a little more, but I was keeping all my feelings inside not wanting to break my promise to Maureen. However, as we got closer to the gate I snapped, unable to contain my turmoil a moment longer. My head was running wild with thoughts and I began to speak them aloud like I did so often at night.

"No she can't go, not Maureen too. Please don't take Maureen. I'll be on my own, please take me too." I cried.

Pauline began to cry too which surprised me, I didn't think she was capable of any emotion. Doreen had also made her way to the gate to say good-bye to Maureen and Caroline, but she wasn't crying. In fact she was quite calm. It was as though she knew she didn't really belong, but I admired her for trying to fit in, and having the decency to make an effort to say goodbye.

I, the opposite to Doreen continued screaming. I pulled at my own hair in an effort to physcially hurt myself, in an attempt to stop the pain I was feeling inside my heart. I felt confused and no amount of consoling from Maureen or Caroline was helping. I just wanted Maureen to stay no matter what. I felt faint and totally out of control. I kept screaming over and over again for Maureen to stay or bring me with them. In the end the Reverend Mother was called, because I was becoming uncontrollable. Neither Sister Martha or Sister Angela could shut me up. I was oblivious to their threats and warnings. All I could think about was being with Maureen. Nothing else mattered. As the gates closed behind Caroline and Maureen leaving me on the inside I really became hysterical. I took hold of those closed gates as though I was hanging on to life itself and screamed viciously after them. I was like a wild cat gone mad screeching on the top of my lungs. "Don't go. Please don't leave me, take me too." I begged, but they didn't answer. They just walked backwards looking at me and crying. They waved to me and begged me to be strong for them and to stop crying, but I couldn't. I was watching part of me leave with them, my heart!

Even when they were out of sight I clutched at the gates and screamed out their names, begging for them to come back and take me too. It was like nightmare that I couldn't wake up from. The Reverend Mother and Sister Martha finally managed to loosen my grip on the gates and I noticed that Pauline and Doreen were already back inside, but I had no memory of them leaving. In fact there was just the three of us here now, the Reverend Mother, Sister Martha and me. When they pulled me off the gate I crumpled to the ground in a massive heap and cried bitterly, repeating the same thing over and over again,
"They're gone, I'm by myself."
The Reverend mother dismissed Sister Martha and allowed me to calm down by myself quielty, just standing over me in silence. When I had reduced my screams to a quiet sob she gently walked me back inside to her room. When we got there she said,

"Now that's better, you made it very hard on your older sisters you know. That's how they will remember you and that's not fair Josephine."

"Fair! It's not fair that I couldn't go too." I said and began crying again. "I miss Maureen already. I can't live without her, I just know I can't."

"That's nonsense, of course you can. Besides your younger sisters need you now, so you have to be strong for them. Next year it will be you going and the year after that you'll be the one coming back for Pauline."

"I'll never come back for Pauline." I hissed, remembering our conversation in the playroom. "I'm sure if she hadn't started arguing with me Caroline would have stayed longer. I hate her, I really do."

"That's not very sisterly Josephine."

"I don't care, I hate her."

"You don't mean that Josephine, she's your sister."

"Oh yes I do mean it. She's awful to me. She's always saying hateful things."

"Now, now, it's not that bad." she said and changed the subject, realising I was becoming hysterical again. "Look, I want you to go and get a drink, then go and rest in the infirmary."

"I don't want to, I want to go back to the others."

"Rest first and after lunch you can join the rest of the girls."

"Okay." I said giving in to her wishes. I was suddenly feeling very lethargic after all my crying and screaming. Not to mention the shock of Maureen leaving.

At Lunch time Linda came running up to me in the dining room,

"Don't run Mitchell." Sister Angela called after her.

"Sorry Sister Angela."

When she was sitting beside me she whispered,
"How are you feeling?"
"Terrible, I want to run away after them. I just can't wait
another year."
Linda's expression changed from concern to outright sadness
and she said,
"But you promised me you'd never leave me until your
sixteeth birthday."
I turned to look at her noticing the strain in her voice, but for
a brief moment it was Maureen that I saw before me, asking me
if I had any messages for dad like she had done at the gate and
I answered her again now, the same way as I did then,
"Yes, tell him he's a very mean man."
"Who's mean," Linda asked wondering what the hell I was
talking about and why my eyes seemed so distant.
"What, oh sorry Linda. My father that's who. I was thinking
about Maureen and a conversation we had before she left. And
don't worry I won't leave you like they left me." I answered
still angry with them for going.
"Look Josephine don't be upset, you only have one year left.
I don't know what will happen to me when you go."
I hugged her tightly. She had gotten through to me where
everyone else had failed. She made me realise with just a few
words how lucky I really was, and how selfish I was behaving.
"If I have my way Linda you'll be leaving with me. I've
already told dad in my sly letters that I want him to take you
too. Although he hasn't given me and answer yet." I said
wondering why he hadn't made any enquiries. Then I thought
that maybe he had, but hadn't told me about them in fear of me
getting into trouble. I turned back to Linda, and in a happier
tone I said,
"If he loves me at all I know he will take you, because that's
the most important thing to me. Having you live with me as a

sister for the rest of my life would make me a very happy person."

Tears rolled down Linda's face as she mumbled "Thanks." Then she hugged me back fiercely. Her grip was so tight I thought she would break every bone in my body!

CHAPTER 50

For the next few weeks I was like a lost lamb. Even though Linda was always there to support me I missed Maureen terribly. I missed her bossy mature ways, not to mention her crazy sense of humour. We had so many good laughs together especially during the last two weeks she had been here. She was forever trying to pretty me up. She would take off my glasses and comb my fringe to one side, and then the other and say,

"Well, maybe when you lose some weight!" and leave the sentence un-finished, which would send the pair of us into fits of laughter.

Now she was gone and I was having such a hard time accepting it. It just didn't seem real. I kept expecting her to creep up to my bed at night. I cried myself to sleep so often as I realised it just wasn't going to happen, she would never come again. I prayed each night, thanking god for Linda's friendship and that dad would take her out of here when I left. I couldn't bear the thought of her being alone and begged dad to take her in each and every sly letter I wrote.

One day I was telling Linda the contents of a letter I had recently written to dad and she turned to me sadly and said,

"We're living in a dream world Jospehine."

"Why?"

"Because even if your father agreed to accept me with five of his own children to fend for, the nuns would never let me go."

"Why not, they can't stop you once you're sixteen."

"They'll find a way, they have their own plans for me."

"What plans?"

"Looking after them! They have already told me I am to start in the laundry right after the holidays."

"When did they tell you that?"

"This morning."

"Well not if I have my way Linda. If I have my way you'll be leaving with me. The very same day," I added with determination.

Linda changed the subject abruptly not wanting to argue about it anymore, and in a happier tone she said,

"We should be getting the results of our exams soon, Then we will have a nice party."

"Yes, but let's not think about that yet. We still have our holidays to enjoy."

"Yea I know." She answered "And they're always fun."

"They sure are." I said happily.

The next day Linda and I were knitting in the playroom getting our quota of jumpers finished when I noticed Doreen knitting in the corner, all by herself. I looked at her with pity then standing up I said to Linda,

"I'll be back in a minute Linda."

"Okay." She answered carrying on with her knitting not bothering to look up.

I walked over to Doreen and looked down at her.

"Why are you sitting on your own Doreen?" I asked.

"Oh, I don't know. I was just sitting here quietly knitting and thinking."

"What were you thinking about?"

"Well I was wondering what was going to happen to me later on and who's going to come for me. It all seems very strange that the rest of my sisters have letters and visitors and I never receive anything. I was also wondering if any one would ever come and get me that's all."

"Yes I was wondering about that too when Caroline was here. I even asked her, but she told me that dad would explain all that to me later so I'm no wiser than you I'm afraid."

"Why do you think he never writes to me or sends me any parcels Josephine?"

"I've got no idea. I have noticed that he never bothers with you, but I really don't know why." I paused for a moment feeling sorry for her. Then in a happier tone I added,

"Look, don't worry about it Doreen. When I leave here next year I'll send you some parcels, in the meantime you can still share my parcels."

"Yes" she answered with very little enthusisam.

"Why don't you come over and sit with me and Linda instead of being by yourself, we don't mind."

"No I'm alright, you go ahead. I'll be fine."

"Okay, but if you change your mind just come over, alright."

"Yea, thanks Josephine."

"That's alright."

I went back over to Linda and after sitting down I said,

"Doreen's very sad Linda."

"How come?"

"She said she doesn't know who's coming to get her when she's sixteen, and that no-one ever bothers with her."

"Oh don't worry, I'm sure she'll cheer up. She's propably having an off day, that's all."

"Yea I guess so, but I just feel so sorry for her." I said still concerned with her demeanour. I took my mind of it by asking Linda if she wanted to have a race with our knitting to see who could finish the row first.

About six weeks after Maureen left the convent I was sitting beside Linda having my lunch, and enjoying her company. It was the first day back at school for me and Linda's first day in the laundry. The pair of us were sitting whispering about how much Linda hated the laundry and how I hated my commercial course when suddenly Sister Angela came into the dining room a little later than usual, and called out from the doorway, "Josephine, Pauline and Doreen Lynch come with me, you have a visitor."

I stood up immediately wondering who on earth wanted to see Doreen. I glanced over at Doreen as she walked towards Sister Angela who was waiting at the door. Her face gleamed with excitement. This was her first visitor in ten years and the excitement she was feeling was more than a apparent. She was walking with such haste to get there that she was almost a jogging.

The news of a visitor cheered me up as well. I was feeling depressed all morning because Linda had been put to work in the laundry during school hours. Apart from missing her I felt bad that she hated it so much. The thought of being confined to the laundry for the best part of her life was breaking her heart, as well as mine. I thought about my commercial classes which I also hated, but I realised how much more lucky I was. I made up my mind to stop complaining about my course when we were together. Instead I would concentrate on making Linda happy and enjoy our reduced time together.

Pauline, Doreen and I followed Sister Angela who was annoyed at having to escort us when she should be supervising the dining room, although I really wasn't paying much attention to her snide remarks. I was still wondering who it was. I started to guess maybe my father, or perhaps an aunt who also knows Doreen, but as we entered the playroom it was yet another stranger who stood before us along with the Reverend Mother. As we entered the room both women turned, but it was the Reverend Mother who spoke first,

"Oh girls, do come in and sit down." she said, "This is your mother."

My body froze to the spot where I stood. I was in a state of shock. This was the last person I expected to see, because she never bothered with us in the past. Then I thought that Maureen had told her to come because we had discussed her never bothering with us just before Maureen left the convent. Feeling happier with having a reason for her visit I finally followed Pauline and Doreen to where our mother was standing and she kissed all three of us on the cheek. As we were about to sit down beside our mother the Reverend Mother, much to my dissapointment, called me away. I hesitated in going to her, I didn't want to miss out on anything our mother had to say. I was just so pleased to see her finally, even though I had no recongition of her at all. She was pretty with a round face and dainty features. She wore little makeup, but her cheeks were rosy on her fair complexion. She had red hair which was short but nicely cut. She was short and plump looking but nicely groomed and there was a certain air of elegance about her. Her figure made me realize who I took after. I found my self desperately wanting to like this person and more than anything I wanted her to love me.

"Jospehine," The Reverend Mother repeated, "could you please come with me for a moment."

I stood up, and followed her outside the room and she closed the door behind me. Then she said in a very quite tone which was almost a whisper,

"Josephine, your mother wishes to take you out for the day, but I'm afraid your father has forbidden it."

I looked at her in a confused manner thinking surely he know's she's here. Then I asked, "Why would he do that?"

"Well that's not for me to discuss right now, but would you like to go?"

"Yes of course I would."

"Okay, I'll permit you and Pauline to go but I'm afraid Doreen will have to stay here because she's too young. There is one condition though, you must promise me that your father will never find out about this."

"Alright, I promise," I said, wondering what all the fuss was about, then I added,

"How come Doreen can't come?"

She seemed to become aggitated with my last question and said,

"I've already told you she's too young. Now stop asking so many questions or I'll stop you and Pauline going too." (The truth was mum had custody of Doreen when she came of age, but not Pauline or I and the Reverend Mother suspected that she may dump us again or send us back in a cab alone, but would probably run off with Doreen and she wasn't prepared to take the chance.)

I decided to shut-up not wanting to spoil my chances of going and nodded my head silently.

When all was agreed the Reverend Mother led me back inside the playroom where we all spoke to mum for the next half an hour or so. Then Doreen was sent out into the yard while Pauline and I were sent for our coats. When we got outside the convent gates Pauline and I expected a long walk instead there was a taxi waiting for us.

We all jumped in the taxi and I opened the conversation.

"I was terribly sad when Maureen left." I said.

"I know you were because Maureen told me all about it." my mother answered.

"How come you haven't been to see us sooner?" I asked, eager to get as much information and questions answered as possible.

"Because I'm a nurse and I get very little time of work."

"But you didn't even answer my letters."

"I'm not very good at writing, your father takes care of all that for the both of us," She said lying through her teeth. She had all the answers for my questions and I never doubted a word.

"Oh I see, so the parcels were from you too."

"Yes of course they were." She answered convincingly.

"Where are we going today" I asked happy to know that our mother loved us after all."

"Well first I'm going to take you to see your aunt in hospital. Then we'll go shopping. I'll buy you both a small gift and something for Doreen as well if you're good."

"How come Doreen wasn't allowed to come with us?" I asked. I still wasn't totally convinced with the the Reverend Mother's answer, it wasn't a good enough excuse for me.

"The Reverend Mother said she was too young and would tire easily and maybe spoil our day. I'm sure she'll be able to come next time."

"But she's not that young she's ten years old."

"Oh never mind Josrephine" she said, getting tired of all my questions,   "At least you two were allowed to come so why worry about it. I'm sure she'll be allowed next time."

I was happy to know that there was going to be a next time, but I still didn't think it was fair that Doreen had to stay behind, so I said

"But I do worry, because no one ever wants to see her. Plus you and dad never send her any parcels and it's just not fair. She always seems to be missing out."

"That's not your concern, so enough of the questions." My mother answered in a harsh tone, surprising me. We sat the rest of the trip in silence then mum finally said

"Here we are at the hospital already."

I looked out of the taxi window and when I saw the Ballinrobe Mental Hospital before my eyes something inside me snapped and I began to scream uncontrollably.

"I'm not going in." I yelled, "Please don't make me go in."

"Don't be silly Jospehine." My mother coaxed. "Look at your younger sister, she's not frightened. It's just a hospital for christ sakes. What on earth has gotten into you, stop that screaming this instant."

She opened the taxi door and let Pauline out. Then she tried to pull me out, but I was filled with a terrible fear which seemed to give me a super strength. I held fast to the door handle and wouldn't let go and I continued to scream.

"Please, no. I can't go in there. Please take me back to the convent."

The taxi driver got out of the car and came around to try and help mum pull me out. With both of them pulling and yanking at me I finally lost grip of the door handle, but then I lost all control. I began kicking the pair of them on the footpath and pulling mum's hair every time she bent down to pull me up. Finally the driver said,

"Look I think we're wasting our time ere, the child is scared outa her wits for some reason. Why don't you two go in and I'll wait with the child outside. She's obviously petrified of the place."

They both released their hold on me and I immediately lept back into the taxi for comfort. I curled up in the far corner of the back seat feeling a little safer but longing to get away from here altogether.

Mum straightened her hair and composed her posture again, then she sat in the back seat with me making me pull further away into my little corner.

"Look luv it's only a hospital." Mum said, "Won't you please come in and say hello to your aunty."

"No" I answered bluntly.

"But why?, What are you scared of?"

"I don't know, I just know it's bad in there."

"But that doesn't make any sense Josephine, what's bad? Why are you so scared?"

"I don't know," I yelled at her, "but I'm sure I'll die if I go in. Please let me wait here." I said, beginning to fear she may try and force me out of the taxi again.

"Okay." she snapped."Wait here if you want, but you're a bloodly nuisance Josephine. I should have left you back at the convent with Doreen." Then she got out of the cab and slammed the door behind her.

I didn't like having her dissaproval, but anything was better than going in the hospital. The taxi driver got back in the front of the car, but neither of us spoke a word. I sat there curled up in a ball wondering why I was so afraid, but I truly didn't know. I just knew it was dangerous in there and something bad would happen if I went inside. I had totally blanked out the memory of being locked in the morgue at such a tender age. However the place itself still held a threat to me, but for no apperant reason, or so it seemed at that very moment. I suddenly felt very tired and drained from my ordeal and decided to lay down across the back seat and rest for a while. I lay there tense and unable to rest with my eyes wide open expecting the worst to happen at any moment.

About fifteen minutes later Mum and Pauline returned to find me still lying down in the back seat. As soon as the doors opened I jumped up and retreated to my little corner for safety. As we drove away Pauline looked at me with a smirk on her face and said,

"I think you should go live in there with all the mental people Josephine. You nearly made me deaf with all that screaming and carrying on. You were like a mad women, the same as you were the day Maureen left."

I felt stupid now that I was safely away from the hospital and not wanting to argue in front of mum, I said quietly,

"I was just so scared to go in, it was like something or someone bad was in there."

"That's idiotic Josephine, it's only sick people in there." Pauline answered.

"Oh shut-up" I snapped, offened by being called stupid not to mention mental, by my younger sister.

Suddenly, the taxi driver turned to mum and said,

"She must ave been there before at some stage ta be acting this way."

"Maybe" mum replied. Then she turned around to me and said,

"Have you been there before Jospehine?"

"Yes when I was little. There was a nice doctor in there who loved me very much." I said smiling as I remembered Dr Mongay.

"So why were you so scared?"

"I don't know, I just don't know. Leave me alone." I said, as a flash of scary memory overwhelmed me."

"Don't take that tone with me young lady," mum retaliated, while I sat wishing she'd just leave me alone. I didn't want to remember my frightening experience of being locked in the morgue.

Suddenly Pauline said,

"I was in there with you for a little while do you remember?" she asked and laughed afterwards.

"What's so funny" I asked,

"Do you remember the time I wet the bed Jospehine and you tried to dry it for me?"

"How can I forget, I got a slap in the face for being on the wrong side of the bed the next morning and all you could do was laugh."

Pauline laughed again and said, "What about the time you slapped the boy's face for calling us orphans. That soon shut him up didn't it?"

Suddenly I screamed as the memory came rushing back,

"Shut-up" I yelled at Pauline, "I don't want to hear about that place."

I began shaking all over becoming hot and cold within seconds of each other, as the memory flashed before my eyes.

"I never want to go back there again," I sobbed.

My shocked mother turned to face me at this sudden outburst and in a strained voice she asked,

"What exactly happended?"

I began to relive my terrible experience in the hospital and as I told mum all about it I shook all over. It was all as clear as day now as though it only happened yesterday. After I conveyed my horrible ordeal I looked at mum for some comfort, but all she said was,

"Never mind it's all over now." but her words were without emotion. There was no love or concern in her voice. She didn't attempt to cuddle or comfort me in anyway. She made me feel extremly unloved and unwanted. Somehow I felt like I was a burden to her even after only a few hours of being together. In a way I wished she had never come at all. None of this would be happening if she had only stayed away.

I sat in silence for the next twenty minutes or so thinking about my mother's attitude towards me. I wondered why she hadn't grabbed me and hugged me tightly after my story of the hospital, like I had hoped and expected she would. My tears had subsided but I still hurt inside. I felt like something had just died inside of me. All my hopes seemed to be slipping away from me. The image of my perfect mother and our future relationship was fading. She was turning out to be just someone else who didn't like me. In an attempt to hang on to my fantasy I began thinking about other things and the Reverend Mother's conversation with me earlier in the morning came to mind. Without thinking about the consequences just wanting to talk to my dream mother again I asked,

"Mum why did the Reverend Mother tell me not to tell dad you were here and taking us out?"

Mum became angry with me, as though just the sound of my voice irritated her and she answered,

"You talk too much Josephine." Her hatred for me rang clear and loud in her voice. I decided to shut-up. I suddenly felt the real threat of her denial of love and I wanted and needed the love of my own mother. It was at that moment that I realised that at this stage of my life I wasn't ready to jeopardise it, or let my image of her die. I needed to hang on to what little I had, which wasn't much!

Finally we arrived at a row of shops and the taxi driver, who must have thought that this was a very strange situation and family, pulled over to let us out.

When we got out of the taxi mum paid the driver. Then ignoring me totally, as if trying to punish me for asking questions she turned to Pauline and said,

"What would you like me to buy you sweetheart?'

"I'd like a ball, a skipping rope and a spinning top." the greedy Pauline answered. I stood there wondering if I had asked for the same would she have objected. She didn't blink an eyelid at Pauline's request. I didn't get a choice of what I wanted, she simply brought me and Doreen the same as Pauline.

Later in the day I asked mum for an ice-cream. However she flatly refused and in the next breath she said, "I'm taking you both back to the convent now."

At the time I felt like I was being punished again for asking for the icecream, and it hurt, but I guess the truth was she was just fed up with both of us by that time. It didn't take our mother long to tire of us, not that day and not at any other time. She really didn't deserve children she was far too selfish, thinking of no one but herself and her needs. It didn't matter what needs we had, mum came first!

When we arrived back at the convent she dropped us off at the gate giving us a small peck on the cheek. I had expected her to come in and give Doreen her presents at least, and give us a big hug telling us how much she enjoyed being with us and how she would miss us dearly. There was none of that. In fact there was no compassion at all. Strangely enough though by that stage I felt the same way towards her. Somehow I knew she didn't love us and that I shouldn't love her either. I walked in with Pauline admiring my lovely gifts. I didn't even stand and watch her drive away, I just walked straight back inside and so did Pauline.

The gateman informed the Revenend Mother via the intercom of our arrival and she came down to meet us at the convent doors.
"Did you have a good time?" she enquired.
"Yes" answered Pauline, "No" answered I!
"How come Josephine?"
I went through the procedure of explaining my day including all about the hospital and even about how mum had refused the ice-cream, and the lack of cuddles. When I had finished with all my complaints she replied in a non-interested tone like she hadn't heard a word I said anyway,
"Ah well never mind." Then she told us never to speak about this day again, and above all never to mention it to our father. She made me feel so confused because mum implied that dad knew everything anyway. My confusion got the better of me and I just couldn't help but ask again.
"Why doesn't our father want us to be with our mother? Our

mother said he knew she was here."

"Josephine I told you before, it's not my place to explain your family business. You will be leaving next year then your father will tell you just how much he want's you to know. Until then stop asking all these questions, it's really quite rude."

I still didn't know what all the secrecy was about and why it was rude to ask questions, but I came to the conclusion that this time I just had to accept what she said and shut-up until dad could fill me in on all the details. However I just hated waiting. I'd spent my whole life waiting, always waiting, and I was sick to death of waiting!

The next day I told Linda all about my day with mum and she said,

"Was your mum angry with you for not going in to see your aunt?"

"I think so but I don't care. At the time I did, but later on when I asked her for the ice-cream and she said no in such a horrible way, I realised that she doesn't really loves us at all. So I don't care now either. In fact I don't care if I never see her again."

"That's not nice Josephine, at least you have a mum and she did buy you all those gifts."

"She never gave me a choice of what I wanted though. Only Pauline got a choice, Doreen and I got the same as what Pauline wanted whether we wanted it or not."

"At least you got the same, that's better than nothing at all."

"Yea I know. I just would have liked to choose one thing, not to mention being refused a lousy ice-cream that hurt me even more. I'm just being silly I suppose. By the way here's the ball, you can have that."

"Thank's Jospehine, are you sure?"

"Course I'm sure, let's go and play with it now."

"Alright."

A few minutes later Pauline came over to us crying. That was about the only time she bothered with me. She only came to me whenever she wanted something or was in trouble.

"What's the matter?" I asked becoming a little impatient with her.

"My new ball fell down the toilet can you get it for me?"

"Okay, come on. I'll go fish it out for you."

However by the time we got back to the toilet the ball was gone, which made Pauline cry and scream louder.

"Oh shut-up Pauline," I said, annoyed with her screams, "You should have got it out straight away. What's the matter didn't you want to get your dainty little hands dirty?"

"No it's not that," she sobbed, "I just didn't know what to do."

"Well now someones flushed the toilet and it's gone down the drain." I said, (It didn't occur to me that someone else might have put their hands down and got it out, only I'd do something like that).

Pauline cried even more which made me feel a little sorry for her.

"Come on stop your crying" I said, "Look we can lift the lid off the drain and while Linda and I hold you by the legs, you can go down and get it."

"No it stinks down there."

"Well I can't do it, I'm too heavy for you and Linda to hold, so you'll have to do it if you want your ball back."

"Alright." she agreed against her better judgement, but desperately wanting her ball back. So the three of us marched off hoping to retrieve Pauline's ball.

When we got to the drain Pauline lay flat on her stomach, while Linda and I lowered her into the drain holding her legs tightly. However when we lowered her deeper into the drain she began kicking us furiously.

"Let me go," she yelled, "it stinks down here."

"Can you see the ball?" I answered

"No just get me up, I'm going to be sick."

"Just get the stupid ball Pauline," I insisted, wanting to do what we came for.

"I can't see it."

"Well stop kicking us and look for it." I yelled back at her, getting tired from all her struggling.

Suddenly someone flushed a toilet and the ball started bobbing up and down.

"I see it. Lower me a little further." Pauline called out.

As I went to lower her deeper into the drain I lost grip of her leg and let out an almighty scream. Linda held on tighter giving me time to grip Pauline's loose leg again. By this stage the terrified Pauline was screaming at the top of her lungs because of her narrow escape.

As soon as I had her tightly in my hands again we pulled her straight back up whether she had the ball or not! However as she hit the surface again we noticed that she was full of smiles.

"I got it," she announced, like the cat who caught the mouse!

"You stink!" I said and we all burst out laughing and began fanning her with our hands in an attempt to make the smell go away before going back inside.

Finally I said,

"Come on Linda let's go and play," and no sooner had I said it when the bell rang for Pauline and I to go inside, whilst Linda had to return to the laundry.

"Thank's Pauline, you wasted all our play time."

"Doesn't matter, I got my ball back that's the main thing." she answered.

I looked at her with disbelief she was so damned selfish.

"You're unbelievable Pauline." I said and just walked away

with Linda.

School wasn't so bad that year. I had started my secretarial
course and although it was relatively easy, I still hated it. It was
just so boring. The only consolation was that it only ran for one
and a half hours each day.
My other subjects were taught by Sister Rosa whom I loved.
Occasionaly I helped the girls like Pauline who were studying
for their leaving exam the following year. So all in all it was
going to be a relatively easy year for me for a change. However
I was missing Linda during the day. It seemed strange not
having her around me all the time. Now we could only spend
lunch and playtimes together and that hurt us both. I remember
one day during the second week back at school. We were in the
playroom during the evening and Sister Rosa was supervising
us and she came over to me and after talking for a little while
she asked,
"Are you looking forward to leaving the convent Josephine?"
"Yes I can't wait," I answered with honesty.
"Who's picking you up?"
"Caroline and Maureeen I imagine."
"Oh yes I remember Maureen. I also met Caroline when she
came to collect Maureen. She's a very pretty young girl."
"Yes she is, isn't she?"
"Then I suppose the three of you will come back and pick up
Pauline when it's her turn to leave."
"No not me. I'll never come back here once I leave."
"Oh," she said, a little shocked at my blatent answer. Then she
changed the subject,
"Who will be picking up young Doreen when she's sixteen?"
I looked at her with a puzzled expression,
"I'm not sure," I answered. (Where ever Doreen was concerned
I was always confused and what was worse, was that whenever

I tried to enlighten my curiousity I was told to ask my father when I left the convent.) "Maybe Caroline and Maureen." I added.

"Oh I see," She said and changed the subject once again. "I heard your mother was in to see you all recently."

"Yes she was. I was surprised when she came because she's never had any contact with us before. It has always been our father who wrote to us and sent us things."

"How come?"

"I don't really know. I did ask mum and she said that she was a nurse and kept very busy and that's why she doesn't visit us. She also told me that dad did all the writing for the both of them. I tried to ask her some more questions, but in the end she told me I talked too much and to shut-up."

"Well she's not too far wrong is she?" Sister Rosa said, smiling down at me and patting my head with affection, "But telling you to shut-up wasn't very nice, was it?"

"No I didn't think so either."

Just then Sister Martha came bursting into the playroom interrupting our conversation.

"Girls, girls, you have all passed!" she yelled with genuine excitement. "I will give you all your individual marks as soon as the Reverend Mother arrives. She's on her way down to congratulate you all."

A few minutes later the Reverend Mother arrived accompanied by Sister Angela and the Matron, and Sister Martha commenced giving the five of us our results.

I got the highest marks for maths and my English composition. Me, the "STUPID ONE" came first. It was a miracle that even I couldn't believe. The Matron was the first to come over and congratulate me,

"Well done Josephine, I knew you could do it."

"I'm so happy knowing for sure I passed" I said, "And real

glad I won't have to go through the year again with Sister Martha."

This last statement made the matron laugh so hard she had tears rolling down her face,

"I can't believe how straight to the point you are." she managed to say during her fits of laughter.

Sister Angela saw the pair of us happy and approached us to see what all the fuss was about. I knew instantly that she was going to try and spoil yet another happy time, so as she came closer I turned away looking at all the other happy people in the room. However that didn't deter her from having her say unfortunately!

"I don't know how you did it Lynch. You're still no smarter now than you were when you came here."

I ignored her totally. I didn't even look at her. I even pretended not to have heard a word she said. I was determined not to let her spoil my day. Not this time. The Reverend Mother called for our attention which stopped Sister Angela having another dig at me and I was really thankful.

When the room was silent the Reverend Mother announced that we would have our party the following day, which made us all clap and cheer with joy. Our party was well overdue. The results had taken much longer than normal to return to the convent, leaving me to wait again, like I had done all my life. Normally they were back during the holidays. I was surprised that they had even let me start my commercial course without the exam results, but I guess it had only been a couple of weeks so there was time enough to pull me out of the course if I had failed.

This was probably the biggest day of my young life. It took precedence over my first holy communion and certainly more than my Confirmation, because it representd freedom and achievement to me. Something I had been deprived of my whole life. I truly had never felt more excited in my entire life as I was right now. I was just bursting with joy. I walked over to share my happiness with Linda and said,

"We did it Linda, We really did it."

"We sure did." She said smiling lovingly at me. "We sure did!"

The Reverened Mother came over to me and said,

"Josephine, you did very well my dear. Congratulations on your high results."

"Thank you Reverend Mother, I even surprised myself." I answered

"I bet you did." She said light-heartedly. "Now I want you to try just as hard in your commercial classes. I know you can do it if you want to and Maureen did exceptionally well at it."

"But Reverend Mother, Maureen did well because she loves it. I hate it already."

"Why?'

"It's boring. What I'd like to do is have the matron teach me dress-making."

"Well that's out of the question."

"But why? Shouldn't I be allowed to choose now that I've passed my exam."

"No, that's not what your father wants for you. He wants all his girls to work in an office and from what I know of him he's a very determined man. I doubt that he will give into your wishes. I'm afraid you'll just have to succeed in your commercial classes if you wish to please your father."

"Oh, I don't know, I might be lucky. Maybe when he knows how much it means to me he will send me to a school for dressmaking when I leave here."

The Reverend Mother laughed in a hopeless manner and shrugged her shoulders in defeat.

"I doubt that very much Josephine, but it doesn't hurt to have hope in life I suppose."

With that she patted me on the head and turned to address all five of us again. When she had our attention she said,

"Congratulations to all of you again and I'll see you at your party tomorrow. Please go back to what you were doing and enjoy the rest of the day." Then she left the room followed by Sister Martha, Sister Angela and the Matron, leaving us alone with Sister Rosa again. Linda and I hugged each other with joy, both of us thankful that the other had passed. The next day we had our long awaited party. We had cake, biscuits, ice-cream and two lollies each and that was our big party! The trouble was we never had parties for our birthdays, just three the whole time you were in the convent, so the few goodies we received were a tremendous treat for us. The whole five of us were in our glory with our two lollies each!

CHAPTER 51

This was my easiest year so far, it was also the most boring! The year never seemed to end. Each night I told myself that another day was over, and each morning I looked forward to the end of the day. Time just wouldn't seem to go, each day seemed longer than the last and I was slowly going mad waiting to get out of the convent. Linda hated this year as much as I did, because she was stuck in the Laundry most of the time, not to mention she dreaded me leaving. Weekends were the best days because I was able to spend my days with Linda, but there weren't enough days in the weekend!

One Saturday afternoon Linda and I were in the small yard near the school, which was usually deserted. Linda was desperately trying to teach me to skip. We were by ourselves so that I wouldn't get too embarrassed and we were killing ourselves laughing everytime I got caught up in the rope, which was quite often! After about twenty minutes Pauline came looking for us, god only knows why, probably because she couldn't find anyone else to play with her. When she found us she said in an annoyed tone,
"I've been looking for you everwhere. Do you want to play ball with me?"
"No go away. Linda's teaching me to skip."
"Fat chance," she said, "You've got two left feet."
"Oh shut-up Pauline." I answered.
"Shut-up yourself," she snapped back and began playing ball by herself, throwing it up against the wall. She knew we wanted to be alone, but because we didn't want to play with her she wouldn't give us the satisfaction of being by ourselves. She threw the ball against the wall about a dozen times or so, then all of a sudden she missed the wall throwing the ball straight

through a classroom window, which just happened to be accomodating Sister Angela. There was a loud crashing noise, followed by a screaming Sister Angela rushing to the window.

"Who threw that ball," she screamed as her hands trembled. She must have been preparing for a class and got a terrible fright when the ball came smashing through the window, because she was as white as a ghost.

Pauline responded to her question,

"It was Jospehine, she was throwing the ball to Linda and she threw it too hard." she said,

I couldn't believe my ears. I was totally shocked at Pauline's blatant lie. Linda and I stood there unable to speak or defend ourselves. We were just dumbfounded at the situation we found ourselves in. Sister Angela left the window and marched out directly to Linda and I and slapped me hard on either side of my face leaving the imprint of her palm and fingers stinging on my face. She seemed to ignore Linda altogether for the moment.

"Your father will pay for that window," she hissed, "because you will write and tell him what you did." Then she decided to address Linda,

"Mitchell you can get up to bed for the day, Lynch get inside and start writing."

Linda quickly walked inside not wanting to be told twice, or be slapped! I remained where I was. I was shocked that only I had been slapped not that I wanted Linda to get hit as well, but it just seemed so unfair and made me sick.

"I'm not writing any letter" I said in an aggressive tone,

"What did you say?"

"I didn't break the stupid window, Pauline did. Linda and I were skipping. Make Pauline write the letter."

"How dare you blame your sister," she snarled, slapping me again. "It's just like you to blame someone else."

"It was Pauline who blamed someone else not me. She was the one who broke the window and if you don't slap her I sure will later. She's nothing but a rotten liar." I said with rage in my voice.

"If you dare lay a finger on her Josephine you will answer to me, and you'll be a very sorry little girl, believe you me. For the time being, you can get to bed with Mitchell, I will deal with you later and you will be writing that letter, you better believe it."

I turned to face Pauline before going inside and said,

"You're going to cop it later Pauline." I headed off to the Matron's room for the dormitory key without thinking that Linda would already have them. I was too angry to think about anything except how bad Pauline was going to get it from me later.

When I got there, the matron saw the slap marks across both sides of my face and asked, "What happened this time Jospehine?"

Pauline smashed a window and blamed Linda and I. I told Sister Angela it wasn't us but she still blamed me. Now Linda and I are being sent to the dormitory for the day as punishment."

"Oh, I'm sorry luv. I can't even interfere, but don't worry about Pauline, I'll get her back for you later."

"How?"

"Never you mind, just leave it with me."

Just then Sister Angela walked in,

"Aren't you in bed yet?"

"I came for the keys but Linda has already taken them. I was just on my way up."

"Well what's taking you so long then, move it, move it." she yelled.

"This isn't fair we didn't break the window." I said as I was walking out.

"Just get up to bed and button your lip before I shut it for you. In fact I'll take you there and get the keys back from Linda."

We walked upstairs in silence, but the whole time I was thinking about how much I disliked this women. When we got there she pushed me inside then walked over to Linda's bed and snatched the keys from her, saying,

"For your back answering Lynch you can both go without food until tomorrow morning." Then she walked out and locked the the door behind her. I turned from the locked door to Linda and shrugged my shoulders. Then I said,

"Well she's gone, the witch. I really hate her Linda and as for Pauline I can't wait to get my hands on her. I could bloody kill her right now, the rotten little pig."

"Ah who cares. This is great, at least we're together."

"Yea, but I can't get over Pauline. How could she lie like that. I'll get her back for this Linda you mark my words. She'll pay dearly for this one." I said, getting angrier by the minute as I thought about how she had deliberately lied to save her own skin.

"Ah don't worry about it."

"But I do. You know I beat her so bad last time I was sure she had learnt her lesson, but she must be plain stupid or something."

Linda laughed at my hopeless expression, "Maybe you should beat her up everyday," she teased "just to remind her not to tell lies or tell tales."

"That's a very good idea."

"I'm only joking Josephine. Hitting her will only get you into trouble and she's really not worth it. Just stay away from her in the future."

I looked at Linda again,

"How come you didn't get slapped, only me?" I asked in a jovial manner.

"Oh Sister Angela loves me," she answered in a mocking tone, "I'm the teachers pet!"

"Oh yea, she hates you more than me." I answered, and the pair of us laughed temporarily forgetting our punishment and happy to be together. The truth was Linda didn't have any parents to pay for the window, so Sister Angela deliberately blamed me so that dad would have to pay for the window. However, I never wrote any letter home about it and she never asked me to. I think I would have died first and she knew it! We spent the rest of the afternoon playing 'I spy with my little eye' and talking about when I left the convent. Linda made me promise that if my dad didn't take her I would write often. We also spoke about our dreams, of Linda being a nurse and I being a dressmaker. It was so nice and peaceful being together and speaking so freely to one another. Somehow we felt safe locked in the room together. However, should I have been locked in the room alone I would have been in a state of panic all day. Even with Linda present I kept remembering the fire in the shoe factory and wondered what would happen if we were trapped in there, but I didn't convey my frightening thoughts to Linda, I was too embarrassed.

The afternoon went by surprisingly quickly. In fact we were both disappointed when the other girls came up to the dormitory for the night.

The following evening after dinner I caught up with Pauline. Well the poor kid must have said sorry a thousand times, but I didn't have an ounce of pity for her. When I had finished releasing my anger, I actually dared her to go and tell Sister Angela,

"Go on." I said pushing her forward, "Go and tell Sister

Angela. I want you to and then I'll break every bone in your body and I'll enjoy doing it."

"No, please. I don't want to." she pleaded.

"But I want you to." I said, nudging her forward again.

"I'll never do it again, I promise. Please Jospehine, I'm sorry, don't make me tell."

"Oh shut-up" I said and walked off on her in search of Linda. The truth was I was starting to take pity on her again and I didn't want her to know it.

Whilst I looked for Linda I wondered if Pauline would report me, but I really doubted it. Not by the way she was begging me not to force her to.

From that day forward Pauline never reported me again. She had finally learnt her lesson and I was glad. The truth was I hated hurting her, because I loved her very much. But on the same token I hated being betrayed by her all the time. That hurt much more than seeing her cry when I smacked her. To me trust and loyalty meant everything, because that was all we had in that place.

Time continued to drag very slowly and my commercial classes were dreadful. I paid very little attention in class and found myself sneaking off at playtimes more and more frequently to practice on the sewing machine. The trouble was I always got caught. I can't count the number of times I was hit over the knuckles with the steel scissors and although it hurt like crazy, it still didn't deter me. I was like a magnet being drawn to the sewing machine.

The matron warned me time and time again but I wouldn't listen. Finally Sister Martha reported me to the Reverend Mother who wrote and told my father. He answered by saying I don't care what you do, tie her up, beat her, punish her, but keep her off that machine. I want no daughter of mine in a factory. After receiving dad's reply the Reverend Mother called me to her room and read me dad's letter. Then she said,

"It seems we will have to skin your knuckles altogether Jospehine. You just have to stop using the machine."

"Alright." I answered in defeat, "I'll stay away if it makes dad so happy."

"Good" she said, and sent me back to my chores. I did stay away from the machine after our conversation but it nearly killed me. However, the need and want to gain dad's approval was greater than the need to practice on a machine. I just couldn't understand why dad was getting so upset about it though. I couldn't see anything wrong with making dresses. In my eyes I was achieving and accomplishing something worth while so why was dad so against it. I just couldn't understand, but the need for his love and approval kept me away from what I loved anyway!

A few weeks later Sister Martha was taking an English Class. I was seated next to a girl called Patricia Kelly. Patricia was one of the girls who was preparing for her exam the following year and I was assigned to help her with her studies. We therefore took part in some of the lessons being taught. However the lessons were not for our benefit, but for those sitting their exams. Sister Martha walked up and down the classroom holding a stick in her hand. The stick was actually the leg of a chair which Sister Martha used to intimidate the students, or so I thought. This was something new as she never use to walk around with it when I was sitting for my exam. As she walked around the room and up and down the aisles, she told a story about an Irish farmer and his horse and cart. The cart was apparently full of hay and the whole story seemed very boring to me! As she spoke I turned to Patricia and whispered,

"It's a wonder, being an Irish farmer an all, that the cart wasn't pulling the horse."

Patricia giggled at the thought of what I'd said, and Sister Martha knew that I said something stupid, but hadn't heard exactly what it was. She walked back down my aisle quietly and quite unexpectedly hit me across the back of the head with the stick. The force of the blow broke the stick in two. Sister Martha hung on to the bottom half and the top half went flying across the room. At first I felt no pain just a numbness and shock. Then I became nauseated and dizzy with the realisation of what had just happened. I sat there wondering how on earth she hadn't cracked my skull with the force of the blow. However I didn't cry, nor did I look at her. I just sat there in silence not sure if another whack was on the way.

Sister Martha carried on with her stupid story as if nothing had happened eyeing me from time to time. Shortly afterwards the lunch bell rang but as I stood up I saw stars, even though I had taken the blow some fifteen minutes before. My head began pounding with pain and I had to use the desks and walls to make my way to the dining room. Somehow I made it to the dining room and with relief I sat down to eat my dinner, except I was having some difficulty lifting my knife and fork. My head felt so heavy that all I wanted to do was go to sleep.

Sister Martha must have realized that she had done something terribly wrong and I was hurt more than she had expected because she approached me in my seat,

"Josephine," she said, "I want to talk to you outside for a moment."

I felt like crying then. I really didn't have the energy to walk again. I just needed to rest for a few minutes. I followed her outside reluctantly which took all my strength and will power. When we got outside I leaned against the wall for support.

"Yes Sister Martha" I mummbled barely able to stand let alone speak.

"I want you to do well in your commercial class this afternoon," she said.

I looked at her and wondered what the hell she was talking about why had she pulled me outside to say that. I studied her through dazed eyes with disbelief and said,

"Pardon."

"Well you haven't been doing very well with the course, so I want you to try hard this afternoon, because your father is going to be very angry with you otherwise and we don't want that do we?"

At that particular moment I really didn't care, all I wanted to do was go to sleep. I looked at her again struggling to keep my head up and said,

"I don't think I should go to class Sister Martha, my head is very sore and I can't see straight."

The tone of her voice appeared to tremble as she said,

"Oh nonsense. I know I hit you a little hard dear, but you'll be fine. I'm sorry for hitting you but you were disrupting my students and that's not fair to them." she said trying to defend her actions by making me feel guilty.

"I'm sorry I only made a joke." I said in a meek tone. It was getting harder and harder to stay on my feet.

"That's alright Josephine," she said in a forgiving tone, "just try and forgot your head and go to your commercial class."

"Yes Sister Martha. Can I please go and sit down now. I don't feel very good."

"Yes child, off you go," She said kindly. The truth was she was petrified that the Reverend Mother would find out what she did, but I didn't realize it at the time. I truly believed that she had forgiven me for disrupting her class, and I was thankful. The trouble was punishment and pain were everyday events in that place, so to me it was nothing out of the ordinary to be hit over the head, today was just a little harder than usual, that's all!

That was my first real headache but they became a regular occurence after that and I still get them now, fifty years on. Everytime I get a headache I remember Sister Martha and that blow I received and wonder if I incurred some serious injury because of it. I never had it checked then and I never bothered afterwards. I just accepted the pain!

I went to my commercial class that afternoon but my concentration span was even less than usual. My head just pounded the whole day. However after a good nights rest, I felt fine. Something good actually came from that blow though because that was the very last time Sister Martha laid a finger on me. I think she truly regretted hitting me so hard and decided to leave me alone. Maybe if she had given me that blow when I had first arrived at the convent my life in there would have been much more bearable!

Christmas finally came around and I swear I was no better at my commercial classes, than when I first started. I failed every test I sat for, but it didn't bother me in the slightest. We weren't punished for failing and I knew in my heart that one day I would do what I always wanted to anyway, which was dressmaking! Pauline and I got four parcels each that year which was great. Maureen sent us toothpaste in her parcel knowing that we were made to use soap to clean our teeth in the convent. At first we didn't know what it was, but she put a note in the parcel and explained how to use it. It took a little while to get used to, but it was far nicer than soap in our mouth. Linda thought it was great too and like me looked forward to brushing her teeth each day.

For the first time in my life I wanted the holidays to be over because it brought me that much closer to leaving. However just the reverse happened, the holidays dragged endlessly. I didn't realize at that stage that I was going to receive yet another disappointment! Eventually the holidays did come to an end and I was very excited about leaving. I only had a few months left and that's all I could think and talk about. Linda became visually sad and withdrawn. Then one day when I went over to sit with her, to my astonishment she snapped my head off.

"Oh go away Jospehine and leave me alone."

I stood there in a state of shock for a moment, then finding my voice I said,

"What's the matter, what have I done?"

"Nothing." she snapped and stormed off leaving me hurt and alone, but most of all surprised at her attitude.

"Okay, fine," I yelled after her, "I'll never bother you again if that's what you want."

"Fine" she yelled back at me without even turning around.

I ran off to the toilet and cried my eyes out. We had never argued before and I couldn't believe that she could treat me this way, it hurt so much. I wanted more than anything to make up with her, but pride stopped me from making the first move. For four days we avoided each other but on the fifth day Linda finally came over to me,

"Hi Josephine," she said softly.

"Hi" I answered back, then rushed straight in with the rest,

"I want to know what I did to you Linda, because I can't think of anything that would make you act so mean to me."

"I'm sorry." she said, "You didn't do anything. It's just that, well, I'm heartbroken over you leaving and that's all you ever talk about. When you leave I'll be on my own and god only knows if we'll ever meet again. It just makes me so sad to think about it and you make it impossible for me to forget about it."

I jumped up off the bench and hugged my friend tightly. Her words made me feel so selfish. I hadn't considered her feelings at all. Tears pricked my eyes just thinking about how much I must have been hurting her.

"I'm sorry Linda. I just wasn't thinking. Look I don't know what lies ahead either, but Linda you know my father's address off by heart, so even if he doesn't take you, though I'm sure he will you can write to me. Then later when the nuns get you a job, maybe a nursing job," (I added to cheer her up,) "you can save hard and come over to England. My father will look after you for sure then, he won't turn you away so cheer up. Besides, I'm not going tomorrow you know."

"Yea I know." she said smiling, but then her smile faded and tears began to roll down her face. She looked up at me slowly and said,

"I love you so much Josephine, and I'm going to miss you terribly. I just can't imagine life without you."

"I know and I'll miss you too, but I know we'll be together again someday, so cheer up."

"I'm fine" she said smiling bravely and rubbing away at her tears with her small fist.

I drew her hand away from her eyes and gently held onto it to comfort her, then hand in hand the pair of us went of for a walk together, friends again. They were the first and last bad words we ever had for each other in eleven years together. It really was a very special kind of friendship, one I miss with all my heart.

The next few months passed slower then ever. Each day seemed to have forty hours and each week ten days, and I did nothing but wish the time would move along at a faster pace.

Then about two weeks before I was due to leave the Reverend Mother called me to her office. I presumed it was to tell me who was coing to collect me form the convent and I went to her room with happy anticipation.

"Oh, Jospehine, sit down please." She said as I entered the room. When I was seated she said,

"I have a letter here from your father. It seems that he isn't going to take you on your birthday after all dear. He intends to wait until Pauline has completed her final exam, then he is going to collect ʸou both at the same time. From here you will all spend two weeks in Ballinrobe at which time Pauline will return to the convent, and you will travel to your home in London."

"But that's another twelve weeks. I was supposed to be leaving in two weeks, why do I have to wait so long?"

"That's the way your father want's it I'm afraid. You happen to be the middle child Josephine, which is unfortunate because you don't get the respect that the older children get, and you're not the baby of the family either. Quite simply you tend to be forgotten about most of the time. You also happen to be the black sheep of your family."

"What do you mean black sheep?"

"What I mean dear, is you never do what you're told. You're the one who has caused your father the most trouble. You're always defying everyone, even with the sewing machine."

"I'm not using the machine any more. Ever since dad wrote I stayed away from it. The truth is I'm not the black sheep, I'm just the unlucky one. This really isn't fair you know." I spat out with fire in my words.

"Well maybe you can do something to help me, seeing your father is being so unfair to you."

"What?"

"Well, I believe your father has no intentions of sending

Pauline back. I think he will take her over to London as well. However we are just as smart as he is and this is what I want you do do. Firstly don't tell Pauline about this letter or our conversation. In fact, don't tell anyone about it. Then later when you're both with your father try to discourage him from taking Pauline. Explain to him how important it will be for Pauline to complete her extra year of commerical studies."

I sat there looking at this women with contempt. She must think that I'm totally stupid, I thought. She had been edgeing me on, degrading my father in my eyes for leaving me here longer than I needed to be and pretending to sympathise with me, just so that she could use me to earn the convent an extra year of weekly payments. However instead of voicing my true feelings I said,
"Alright, I'll do my best," I said, "Can I go now."
"Yes you may and I'm so sorry your father has disappointed you. I know how betrayed you must feel, but it's only a few weeks dear." She added.
"Yes," I answered and left the room disgusted with her and my father.

As I walked back to class I thought, Reverend Mother, if you think I'm the black sheep of the faimily I'll behave like one. I'm going to encourage Pauline to leave not to stay. If you think I'm so bad then I'll act that way."
I went back to class and couldn't wait for it to finish. I wanted to tell Linda all the news, even though I was hurting inside just thinking about it. I kept asking myself why I was always the one missing out. I knew I promised the Reverend Mother not to discuss it with anyone, but after our conversation I held little respect for her. I wasn't sure whether to tell Pauline though. I couldn't trust her to keep her mouth shut, so after thinking

about it all during class I decided not to mention it to her.

After class I told Linda all the news and how I intended going against the Reverend Mother's wishes. I told her that I was going to try and convince Pauline to travel to London with us. It wasn't that I wanted Pauline to come with us, it was more out of spite for the Reverend Mother's attudide.

Linda smiled and said, "Well it's good news for me anyway, I'll have you a while longer."

"Yea, I'll have you a while longer too." I answered, but the truth was I wanted nothing more than to be out of the convent. However it was true I'd miss Linda with all my heart.

"I'm still disappointed with my dad though. It's really unfair he took all the others out on their birthday."

"It's propably cheaper for him Josephine. I don't think he's doing it on purpose."

"Yea I guess so, but that's no consolation to me."

"I guess not, but there's nothing you can do about it either."

"I know and that's even more frustrating."

"Come on let's go for a walk and forget about it, there's no use dwelling on it."

"Alright," I answered, but it wasn't that easy for me to forget about it. In fact I couldn't stop thinking about it and that night I lay in bed, like so many other nights before, wondering why dad had let me down so badly. Maybe he knows I'm ugly I thought and isn't interested in me. I cried myself to sleep once again truly believing that my father didn't love me because of the way I looked.

My sixteenth birthday came, but no one came to collect me. It was the saddest day of my life. I still hadn't told Pauline of the conversation with the Reverend Mother, so as far as she was concerned I was going on my birthday, not that she made any effort to spend some time with me, she couldn't have cared less.

Later on in the evening Pauline came up to me and asked,

"How come Caroline and Maureen didn't come for you Josephine? Dad got them out when they were sixteen."

I already felt depressed and really didn't want to get into any long discussions about why I was still here, especially with her, so I answered,

"I have no idea Pauline, just go away please."

"Maybe he knows how stupid and ugly you are" she yelled at the top of her voice.

I can't explain how hurt I was by her words because I had been thinking the exact same things the night before, but hearing them from someone else, especially my own sister, was like a knife going through me. I was too hurt to even hit her, which would have been my normal reaction. Instead I answered her in a sarcastic tone,

"You could be right Pauline, but who gives a damn." I wanted badly to tell her the real reason no one came to collect me, but I just couldn't take the chance not with her big mouth, no matter how embarrassed I was.

Linda heard her every word, I think the whole convent did because she yelled so loud, and Linda was immediately by my side,

"Give her a slap in the face," Linda said hating Pauline as much as I did at the moment.

"No, she's not worth it. Besides she gets enough from Sister Martha now."

"Well it hasn't taught her any manners, she's still just as nasty." Linda added.

Pauline walked away quickly just in case I decided to take Linda's advice and belt her one. When she was gone Linda turned to me and said,

"I can't understand why you didn't whack her one."

"I just couldn't be bothered, not today. I'm too upset about other things, she's the last of my troubles. Besides she's not worth worrying about."

"Yea I guess you're right. Come on let's forget about her. I'll try and teach you to skip again, how does that sound."

I laughed at the hopeless expression on her face and said,

"It's my birthday, give me a break."

"Alright let's just go for a walk then."

"Sounds good to me." But as we walked away I couldn't help wondering why Pauline was as mean as she was. She truly didn't care about anyone.

The day finally arrived for Pauline to sit for her exams and against my better judgement, I went to wish her good luck. She wasn't in the least bit nervous like I had been, in fact she was very confident.

At the end of the day I was there to see how she went, just like Maureen had been for me.

"How did you go?" I asked,

"I went fine. I'm not stupid like you, you know?" she snapped back at me in a cocky manner.

Sister Martha who was standing in the gathering, heard her sharp words and strangely enough jumped to my defence. She hated me but she hated Pauline more.

"That remains to be seen when the results come back madam" She snapped. "It would pay you to try to be nice to people instead of being so hostile, you little brat." Sister Martha said, which was really hypocritical coming from her. She was the most hostile person I had ever met, with Sister Angela coming a close second!

Pauline blushed and turned away without saying another word and for that I was thankful.

A week later the summer holidays began and after spending a week revising the exam answers, Sister Martha believed that all four girls had passed their exams. Not that it was of any interest to me all I was concerned about was getting out of here. I knew I would be leaving at any time I just wasn't sure when, so I waited patiently to hear from the Reverend Mother. Another week passed and during the weekend something that I never expected happened. Sister Angela came up to me and gave me a brand new pair of shoes. My first new pair in eleven years. I was really surprised and instead of saying thankyou, I said,

"Oh," but then it clicked. It was because I was leaving and they wanted to impress dad.

"Are these to show my dad." I asked sarcastically.

"Enough of the lip Lynch," she answered and literally threw the shoes at me saying,

"Try them on."

I tried the shoes on as she hovered over me staring at my feet with her small beady eyes.

"Do they fit?"

"Yes they're fine," I answered.

The next day was Sunday and they decided to take us for a Sunday walk. Usually I enjoyed getting out but today I was disappointed because it meant that I wasn't leaving today either. I was sure that's why I'd received the new shoes, but now I wasn't quite so sure.

It was late July now and very hot. As we walked to town Linda and I were side by side and we saw some workmen repairing bitumen roads and I turned to Linda and said,

"Look Linda, look at that hot tar, it's actually smouldering."

"Oh yes and doesn't it stink."

"It sure does." With that I looked down at my new brown shoes and as if on impulse, I walked straight into the hot, melting tar before Linda could say or do a thing to stop me. She just stood there gazing at me with her mouth wide open.

"Oh Jesus, you're gonna get killed now Jospehine. What on earth possessed you to do that?" she asked, still shocked at my impulsive action.

"I don't know, I just felt like doing it. I don't even care about being in trouble."

"You've gone mad, the heat has gone to your head."

I laughed and looked down at my shoes which were totally ruined. As I walked along after that I stuck to the ground with each step I took, making walking diffucult but amusing. I nudged Linda to take a look and the pair of us started to quietly giggle. However, on the way back to the convent I lost my sense of humor and began to panic. As soon as we arrived back, much to my relief we were told to change ouy of our walking-out clothes in the dormitory. I took my new shoes off and hid them under my bed. Lucky for me my old ones were still under there.

Later in the playroom Sister Angela approached me and said, "Where's your new new shoes Lynch?"

"They're under my bed, they were hurting me after our long walk today."

"Get them back on," she snapped, "they obviously still need stretching."

Then she grabbed me by the ear and marched me back up stairs and I trembled the whole way. I knew all hell was going to break loose when she saw the state of my new shoes.

As I pulled the shoes from under my bed she saw the tar stuck all over them, and she stood there gaping in a horrified manner. She looked terrible stupid for a moment and I almost laughed at her expression.

"What on earth happened to them?" she asked with disgust.

At first I stood speechless searching for the right words to say, unfortunately I didn't find them. Instead I said,

"Well I've been so used to old ones my whole life I decided to christen these to make them old looking."

She slapped my face hard, "Brat" she growled, "Well let me tell you something these are the shoes you will be wearing when you leave the convent. Ruined or not this is what you shall wear."

I held my face and looked at her straight between the eyes,

"I'm sure my father will buy me a new pair in Ballinrobe." I said defiantly.

"How did you know you were going to Ballinrobe first?'

"The Reverend Mother told me weeks ago." I answered with satisfaction.

"Did she also tell you about Pauline going with you?"

"Yes"

"Did she tell you that your father might try and steal Pauline and take her to London with the rest of you."

"Yes, and she asked me to persuade dad to send her back if he tries."

"And are you going to do that?"

I felt like saying no I'm not, the lot of you can go to hell, but I lost my nerve and said nothing,

"I'm asking you a question Lynch" she snapped

Her tone angered me giving me the nerve to speak my mind after all,

"No I'm not, why should I."

"What did you say?"

"I said that I won't try and change dad's mind. Even if I wanted to, how do you expect me to change my fathers mind. There's nothing I can do. But if I was in Paulines shoes I wouldn't come back to this hell hole."

"But you're not Pauline and you never could be. She's a fine young girl, and you're rotten to the core. She know's how important it is to finish off the last year, she's not as stupid as you. Furthermore you will remind her of that. For some stupid reason that I just can't begin to understand, Pauline listens to you, so you will advise her correctly.

"Maybe she listens to me because I'm not so stupid after all." I retaliated.

She slapped my face again, only harder this time.

"You're nothing but an ignorant little brat and that's all you'll ever be." I didn't answer her. I just wanted her to go away. The sight of her witch-like face was getting on my nerves. I hated this woman as much as I hated Sister Martha and I'm sure both of them knew how I felt. However, I didn't care if they knew, not anymore. This was the last straw.

When she saw that I was staying quiet she took it as a sign that she had won the battle and in a condescending voice she said,

"That's a good girl. Now I'll take these new shoes and try to clean them up for you dear. You will get them back the day you leave. If anyone ever comes to collect you that is." she added smugly.

"Clean them if you want," I said trying to get back at her for her last remark and then I added, "And my sisters will be here any time now to collect me, don't you worry?"

She turned back to comfront me with a smirk on those silly thin lips of hers.

"I'm not worried, the sooner they come the better for everyone here, but you must be worried. They are taking their time, aren't they?" she answered slowly and with malice in her tone.

I couldn't stand looking at her for a moment longer. I actually felt like slapping her, so I said,

"May I go back to the playroom now?"

"Yes of course you may," she said in the same condescending tone of voice. Then she turned and led the way back downstairs and I truly had the urge to push her down them a few times.

All my life she had tormented me and hit me at every opportunity, sometimes just for the sake of it and I was sick to death of it. During my last few weeks my anger soared higher and higher with each passing day and I answered back on several occasions. I was frustrtated at not knowing when I was leaving and angry with dad for leaving me behind for the extra twelve weeks. I was fast losing hope of ever getting out of here. I think the waiting made me grow up too and I finally realised that these people who called themselves nuns, that I'd grown up with, weren't to be worshiped and treated with respect. They were cruel human beings and I detested them. I also refused to hide these feelings a moment longer. Even the Reverend Mother and her sneaky tactics turned my stomach now. I think Sister Martha and Sister Angela saw the growing anger inside of me, because they avoided me during my last weeks there and didn't try to slap me or even reprimand me for answering their every statement with sarcasm. In fact, they chose to ignore it. I think they realised that I was on the edge and would snap at the slightest provaction, so they avoided me totally most of the time, and spoke to me only when they had to.

CHAPTER 52

The following Wednesday a letter arrived from dad, advising the convent that Caroline and Maureen would be picking up Pauline and I that Friday. It also gave the date when Pauline would be returning to the convent. When the Reverend Mother gave me the news I was ecstatic at first, but then I began to worry about Linda. How was I ever going to persuade dad to take her to live with us. At the time I truly believed with all my heart that he would take her, but how wrong I was. I just didn't know my father and how determined he was, once he made a decision. Nor did I realise that he couldn't cater for his own children let alone an extra one. I didn't realise that he was seperated from mum either, especially since she never mentioned it to us when she came to see us. In fact, she had implied that they were very happy together.

Over the next two days Linda and I were inseparable clinging to each other to savour the few remaining moments we had together. I even joined her in the laundry as much as possible and helped her with her work. The nun's didn't object either. It made no difference to them any way, I shouldn't have even been in the convent now. My commercial classes had long finished and I was now bascially just sitting in on the senior classes going over what ever they were doing, just filling in time waiting to be claimed!

Linda and I were both torn apart by me leaving. My only consolation was that I was the lucky one this time. I wasn't the one being left behind. However I pitied Linda with all my heart, because I knew from first hand experience exactly what she was going through. Friday finally came and I awoke in a strange mood. I was overwhelmed with a feeling of internal peace which I had never experienced before. In a way it frightened me because it was such a new experience. Suddenly Linda came to mind and my chest became heavy, like a brick was on top of it and I nearly burst into tears, but then just as suddenly the peaceful easy feeling engulfed me again, giving me the feeling that everything was going to be just fine and I got up to face my day. A day that I knew would bring a lot of tears, as well as happiness.

Lunch time came, but Caroline and Maureen still hadn't arrived for us. As I ate my lunch I sat wondering if they were coming after all, and I became quite concerned. However about an hour later the matron came to find me in the laundry. She had Pauline and Doreen beside her as well and I gathered that Caroline and Maureen had arrived. When she approached me she told me I had to get changed now and confirmed that my older sisters had arrived. Althought I was excited, I also felt like someone had just given me a blow to the head as the reality of leaving Linda became overwhelming. I turned to Linda to see her drying her hands with her head hung low. Then she looked up at me and big tear drops formed in the corner of her eyes. I too dried my hands on my skirt, instead of a towel, I didn't want to waste time, I wanted to hug my friend quickly and dry away those large tears that threatened to spill over.

"Don't cry please. I'm not leaving yet and I won't go before saying goodbye to you, I promise."

"Alright I'll see you after." she said, but she couldn't stop her tears from flowing down. I ran out of the laundry not wanting to cry myself and waited for the others to catch up with me outside.

When we were inside the main building Doreen was sent

straight into the playroom, while Pauline and I were taken to the dormitory to get changed. Doreen seemed excited about seeing Caroline and Maureen, but her big brown eyes showed how sad she really was about me leaving. Every time I looked at her I couldn't help but feel sorry for her. She knew that I wasn't coming back which was bad enough, but she was expecting Pauline to be back. I was the only one who knew she probably wouldn't be and I felt a real heel deceiving her like this. Doreen and I had become much closer over the past year and she trusted me. Now I felt that I was betraying her, but what other option did I have. I had nearly told her on several occasions, but figured why hurt her any more than she needed to be. She was already hurting enough because of being rejected by our parents, not to mention the uncertaintly of her future, she didn't need any more worries in her head.

When we arrived at the dormitory the matron organized Pauline first and sent her off to the playroom. Then she began to prepare me which seemed strange at first, since we both could have got ready and left together. However when we were by ourselves her reasoning became clear because she began giving me some motherly advice about my future, telling me to listen to my father and so on. When I was all dressed and ready to leave she hugged me tightly as she had on so many occasions and we said our goodbyes.

"God bless you Josephine." she said, then she abruty let me go and turned to leave before her tear filled eyes overflowed.
I turned and watched her hobble out of the room filled with a sense of love and yet emptyness. Then before she could reach the door I ran to her and hugged her tightly again.
"Thank-you," I said, holding her tightly, "thank-you for loving me."

"Oh, Josephine, you'll never know how much I loved you." she said struggling to hold back the tears. "You take care my love and remember me always." she added in a shaky voice.

"I will" I said, "I'll never forget you and all the kindness you've shown me." Then I released my hold on her and she quickly walked out of the room with her tears and pride intact.

As I watched her walk through the door I thought to myself, you really did love me Kathleen Corgorgan and I was the only one you ever did. "Thank-you again" I said aloud and my tears rolled gently down my face. I stood there for several minutes remembering all the times she had helped me and all the times I had woken her during the night. I wondered if I'd ever see her again. However, I doubted it because I never wanted to return to this place as long as I lived. Suddenly I dried up my tears with an urgency to leave this place. I quickly ran down stairs to my awaiting sisters in the playroom.

I walked in and both Caroline and Maureen looked stunning. I couldn't believe how much Maureen had changed in just one year. She was wearing a Navy Blue suit, which had a tight fitting pencil skirt which enhanced her slender figure. Her hair was still short but nicely styled, which gave her an older appearance. The heels on her shoes were so high I wondered how she ever managed to walk in them. I was sure I would lose my balance just standing in them. Then I turned and looked at Caroline again. She also looked beautiful and her hair hung long and free down her back.

"You two look terrific," I finally managed to say.

"Ha," Sister Angela answered, "Caroline's hair spoils her looks altogether."

"I don't think so. I think she looks beautiful and I'm going to grow mine the same way commencing right now." I answered her bravely and with absoulute confidence. I was displaying the true Lynch pride, if ever I had. Besides she couldn't touch me anymore and that made me feel strong. I truly believe that if she had tried to strike me that day I would have retaliated and hit her back just as hard. I just hated her so much and had allowed my hate to show through especially over the last two weeks.

"Hair is dirty Josephine. I'm not surprised you should want it, I just expected more from Caroline that's all. Besides, as I've said on many occasions, nothing could improve your looks."

"Nor yours Sister Angela," I answered emphasising her name and laughed into her face. I stole a glance at Caroline and Maureen expecting their disapproval, but they too were struggling to hold back their laughter. When I returned my gaze to Sister Angela she had turned her back to me and was retreating to the other side of the room. Not far from where Pauline and Doreen had seated themselves quietly. When I look back on it now, what I said was terribly rude and disrespectful and in all truth I shouldn't have said it. However this woman had constantly torn at my very soul, stripping me of everything that I was and it was my turn to return her insults. At least that's how I felt at the time. Now I wish that I had held my tongue because that day I was no better than her. In fact I was even worse because I was only a child in her eyes. I must have offended her quite badly for her to walk off the way she did, but I didn't feel an ounce of pity for her at the time. In fact, quite the opposite, I felt triumphant. Now I realise how wrong I was. She was a lonely old woman who needed to be pitied not hated, and I wonder if she only became a nun because no man loved or wanted her, but who can say for sure. I do know she was very a bitter person who wanted everyone else to be as miserable as she was.

A few minutes later as we were talking amongst ourselves Doreen came over to me with tears in her eyes and asked, "Josephine how come I'm not going on holidays with Pauline?"

I looked at her pitiful face and my heart reached out to her, "I don't know Doreen, I really don't." I answered

She didn't answer me, she just turned and walked away and sat beside Sister Angela, then in a pleading tone she asked, "Why can't I go too Sister Angela."

"You can go next time" Sister Angela lied with sincerity and compassion in her voice,

Doreen, as if in a state of confusion stood up again and walked back to me as if she wanted me to confirm Sister Angela's promise.

"Is that true Josephine? When you come back for Pauline next year will you be taking me for a holiday."

"I told you once before Doreen, I'll never come back here after today, but someone else will pick up Pauline and maybe they will take you on a holiday. Although, I can't be certain." Not wanting to make any false promises to her and deceive her any more. I knew deep in my heart that Pauline wasn't coming back and I longed to tell Doreen the truth but I couldn't because Sister Angela had her eyes glued to me. I think she suspected that I wanted to be honest with Doreen.

"Oh Josephine I know you said you would never come back here, but will you for me. You're the only one who cares about me. Please come back just one more time for me." She begged.

Her begging made me ashamed of myself even more and I was just about to tell her the truth because I couldn't bear Doreen's pain a moment longer.

"Pauline wont' be...."

"Lynch, what do you think you're doing," Sister Angela

snapped.

"I want to tell her the truth because I love her. I don't want to hurt or deceive her any more." I answered abruptly. Then just as abruptly I had second thoughts about telling Doreen the truth. After all I didn't know for certain that Pauline wasn't coming back. Even the nuns only presumed that fact, so why worry Doreen unnecessarily I thought, so I said,

"Doreen, it will be your turn to leave soon. Now I'm not sure who will be picking you up, but someone will. In the meantime I promise to write to you often and send you plenty of parcels, alright." I had hoped my words would bring a smile to her face, but they didn't. It was depressing me so much seeing her so dispondent. I knew that apart from staying here with her there was nothing I could do to cheer her up. It was making me feel so desperate and anxious inside.

Caroline realised how distressed I was becoming and interrupted us,

"Look we better go, our uncles are waiting in the car outside for us." she said gently.

"Fine." Sister Angela said, annoyed at the Caroline's urgency to leave, "go and get your things if you must." she added nastily.

I was in a desperate hurry to leave, but I had promised to say a final goodbye to Linda. I wanted to refrain from leaving until recess at least, until Linda got out of the laundry.

"Well go on," Caroline urged as she saw me hesitating and having no idea why I wasn't moving.

"Alright" I said with some annoyance in my voice, but before she could answer, I turned and slowly walked out of the room with Pauline to get my jacket and glasses. Pauline was up in a flash as soon as she heard Caroline suggest that we leave but she had no one to say goodbye to. No one wanted to see her off!

When we reached the dormitory Pauline ran in, grabbed her jacket and ran back down stairs, not bothering to say a word, or wait for me! I was glad in a way though, I wanted to waste some time, I knew recess was close by and I had promised Linda that I would wait to say goodbye and I wasn't about to break that promise for anything. I didn't mention why I was going so slow to Caroline just in case Sister Angela had deliberately prevented Linda from saying goodbye just to spite me after my verbal attack on her.

I picked up my tin-rimmed glasses from the window sill and remembered the first time I had place them on this ledge. I studied them for a moment then I placed them back on the ledge.

"You can stay there" I said out loud, "I never want to see you again." Then I turned without looking back and ran downstairs. Just as I reached the top of the staircase the recess bell rang and my heart fluttered with joy and sadness at seeing Linda for the last time. When I got back down stairs Linda was already waiting outside the playroom for me. I smiled when I saw her wondering how she got from the laundry room so fast she must have run the whole way. I took a bag of toffees out of my pocket that I had saved from my birthday parcel just for this occasion, and when I got to her I handed them to her and said,

"Here, these are for you. Think of me when you eat them."

She had tears in her eyes as she took the toffees from me and she bowed her head to hide the tears and in a strained voice she said,

"How could I ever forget you, you are my very best friend and I'll miss you with all my heart."

"Oh Linda, please don't cry." I begged as my tears spilled

down my face as well. "I just can't bear it."

"I'm sorry, I'm just so sad." she said trying in vain to control herself.

"I know, me too. I hate leaving you, but it's only for a short while" I assured her. "You promise to write any chance you get and hopefully one day soon we'll be together again."

"I hope so Joesphine and please take care."

"I will." I paused for a moment and then added, "Linda will you take care of Doreen when I'm gone. No one else seems to want the poor thing and I feel so helpless to do anything. I can't wait to tell dad how sweet and good she is and find out why he has ignored her all these years."

"Don't worry, I'll watch out for her."

"Thanks" I said and then in and effort to cheer us both up I said,"Guess what?'

"What?" Linda answered brightening up a little.

"I left my glasses on the window ledge. That's their home now."

Linda laughed making me happy just seeing her smile again. That was the way I wanted to remember her. I was going to miss her so much and I felt like my heart was going to break in two leaving her behind. She had been my saviour in this place and I owed her so much. Nothing I could ever say or do would ever repay her.

"I went in there before," Linda said, pointing with her head to the playroom door, "but Sister Angela gave me my marching orders, so I waited here. I saw that you weren't inside anyway, so I didn't mind getting kicked out."

"I'm glad you waited."

"Of course I waited. I would have waited here all night if I had too," she said hugging me. Then so as not to start crying again she said,

"Your sisters looked great, I stole a glimpse at them when I was in there."

"Yea, they sure do."

"I can imagine you in six months looking just as beautiful Josephine."

"I doubt that very much."

"Ah don't be silly, you're beginning to sound like sour puss in there," she said laughing as she referred to Sister Angela. Then she added,

"How's Doreen handling the fact that you're leaving? She didn't seem too happy when I went in before."

"No, she's not taking it very well at all, she's broken hearted. I feel so sorry for her sometimes, it's as though she doesn't exist in this family. It really breaks my heart. She can't understand why she's not going on the holiday with Pauline either. She doesn't realise that Pauline probably won't even be coming back which is even worse."

"It all seems very strange to me. I mean why are they letting her go if they think she won't be coming back?"

"Because they can't be sure she won't and they can't stop dad taking her on a holiday once a year."

"Oh, that's why they asked you to try to encourage her to come back."

"Exactly, but they can go to hell."

Suddenly Linda became sad again and for a moment I thought my show of temper had somehow upset her.

"What's the matter?" I asked,

"Oh nothing, it's just that I hate you going and I can't stop thinking about it."

"You'll be leaving yourself soon Linda as soon as I can get dad to arrange it all. So don't be too disillusioned.

"Yea, if he takes me. We don't know for sure that he will. I know if he doesn't, that I don't have anywhere else to go, so I may as well stay here and work for them. I mean anything could happen to me out there all alone Josephine. I might even starve to death."

"Don't be stupid. If dad won't take you I'll let you know straight away, then you can leave and become a nurse just like you've always dreamed about. You'll earn lots of money and come to join me in London by yourself."

"You have it all planned don't you? I just wish I had your confidence. The truth is I'm scared stiff about being on my own and having to fend for myself, at least in here I'm assured of my safety and food if nothing else."

"Rubbish, your're a prisoner in here. Any place is better than this place Linda. Promise me you won't stay here no matter what happens."

"We'll see," she said still in a depressed state. She was making me feel terrible about leaving. Like I was deserting her or something. I guess in a way I was!

"Linda, please don't be downhearted. Things will work out, you'll see. But you can't be scared to leave or you'll get stuck in here forever and that would be a fate worse than death."

"Ah, what will be will be" she said trying to smile. "Come on, maybe Sister Angela will let me into the playroom now that you're with me."

"Alright," I said and the pair of us walked back inside. I was amazed to find so many nuns in here now. When I had left only Sister Anegla had been here and no-one had passed us while we were outside. I giggled to myself thinking that they must have all rushed here to see my sisters, like Linda had rushed to see me and the thought amused me as my mind's eye saw all these nuns running down the corridor. All the nuns were crowding around Caroline and Maureen like flies would around food, all of them quizzing my sisters about their life in London and what they had been doing with themselves. However, neither of them were giving too much away.

I for one was glad that there was so much commotion going on because Linda and I entered practically unnoticed, which meant I could have a few extra moments saying goodbye. Plus the fact Linda wasn't thrown out of the room again. As soon as we walked in we both walked over to Doreen who was sitting in a far corner by herself as usual. I sat down beside her and put my arms around her affectionately. Then in an attempt to cheer her up I promised to send her plenty of parcels. (In those days, a parcel represented love. It was the only love we really got.) When my promises didn't work, I reminded her that she would be leaving one day herself, and not to be upset by us leaving now because one day we would all be together on the outside, but nothing seemed to be working. She was too upset to even listen to me, let alone understand me. She truly was quite distraught.

Caroline suddenly looked over and realized that I was back and I saw her smile with gratitude. The poor thing was sick to death of all the questions coming her way. However Maureen seemed to be lapping up all the attention. Suddenly she walked away from all the nuns and said,
"Oh Josephine, you're back. We should be leaving now."
I stood up reluctantly. I was dreading having to say my final farewells to Linda and Doreen. I looked at them both and a lump formed in my throat. They were both crying making my insides feel as though they were being torn apart. It was Linda I hated leaving the most even though Doreen was my step sister. Linda had been my whole life. Most of the time my reason for living. Memories of the good times we experienced together flashed before me and I burst into tears.
"I'll miss you Linda" I said, "Thank-you for everything."
Linda let the quiet tears she had been crying burst into hysterical tears, which made it impossible for her to speak.

Instead we both just stood there holding on to each other tightly, letting the love flow freely between us. Finally we released each other and made our way out of the room.

Linda and Doreen walked us down the long path that I had walked up so many years before. The three of us walked hand in hand with me in the centre of both of them. When we reached the gates we said our tearful and emotional goodbyes and hugged each other with passion once again.

As I walked outside the gates it was like a dream come ture. I was really out for good, free at last. Yet I had never felt more miserable in all my life. I had this awful tight feeling in my chest and throat and I couldn't control my sobbing. I walked backwards waving to Linda and Doreen and it was a terrible fight for me to keep from running back to touch them both one more time, but I was scared to do that in case I couldn't let them go again.

I got into my uncle's waiting car not acknowledging my two uncles at all. Instead I knelt on the back seat just staring out the window at my step-sister and my very precious friend. I could see Linda waving and the tears that streamed down her face. They reminded me of a waterfall, fast and steady. I could even see her heaving chest as she fought to control her emotional tears.

"I love you Josephine," she screamed after me, "please don't forget me."

"I won't," I yelled back through the side window, "and I love you too, with all my heart."

I looked at Doreen standing beside Linda and without a word from her I could see how tormented she was. Her eyes were like mirrors screaming out her pain and suffering to me. I can still see those large sorrowful eyes looking at me. Pleading and begging silently for me to come back for her some day. Her eyes expressed all the hurt she was feeling and I was helpless to do anything for her. So I turned away and looked back at Linda.

Suddenly the car started to pull away, making me tense all over as I realised that this was it. I was finally leaving the convent. I kept waving until I couldn't see them anymore, but the memory of Doreens big expressive eyes and Linda's heaving chest will be etched on my brain until the day I die. I will never forget their faces the day I left and it breaks my heart everytime I think about them.

When I couldn't see them anymore I turned to face the front of the car, but I continued crying my heart out for a good twenty minutes. When my crying finally subsided, Maureen re-introduced me to my two uncles and explained that they were our father's brothers. They seemed to be very happy-go-lucky people, which made me feel relaxed if nothing else. After all the introductions Caroline and Maureen lit a cigarette and my uncle Shamous (my youngest uncle) lit his pipe.

"Poo that stinks." I said, feeling at ease with my uncles, "Hurry up and put it out."
For some reason that tickled everyone's fancy and they all began laughing. Then uncle Shamous said,
"Open ya window lass if the smell bothers ya. I'm enjoying this ere pipe. Ya a true Lynch though, I'll say that for ya. Not afraid ta speak ya mind are ya lass?"
Everyone began laughing again at my uncles remark, but I had trouble even understanding him, not alone catching the joke. He talked so fast it seemed like a hundred words a minute to me

and his words made no sense at all, because he cut off the end of most of them. I looked at Maureen in hope she could translate for me, and said "How come you can understand him?", but she didn't answer, like everyone else in the car just burst out laughing again and for a minute, it seemed that they were laughing at me, but I didn't know why. Maureen finally calmed down enough to answer me after noting my confusion.

"Because dad speaks like that too. You'll get used to it soon enough, don't you worry." she assured me.

I decided that I'd best keep my mouth shut for the rest of the journey. It seemed that every time I opened it, everyone laughed at me. I was starting to believe that my uncles thought that I was an idiot and I was losing confidence quickly. These men were little more than strangers to me, even if they were my uncles. And I didn't want them telling dad I was an idiot.

Then out of the blue I looked over at Pauline and she sat staring out the other window. I hadn't heard her speak one word since we got in the car and I began to wonder what she was thinking about, but with Pauline it was impossible to say, she never showed her emotions. However I decided to join in her silence. I mean if dad's brothers told him I was stupid as well as ugly he might reject me altogether.

It didn't take long to arrived at the cottage where my father was born and rasied until he married our mother. When we walked in my aunt Kathleen was busy cooking and the whole place smelled of freshly baked bread, which made me instantly hungry. The sweet aroma gave a real homely and welcoming feeling which was more than just nice, it was refreshing to the soul, and I welcomed it gladly. As I looked around I found that the surroundings were not quite what I was used to. The cottage was run down and neglected, but on the same token, you couldn't call it dirty. The convent was always so clean and sterile, everything in it's place and a place for everything, so to speak. I looked up, and there was bacon hanging from the ceiling. The floor was cold concrete with no coverings at all. This surprised and puzzled me because I had only ever seen timber floors at the convent, even at the hospitals I had stayed in. I had never seen concrete in a building and it looked so cold and uninviting, which spoiled the otherwise cosy atmosphere. There was also baby chicks running all over the kitchen floor and dropping their loads freely everywhere. This did seem a little disgusting at the time, but I didn't comment on it. No one else was complaining so why should I. After all it was quite normal on Irish farms. However the chicks in the kitchen were less disturbing to me than using the field for the toilet. I remember my aunt telling me years before in the convent that she wasn't used to toilets, but as they say, seeing is believing. It was really terrible having to shit with the cows and wipe yourself with a leaf!

However from the moment I tasted my aunt Kathleens cooking I soon forgot about my surroundings. The truth was I had never tasted anything so good. Suddenly after taking in all my surroundings I started to worry about more important things like where my dad was and why wasn't he here! Then out of the blue while I was still eating the most delicious meal I'd ever had, I said
"Where's our dad?" I had always had trouble keeping my thoughts to myself and today was no different. I was really disappointed because in my heart I had expected him to be waiting with open arms to greet us. Then when that didn't happen I fully expected him to join us for dinner, believing that uncle Leonard was going to go and collect him. However uncle Leonard didn't return either. He apparently had work at the pub

to do.

"He's in Dublin luv, you'll be seeing em in a couple of days." my uncle Shamous answered, shocking me unbelievably. He didn't even care enough to be here I thought.

"Oh," I answered very disappointed, but I didn't look up, instead I continued eating my meal in silence. I didn't want to show everyone just how disappointed I really was. However Maureen, who was very perceptive of my emotions, noticed how hurt I was and after dinner in an effort to cheer me up she said,

"Jospehine, I've got a surprise for you."

"What is it?" I asked instantly cheering up.

"Wait here, I'll go get them for you."

When she returned she handed me my first pair of nylon stockings. They were just like the ones her and Caroline wore.

"Oh they're beautiful," I said, and jumped up to hug her, "Thank-you."

"Well put them on," she insisted

"Here?" I said, looking at my uncle Shamous.

"I was just going." my uncle Shamous said with an amused smile on his face. Then he stood up and walked into the sitting room, lighting his pipe as he went. "Yes here," Maureen continued, but then frowned and looked at Caroline, "I forgot to get her a suspender belt." she said,

"Well that was stupid," Caroline answered in a motherly manner.

Maureen laughed at Caroline's cross tone and said,

"Never mind, I'll get her one of mine," and she ran back upstairs before anyone could say a word. A few minutes later she burst back into the kitchen puffing and panting from her run up the stairs and approached me with one of her suspender belts and tried it up against me. The trouble was I was far too fat and it didn't even go half way around me.

"Oh" she exclaimed pretending to be shocked. Then she looked me in the face and buckled over with laughter at my expression.

"Wait a minute." she added through her laughter and ran back upstairs, leaving me waiting like a stupid idiot. When she returned she was holding another suspender belt.

"Maybe if we could somehow tie two together it might fit." she said, with tears of laughter running down her face. By this stage everyone in the room was in hysterics. Everyone except me that is. My sense of humour was non existent at the moment. In fact, I had never been so embarrassed in all my life. My aunties were little more than strangers to me and I couldn't believe that Maureen was doing this to me in public.

I stood there like an idiot for a little while allowing her to try both suspender belts around me and then I lost my temper and pushed her away.

"Go away Maureen." I said in a dejected tone. "You think you're very funny don't you? Well you're not and I'm not wearing the bloody nylons, you can keep your stupid present." I yelled.

Her laughing stopped instantly and she became serious. Then in a concerned tone she said,

"What's the matter Jospehine?, I was only messing around with you."

"Well don't. I don't need you to remind me I'm fat, I know that. There's no need for you to laugh at me, I can't help the way I am."

"Oh Josephine don't be like that, I was only joking with you. You know I wouldn't hurt you on purpose, sure you used to laugh at these sort a things yourself. Besides we really do have to get these nylons to fit. It was dad who gave me the money for them, and he might get offended if you're not wearing them when he see's you."

"I don't care, I'm not wearing them and that's final." I said with determination.

No one was laughing any more, in fact the room was deadly silent. Suddenly Caroline stood up from the table and came over to me. She put her arms around me and kissing my cheek she said,

"We're sorry love, we didn't mean to hurt your feelings. We were just having a laugh that's all. And you don't have to wear the nylons if you don't want to alright."

"Okay." I answered, happy for the comfort her arms were bringing me. However Maureen didn't agree and looked over at Caroline with a genuine look of concern on her face.

"Caroline, you know dad, he'll go mad if he doesn't see them on her after paying out good money for them."

"Well that's your fault, you should have thought about that before you started taking the piss, shouldn't you?" Caroline snapped back at Maureen.

Suddenly I saw the funny side of the situation and Maureen's intense expression made me laugh. However I still had no intentions of wearing the nylons. At least not until I got a suspender belt my size.

Everyone smiled when I laughed and the atmosphere became relaxed again. We all started to clean up the kitchen, then joined uncle Shamous in the sitting room. When we entered, uncle Shamous was sitting next to the cosy fire puffing away on his pipe and it was a sight for sore eyes. The smell of the pipe didn't even bother me, it seemed to blend in with the fire which brought a certain kind of warmth, not only to the room, but to my very being. It was a feeling of belonging which gave me a sense of security that was most inviting to my insecure world. I sat down near the fire and I felt instantly relaxed and happy.

At about eight thirty, we all had some hot cocoa and said the rosary together. Then Pauline and I were sent to bed. Our bedroom was a large room with one double bed in it, but after the warmth of the cosy sitting room this room appeared overly large and extremely cold and uninviting. In fact I found myself wishing I could stay up longer to recapture that warm and safe feeling.

When Pauline and I were alone I turned to her and told her what I had been dying to say for months. Now seemed like the perfect time to get it off my chest.

"Pauline, I don't think you will be going back to the convent," I splurted out as if I were in some sort of hurry. "I think dad is going to sneak you over to London with us."

"Oh he can't Josephine, I must go back. The nuns will send the guards out looking for me and I'll be locked up in prison when they find me." she answered, sounding really terrified.

"No they won't. You will be in England long before you're supposed to be back in the convent and they won't come to another country for you."

"But I'm scared. Sister Angela told me last week about someone else that went to prison for trying to run away many years ago. Then she told me how bad prison was, how they starve you in there, giving you only bread and water to eat. Plus you have to piss in your own cell and sleep there too."

"Oh don't be stupid, she's just trying to scare you. Besides, if anyone gets into trouble it will be dad not you, stupid. And you have the cheek to call me stupid." I added, laughing at her for a change.

"But why would Sister Angela say all those things if they weren't true?"

"Because she wants to make sure you go back, then they'll get dad's money for another year, that's why. They told me months ago that if dad tried to bring you to London that I should try to convince you to go back, but the truth is, I think you would be crazy to go back if dad wants to take you with us."

"How do you know all this?"

"The Reverend Mother told me."

"What?" she told you that dad was going to kidnap me. How does she know?"

"Well she doesn't know for sure. Neither do I for that matter, but she thought he would. Maybe he won't, who knows for sure. By the way now that we're on the subject, that's the real reason I had to wait until now to leave the convent, not because I was too ugly or because dad didn't want me like you said on my birthday. I had to bloody wait for you to finish your exam."

"Oh!" she said laughing into my face as she rememered our arguement in the playroom on the sixteenth birthday.

"Yea you can laugh. Along with having to wait an extra twelve weeks in there, I had to put up with your insults as well."

"They were only jokes." she answered and continued to laugh.

"Well they weren't very funny." I answered and turned over in the bed putting my back to her. Then I tried to go to sleep but I couldn't. I was too anxious about meeting my father for the first time. I began to wonder again why he hadn't been here to meet us and my disappointment overwhelmed me to the point of tears, but I held them back, reminding myself that a couple of extra days after all these years of separation wouldn't make much of a differece.

To take my mind off the negative thoughts I was having I began to count sheep and shortly after I fell into a deep and blissful sleep. It had been quite a tiring day on the whole, first with saying goodbye to Linda and Doreen which had been most distressing, and then getting to know my relatives again, had made me more tired than I realised. The next morning I was awoken by the smell of fresh bacon cooking instead of Sister Angela's whistle. At first I thought it was a lovely dream, but as the smell became more evident I started to get hunger pains and realised that I was awake. So I nudged Pauline quickly to wake her up.

"Wake up," I coaxed, "they're cooking breakfast." then jumped out of bed. I was a little concerned in case I would be left without any. Pauline jumped out of bed too and we washed our face and hands in a small basin of water which was placed beside our bed the night before. Then we made the bed and got dressed quickly and ran down stairs. We must have looked like a pair of hungry savages the way we burst into the room!

Apart from aunt Kathleen we were the only ones there and I for one felt embarressed by our eagerness, not to mention scaring aunt Kathleen out of her skin by our sudden entry, the poor thing jumped when we entered and the pair of us burst out laughing at her startled expression. It was a nice feeling getting up and going straight to breakfast without having to do any chores first. In fact it was almost strange and gave me a feeling that just maybe I was going to be slapped or reprimanded at any given moment. I had to keep reminding myself that I wasn't in the convent anymore and that things were going to be different from now on. Now dad was going to take care of me and love me forever. Life was going to be grand for evermore, or so I thought! Unfortunately it wasn't going to be quite that simple, I still had to face a lot more disappointments in life, much more than any one person should have to endure!

After our lovely breakfast of fried eggs, sausages, bacon and tomatoes, (all home made or grown) accompanied by heaps of freshly baked bread and butter, we cleaned up the kitchen together. However it was a slow procedure without tension.

Everyone chatted away happily to each other and there was a calmness in the air making me feel at ease. Later in the morning when uncle Shamous was working on the farm, our aunties showed us around the property which seemed to be quite large. We walked around it for hours which was very tiring, but enjoyable. There were many different kinds of animals to look at too, but they made me nervous and I wasn't tempted to pat them the way my sisters were, although I did enjoy looking at them from a distance. Ever since I was bitten by the dog at the convent, I had no desire to go near any animal. They all had teeth and they could all bite as far as I was concerned!

Later that night Caroline and Maureen asked if they could go to the Ballinrobe dance hall for the evening and uncle Shamous said they could. So aunt Kathleen and uncle Shamous escorted them out for the evening. Pauline and I stayed home with aunt Phyllis which I resented. I felt like Caroline and Maureen was deserting us. I thought that they would have wanted to be with us since they hadn't seen us in so long, but I guess in their eyes they weren't doing anything wrong. They were just enjoying life to the fullest after being deprived of the good things for so long. However that didn't stop me from feeling dejected at the time.

Caroline was nearly twenty two years old now and well able to take care of herself yet she didn't dispute being chaperoned to the dance. I guess she knew the traditions in Ireland and that having her aunt and uncle with her was better than not going to the dance at all no matter how embarressing it was. In England things were different though, she was free to come and go as she pleased as long as she obeyed dad's rules and curfews and this applied to Maureen as well.

As for Pauline and I the only place we got to go was to bed and much earlier than the night before, because we had an early train to catch. But so did Caroline and Maureen yet they were out dancing, which annoyed me even more. What was worse we couldn't even go to sleep. Apart from it only being early in the evening we were both too excited about meeting our father the following day and couldn't help wondering how it would be and what he was like. We spent most of the night talking to each other in the darkness.

I must have fallen asleep while we were talking because the next thing I remember was the smell of breakfast again. However when I opened my eyes I realized it was still dark outside and turned over to go back to sleep, but the aroma from the kitchen was persistent and wouldn't allow me to sleep. It was calling me downstairs quickly, so I sat up and woke Pauline just like I had the previous morning. We went down to breakfast, but we didn't burst in like we had the day before and to our surprise we were the last ones there today, needless to say there was still plenty of food left for us!

After breakfast we walked to the train station to catch the early train to Dublin. When we got there our train hadn't yet arrived, which gave us time to say our goodbyes. Although these were affectionate farewells, they weren't emotional and no one cried. In fact I was eager to be going even though our relatives had treated us with kindness and love, I wanted to be with my father.

As we pulled into Dublin I gazed out of the train window looking for dad, who I was positive would be there to meet us. However I was disappointed yet again, because just like at the farm house he didn't show up. I really couldn't comprehend why he wasn't here to meet us. He was our father for Christ sake, he hadn't seen or touched me since I was barely three years old and he had never seen Pauline. What the hell was the matter with the man I wondered.

The train stopped and as we got off I looked around again, in hopes I had missed him from the window, but when there was still no sign of him. I became angry, and turned to Caroline.
"Where's dad Caroline?"
"He's at the hotel, I have the address here and some money to catch a taxi."
"He doesn't seem too eagar to see us, does he?" I accused, as if it were all Caroline's fault.
"That's his way Josephine, he's not trying to hurt you." she answered me flatly.
"Well he is hurting me." I spat back at her.
She didn't bother answering me, instead she walked forward and hailed a cab for us.

When we reached the hotel the first person I saw was dad waiting outside the hotel for us. There was another woman standing beside him but I was oblivious to her, all I could see was my father who was going to shower me with love forever. All the horrible thoughts I had of him back at the train station disappeared instantly and were replaced with love and devotion. As soon as the taxi came to a halt I pushed open the door and ran with open arms to my father and hugged him with relief and affection. He bent down and kissed my cheek affectionately. Then he turned to Pauline who was slowly climbing the stairs of the hotel not in any hurry at all. As soon as she reached us he bent and kissed her too. Then he put his arm around the women standing beside him and said,
"This ere, is ya Ma girls." shocking me to my very core. I

immediately turned to Pauline for confirmation that I wasn't going mad, but when I saw her frowning as well I turned back to dad and said,

"That's not our mother."

Dad appeared shocked by my response to the introduction, "What?" he said, wondering how I could have known.

I looked from dad to Pauline, and then back up at dad.

"Our mum came to see us at the convent a little while back and it wasn't her." I said looking at Edna. I stood staring at dad for a moment waiting for an explanation to end my confusion. However I didn't get one. Dad smiled and changed the subject altogether, leaving me even more confused and unsettled. He turned to Edna and said,

"Ma, why don't we take the girls ta the pictures this afternoon?"

"That's a great idea love, but why not go to the evening session instead. Then we can spend the day shopping and getting the girls some new clothes."

"That sounds a much better idea." dad answered with a smile on his face and added, "but first, let's go inside and let the girls freshen up a bit."

"That's the best thing I've heard all day." Maureen said and burst out laughing putting a lightheartedness back in the air.

We all went into the hotel and after unpacking our few belongings and brushing our hair, we went downstairs for a cool drink. Then we went on a spending spree. The afternoon's shopping was fantastic. Pauline and I both received several new outfits and an overcoat each. I got new shoes with a small heel too, which made me feel quite grown up. I also got a suspender belt my size!

After the shopping we both went to the hairdressers and had our hair cut and styled. In all honesty, by the end of the day I felt like a princess because of all the attention I was getting. I truly couldn't remember being so happy and loved in my whole life. My only wish was that Linda was there to share it with me. I missed her so much already. I was even tempted to ask dad about adopting her now, but decided against it in case he thought I was taking advantage of his generosity. The last thing I wanted to do was spoil things between us when they seemed to be going well.

When we were all too exhausted to take another step we caught a cab back to the hotel. The first thing I did when I entered my room was try on all my new clothes again and admire myself in the mirror. Then I joined Pauline who was taking a nap on the bed and had a peaceful sleep before dinner.

After dinner Caroline and Maureen announced that they had decided not to go to the pictures, that they were going to a dance instead, which dissapointed me and then dad gracefully declined as well, saying that he was tired after our shopping spree and wanted to relax at the hotel bar for the night, which really broke my heart. I wanted so much to be with all of them as a family, but it didn't seem to worry them in the slightest.

That left Edna to take Pauline and I to the pictures. This fact left me wondering about my mum and where she was and why dad had told us that Edna was our mother. Suddenly I wondered if the lady who had come to see us at the convent was an imposter, but surely the nuns would have known if she was, I told myself. It was all very mysterious and confusing but as much as I wanted to know all the details I was too scared to ask anyone except Caroline and Maureen and I could never get them alone long enough to ask them anything. Pauline was no wiser than I, so it was pointless asking her and I daren't ask dad, not yet anyway. As for Edna, as far as I was concerned she was no more than a stranger to me.

Although I would have preferred to go out as an entire family the night out at the pictures was very exciting. Dublin city was a buzz of entertainment and bright lights. Not to mention I had never been out so late, I was usually in bed by this time. The not knowing what to expect either added to our excitement. As we stood in line to get our tickets I noticed that people had to pay for them and realized that I had no money. I turned to Pauline and in almost a whisper I said,
"Did dad give you any money Pauline?"
"No, why?"
"You have to pay to get in, who's going to pay for us?"
Even though I was talking very quitely, Ma who was standing close in front of us heard me and looked back. Then she said,
"Me of course Josephine."
I looked up at her and hesitated for a moment before saying,
"But the nuns said we weren't allowed to take from strangers Ma." My words held no ill feelings they were just expressing an inbuilt fear. I truly thought that I would be in trouble if I accepted Ma's money."
"It's your father's money Josephine," she answered in a sombre tone. Then as she regarded me for a moment and her hurt expression turned to an angry one and she said,
"Besides, I'm no stranger I'm your father's wife." For a moment her cold stare reminded me of Sister Angela and I knew instantly that she didn't like me very much. I began to wonder fearfully if she could or would send me back to the convent and wished that I had kept my big mouth shut even though I didn't know exactly what had caused her to be so angry with me.

When we had our tickets we went into the foyer and Ma brought us an ice-cream. As she handed me mine she said,

"Your father bought this too Josephine so you can eat it in peace," The sharpness of her tone frightened me and I sat through the whole movie worried sick that I would be sent back to the convent the next day. I don't even remember what the movie was about.

When we arrived back at the hotel Ma tucked us into bed. She seemed as though she had forgotten the whole affair, talking to me in a normal tone again which settled my nervous stomach. A few minutes later dad entered the room to give us a kiss goodnight as well.

When he leaned over to kiss me he smelled so bad I almost heaved. However I didn't tell him that he was making me sick. Instead I held my breath and hugged him tighly, thankful for his long awaited cuddles. Then Pauline and I were left alone while dad and Edna retired to their own room. I had no idea if Caroline and Maureen were back yet when I lay down in the bed. If they were they didn't bother coming in to say goodnight!

The next morning at breakfast dad suddenly turned to me and said,

"Josephine, ya weren't very nice ta ya Ma last night lass."

I looked up surprised, not realizing what he was refering to and said,

"Why, what did I do?"

"Ya tried to embarrass ya Ma, when she was buying the tickets."

"I'm sorry dad. I wasn't trying to embarrass her. I was trying to be considerate actually by not taking advantage of people. That's the way we were brought up by the nuns." I answered in a shaky voice, worried in case he would send me back again for being rude.

"Well don't worry about it this time lass, but ya mind ya manners in the future okay."

"Yes dad." I answered, hoping that this really was the end of it all. I had believed that it was all over and done with the previous night when Edna had tucked us into bed. At least it had appeared to be forgotten, she had been extremely nice to me then. I began to feel very insecure and quickly realized that Edna, our new Ma, was far more important then we were and I didn't like that idea.

Dad turned away from me and addressed Pauline, "Ya don't talk much, do ya child?" he said in a mocking tone.

"There's nothing to talk about." Pauline answered in a tone that suggested she had no interest in talking to him now either.

"Well what would you like to be when you grow up?" dad asked trying to keep the conversation going.

"I'm not sure, I've never thought about it," she answered in a grown up manner. However, I knew what I wanted to be and was more than eager to talk to my dad.

"I know what I want to be dad, I want to be a dressmaker," I said with real excitment in my voice.

"Over my dead body ya will, not if I can help it." he said in a stern voice which caught me of guard. But before I could even apologize or justify my statement he added,

"Don't let me ever ear that coming from ya mouth again lass."

I sat there dumbfounded with his abruptness. I instantly decided to eat my breakfast in silence and speak only if and when I was spoken to. It was far safer. Pauline had the right attitude after all I thought, she hadn't been reprimanded once!

We spent the next two days in Dublin just getting to know dad and his new wife. I spent all my spare time wondering what life was going to be like in England and was eager to get there. Caroline and Maureen seemed ever so happy and I wondered if I would ever be as happy as them one day. They were so comfortable with dad but for some reason I still felt uneasy with him. I hoped that time would help me adjust and gathered that Caroline and Maureen must have been just as uncomfortable with him at first. I also wondered if when we got to England they would take me out to the dances that they seemed to enjoy so much, which was strange to me because neither of them enjoyed dancing at the convent. In fact Caroline hated it back then. I couldn't see them taking me along with them though, at the moment all they seemed to want was each other. They were so close that I was almost envious of their relationship. Right now I didn't think I'd ever fit in. I felt like a lost sheep that no one cared enough about to look for.

The day finally arrived for us to return to London and I woke up extremely excited about the trip. I guess I felt that arriving in London and my new home represented my true freedom and security. When I arrived there my ordeal would truly be over and I could live a life of peace with my family.

As soon as we went aboard the ship Caroline and Maureen ran off flirting with the crew, reinforcing my feelings that they were deserting us all the time, not that it bothered Pauline at all. While they were off having fun Pauline and I stayed by dad's side, like a couple of five year old children. We were scared of getting lost or forgotten in this big wide world and weren't prepared to take any chances. I did ask dad if we could walk around the ship and have a look at everything but dad didn't like that idea, he was happy to sit on deck drinking one beer after the other.

At first the smell of the beer didn't bother me, but as we got further out to sea and the ship started to rock to and fro, the smell of the beer and cigarettes became overwhelming and I became violently ill and threw up everywhere including all over dad's vacant knee. I've never seen anyone move as fast as dad did right then and if I hadn't felt so awful, not to mention embarrassed, I would have been in hysterics laughing. Edna jumped up also and came rushing to my side and led me to the railings behind us in case I had to vomit again. Then she began rubbing my back in an effort to comfort me.

"What's the matter child?" she asked in a concerned voice.

But I was still heaving too much to answer her. Dad who was standing close to us, trying to clean his pants with a hankerchief, started to laugh and said, "She's foocking sea-sick woman, can't ya tell."

I looked over at him gaining confidence with his hearty laugh and said,

"It's the smell of your beer and cigarettes dad, they smell terrible."

Edna burst out laughing at my statement, then she said "Sea-sick my foot." which made dad laugh again. Then she turned back to me and said,

"Come on child, I'll bring you to the rest room to get cleaned up."

"Thank you" I said gratefully. I was having trouble believing that I hadn't been slapped for throwing up let alone getting help to clean up my mess. Things were so different in so many ways now, but I still had trouble being totally relaxed. I kept expecting something to go wrong at any given moment.

When I was cleaned up a little we went back on deck to join dad. When we got there Maureen was there laughing and joking around with dad. It made me happy seeing them together like that and I couldn't wait to join them as well. As soon as I got there dad turned to me and said,

"Are ya feeling better now lass, after christening ya old man?"

"Yes dad, much better," I answered overjoyed with his concern for me and his humour at the situation.

"So I smell bad do I love?" dad asked in a mocking voice, but I wasn't sure how to answer him. I wasn't sure if he was joking or not. However Maureen doubled over with laughter at dad's comment and I let out my tense breath. Then in a timid voice I said,

"Sorry dad, I'm not being rude. It's not you that smells anyway, it's that beer stuff you're drinking. I've never smelt anything so bad in my life," and before I knew it everyone was laughing even Pauline who rarely laughed. For the first time since the pictures I felt happy and content. For once in my life I wasn't scared of my own shadow and that felt great. I had a feeling that dad and I were going to get along just fine, so long as I didn't try to dispute his decisions or go against him!

FINALE

Maureen only stayed with us for a few minutes. Then she was gone again in search of Caroline. As for dad he returned to his beer and cigarettes. So I spent the rest of the trip looking out to sea a few feet away from dad, just taking in the soft sea breeze and warm sunshine. I daydreamed about my new life and wondered what it had in store for me. I wondered if I would always be as happy as I was right now, or would the bubble pop at any minute.

Suddenly Linda and Doreen came to mind and I contemplated discussing them with dad right now while we were getting along so well, but quickly decided not to disturbe him at the moment. He looked like he was half asleep in his seat anyway, (more than likely already drunk). I thought it would be best to wait until I was safely in my new home and was settled before bringing them up into the conversation.

I had my whole life in front of me now and I was happy with anticipation that it would be a good life from here on in. My younger years had been hard and cruel and I hoped that god would take care of me from now on.

I didn't realize it then, but so many more bad things were going to happen before I was going to become truly contented in life. At that time all I could see was my freedom from the convent and that was all I had ever wanted, but I guess freedom has a price too and I had to pay that price many times over. But that's another story!